In *Fashion Advertising and Public Relations: A Historical and Sociological Perspective,* Dr. Martina Topić-Rutherford grounds readers in a thorough understanding of the business of fashion. Through her extensive research, she demonstrates why education in the history and industry itself is critical to effective advertising and public relations. I found Chapter 3 to be quite fascinating, which provides a detailed history of 100 years of fashion trends. I also appreciated the fact that her book includes specific, engaging class activities to contribute to learning. This book will be an excellent resource for public relations and advertising students as well as apparel design and merchandising programs. After reviewing the book and the class activities, I wanted to be a student in Dr. Topić-Rutherford's class.

Marlene S. Neill, *Professor, Baylor University, US*

By writing this book, Martina Topić-Rutherford has joined an elite group of authors who can write with passion and, at the same time, are experts in their subject areas. By invoking a sociological lens, the book explains the role of PR in the fashion industry in its context: without the history, the changes in society, and the evolutions of habits (and the habitus), practicing fashion public relations would be impossible. That is why *Fashion Advertising and Public Relations: A Historical and Sociological Perspective* is an essential resource for PR students and fashion enthusiasts. Everyone already involved in fashion PR professionally should read this book, too. For them, the book will be an ultimate source of knowledge, providing an industry-standard practical insight. Martina has achieved one additional goal. After reading the book, you will see that the gap between the theory and the practice of PR becomes smaller.

Michał Chmiel, *Senior Lecturer, Royal Holloway, University of London, UK*

This is such a fascinating read, providing a captivating incursion into fashion advertising and public relations through a historical and sociological lens. This interdisciplinary perspective makes the whole journey of reading the book worthwhile, more so as it provides critical guidance and commentary. The Reflection boxes are particularly interesting, extremely useful either as individual reflection moments or class exercises. This book is a must-have for any communication student interested in fashion, as well as for any fashion enthusiast interested in communication!

Anca Anton, *Associate Professor, University of Bucharest, Romania*

The textbook *Fashion Advertising and Public Relations: A Historical and Sociological Perspective,* authored by Martina Topić-Rutherford, is an exciting journey into the world of fashion and fashion communication. It's a fascinating read that will interest not just students and academics but also fashion enthusiasts, journalists, and professionals. The book isn't just about how to communicate in fashion; it's about understanding the industry's rich history and trends, with special emphasis on distinctive advertising and PR practices in fashion. This textbook is a valuable resource that successfully bridges the gap between theory and practice, making it a must-read for anyone with an interest in the dynamic world of fashion communication.

Mirela Holy, *Professor, Institute for Migration Research and VERN' University, Zagreb, Croatia*

A historical and sociological exploration of fashion history within the context of media, advertising, and PR industries, *Fashion Advertising and PR: A Historical and Sociological Perspective* provides a wealth of resources and increases students' knowledge of the fashion industry and its distinctive practices. Using a mix of journalistic and academic styles, and drawing on sources from academia, popular culture, research archives, and fashion magazines, this textbook will keep readers engaged and eager to learn more. Martina Topić-Rutherford provides readers with a wealth of knowledge and sources for further exploration. She meets her unique textbook objective of creating cultural capital for those who want to work in the fashion industry but don't know where to start.

Ioannis Kostopoulos, *Reader in Digital Marketing, Liverpool John Moores University, UK*

Dr. Martina Topić-Rutherford creatively interweaves powerful industries – fashion, advertising, and PR – opening a new niche that successfully bridges academic insight with real-world business practice. Written in an inspired style and enriched with visual appeal, this groundbreaking textbook is an invaluable guide for students, lecturers, and practitioners alike. Thanks to its relevance and breadth, the book will also resonate with readers beyond academic and professional circles.

Marija Geiger Zeman, *Senior Research Scientist, Institute of Social Sciences Ivo Pilar, Zagreb, Croatia*

In *Fashion Advertising and Public Relations: A Historical and Sociological Perspective,* Dr. Martina Topić-Rutherford critically examines the role of PR and its influence on the fashion industry for over a century. It is brilliantly presented through an interdisciplinary lens that examines the industry's intersection with feminism, technology, social class, luxury branding, and the ever-shifting sources of social power. Readers will gain a profound understanding of why, and most importantly how the fashion industry has changed since the turn of the 20th century.

Kenneth Henrie*, Assistant Teaching Professor of Marketing Penn State, University-Greater Allegheny, US*

This book is a significant and timely contribution that addresses a long-standing gap in the study of Fashion PR. Beyond emphasizing the central role of PR and advertising in the fashion industry, it offers a compelling sociological perspective that deepens our understanding of the field. Its historically grounded analysis is both original and rigorous, while the carefully curated case studies provide invaluable opportunities to bridge theory and practice. A highly commendable addition to academic scholarship and professional development alike.

Anastasios Theofilou, *Principal Academic in Public Relations, Bournemouth University, UK*

Fashion Advertising and Public Relations

Fashion Advertising and Public Relations offers a historically grounded analysis of advertising and public relations in the fashion industry.

It provides an in-depth introduction to the history of styles and leading designer innovations in advertising from the early 1900s to the modern day, which took place in tandem with societal developments. The text aims to equip the reader with the cultural capital necessary to pursue a career in fashion communication by providing foundational knowledge of the fashion industry's rich history. In line with this aim, it also covers a broad range of advertising and public relations practices in fashion, including fashion event management, press releases, digital media strategies, fashion magazine strategies, crisis communication, and CSR communication. A wealth of pedagogical features are included throughout the book, including reflection points, student exercises, and end-of-chapter discussion questions.

This unique textbook will be valuable for students of fashion marketing, business, and communication and for undergraduates studying public relations and advertising considering a career in fashion.

Comprehensive and ready-to-use instructor resources, such as dedicated case studies for each chapter, assessment strategies, quizzes, essay topics, and scenario assignments, are also offered online to augment teaching.

Martina Topić-Rutherford is a behavioral sociologist and mass communication scholar. She is currently an associate professor at the University of Alabama, College of Communication and Information Sciences, Department of Advertising and PR, US.

Mastering Fashion Management

The fashion industry is dynamic, constantly evolving and worth billions worldwide: it's no wonder that Fashion Business Management has come to occupy a central position within the Business School globally. This series meets the need for rigorous yet practical and accessible textbooks that cover the full spectrum of the fashion industry and its management.

Collectively, *Mastering Fashion Management* is a valuable resource for advanced undergraduate and postgraduate students of Fashion Management, helping them gain an in-depth understanding of contemporary concepts and the realities of practice across the entire fashion chain – from design development and product sourcing, to buying and merchandising, sustainability, and sales and marketing. Individually, each text provides essential reading for a core topic. A range of consistent pedagogical features are used throughout the texts, including international case studies, highlighting the practical importance of theoretical concepts.

Postgraduate students studying for a Masters in Fashion Management in particular will find each text invaluable reading, providing the knowledge and tools to approach a future career in fashion with confidence.

Customer Experience in Fashion Retailing
Merging Theory and Practice
Edited by Bethan Alexander

Fashion Business and Digital Transformation
Technology and Innovation across the Fashion Industry
Charlene Gallery and Jo Conlon

Luxury Fashion Marketing and Branding
A Strategic Approach
Alice Dallabona

Creativity and Innovation in the Fashion Business
Contemporary Issues in Fashion Design and Product Development
Helen Goworek and Fiona Bailey

Fashion Marketing and Communications (2nd edition)
Theory and Practice Across the Fashion Industry
Olga Mitterfellner

Fashion Trends and Forecasting
The Fashion Futurists' Toolbook
Eunsuk Hur, Caroline Hemingway, and Stephen Westland

Fashion Advertising and Public Relations
A Historical and Sociological Perspective
Martina Topić-Rutherford

For more information about the series, please visit https://www.routledge.com/Mastering-Fashion-Management/book-series/FM

Fashion Advertising and Public Relations

A Historical and Sociological Perspective

Martina Topić-Rutherford

Routledge
Taylor & Francis Group
LONDON AND NEW YORK

Designed cover image: 'INF14–147 Carnaby Street, London, 1969' / The National Archives, UK

First published 2026
by Routledge
4 Park Square, Milton Park, Abingdon, Oxon OX14 4RN

and by Routledge
605 Third Avenue, New York, NY 10158

Routledge is an imprint of the Taylor & Francis Group, an informa business

British Library Cataloguing-in-Publication Data
A catalogue record for this book is available from the British Library

ISBN: 978-1-032-84806-8 (hbk)
ISBN: 978-1-032-84023-9 (pbk)
ISBN: 978-1-003-51504-3 (ebk)

DOI: 10.4324/9781003515043

Typeset in Optima LT Std
by codeMantra

Access the Support Material: www.routledge.com/9781032840239

Contents

Acknowledgments

First and foremost, I would like to thank David S. Rutherford for his help in editing my teaching slides, structuring the proposal and textbook as a whole, as well as developmental editing of the textbook. Without exaggeration, I could not have done this textbook without David, as his guidance has been instrumental in developing and creating the content in a way that is suitable for a textbook. He also helped me with the index. David is an acquisition editor in a large publishing corporation in the US, and also my wonderful husband and an amazing daddy to my British-born cats.

Many thanks to the Dean of the College of Communication and Information Sciences, the University of Alabama, Professor Brian Butler, and Dr. Matthew VanDyke (interim chair of the department of Advertising and PR at the time I joined UA) for start-up funding, which helped fund images from the UK National Archives. #RollTide

The cover page (Carnaby Street, London, 1969) is a homage to my career in the UK, where I originally developed the Fashion PR course and started to teach it at Leeds Business School, Leeds Beckett University (also my lovely alma mater).

Finally, many thanks to Carla Fernández and the House of Dior for their kind assistance with images for the textbook.

Author's Biography

Dr. Martina Topić-Rutherford is a behavioral sociologist and mass communication scholar. She joined academia in 2007, first as a research and teaching assistant at the University of Zagreb, Faculty of Political Science (2007–2013). She worked at Leeds Beckett University, UK, where she held roles such as graduate teaching assistant, lecturer in public relations, senior lecturer in public relations, and reader at Leeds Business School (2014–2023). Currently, she is an associate professor in public relations leadership at the University of Alabama, College of Communication and Information Sciences, Department of Advertising and PR, US (since 10/2023). She holds a PhD degree in Sociology (University of Zagreb, Faculty of Humanities and Social Sciences, Department of Sociology, 2013) and a PhD in Marketing, Communications and Public Relations (Leeds Beckett University, Leeds Business School, UK, 2019). She also holds a PG Diploma in Global Journalism from City University of London, UK (2007). She is editor-in-chief of *Corporate Communications: An International Journal* and *Northern Lights: Film & Media Studies Yearbook*, and editor-in-chief of the book series *Women, Economics, and the Labour Relations*, and co-editor of the book series, *Routledge New Directions in PR and Communication Research*. Since 2021, she has been leading the EUPERA research network, Women in PR (previously a research project, 2018–2021). She was also a research lead for the #WECAN (Women Empowered through Coaching and Networking) project funded by the Department of Work and Pensions (UK), and she was an author and lead of the British Academy project on Women in Advertising. She is the author of *Corporate Social Responsibility and Environmental Affairs in the British Press: An Ecofeminist Critique of Neoliberalism* (Routledge, 2021) and *Workplace Culture in Mass Communication Industries* (Routledge, 2023). She is a member of the British Sociological Association, AEJMC, and EUPRERA. She is the author and lead of the CommsWomen advocacy initiative (https://www.commswomen.uk).

List of Tables

Introduction: Why Read This Textbook?

At one point in 2015 or 2016, when I worked at Leeds Beckett University in the UK, my program lead came to me saying one of his students was doing an internship with a major fashion retailer and had a problem with a press release. Her manager kept returning the press release as poorly written, and the student did not know what to do anymore; thus, she sought help from our program lead, asking if there was someone to look at her press release and help her revise it. The program lead came to me knowing I always had an interest in fashion, and work experience from before joining academia. I opened her press release and immediately agreed with her manager that the press release is poorly written because it was using conventional press release writing and described the new collection as beautiful (that's it). I opened the website of the retailer and immediately saw that the new collection was inspired by the 1970s. I then advised the student on how to rewrite the press release, commenting on the 1970s style and colors, and gave her some references. I suggested a title, something along the lines of 'The Crazy '70s are back…'. This incident made me realize that there is a lot of interest in working in fashion among PR and advertising students, but that these students traditionally do not have fashion content in their programs and thus do not have the cultural and symbolic capital to craft press releases and other communication content that would read as compelling and industry-specific. In 2017, during the program revision at Leeds Beckett University, I authored the Fashion PR undergraduate course, which I successfully taught until 2023, when I moved to the US. In the US, I teach the same course (from academic year 2025/2026 called Fashion Advertising and PR).

I always approached teaching fashion advertising and PR from the perspective of first learning about fashion history and fashion styles, and the societal developments that the fashion industry followed. I also focus on history, legacy, innovation, and the distinctive character of communication of fashion brands, particularly haute couture and luxury ready-to-wear, as agenda-setters and innovators. Then, within that, I teach about the distinctive character of fashion advertising and PR and developments in the media and advertising industries that happened at the same time as fashion developments. The focus on haute couture and luxury ready-to-wear is not for elitist reasons; it is simply that these houses have historically innovated and influenced fashion and continue to do so to the present day. As a result, these brands are talked-about issues in the industry, and one needs to know that when writing or working in fashion.

This textbook follows my course and approaches learning about fashion advertising and PR in the same way as my course. We first examine the importance of fashion, refuting

DOI: 10.4324/9781003515043-1

some common stereotypes. Next, we consider fashion and society drawing particularly on sociological theory, for I am a sociologist and see fashion as a fundamentally social phenomenon. I am also a historical and behavioral sociologist and thus, look at fashion and fashion advertising and PR from a historical perspective, tracing developments and changes that impacted the industry and societies at large. We move on to study fashion history, focusing particularly on fashion styles and the societal context within which these styles developed. Then, we explore haute couture and ready-to-wear (prêt-à-porter). From there, we go into fashion advertising and PR practice, looking at how that practice changed historically, covering topics such as digital communication in fashion, corporate social responsibility (CSR) in fashion, working with magazines, press releases, and event management. Finally, the last chapter focuses on the distinctive advertising and PR practices in haute couture and luxury ready-to-wear that focus on asserting history, innovation, and legacy. Haute couture and luxury ready-to-wear sell a lifestyle rather than products and communicate differently from retailers. Due to the restrictiveness of the word count, online materials include additional designer analyses and various case studies. I have opted for more in-depth content in the textbook rather than excessive case studies, which I hope is a good decision that will keep readers engaged.

This textbook is not about how to write in fashion, but about creating cultural capital to work in the fashion industry. It does so by exploring the industry's distinctive advertising and PR practices, its rich history, and the cyclical nature of its styles, knowledge that provides cultural and symbolic capital to advertising and PR students who do not traditionally have that content in their programs. The insight gained from this textbook can then be applied to fashion writing, as well as job interviews and later office culture.

The course I teach has so far been very successful both in the UK and the US, and I hope that readers will enjoy the textbook and find it valuable. If the book helps you in any way, please feel free to connect with me on LinkedIn and let me know. I would love to hear about it. I spent years researching this content and then 1.5 years writing this textbook. If the textbook proves itself valuable to just one person, the effort will be worthwhile.

Martina Topić-Rutherford,
On the 25th day of August 2025, in Tuscaloosa, United States

PART 1
THE FASHION INDUSTRY

CHAPTER 1

The Importance of Studying Fashion for Advertising and PR

Learning Objectives

- Explain the social and cultural significance of fashion, including its role in expressing identity, status, and social change.
- Describe the evolution of fashion from early costume to modern trends, including the influence of haute couture, prêt-à-porter, and mass production.
- Analyze how fashion functions as a form of cultural and symbolic capital.
- Evaluate the role of gender and societal norms in the development and perception of fashion.
- Understand the specific challenges and functions of fashion advertising and public relations.

Fashion as Expression

In 2010, Lady Gaga appeared at the MTV Video Music Awards Ceremony in a dress made of raw meat to send a message about her disapproval of the military's 'Don't Ask, Don't Tell' policy. She said, 'If we don't stand up for what we believe …, pretty soon we're going to have as many rights as the meat on our own bones' (Malach, 2024, n.p.). The meat dress was a much-talked-about fashion statement, drawing criticism from environmental and animal rights organizations. Lady Gaga's use of her outfit at an awards ceremony to make a political statement shows that fashion is much more than just clothes.

Clothing is a fundamental aspect of our lives. Humans need clothes to protect themselves from cold, heat, rain, snow, and sun. However, clothes are also used to decorate our bodies and differentiate ourselves from others. In choosing the clothes we wear, we make statements about ourselves. Therefore, fashion is often linked to identity and choice. This is because we do not just declare who we are with fashion, but also who we want to be. For example,

> through fashion, people rebel, challenge assumptions about their station in life, or traverse boundaries set by class, race, or gender, all by simply grabbing something different from the closet in the morning. Many fashion trends have sprung

DOI: 10.4324/9781003515043-3

> from individualistic or rebellious sartorial choices, and over time those trends have become the norm—giving future generations new ideals to either accept or reject (Croll, 2014, p. 7).

Coco Chanel also said, 'fashion changes, but style endures' (Britannica, n.d.). This quote captures the way many fashion enthusiasts and professionals see fashion, not just as something trendy and trivial, but as something that fundamentally shows who we are through our style and fashionable expression.

REFLECT

Look at your wardrobe and think about how you would describe your fashion style. Do you have a style? If so, what is it? If you do not think you have a style, think about someone, whether from your personal circle or a famous person (celebrity, influencer), whose clothes you like.

Social Significance of Fashion

Fashion – in the form of early costumes – has also historically been used to signify belonging to a group. Early costumes expressed a belief in permanence and archetype (Fishenich et al., 2000). Fashion can be seen as 'the outward and visible sign of a civilization, it is part of social history' (Ewing, 1992, p. 1), and a 'visual representation of a given historical period' (Stephens Frings, 1987, p. xxv). For example, reading historical editions of any fashion magazine shows readers not just the fashion of the time, but also social conventions, such as modesty in clothes during the Edwardian period of the 1900s or the social reformation of the 'roaring' 1920s, when women started to show their bodies. Fashion is indeed fundamentally linked to women, even though men dress themselves and have historically also used clothes to showcase belonging and identity. But, because of the media industry's emphasis on fashion as a woman's preoccupation, which particularly happened during the 1950s following the return of men from WWII, when working women were pushed toward returning to the private sphere (Friedan, 1963, Churchill, n.d.), fashion remains associated with women.

Fashion has always had a social significance. Clothing was linked to social status and used to emphasize differences between social groups. For example, until the 19th century, clothing was socially regulated, and there were rules for who could wear what kind of clothing. In France, during the rule of Louis XIV, upper-class men had to wear shoes with red heels, a sign of their upper-class status (Croll, 2014), which furthers the cause that fashion is a sign of identity and something that separates and distinguishes us from others. Breaching rules brought consequences, but this did not stop people from decorating themselves. Fischenich et al. (2000) argued that,

> fashion begins when people take pleasure in dressing up when the desire for novelty relegates functional considerations to a secondary level. Fashion enables the

> realization of a paradox: it allows people to be unmistakably themselves and, at the same time, enables them to show that they belong to a certain group. Unlike costume, fashion is subject to constant change. It emphasizes individuality and transience, and this is where its great appeal lies (p. 6).

We regularly make assumptions about people based on what they are wearing. For example, we assume people's values, occupation, origin, style, identity, and social class. Our wardrobe reflects more about us than we often realize. Fashion is sensitive to the time in which one lives, which is why societal history can be read through the history of fashion. However, unlike art, which is pursued by the few, fashion is pursued by everyone because everyone wears clothes (Croll, 2014). This is not to say that fashion cannot be art. Fashion can indeed be described as a form of art because people often have a desire for beautiful things (e.g., colors, lines, shapes). Like other forms of art, fashion follows its own rules, and the fashion industry has historically interpreted the human world in its own way. Thus, fashion is more than just a product that stems from the rise of consumerism; it sits between consumerism and art (Fischenich et al., 2000). Most people who 'collect and wear designer fashions do so simply because of the sheer pleasure involved. The hunt for a good piece, the knowledge you gain in the process, and the personal stories you hear along the way can be as compelling as finding and purchasing a highly desired, sought-after piece' (Clarkson, 2011, p. 52). This aesthetic pursuit is the reason many fashion designers see themselves as artists, and fashion shows and photography were historically more about the art of fashion than the practicality of clothing.

One form of fashion is haute couture or high fashion. Haute couture items are not always something one would wear every day; these creations are presented in fashion shows intended to showcase the talent of the collection's designer and instigate public interest. In 2011, Alexander McQueen created a fashion show in the New York Metropolitan Museum of Art, which stretched over two city blocks and broke attendance records (Freeman, 2011). Fashion enthusiasts claim that fashion is art, refuting critics who see fashion as commercial and vain and who argue that fashion cannot match the aesthetic purity and conceptual complexity of other forms of art (Croll, 2014). Some authors even argue that 'favourite items of clothing have the power to transform the body and spirit' (Clarkson, 2011, p. 4).

Historically, clothing evolved into fashion when people agreed to replace loosely fitted robes with fitted clothes. Men and women were initially equal in their fashion expectations. In early periods, such as medieval, Tudor, and Stuart times, men were seen as *peacocks* and outshone ladies in their fashion (Ewing, 1992). This changed later, with exceptions being the 1960s and 1970s when men also wore clothes that would be, in other periods, seen as somewhat feminine (e.g., flared trousers and platform shoes of the 1970s). The mid-19th century coincided with the rise of couture, with couturiers seeing themselves as artists fostering self-expression and individualism through the fashion worn by the upper class. Modern fashion styles are linked to the mass production and standardization that first appeared during the Industrial Revolution, which increased the availability of fashionable clothing to the middle classes, who also started to seek individualism and self-expression.

Before mass production, the manufacturer of clothing relied on hand-working techniques that were labor-intensive. The off-the-rack clothes and prêt-à-porter (ready-to-wear) fashion that became available after WWII ended the work of many seamstresses who were copying couture patterns and styles promoted by Parisian haute couture and fashion magazines (Clarkson, 2011). The most revolutionary period in fashion started during the 1920s, when layers started to drop and women's fashion moved in line with societal trends. A large influence during this time was Coco Chanel and the rise of the department stores in the US, which started to sell fashion labels. While fashion has been accused of perpetuating patriarchy and women's traditional societal roles, as discussed in Chapter 2, fashion has also contributed to women's empowerment, and this is visible in the way fashion styles developed and changed over time.

Fashion changed significantly during the 20th century. What used to be reserved for a privileged few became available to all; thus, fashion changed in all but name (Ewing, 1992). Some of the novelties developed in the early decades of that century are nowadays classics. The 'shift dress, the twin set, the tailored suit, the bias-cut gown, the little black dress and many more have not drastically changed since their inception' (Clarkson, 2011, p. 4). Indeed, the period precipitated a revolution in fashion, with the pace of change becoming part of fashion's very essence as styles and silhouettes evolved ever more rapidly. For example, skirt lengths changed considerably during this period: while in earlier centuries hemlines went all the way down to the ankle, in the 20th century, hemlines moved up and down and became shorter than ever in some decades. Shorter skirts and showing legs were no longer seen as a social taboo (Fischenich et al., 2000). Most of the changes that happened during the 20th century would previously have been considered immoral, when women's bodies were hidden from view. Yet during this period, the silhouette became a central point of fashion. Designers followed societal progress in women's rights and increased women's empowerment. It was also in the 20th century that women started to wear men's clothes or male-like clothes for the first time, with trousers becoming a standard fashion and rising in popularity as the century progressed. This might not seem relevant today, but the introduction of women's trousers was a revolutionary act that changed fashion forever and empowered women. Thus, fashion changes went along with societal progress and contributed to women's equality. Indeed, it is hardly the fashion industry that confined women to the domestic sphere; almost every time there was a progressive initiative, fashion went along with the times and supported women's empowerment, and this trend has lasted up until the present day. Gender fluidity is not new to fashion, and the industry tried to push societal boundaries when some designers introduced gender fluidity during the 20th century. Recently, with the rise of gender activism, support for gender fluidity has been championed by many brands (Sanders, 2019). Thus, fashion continues to stand for progressiveness and support of all communities.

What is central to fashion is the cyclical nature of the industry, where old styles re-emerge as the latest styles and regain their popularity. Even couture designers 'plunder the back catalogues in order to study, copy and learn from the masters of years before, often mimicking details, such as pin tucks or seam-finishing, as well as prints, pattern-cuts or surface decoration, such as beading, lacework or ribbonwork, in their own designs' (Clarkson, 2011, p. 4–5). Many designers have developed different fashion styles over the decades that have changed the world forever. However, the cyclical nature of fashion is not a historical anomaly. Couturiers were always inspired by the past, first a distant past, then a more immediate one. *La Belle Époque* inspired Christian Dior's New Look of 1947, the Directoire fashion of Paul Poiret, and the 'sack' dresses of the fifties (Peacock, 1993). The mid-1920s 'influenced the fashions of the early sixties, a decade which was to end, in complete thrall to the thirties, with the Retro/Biba look' (Peacock, 1993, p. 7). During the 1970s, Yves Saint Laurent took inspiration from the 1940s, and during the 1980s, designers continued to explore and re-explore the 1950s and 1960s (Peacock, 1993).

REFLECT

Think about a period in history or a cultural group whose fashion you find interesting or distinctive. Look up images of their clothing styles online and consider: What social values or norms are reflected in their clothing? How did their fashion express identity, status, or group belonging? Can you identify any modern fashion trends that have been influenced by this style?

Fashion Advertising and Public Relations

Advertising and public relations (PR) in the fashion industry tend to be more complex than in many other industries because of constant innovations in fashion, new trends emerging in seasons, and the cyclical nature of the fashion industry. There is also the issue of velocity and vastness of the industry, which further complicates advertising and PR efforts (Fionda & Moore, 2009; Easey, 2002). Brand image also contributes to the complexity of promotional efforts in the fashion industry because a brand image is not just a name, logo, slogan, and design. It is also a concept conveying symbolic meaning and associations with a brand's name, ideas, and attitudes. Advertising and PR professionals must create and maintain a distinctive and desirable image of the brand and differentiate themselves from other brands, which in the fashion industry is difficult due to the large size and competitiveness of the industry at all levels (haute couture, prêt-à-porter, and smaller brands). For example, Levi Strauss & Co. is not just about the red label of the brand but also about urban consumers' imagination (Lee et al., 2000). Another reason for focusing on differentiation and brand image is the issue of copying and intellectual property (IP) rights, which do not exist in fashion (Blakley, 2010). Fashion products cannot achieve IP rights, and therefore, anyone can copy styles and designs and sell them, which mass manufacturers have done for decades. As a result of this problem, many fashion brands nowadays foster partnerships with retailer brands, such as Versace and Swedish retailer H&M (Suhrawardi, 2011), and they are also trying to create patterns and styles that make copying obvious, such as the checkered pattern typically associated with Burberry. Advertising and PR professionals work toward creating brand awareness and associating certain patterns and styles with certain brands. This is also why haute couture houses go to great lengths to communicate their innovations and long-standing fashion traditions.

The image of fashion advertising and PR mirrors general perceptions of the fashion industry as trivial and easy work. However, the fashion industry moves fast, and new products are constantly developed, which makes the job of a fashion advertising and PR professional engaging but also demanding. This is not always recognized, and other forms of advertising and PR work get more recognition, e.g., crisis and health PR. There are very few scholarly works that tackle fashion PR work, with even fewer tackling advertising. Cassidy and Fitch (2013) argue that fashion PR is often perceived as "frivolous, glamorous and primarily image management and promotion" (p. 1). In their study on practitioners, Cassidy and Fitch (2013) argue that fashion PR work is incorrectly described as only promotional work, with some practitioners saying that 'people believe PR is all about parties, air-kissing and long boozy lunches' and that even some PR practitioners believe that,

> it is very glamorous and they think you just teeter around in high heels and get to go to all the shows and drink champagne and that it's all quite relaxed. The reality is long hours and you are the spokesperson for an entire brand, so there is a lot of pressure on you to deliver' (p. 5).

However, many still see fashion PR simply as a promotional activity and a common definition is that fashion PR is 'to communicate information about a client's product or designs to various publics through various media channels' (Noricks, 2009, p. 48). Fashion advertising and PR indeed encompass a lot of communication through multiple channels; however, it also includes building relationships with the *publics*.

The professionalization project of PR, where the focus is on PR as a strategic management function, led to the marginalization of fashion PR, which still largely focuses on communication (Cassidy & Fitch, 2013). Fitch (2017) argued that 'corporatist approaches to understanding PR as a strategic, management discipline, which continue to dominate public relations scholarships, make little sense in relation to day-to-day public relations practices' (p. 159). Fashion advertising and PR include a lot of media work and promotional activities, such as organizing and attending events, fashion shows, and fashion weeks; communicating corporate social responsibility (CSR) policies and crisis management strategies; and digital outreach, which includes communication on social media channels and working with bloggers, vloggers, social media influencers, and traditional celebrities. For example, working with bloggers and influencers includes generating electronic word of mouth (eWOM), which occurs when fashion PR practitioners launch 'a campaign or in some other way encourage others to speak about a product or a company' (Kulmala et al., 2013, p. 21). This process focuses on storytelling to influence attitudes (Esteban-Santos et al., 2018) positively. We explore digital communication in fashion in Chapter 5, and CSR in Chapter 6.

In advertising, research has mainly centered on studying fashion advertising in magazines and images because fashion advertising is largely image-based (Santaella et al., 2012, Taylor & Costello, 2017). In addition, research into fashion advertising focuses on what makes fashion advertising effective, consumer responses to fashion advertising, the segmentation of consumers, and involvement with advertising using theories such as the elaboration likelihood model (Taylor & Costello, 2017, Santaella et al., 2014). Scholars have so far not tackled the work of fashion advertising, and the only industry knowledge so far remains in the realm of PR.

REFLECT

Choose a current fashion brand or designer you admire. Visit their website or social media platforms and reflect on the following: How does the brand communicate its identity and values through images, slogans, or collaborations? What kinds of media channels are they using (e.g., Instagram, TikTok, LinkedIn)? How do they distinguish themselves from competitors?

Cultural Capital and the Importance of Studying Fashion

For centuries, Paris has been the center of the fashion world, with haute couture and *la mode* elegance created and promoted by Parisian designers. With the rise of prêt-à-porter (ready-to-wear), Paris continued to influence fashion, but the most influential fashion city is now New York, which was influenced by the rise of ready-to-wear fashion sold by department stores, and the American designers' focus on working women. Even though fashion is no longer dictated by elites and haute couture, haute couture houses still influence fashion and trendsetting, albeit their influence coexists with prêt-à-porter and consumer influence, such as youth or street fashion in some decades.

Parisian haute couture initially led the way in revolutionizing fashion, but it is also important to mention the influence of anti-fashion movements, punk, and the power suits of the 1980s, which are all important elements of fashion as we know it today. While haute couture, in its early decades, set trends for fashion, later, its influence faded as many fashion houses increased their focus on prêt-à-porter fashion. It is still important to understand haute couture, not just because of its historical relevance but also because haute couture gives fashion houses a distinctive legacy. Thus, doing fashion advertising and PR for haute couture is distinctly different than doing advertising and PR for retail fashion. Haute couture fashion is also a talked-about issue in the fashion industry, and knowing the history of haute couture and the legacies of couture houses presents a form of cultural capital for working in fashion. The importance of this cultural capital is well represented in popular culture. For example, in the *Devil Wears Prada* book (and the film of the same name), Lauren Weisberger (2003) narrates her experience of working for a big fashion magazine through the character of Andrea. The book was likely based on Weisberger's real-life experience of working for *Vogue,* albeit, presumably for legal reasons, the book is written as fiction. A large part of Andrea's fashion magazine work experience, as vividly portrayed in the book, is centered on her learning about fashion and understanding it, including designers and their legacies and notable products, as well as knowing how to present herself and dress appropriately. Similarly, Plum Sykes (who worked for *Vogue*) writes about New York society and high-profile women, colloquially known as Park Avenue Princesses, in her book *Bergdorf Blondes* (Sykes, 2004). While these types of novels are often labeled as *chick-lit,* their sociological value is immense because they portray fashion in everyday life and show how knowing about fashion, its history, social significance, and particularly understanding designers, can include or exclude members from high society and exclusive social circles. Equally, for working in the fashion industry – as portrayed in *The Devil Wears Prada* – one is expected to have an in-depth knowledge of fashion, and this textbook aims to support that endeavor and provide a starting point for gaining the cultural and symbolic capital necessary to understand fashion and be more employable in this distinctive industry.

Capital as a sociological concept was introduced by Pierre Bourdieu, a French sociologist. Cultural capital is knowledge relevant to a particular field. Capital is normally gained from family, schools, and academia. However, it is also linked to habitus – one's area of growing up that influences our capital and understanding of the world. Bourdieu (Bourdieu, 1977, 1977a; Bourdieu & Passeron, 1977) spoke of doxa or taken-for-granted knowledge that creates a disposition to succeed in certain fields. For example, in mass communication industries, dispositions are linked to behavioral and communication styles, the ability to communicate and build relationships with others, engage in networking (Bourdieu, 2001; Topić, 2023) but also having cultural knowledge such as understanding of arts, theatre, and being able to strike up conversations about those topics (Crossley, 2001; Edwards, 2013). Bourdieu argues that capital is central to a field because all forms of capital (economic, social, and cultural) can be transformed into symbolic capital if the capital a person possesses is seen as valuable in that field (Bourdieu, 1986). Each field has its own rules, and people who compete for positions try to master what Bourdieu calls the 'rules of the game' within their chosen field (Bourdieu, 1986; Topić, 2023). In other words, people maximize the amount of symbolic capital they have because it is linked to status, authority, and prestige (Schwartz, 1997; Webb et al., 2000).

The theory has been applied to many areas, such as education, employment, career progression, and gender relations at work, to name a few. In fashion, symbolic capital is often knowledge of the fashion industry, designers, collections, most memorable and relevant items from big designer names that would be seen as collectibles, knowing about fashion capitals and big fashion shows, fashion magazines, etc. Being able to talk about fashion and having in-depth knowledge of the industry and its history constitutes symbolic capital. Therefore, this book takes a sociological and historical approach to fashion and fashion advertising and PR to provide readers with a starting point in gaining symbolic capital for working in fashion.

REFLECT

Think about a time when knowledge of fashion affected how someone was perceived in a social or professional setting. This could be a personal experience, something you observed, or a scene from a book, film, or TV show.

What forms of cultural or symbolic capital were at play in that situation? How did fashion knowledge – or the lack of it – influence status? How might gaining more fashion knowledge improve someone's ability to succeed?

Write a short reflection connecting your example to Bourdieu's concept of capital.

DISCUSSION QUESTIONS

- What skills and qualifications are increasingly necessary for a professional career in fashion PR or advertising today?
- To what extent does the professionalization of PR in fashion legitimize the industry as a serious discipline compared to other sectors like tech or healthcare?
- How does advertising in fashion go beyond selling products to constructing cultural meanings, identities, and lifestyles?
- How does Pierre Bourdieu's concept of cultural capital apply to the fashion industry? Can clothing choices function as a form of symbolic power?

- In what ways does fashion operate as a marker of social class, education, and cultural knowledge?
- Can fast fashion democratize cultural capital, or does it simply replicate elite styles in a diluted form?
- How do influencers and celebrities transform personal style into cultural capital, and how does this affect everyday consumers?

EXERCISE: FASHION AS EXPRESSION

Think about how your clothing choices reflect who you are or how you want to be seen.

- In what ways do you use fashion to express your identity (e.g., personality, beliefs, culture, gender, mood)?
- Do you change how you dress based on the setting? What do those shifts say about how identity is shaped by context?

Discuss how cultural or geographical background might shape each person's fashion choices and expressions of identity.

EXERCISE: CULTURAL CAPITAL AND THE IMPORTANCE OF STUDYING FASHION

Create a list of five items that represent cultural or symbolic capital in the fashion industry (e.g., knowing the name of a designer, identifying a famous style like the 'New Look').

- For each item, briefly explain why it holds symbolic value in fashion or media professions.
- Reflect on which items you personally already know, and which ones you would like to learn more about.
- Consider how building cultural capital could benefit your future career in PR or advertising.

Further Exploration: Exploring Fashion Capital Through Film

Watch *The Devil Wears Prada*. Write notes as you watch and note the challenges Andrea faced when she first got a job at a fashion magazine. Pay attention to her conversations with stylists and editors. After that, discuss with your peers which of these conversations reveals the lack of knowledge and cultural and symbolic capital for working in fashion.

References

Blakley, J. (2010). Lessons from fashion's free culture. *Ted Talk*, May, 25th. Retrieved from https://www.ted.com/talks/johanna_blakley_lessons_from_fashion_s_free_culture?subtitle=en

Bourdieu, P. (2001). *Masculine Domination*. Redwood City: Stanford University Press.

Bourdieu, P. (1986). The Forms of Capital. In Richardson, J.G. (ed.), *Handbook of Theory and Research for the Sociology of Education*. New York: Greenwood Press (pp. 241–258).

Bourdieu, P. (1977). Cultural Reproduction and Social Reproduction. In Karabel, J., & Halsey, A.H. (eds.), *Power and Ideology in Education*. Oxford: Oxford University Press (pp. 487–511).

Bourdieu, P. (1977a). *Outline of a Theory of Practice*. New York: Cambridge University Press.

Bourdieu, P., & Passeron, J.-C. (1977). *Reproduction in Education, Society, and Culture*. Beverly Hills, CA: Sage.

Britannica (n.d). Coco Chanel. 100 Women. *Encyclopedia Britannica*. Written by The Editors of Encyclopedia Britannica. Retrieved from https://www.britannica.com/explore/100women/profiles/coco-chanel

Cassidy, L., & Fitch, K. (2013). Parties, air-kissing and long boozy lunches? Public relations in the Australian fashion industry. *Prism, 10*(1), 1–13. Retrieved from http://www.prismjournal.org/fileadmin/10_1/Cassidy_Fitch.pdf

Churchill, L.B. (n.d.). The Feminine Mystique Work by Friedan. *Britannica*. Retrieved from https://www.britannica.com/topic/The-Feminine-Mystique

Clarkson, K. (2011). *Vintage Fashion Sourcebook*. London: Carlton Books Ltd.

Croll, L. (2014). *Fashion that Changed the World*. Munich: Prestel Verlag.

Crossley, N. (2001). The Phenomenological Habitus and Its Construction. *Theory and Society, 30*(1), 81–120.

Easey, M. (2002). *Fashion Marketing*, 3rd edition. Oxford: Blackwell.

Edwards, L. (2013). Institutional racism in cultural production: The case of public relations. *Popular Communication, 11*(3), 242–256.HYPERLINK "https://doi.org/10.1080/15405702.2013.810084" \h

Esteban-Santos, L., Garcia Medina, I., Carey, L., & Bellido-Perez, E. (2018). Fashion bloggers: Communication tools for the fashion industry. *Journal of Fashion Marketing and Management: An International Journal, 22*(3), 420–437.

Ewing, E. (1992). *History of 20th Century Fashion*. London: BT Basford Ltd.

Fionda, A.M., & Moore C.M. (2009). The anatomy of the luxury fashion brand. *Journal of Brand Management, 16*(5/6), 347–363.

Fischenich, S., Horbas, C., Kaiser, A., Kothe, R., Meisner, J., Roth, A., Willemsen, C., Wolter, G., & Zipperer, A. (2000). *A History of Fashion in the 20th Century*. Cologne: Konemann Verlagsgesellschaft.

Fitch, K. (2017). Seeing 'the unseen hand': Celebrity, promotion and public relations. *Public Relations Inquiry, 6*(2), 157–169.

Freeman, H. (2011). Alexander McQueen exhibition becomes New York's latest blockbuster. *The Guardian*, 9 August 2011. Retrieved from https://www.theguardian.com/lifeandstyle/2011/aug/09/alexander-mcqueen-exhibition-new-york

Friedan, B. (1963). *The Feminist Mystique*. New York: W.W. Norton.

Kulmala, M., Mesiranta, N., & Touminen, P. (2013). Organic and amplified eWOM in consumer fashion blogs. *Journal of Fashion Marketing and Management: An International Journal, 17*(1), 20–37.

Lee, T.S., Leung, C.S., & Zhang, Z.M. (2000). Fashion brand image marketing: Brand image and brand personality. *Research Journal of Textile and Apparel, 4*(2), 60–67.

Malach, H. (2024). Lady Gaga turns 38: A look at her career-defining fashion through the years, from the meat dress to Met Gala drama. *WWD – Women's Wear Daily*, October 28, 2024. Retrieved from https://wwd.com/

feature/lady-gaga-fashion-through-the-years-1236287053/

Noricks, C. (2009). *Exploring Fashion PR*. Retrieved from https://www.slideshare.net/prcouture/exploring-fashion-pr-1267609

Peacock, J. (1993). *20th Century Fashion*. London: Thames & Hudson Ltd.

Sanders, W. (2019). There's more at stake with fashion's gender-fluid movement than you realise. *Vogue*, August 11. Retrieved from https://www.vogue.co.uk/article/the-meaning-of-gender-fluid-fashion

Santaella, M., Summers, T.A., & Belleau, B.D. (2012). Involvement in fashion advertising: The role of images. *Academy of Business Journal*, 2, 66–77.

Santaella, M., Summers, T.A., & Kuttruff, J.T. (2014). Involvement in fashion advertising: Image versus text. *Academy of Business Journal*, 1, 8–23.

Schwartz, D. (1997). *Culture and Power: The Sociology of Pierre Bourdieu*. Chicago, IL: University of Chicago Press.

Stephens Frings, G. (1987). *Fashion: From Concept to Consumer*, 2nd edition. Englewood Cliffs, New Jersey: Prentice-Hall, Inc.

Suhrawardi, R. (2011). Versace for H&M. *Vogue*, 17 November. Retrieved from https://www.vogue.co.uk/gallery/versace-for-hm-party

Sykes, P. (2004). *Bergdorf Blondes*. New York: Hyperion.

Taylor, C.R., & Costello, J.P. (2017). What do we know about fashion advertising? A review of the literature and suggested research directions. *Journal of Global Fashion Marketing*, *8*(1), 1–20.

Topić, M. (2023). *Workplace Culture in Mass Communication Industries*. London: Routledge.

Webb, J., Schirato, T., & Danaher, G. (2000). *Understanding Bourdieu*. London: Sage.

Weisberger, L. (2003). *The Devil Wears Prada*. New York: Broadway Books.

CHAPTER 2 Fashion and Society

Learning Objectives

- Analyze sociological theories that explain the role of fashion in society.
- Trace the major milestones that shaped the fashion industry's historical evolution.
- Explain how industrialization accelerated mass production and global distribution of fashion.
- Assess diverse feminist perspectives on fashion, power, and identity.
- Analyze and evaluate consumer culture in fashion and the diverse ways in which publics respond to it.

Fashion and Elites

In November 2010, the British Royal Palace publicly announced the engagement of Prince William and Kate Middleton. A few days later, Prince William and Kate Middleton (now known as Princess Catherine) gave an interview which was broadcast by ITV. The *Issa* dress Kate Middleton was wearing during the interview sold out within 24 hours of the broadcast (Us Weekly, 2010). This phenomenon gave rise to the so-called *Kate Effect*, with Kate's outfits selling out within hours of any event she attended (Hinsliff, 2023). The contribution of Princess Catherine to the British fashion industry has been estimated to be so high that Princess-promoted brands, such as Issa, Reiss, and LK Bennett, have achieved global popularity thanks to her endorsement (Thomas-Bailey & Wood, 2012; Henley, 2017).

The influence of elites like Kate Middleton on fashion is not new. Historically, fashion was dictated by elites, and trends came from the top. The fashions adopted by the ruling classes, such as the court or aristocracy, spread downwards to the other classes. Fashion was often connected to mass hysteria and consumerism because trends were set by elite groups, whose trends then spread to non-elite groups trying to identify with elites or upper classes by copying their style (Simmel, 1904, 1957). The spread of fashion trends was a minority movement initially and not fully embraced by the masses (Ewing, 1992). However, things started to change as new trends started to emerge, and fashion trends gained mass following. This resulted in elites trying to distinguish themselves from others by

DOI: 10.4324/9781003515043-4

re-inventing their style once the existing style got copied (Simmel, 1904, 1957). Changes to elite style eventually gave rise to fashion cycles and trends emerging and re-emerging, which created the fashion industry as we know it today.

REFLECT

Who is a well-known public figure in your country (American readers, think of national influencers vs influencers from your home state)? Are they a fashion influencer or a leader? Who follows them? Who is their fashion demographic? Think about how this person influences the way others dress and whether and how this person has influenced you personally. If you have been influenced by this person, think about why you follow them. If not, why not?

Sociological Understanding of Fashion

Early sociologists viewed fashion as an abstract and socially negotiated idea separate from clothing or dress, which is material and tangible. They saw fashion as imitative and crucial to understanding society and the social hierarchy embedded within the system, implying that the imitators are on the lower end of the social spectrum, while those who are imitated are on the upper end (Kawamura, 2019). This view has been proposed by sociologists such as Herbert Blumer, whose view of fashion fits into the social differentiation approach to fashion, which is linked to one's social class. Spencer (1966[1896]) saw fashion as imitative at its beginning, and only later growing into the realm of individuality as people developed their own styles. Thorstein Veblen (1957[1899]) also wrote about patterns of fashion dispersal in his classic sociological text, *The Theory of the Leisure Class: An Economic Study of Institutions*, arguing that fashion starts with the so-called 'leisure class', which is a group with the most money, who are attracted to fashion because fashionable items cost more than regular items. This argument centered on defending fashion, which many early sociologists did when they offered a social theory of fashion. Veblen (1957[1899]) argued that fashion has three properties,

a. An expression of the wearer's wealth, which becomes conspicuous consumption because what people wear is a sign of their economic status.
b. The less the dress is practical and functional, the more it becomes a symbol of high class because an extravagant dress symbolizes that one does not have to work for a living.
c. Fashion is *up to date*, and to be *in fashion* means that fashion must be appropriate for a certain period in time.

Social class has been one of the central features of sociological thought for many decades, and Simmel argues that fashion is never the same for different social classes. Class distinction is seen as a feature of fashion in an open-class society (Simmel, 1904). Elites seek to set themselves apart from others through a distinctive form of dress. However, as the elites see a preparation for appropriation by lower classes, they abandon their fashion (Simmel, 1957). Thus, fashion can illustrate historical class relations. Simmel (1904) spoke of a class pyramid in fashion where elites first set the trend, then those classes below them copy that trend, and so on (e.g., aristocracy → middle class → working class), until a trend spreads to society at large. This process results in elites eventually losing marks of a separate identity and adopting a new insignia to distinguish themselves from others. As a result, fashion constantly finds itself in a cycle of innovation and emulation, which also means that once a cycle starts, it will inevitably march toward its doom. Blumer (1969) has taken the understanding of the fashion process forward to the realm of trends and cycles, arguing that repetition of cycles is a fundamental aspect of the fashion process.

However, regardless of calls from early sociologists for more work on fashion, jobs in fashion, as well as having an interest in fashion, are not always taken seriously due to the cyclical and trendy perception of fashion. Fashion continues to be seen as trivial and linked to aesthetics, emotional well-being, and a personal sense of gratification when purchasing clothing items (Tranberg Hansen, 2004; Abrahamson, 1996; Blumer, 1969). A particular criticism of the fashion industry has always been that the industry attracts too much excitement, conformity, and mass hysteria (Tranberg Hansen, 2004; Abrahamson, 1996; Blumer, 1969). Some sociologists argue that fashion is not trivial. Indeed, we can learn social history through studying fashion in the arts, entertainment, medicine, and literature (Blumer, 1969). Therefore, fashion can be seen as evidence of a *social contract* for what was appropriate to wear at a certain time.

Blumer (1969) specifically argues that fashion should not be seen as something only linked to the area of costume and adornment because these are not the main aspects of fashion, which operates in 'many diverse areas of human group life' (Blumer, 1969, p. 275). Yet only a handful of early sociologists had studied fashion; apart from Blumer, notable examples include Simmel (1904), Sapir (1931), and Lang and Lang (1961). Things have not changed significantly, even though sociology as a discipline has developed, and some sociologists still call for more studies of fashion (Crane & Bovone, 2006; Kawamura, 2019). However, many sociologists remain uninterested in fashion and continue to view it through a Marxist lens, seeing it as a capitalist manipulation of the public or as something associated with 'consumption of women's pursuits' (Crane & Bovone, 2006, p. 320). A widespread position in sociology is that fashion became relevant in societies after the development of the European bourgeoisie and capitalism (Aspers & Godart, 2013).

Blumer (1969), speaking in the 1960s when fashion styles and the cyclical nature of fashion had already been established, argues that fashion is an individual and very calculating act because,

> the fashion conscious person is usually quite careful and discerning in his effort to identify the fashion in order to make sure that he is "in style"; the fashion does not appear to him as frivolous. In turn, the person who is coerced into adopting the fashion contrary to his wishes does so deliberately and not irrationally. Finally, the person who unwittingly follows a fashion does so because of a limitation of choice rather than as an impulsive expression of aroused emotions or inner anxiety (p. 277, emphasis in the original).

Blumer (1969) adds that there is no evidence that people follow fashion because of *craze* fashion causes, and that the behavior of people who adopt fashion does not show any more irrationality than voters casting ballots. Therefore, fashion,

> carries the stamp of approval of an elite – an elite that is recognized to be sophisticated and believed to be wise in the given area of endeavor. It is this endorsement which undergirds fashion – rather than the emotional interaction which is typical of crazes (Blumer, 1969, p. 277).

Based on ethnographic research conducted in the Parisian fashion industry, Blumer (1969) argues that fashion is a highly selective process, exemplified by his observations from a Parisian fashion event:

- A hundred or more designs were presented to 100–200 buyers, with only six to eight designs being selected by buyers.
- It was impossible to predict which designs would be chosen by buyers.
- Buyers were preoccupied with intense discussions about women's fashion, and what fashion publications were writing, in an attempt to predict the taste of the public.
- Most buyers made almost identical choices on new designs independently of each other, probably due to a consensus arising from discussions among buyers and a shared taste.
- Designers were preoccupied with translating themes from media and existing fashion into new designs, trying to capture the modernization of society and following the spirit of new societal developments.

Blumer also criticized Simmel's (1904) view of elites and argued that instead of styles coming into fashion because of the distinction offered by elites, what is central to fashion is to 'be in fashion' (p. 280). This is because,

> it is not the prestige of the elite which makes the design fashionable but, instead, it is the suitability or potential fashionableness of the design which allows the prestige of the elite to be attached to it. The design has to correspond to the direction of incipient taste of the fashion consuming public. The prestige of the elite affects but does not control the direction of this incipient taste. We have here a case of the fashion mechanism transcending and embracing the prestige of the elite group rather than stemming from that prestige (Blumer, 1969, p. 280).

Blumer (1969) further adds that both elites and non-elites want to *be in fashion*, and they also conduct a selection process from designers trying to find a new trend. Prestige does not guarantee anything because fashion has, time and time again, bypassed leaders and invented something new. Blumer (1969), therefore, saw fashion as a collective decision of people to be *in fashion* because of a developing taste. Finally, Blumer (1969) also argued that fashion is often seen as an aberrant and irrational *social happening* because of the mass hysteria it can cause, and those who make this argument misunderstand fashion. He says,

> to view fashion as an aberrant and irrational social happening, akin to a craze or mania. Presumably, this ill-considered view of fashion has arisen from considerations which suggest that fashion is bizarre and frivolous, that it is fickle, that it arises

> in response to irrational status anxieties, and that people are swept into conforming to it despite their better judgement. It is easy to form such impressions. For one thing, past fashions usually seem odd and frequently ludicrous to the contemporary eye. Next, they rarely seem to make sense in terms of utility or rational purpose; they seem much more to express the play of fancy and caprice (Blumer, 1969, p. 266).

REFLECT

Discuss the following questions: Can you identify a fashion trend today that seems to follow Simmel's theory? Who are the trendsetters, and who are the imitators? How do these early sociological ideas help you think differently about fashion choices in your own life or community?

In modern sociological thought, fashion remains within the realm of material; however, some authors have added symbolic value to fashion's material culture. For example, Crane and Bavone (2006) argued that fashion should be studied through the prism of the symbolic value of fashion to material culture. This means that we should see fashion through sociology of consumption, sociology of material culture, and the sociology of cultural production, where new interpretations of symbolic values are created and attributed to material culture. Crane and Bovone (2006) argued that consumers create meanings from material goods after purchase, which contributes to experiencing a social life. This argument aligns with Blumer's work because it assigns fashion a symbolic value; thus, fashion is seen as material, and material is also symbolic. The process of creating meaning through fashion contributes to consumption, expressing symbolic values (not just economic ones) and material goods, such as fashion items, because fashion also participates in communicating values since consumers communicate messages about values they hold when making a purchase (Dolfsma, 2004). Crane and Bovone (2006) argued that clothing can be seen as a type of visual text used by people to communicate about themselves and that visuals of fashion are comparable to advertisements or photographs. The fashion industry can be seen as engaging in a process that produces fashion values, similar to artistic values, and this process is a highly cooperative activity because professionals and workers have different skills to participate in the fashion industry and must rely on many different people. Therefore, fashion can be seen as 'the product of a chain of a great many individual decisions made by people interconnected within the various niches in the industry' (Kawamura, 2005, p. 53).

Fashion is a cultural production because there is a need to innovate by altering the symbolic values attached to each style of clothing. Since fashion collections are produced several times a year, this means that previous styles need to be combined with new ideas, and there is a necessity to produce clothes that have a symbolic value that resonates with consumers and resolves the 'demand uncertainty' (Dowd, 2004, p. 1). By communicating fashion items, the symbolic value of fashion is presented through media and advertising because brands are communicating values that imply ideology and specific lifestyles. Equally, editorial pages in fashion magazines and fashion advertisements, catalogs, and TV programs disseminate images of clothing, and this communication relies on redefining symbolic values of each style of clothing (Crane & Bovone, 2006).

REFLECT

Think of a specific item of clothing you own. Consider the following:

Material Aspect: Describe the item (e.g., fabric, color, style, brand). Where did you get it, and why did you choose it?

Symbolic Aspect: What does this item represent to you or others? Does it signify a role (e.g., student, professional), a cultural identity, a value (e.g., sustainability, luxury), or a memory?

Communicating Fashion and the Changed Role of Elites

The concept of communicating fashion goes back to the concept of elites and who decides what is fashionable. Blumer (1969) was not entirely wrong in criticizing the concept of elites setting up trends to distinguish themselves from others because things had indeed started to change during his time, and the pace of change has increased, particularly during the 21st century. It would be wrong to argue that elites no longer set trends; they do, but the nature of setting trends has changed. For example, British Royal Family members are often the fashion trendsetters, such as Princess Catherine, whose style is praised and copied by fashion retailers, elites, and non-elites. Since the rise of digital communication, some websites carefully follow the royal fashion style, such as the 'What Kate Wore' website, which follows the fashion choices of Princess Catherine (https://whatkatewore.com) and helps others copy her style. The British Royal Family does not seek to distinguish itself, because Princess Catherine has not changed her style once others started to copy her. Therefore, we now talk about mass following and the contribution of the Royal Family to fashion. We could argue that elite trendsetting has changed, and while previously, elites wanted to distinguish themselves from non-elites, nowadays, elites try to remain socially significant and exert influence by creating a mass following. This is linked to the desire for imitation, which Simmel (1957) tackled in his work arguing that individuals imitate others because it gives them the satisfaction of not standing alone in their actions, and this applies to all forms of trendsetting today where people still imitate famous personas in their style; the main difference is that nowadays famous persons or elites no longer seek to distinguish themselves from others but to influence them.

The desire to influence has been exacerbated with the rise of bloggers and vloggers. Many influencers start as members of the public but later, with their rise in popularity, become a form of elite themselves and start setting trends, which creates a new cycle among influencers with new influencers continually emerging. Many influencers, once they gain popularity, engage with brand endorsements, and launch their own brands and labels, which makes them a form of micro-elites. For example, Italian influencer Chiara Ferragni has created a business empire from her blog, *The Blonde Salad*, which started in 2009. She launched her fashion label in 2013, first as a shoe line, but then she expanded her business and introduced other products, such as accessories, clothing, swimwear, makeup, jewelry, and children's wear (Herndon, 2022). Rather than focusing on design, since Ferragni is not a designer, the brand has been described in a way that appeals to modern women: 'Chiara Ferragni is the brand of sharing, happiness, positive values and good vibes, both in real and digital universe. Chiara Ferragni women are international, dynamic, cool, modern and strong' (Morelatto Group, n.d.). *The Blonde Salad* blog evolved into a talent and marketing strategy agency, and Ferragni is a board member. The blog still features fashion news and reads like an online magazine (The Blonde Salad, n.d.). In 2015, Harvard Business School dedicated a case study to Chiara Ferragni's brand, recognizing her business acumen in monetizing her popular blog and turning it into a business empire (Keinan et al., 2015). Given the rise of influencers that expanded imitation and widened participation, fashion remains in the domain of imitation, be it from elites and celebrities or micro-influencers, such as bloggers and vloggers.

The type of symbolic values associated with fashion items changes and depends on the cultural and political history and the characteristics of ethnic groups that participate in consuming fashion and attaching symbolic values to fashion items. Different countries have distinctive fashion cultures, which depend on the nature of the fashion industry, clients, influences of marginal subcultures, and the role of arts and culture in the country's heritage (Crane & Bovone, 2006). Fashion is often associated with Europe, due to the rise of haute couture which started in Paris; however, the lack of knowledge of fashion theory and history in other parts of the world likely comes from a historical lack of Western interest in other civilizations, as well as language barriers. The relevance of fashion, however, increased with the modernization and industrialization that happened in the West during the 19th century. Already in 1923, Marshall (1923) argued that 'until a while ago it was only the rich who could change their clothing at the capricious order of their dressmakers: but now all classes do it' (p. 260). Therefore, to consider fashion as a societal phenomenon, we must also use a historical approach and study fashion within the context of industrialization.

REFLECT

Choose one fashion blogger or vlogger, and reflect on the following questions:

In what ways does this person influence your or others' fashion choices?

What gives them authority or credibility – style, storytelling, follower count, brand collaborations, or something else?

Do you think their influence reflects democratic access to fashion culture or reproduces a new form of elitism?

Historical and Societal Developments in Fashion During and After the Industrial Revolution

The growth of manufacturing supported the fashion industry, with one of the most significant developments being the introduction of the sewing machine. The first sewing machine was introduced in 1851 in the US by Isaac Merrit Singer, who spearheaded further developments, such as those from Wheeler and Wilson of Michigan and Wilcox and Gibbs of Virginia. The invention of the sewing machine revolutionized fashion in a similar way that the telegraph revolutionized communication and the steam engine revolutionized travel (Stewart & Hunter, 1964). It took until the 20th century for the fashion industry to start rising and for a true societal revolution to happen, but the invention of the sewing machine cleared the way. In the UK, John Barran is credited with being the first to use sewing machines in his factory. Even though Barran's Leeds factory did not start producing women's clothes until 1927, they were the first to engage with high-grade men's tailoring manufacture and, later, also conveyor belts for women's outerwear (Ewing, 1992). In London, Selincourt and Colman started making coats, mantles, and fur garments in 1857, later expanding their range to include dresses (Ewing, 1992). The invention of the sewing machine democratized fashion, as it made mass production of fashion possible – without it, fashion would never have become available to all (Stephens Frings, 1987).

Men's clothes entered mass manufacturing first because of the perception that men's fashion is more stable and less prone to changes in trends. Thus, women's fashion was mainly made in department stores, which had their own workrooms (Stephens Frings, 1987). Women's fashion was also produced by the so-called little dressmakers, who were working-class women sewing clothes for ladies and Court dresses, producing a British equivalent of haute couture (Ewing, 1992; Gayle, 2012). The dressmakers were poorly paid, which was recorded by some fashion writers who wrote about a silk blouse during the Edwardian period and spoke of the wages of dressmakers in the early 1900s,

> many blouses of handsome material and of excellent workmanship are made ... by girls who are paid considerably less than 10s. a week. A silk blouse was shown to one of us for the making of which 10d. had been paid. Back and front were composed entirely of small tucks and of insertions of lace. The retail price of the garment would have been from 18s to 25s. The worker, a skilled young woman, could not make two such blouses in a day (Ewing, 1992, p. 56–57).

This issue was explored in detail in a book by Mayer and Black (1909), who explained how poorly women sewers and dressmakers were paid and compared their pay with that of men who worked in manufacturing, arguing that women were paid a fraction of men's pay. Brittain (1953) argued that between 1900 and 1914, the average wage of a British male worker was 30 shillings, whereas women who were sewing clothing were making no more than 18 shillings. Women were also working 18-hour shifts, but trade unions were not concerned with women's rights, which only started to change when Mary McArthur founded the National Federation of Women Workers in 1906. The progress in campaigning for women's working rights was slow, with only 107,000 members of the women's working federation, which rose to 878,000 in 1913, with two-fifths of members being from the textile industry. In 1914, there were five million women workers, of which 612,000 were in clothing, 86,000 were in textiles, and around two million were in domestic services, earning about £20 a year and generally overworked (Ewing, 1992).

In the US, women's work organizing started even earlier than in the UK. The International Ladies Garment Workers' Union was founded in 1900 by 11 men representing 2000 organized members, but the pay did not immediately improve. Even when the ready-to-wear clothes started to rise in the US, ladies were purchasing clothes produced by poorly paid women workers, which resulted in strikes in 1909 in New York, the biggest female strike of the time. Agreement was only reached in 1910 after further strikes, but working conditions did not improve until after WWI (Ewing, 1992). This period was also known as the time when the fashion industry was accused of operating in sweatshops and criticized for unsafe working conditions. For example, a fire in a textile company in New York in 1911 influenced the changed views of fashion because 146 workers, mostly girls, died due to the factory's main exit door being bolted. This then resulted in action on working conditions, pay, sick benefits, and regular hours (Stephens Frings, 1987). However, these poor working conditions led to criticism from feminists and influenced a forever difficult relationship between fashion and feminism.

Fashion and Feminism

The relationship between fashion and feminism has suffered due to two opposing ideas: 'that fashion is a powerful tool women can use to forge identity and influence others, or that fashion is a force that oppresses women' (Croll, 2014, p. 98). Historically, feminists opposed fashionably dressed women, such as the famous case of Susan B. Anthony and Elizabeth Cady Stanton, who were proponents of this philosophy. At the 1852 Women's Convention, Stanton opposed the leadership bid of Elizabeth Oakes Smith because of her stylish attire. This attitude has held throughout feminist history; somehow, being both fashionable and feminist is impossible (Croll, 2014). There is a good reason for this opposition, though. Before the birth of feminism and during its First Wave, women were suffering under tightly laced corsets and heavy skirts, which were harming their health and making them uncomfortable due to difficulties in moving. Corsets were stiffened with metal or whalebone and tightened hard. Therefore, one of the first feminist fashion statements was Bloomers. In 1851, this outfit – a dress with trousers underneath inspired by Turkish women's fashion – was born by Amelia Bloomer, who showed it in *The Lily*, a temperance and women's journal. The outfit was worn by Elizabeth Cady Stanton and featured in the journal, which started a fashion craze and even ended up being featured in *Harper's Monthly* (Croll, 2014). The trend did not last, but it is sometimes seen as the first Western experiment with women's trousers. In England, suffragettes protested corsets in 1904, launching a campaign against this restrictive garment, which also influenced French campaigners to do the same (Worsley, 2011).

Feminists were also hostile to fashion because of women's working rights. The fashion industry was seen as a bastion of capitalism, and thus, many feminists historically called for resistance to fashion (Parkins, 2006; Moi, 1988). Another reason for feminist hostility toward fashion is that many textile and factory workers are women who have faced sweatshop working conditions and health harm from factory chemicals, and thus, feminists also see the fashion industry as exploitative of women. Fashion is often blamed for the beauty myth and overly focusing on White, thin, and tall women (Mellicker, 2016). Feminists often use Simone de Beauvoir to criticize fashion. In her work, de Beauvoir (1952) argued that one is not born but becomes a woman, and she eloquently argued that rationality is ascribed to men, while women are seen through their material bodies, an issue that has later been explored by the ecofeminist movement (Topić, 2021). As a result of de Beauvoir's work, many feminists argued that women's self-presentation is a cultural body practice (Entwistle, 2000), which led to the argument of a beauty myth (Wolf, 1991) that women can only achieve a high social status if they have a socially approved appearance, which is defined by youthfulness and thinness. The focus on appearance is something feminists see as oppressive because women are nudged to focus on unhealthy beauty routines, which bring them no reward and prevent them from focusing on social and political issues of the day (Wolf, 1991; Faludi, 1991). Other scholars have argued that preoccupying women with appearance was a result of the work of the media industry, dominated by men, which happened in response to the threat of Second Wave Feminism (Friedan, 1963; Churchill, n.d.), however, many commentators and feminists still express hostility toward fashion even though, the fashion industry has rarely gone against social progress and has almost always supported women's empowerment.

What is more, fashion is an industry that has historically empowered women not only with designs but also with employment. Women designers played a key role in modernizing women's fashion and advancing women's liberation, suggesting that feminist hostility toward fashion merits reconsideration. For example, Madeleine Vionnet abandoned corsets before other designers and relied on natural women's curves. Her designs 'utilized draping and – her great contribution to couture – the bias cut, which made her dresses cling to the body in an appealing way. Vionnet's designs were radical, but they were also the first triumph of the female figure in modern fashion' (Croll, 2014, p. 100). Other than Vionnet, Coco Chanel also revolutionized women's fashion by drawing inspiration from men and introducing and popularizing trousers (Cerini, 2021). Popularizing masculine-inspired fashion items such as blazers, sweaters, and jersey suits, as well as trousers, Chanel also contributed to women's liberation. Chanel's fashion brought 'a new meaning to chic, but at the same time were highly versatile and allowed women to live an active life while remaining stylish' (Croll, 2014, p. 102). This fashion empowerment happened during the First Wave of Feminism, while women fought for the right to vote, and lasted until WWII. After that, conservativism returned with Christian Dior's New Look, which focused on ultrafeminine styles, including tiny waists. The New Look horrified Chanel, who returned from retirement in 1954 at the age of 71 to bring back practical clothing to women (Croll, 2014) and fought the New Look, which, in comparison to Chanel's empowering clothes, could have been seen as a step back even though proponents of the New Look argue that Dior brought hope after the misery of war with his glamorous and luxury designs.

The Feminine Mystique by Betty Friedan (1963) also criticized the new domestication of women and the return of conservative values, which became the focus of the Second Wave of Feminism due to the portrayal of women as housewives, with feminists fighting and arguing that women's destiny and happiness are not just in households. This work opened the neglected question of why so many White, suburban, stay-at-home moms and housewives struggled with neurosis, anxiety, and depression, which was common for these women in the period between the 1940s and 1960s, with the issue reaching its peak during the 1950s (Gershon, 2017). There was also a corresponding rise in the prescription of tranquilizing drugs and antidepressants, with some studies showing that women increasingly received such medications (Gove, 1972, 1987). Thus, the Second Wave of Feminism focused on achieving equality of women in the workplace, including launching a sex revolution (Croll, 2014). However, the division between feminism and fashion remained. Betty Friedan, a notable American feminist argued that it is not wrong for a feminist to look beautiful saying, 'Women could all stop wearing lipstick and blusher, eye shadow and moisturizing cream tomorrow, and I doubt it would help them break through the glass ceiling or get childcare or parental leave within the structures of the workplace' (Feldman, 1992, p. 45).

During the 1970s, Gloria Steinem became a symbol of both feminism and fashion. While she was critical of fashion and somewhat hostile toward the industry, her style, including aviator sunglasses, became widely imitated, provoking hostility from other feminists who saw her as too fashionable. Steinem founded a magazine, *Ms*, in 1972, that tackled politics, not just beauty and fashion. She was also feminism's cover girl bringing positive visibility to feminism (Croll, 2014). This visibility of feminism and the popularity of *Ms* magazine also instigated changes in *Vogue*, a leading fashion magazine, where eccentric editor Diana Vreeland was replaced by Grace Mirabella, who focused on working women. Mirabella featured clothes that were for both home and office, smart, affordable, and often power-suited (Croll, 2014; Mirabella, 1995), which supported the feminist cause but somewhat diminished the artistic component of fashion (e.g., haute couture). On the other side of this approach to working women was Helen Gurley Brown, a *Cosmopolitan* editor who identified as a feminist, featuring articles about the workplace and women's success in workplaces, but feminists criticized her because she advocated the use of sexuality as a tool for career advancement (Croll, 2014). For example, in the book *Having It All,* Gurley Brown (1982) writes about 'mouseburgers', which she defines as non-appealing women (she includes herself in this description), and teaches them how to satisfy a man, using men for funding and career advancement, not surprisingly outraging feminists. In *Sex and the Single Girl,* published 20 years before *Having It All,* Gurley Brown (1962) wrote about women gaining financial independence and having sex before marriage, which caused a scandal at the time. Because of advocacy for the sexual liberation of women in this book, some have celebrated Gurley Brown as a second-wave feminist on par with Betty Friedan; however, others criticized her. Gurley Brown responded to criticism by saying,

> This is how it was for me. This is how I played it. It's just a pippy-poo little book and people come back with this diatribe about its great social significance. Well it's just because nobody ever got off his high horse long enough to write to single women in any form they could associate with. If they had, somebody else would be the arbiter for single women at this point instead of me (Doll, 2012, n.p.).

It was only the Third Wave Feminism of the 1990s that embraced women's diversity, including the desire of some women to be fashionable. One aspect of this change in the feminist approach to fashion was the so-called 'Riot grrrl' influenced by punk. This fashion was girly and aggressive at the same time, and sometimes 'protest slutty' (Croll, 2014). The Girl Power slogan originates from this movement, and it was popularized by a British girl band, the Spice Girls. Madonna was, at the same time, wearing sexualized fashion, and this became the embodiment of Third Wave Feminism. The question of whether a feminist can also love fashion remains open. While feminists are no longer as aggressive and hostile to women who like fashion, old attitudes have not entirely disappeared. However, some feminist magazines, such as *Jezebel,* have fashion articles covering labels, trends, and icons, and they provide criticism when things are too centered on men in fashion shows or big celebrity events. Some bloggers also feature fashion, such as the now-defunct *Man Repeller* blog, which wrote about silhouettes that turn men off and, rather than arguing that fashion oppresses women, argued that women can dress up for each other and themselves (Croll, 2014). The Fourth Wave of Feminism, which started between 2010 and 2012, focused on sexual harassment, body shaming, girls' fan culture online, rape culture, reproductive rights, LGBT+ rights, and intersectionality. The relationship with fashion continues to be softer and now focuses on sustainable fashion and body positivity, and while some feminists still might see fashion as patriarchal, capitalist, and oppressive, in the Fourth Wave, some feminists also promote the power of choice and inclusivity. A famous example is *The SlutWalk* movement, which happened in response to a Canadian police officer claiming that women invite assaults because they dress like sluts, so feminists reclaimed the term slut through fashion and protested victim blaming that argues women are assaulted because of the way they dress (WGRC, n.d.).

It can be argued that the third and fourth waves of feminism did the right thing in softening criticism of fashion. Women's interest in clothes is reasonable because, for a long time, women were only allowed to own their clothes and nothing else (Stephens Frings, 1987), and thus, a long-term woman's interest in fashion is a logical continuation of historical social conditions and societal developments. Some scholars argue that even though many fashion designers are men, they still narrate women's history with their designs, and, since fashion is so deeply connected with women and women generally express interest in fashion (regardless of why this is the case), trivializing fashion means also trivializing women (Parkins, 2012, 2006).

REFLECT

Can fashion be a feminist act? In what ways can dressing up be a form of empowerment rather than objectification?

How have feminist movements historically influenced fashion styles and choices (e.g., bloomers)?

Is it possible to separate fashion choices from patriarchal standards of beauty? Why or why not?

How does the labor behind the clothes we wear relate to feminist concerns about exploitation and agency?

If we accept the view that trivializing fashion means trivializing women, how do we provide a meaningful critique of the fashion industry?

Consumerism, Commercialization of Fashion, and Understanding Publics

After the invention of the sewing machine, a logical development for the fashion industry was to further commercialize fashion, which happened with the introduction of commercial patterns that replaced home-sewn garments cut and fitted by trial and error (Stephens Frings, 1987). In the US, this business particularly grew with the first paper patterns becoming available in 1850 in Philadelphia by Ellen and William Demorest, who also brought out their first issues of *Madame Demorest's Mirror of Fashions* in 1860 in New York. This magazine enabled customers to order patterns via mail order, and many patterns were from French fashion. However, since Americans were more conservative than Europeans, the Demorests adapted European styles to American taste (Stephens Frings, 1987). These patterns created fashion consciousness and contributed to fashion mass production and the popularity of fashion. The mass character of the fashion industry has also been exacerbated by early mail order, which started in the US, where most of the population lived in rural areas with limited store offers. With the rise of the railway, these areas were able to order goods by mail order. People started to order merchandise from catalogs and pay at delivery (Stephens Frings, 1987). The rise of consumerism and customer service in the

US also increased the mass production of the fashion industry and the demand for fashion products. For example, Marshall Fields from Chicago and their famous mantra 'customer is always right', or Montgomery Ward and their money back guarantee ('satisfaction or your money back') started in the 19th century at the onset of the Industrial Revolution.

Society has had a class division for centuries, and class is often determined by income. Historically, the wealthiest were always the most fashionable because they could afford lavish clothes, which became a status symbol rather than just a sign of good taste (Stephens Frings, 1987). To this day, people try to prove their success with clothes. The traditional class division that originally existed and separated haute couture from retail no longer exists, and clothing is now mass-produced. The largest spending power rests with the middle-income group in the West, and most people can enjoy fashion at least to a certain level.

Fashion, like many consumer goods companies, is directed toward those who have the most purchasing power, and this sometimes results in whole clothing lines specifically targeting certain groups, such as the baby boom generation that came of age during the 1960s and created a mass market, firstly for junior consumers (due to this generation being around 25 years old) and then a more sophisticated look during the 1970s as this group grew older (Stephens Frings, 1987). Society is now segmented even more, and fashion companies often target publics based on their education, interests, location, lifestyle, income, etc. (Stephens Frings, 1987). However, the fashion industry is more sensitive to economic situations than some other industries (e.g., food) because when the economy is good, profit rises in the fashion industry, and equally, if there is an economic downturn, fashion suffers. What sometimes happens is that when the economy is bad, people only look to buy what they need, which is reflected in colors that tend to be cheerful and happy during an economic upswing and greyer when the economy is struggling (Gall, 1985; Walch, 1983). However, fashion moved from people buying clothes when they need them to something people buy more frequently due to different motives, such as:

a. *the desire to be fashionable* (consumer obsolescence, discarding fashion that is not the latest trend);
b. *the desire to be attractive* (clothes show our physical attributes and/or make us look better),
c. *a desire to impress others* (exhibiting our taste, level, or income),
d. *a desire to be accepted by friends or colleagues* (peer groups and fitting in):
e. *a desire to fill an emotional need* (new clothes help people feel better psychologically) (Stephens Frings, 1987).

When buying clothing, people use several criteria when choosing what to buy, including colors, texture, style, price, fit, appropriateness, brand, fabrics, and workmanship (Table 2.1).

Consumption is largely seen as relational (Aspers & Beckert, 2011) because the act of purchase relates to what others think and do, and an individual making a purchase relates to these views when deciding what to buy. Therefore, individuals are not born with an interest in fashion. Instead, individuals are born into 'a society in which fashion and social distinctions are taken for granted and valued' (Aspers & Godart, 2013, p. 183). Fashion comes into being through use and consumption, for example, when companies use a certain type

Table 2.1 Fashion Purchase Criteria

CRITERIA	DESCRIPTION
Color	• People relate personally to colors and some colors fit certain people better than other colors
Texture	• The surface interest in the fabric; fabrics evoke a sensuous appeal in people
Style	• Line, silhouette, and details • Hanger appeal • Style can be personal or linked to current trends (depends on consciousness levels of each individual)
Price	• The total worth of a clothing piece and its relationship to the retail price
Fit	• Size is not a guarantee of a fit • Sizing standards exist but each company is different • Some companies use sizes suitable for their target consumer group
Appropriateness	• Clothing item needs to be suitable for desired occasion and for lifestyle needs of consumers
Brand	• Some consumers recognize brands and buy based on their reputation; others are influenced by advertising
Fabric performance and care	• The durability of clothing items and the ease of caring for each garment • Most consumers prefer easy-care, easily wash-and-wear garments • Designer garments require more care but consumers who buy designer clothing are often willing to pay for extra care • Fiber content and care instructions are available on labels
Workmanship	• The quality of construction, stitching, and finishing. The finest workmanship is usually found in designer garments whereas mass production can often suffer from the quality of stitching and finishing, however, many consumers who buy mass clothing do not pay attention to these details

Source: Author's work; information adapted from Stephens Frings (1987, pp. 37–38) and Marcus (1979, p. 1)

of advertising directed at consumers or when people display their bodies in a certain way (Aspers & Godart, 2013). Fashion also represents the general 'aestheticization of social life' (Postrel, 2004), which includes both material (consumer objects and the body appearance) and immaterial (ways to talk and express oneself). For that reason, some sociologists study fashion consumption as an economically important phenomenon and look at 'aesthetic markets' (Aspers, 2001) or 'aesthetic economy' (Entwistle, 2009). Consumption is linked to the meaning of clothes, and consumers attribute meaning to clothes through the act of consumption.

REFLECT

List three fashion items you purchased or desired in the past six months. For each item, note:

Trigger: Where did you first encounter the item (e.g., Instagram ad, friend, store display)?
Narrative: What story did the brand or medium tell you about the item?
Public Identity: Which 'public' did the narrative imply you belonged to?

DISCUSSION QUESTIONS

- Simmel described fashion as a tool of social distinction – first adopted by the elite, then copied by the masses. Do you think this model still holds true? Why or why not?
- How does Simmel's idea of fashion as a class-based cycle compare to today's influencer-driven fashion trends?
- In what ways are Simmel's and Blumer's theories complementary? Where do they conflict?
- How might each theorist interpret the influence of social media platforms like Instagram or TikTok on fashion trends?
- Can we still apply early sociological theories to today's global and digital fashion industry, or do we need new frameworks?
- How do clothes function as more than just practical items? What cultural meanings do garments carry beyond their material form?
- How can garments reflect or challenge social norms, values, or ideologies?

FASHION AND FILM

Fashion in Film

1930 – Morocco – Marlene Dietrich caused a sensation by wearing trousers
1934 – It Happened One Night – Clark Gable took off his shirt and scandalously revealed his bare chest
1936 – The Jungle Princess – curves of Dior's New Look adapted to the screen by Edith Head, the chief designer
1954 – Sabrina – Audrey Hepburn requests to work with a couturier and not Edith Head – jumpstarted the career of Hubert de Givenchy

1961 – Breakfast at Tiffany's – Audrey Hepburn works again with Givenchy and popularizes the little black dress (originally introduced by Chanel)
1974 – The Great Gatsby – Ralph Lauren designs a 1920s collection for the film to a wide acclaim
1980 – American Gigolo – Richard Gere wears Armani suits
1980s – The Cook, The Thief, His Wife and Her Lover, The City of Lost Children, The Fifth Element – Jean Paul Gaultier designs couture for these films. In 2008, Jean Paul Gaultier released a collection inspired by the Pirates of the Caribbean 3
2013 – The Great Gatsby – re-popularizing the 1920s style with Ralph Lauren launching a new collection to remind audiences about his work in the original film

Fashion as a Film Topic

1995 – Clueless
2008/2010 – Sex and the City: The Movie and its sequel
2006 – The Devil Wears Prada
2009 – A Single Man
2013 – The Bling Ring

References

Abrahamson, E. (1996). Management Fashion. *Academy of Management Review, 21*(1), 254–285.

Aspers, P. (2001). A market in vogue, fashion photography in Sweden. *European Sociology,* 3, 1–22.

Aspers P., & Beckert, J. (2011). Introduction—value in markets. In Beckert, J., & Aspers, P. (eds.), *The Worth of Goods: Valuation and Pricing in the Economy.* New York: Oxford University Press (pp. 3–41).

Aspers, P., & Godart, F. (2013). Sociology of Fashion: Order and Change. *Annual Review of Sociology,* 39, 171–192.

Blumer, H. (1969). Fashion: From Class Differentiation to Collective Selection. *The Sociological Quarterly, 10*(3), 275–291.

Brittain, V. (1953). *Lady Into Woman: A History of Women from Victoria to Elizabeth II.* London: Andrew Dakers Ltd.

Cerini, M. (2021). How Coco Chanel changed the course of women's fashion. *CCN Style,* January 9. Retrieved from https://www.cnn.com/style/article/coco-chanel-fashion-50-years

Churchill, L.B. (n.d.). The Feminine Mystique Work by Friedan. *Britannica.* Retrieved from https://www.britannica.com/topic/The-Feminine-Mystique

Crane, D., & Bovone, L. (2006). Approaches to material culture: The sociology of fashion and clothing. *Poetics,* 34, 319–333.

Croll, J. (2014). *Fashion That Changed the World.* Munich: Prestel Verlag.

De Beauvoir, S. (1952). *The Second Sex.* New York: Vintage Books.

Dolfsma, W. (2004). Paradoxes of modernist consumption – reading fashions. *Review of Social Economy, LXII*(3), 351–364.

Doll, J. (2012). Sex and the Single Girl: The Legacy of Helen Gurley Brown. *The Atlantic,* August 13. Retrieved from https://www.theatlantic.com/international/archive/2012/08/sex-and-single-girl-legacy-helen-gurley-brown/322898/

Dowd, T.J. (2004). Editorial: The embeddedness of cultural industries. *Poetics,* 32, 1–3.

Entwistle, J. (2009). *The Aesthetic Economy of Fashion: Markets and Value in Clothing and Modelling*. Oxford: Berg.

Entwistle, J. (2000). Fashion and the flesh body: Dress as an embodied practice. *Fashion Theory,* 4, 323–348.

Ewing, E. (1992). *History of 20th Century Fashion*. London: B.T. Batsford Ltd.

Faludi, S. (1991). *Backlash: The Undeclared War Against American Women.* New York: Doubleday.

Feldman, E. (1992). *Fashions of a Decade: The 1990s.* New York: Facts on File.

Friedan, B. (1963). *The Feminine Mystique*. New York: W.W. Norton.

Gall, B. (1985). Textile and Apparel Industry Analysis. Merrill Lynch, *Wall Street Week,* NET, March 22, 1985.

Gayle, J. (2012). *Fashions in the Era of Jane Austen: Ackermann's Repository of Arts.* London: Publications of the Past.

Gershon, L. (2017). What Really Made 1950s Housewives So Miserable. *JSTOR Daily,* June 8. Retrieved from https://daily.jstor.org/what-really-made-1950s-housewives-so-miserable/

Gove, W. (1987). Mental illness and psychiatric treatment among women. In Walsh, M.R. (ed.), *The Psychology of Women: Ongoing Debates*. Newhaven: Yale University Press.

Gove, W.R. (1972). The relationship between sex roles, marital status and mental illness. *Social Forces,* 51, 34–44.

Gurley Brown, H. (1982). *Having It All: Love, Success, Sex, Money ... Even If You're Starting With Nothing.* New York: Simon & Schuster.

Gurley Brown, H. (1962). *Sex and the Single Girl.* New York: Bernard Geis Associates.

Henley, T. (2017). The Kate Effect: Designers open up about how the royal has impacted their business. *Hello Magazine,* August 22. Retrieved from https://ca.hellomagazine.com/royalty/02017081638037/kate-middleton-effect-designers-talk-boost-in-business

Herndon, A. (2022). Top Leading Fashion Influencers Who Have Their Own Clothing Brands. *WWD*, July 12. Retrieved from https://wwd.com/feature/top-fashion-influencers-with-clothing-brands-1235217785/

Hinsliff, G. (2023). The 'Kate effect': How the Princess of Wales became the royals' not-so-secret weapon. *The Guardian*, May 6. Retrieved from https://www.theguardian.com/uk-news/2023/may/06/the-kate-effect-how-the-princess-of-wales-became-the-royals-not-so-secret-weapon

Kawamura, Y. (2019). *Fashion and Sociology.* New York: Bloomsbury Publishing.

Kawamura, Y. (2005). *Fashion-ology: An Introduction to Fashion Studies.* Oxford: Berg.

Keinan, A., Maslauskaite, K., Crener, S., & Dessain, V. (2015). The Blonde Salad. *Harvard Business School Case Study,* January 9. Retrieved from https://store.hbr.org/product/the-blonde-salad/515074?sku=515074-PDF-ENG

Lang, K., & Lang, G. (1961). *Collective Dynamics*. New York: Crowell.

Mayer, Mrs. C., & Black, C. (1909). *Makers of our Clothes.* Duckworth: Leopold Classic Library.

Marcus, S. (1979). Who's Minding the Customer? *Commonwealth*, November 5.

Marshall A. (1923). *Money, Credit and Commerce*. London: Macmillan.

Mellicker, R. (2016). *The Feminism of Fashion.* Retrieved from https://www.huffpost.com/entry/the-feminism-of-fashion_b_9705262

Mirabella, G. (1995). *In and Out of Vogue: A Memoir.* New York: Doubleday.

Moi, T. (1988). Feminism, Postmodernism, and Style: Recent Feminist Criticism in the United States. *Cultural Critique*, 9, 3–22.

Morelatto Group. (n.d.). *Chiara Ferragni.* Retrieved from https://morellatogroup.com/en/chiara-ferragni

Parkins, I. (2012). *Poiret, Dior and Schiaparelli: Fashion, Femininity and Modernity.* London: Berg.

Parkins, I. (2006). Building a feminist theory of fashion. *Australian Feminist Studies, 23*(58), 501–515.

Postrel, V. (2004). *The Substance of Style: How the Rise of Aesthetic Value Is Remaking Commerce, Culture, and Consciousness.* New York: Perennial.

Sapir, E. (1931). Fashion. In *Encyclopedia of the Social Sciences VI.* New York: Macmillan.

Simmel, G. (1957). Fashion. *American Journal of Sociology, 62*(6), 541–558.

Simmel, G. (1904). Fashion. *International Quarterly,* 10, 130–155.

Spencer. H. (1966[1896]). *The Principles of Sociology,* Volume II. New York: D. Appleton and Co.

Stephens Frings, G. (1987). *Fashion: From Concept to Consumer,* 2nd edition. Englewood Cliffs, New Jersey: Prentice-Hall, Inc.

Stewart, M., & Hunter, L. (1964). *The Needle is Threaded.* London: Heinemann/Newman.

Thomas-Bailey, C., & Wood, Z. (2012). How the 'Duchess of Cambridge effect' is helping British fashion in US. *The Guardian,* March 30. Retrieved from https://www.theguardian.com/uk/2012/mar/30/kate-duchess-of-cambridge-fashion-lk-bennett

Topić, M. (2021). *Corporate Social Responsibility and Environmental Affairs in the British Press: An Ecofeminist Critique of Neoliberalism.* London: Routledge.

Tranberg Hansen, K. (2004). The World in Dress: Anthropological Perspective on Clothing, Fashion, and Culture. *Annual Review of Anthropology,* 33, 369–392.

The Blonde Salad. (n.d.). *Chiara Ferragni.* Retrieved from https://www.theblondesalad.com/en/chiara-ferragni/

Us Weekly. (2010, November 18). *Kate Middleton's Engagement Dress Sold Out Within 24 Hours.* Retrieved from https://www.usmagazine.com/stylish/news/kate-middletons-engagement-dress-sold-out-within-24-hours-20101811/

Veblen, T. (1957[1899]). *The Theory of the Leisure Class: An Economic Study of Institutions.* London: Allen and Unwin.

Walch, M. (1983). Color Association of the United States. Cited in A. Toufexis, Living: The Bluing of America. *Time,* July 18, p. 62.

WGRC. (n.d.). SlutWalk. *Women & Gender Resource Center, the University of Arizona.* Retrieved from https://wgrc.arizona.edu/slutwalk#:~:text=Violence%20and%20sexual%20violence%20affects,to%20prevent%20being%20sexually%20assaulted

Wolf, N. (1991). *The Beauty Myth: How Images of Beauty are Used Against Women.* New York: W. Morrow.

Worsley, H. (2011). *100 Ideas That Changed Fashion.* London: Laurence King Publishing Ltd.

CHAPTER 3

Fashion Styles (1900–2000)

Learning Objectives

- Analyze how fashion reflects societal changes and the evolving roles of women.
- Compare fashion styles across decades and identify key innovations characteristic of each era.
- Explain the origins and development of fashion's cyclical nature.
- Identify significant transformations within the fashion industry over time.
- Distinguish between the evolution of haute couture and the emergence of ready-to-wear fashion.

The Edwardian Time

The period before 1900 was centered on conservative values and influenced by upper-class moral standards of what constituted appropriate dressing for a lady. This means that women were expected to wear corsets and appear slim, but their fashion style was also meant to support a changed social presentation of men. Until well into the 19th century, aristocratic men wore clothes that were not that distinctive in style from the women's: 'they wore rich, puffed materials in all sort of colors, decorated with lace, ruches and embroidery' (Fischenich et al., 2000, p. 12). However, as men started to emphasize their work ethos, this created a change in their outfits, which had to be more practical and functional, while women were left to demonstrate their status by differentiating their clothing from other women. It was at this time that fashion became the domain of women who were showcasing the economic success of their husbands. The men's clothing style established in the 19th century remains a cornerstone of men's fashion, suits with vests and ties; for many years, this dressing style involved a hat, which is no longer socially required.

During the Edwardian period, women were confined to a private sphere and expected to have an *S figure*, which meant wearing tight corsets to showcase a wasp waist. Women of the 19th century looked as if their bodies were 'split in two: on the upper side her bosom, and on the underside her bottom, divided by a tiny waist with hips and stomach laced away' (Fischenich et al., 2000, p. 12). The Edwardian period (called *La Belle Époque*

DOI: 10.4324/9781003515043-5

Figure 3.1 A picture of the Edwardian lady from 1912 wearing Edwardian fashion
UK's National Archives. Reprinted with permission

in France) was, therefore, conservative, and fashion rules were dictated in a top–down way, with only a privileged few having some freedom in their lives.

However, this changed in 1909 when 'a new linear silhouette came into fashion. Societal norms were challenged, and an explosion of originality and progressive ideas in art, film, psychology, and the role of women was established' (Clarkson, 2011, p. 7). The new *S silhouette* was a result of the new corset invented by a Frenchwoman, Mme. Gaches-Sarraute, who studied medicine; a corset that would remove the extreme pressure from the waist and improve women's health. This new corset, the so-called health corset, 'came high up on the bust and had a curved front busk indented at the rightly laced-up waist. The new design had a straight busk, began lower down on the bosom, which it released, and extended more deeply over the hips' (Ewing, 1992, pp. 8–9). However, this corset did not gain popularity as fashionable Edwardian ladies did not accept it because the new corset was laced up over the large curves that were not fashionable at the time. The general fashion style, therefore, changed very little during this period, and women continued to wear corsets, corset covers, flannel petticoats, and silk gowns on top of these garments, accompanied by large and expensive hats. The sign of elegance of the time was tea gowns made of pleated chiffon, lace, and regal furs or satin, which were day gowns, and ladies would change into something different for evenings. Department stores, such as Debenham & Freebody and Marshall and Snelgrove, specialized in these gowns and featured them in their catalogs (Ewing, 1992). However, reformers started to protest these conventions around 1900 (doctors, sociologists, educationalists, artists) and called this fashion style unhealthy and unnatural because corsets caused a curved spine, made natural movements difficult if impossible in some cases, and contributed toward creating a deformed female shape with many women suffering injuries due to breathing difficulties and injuries caused by metal corsets (Fischenich et al., 2000). The Edwardian-lady style started to fade away around 1909, particularly,

> those immense, yard-wide hats, laden with plumes and feathers or bell-shaped skirts that swept the ground; that giddy confusion of ribbons, lace, embroidery, frills, jewels and beads at every point … she was becoming an anachronism … great formality and immense luxury in women's dress and also demanded close attention to being in the height of fashion and to wearing the correct clothes on all occasions. On the famous weekend country visits, which were a feature of high life, the fashionable lady would change her dress, with all its accessories, five or six times a day. And no outfit should be seen twice during one weekend (Ewing, 1992, p. 6).

It took a long time to remove the *S shape*, which was distorting women's bodies. The revolution happened in Paris, and it was led by Paul Poiret, a Parisian couturier who rejected *S*-shaped silhouettes and corsets and introduced a natural line (Poiret, 1934). Poiret said that he made the change, 'it was in the name of Liberty that I proclaimed the fall of the corset and the adoption of the brassiere…. Yes, I freed the bust' (Pearce Rotondi, 2025, n.p.). The skirt was a reference to his 'hobble' skirt innovation, which could prevent the wearer from walking, and thus, Poiret was still speaking to the aristocracy more than the masses, showing health concerns but not widening access to fashion. Poiret was not the inventor of the brassiere, which was mentioned in the American *Vogue* in 1907, but

Figure 3.2 An Edwardian lady of 1894 wearing a corseted dress
UK's National Archives. Reprinted with permission

he did loosen the waist and remove the pressure on the stomach created by an *S*-shaped corset, and this then removed exaggerated curved hips and created a more natural figure (Ewing, 1992). Poiret paved the way toward revolutionizing fashion, and fashion began to express women's societal attitudes, which started to change at the time Poiret innovated his clothing. These changes coincided with women everywhere beginning to work more than ever before, which resulted in a changed consciousness and requests for societal change, followed by changes in fashion. Poiret is also often credited with introducing vibrant colors into the Edwardian period, which presented a change from the pear, almond, grey, and brown, which were colors of the time (Ewing, 1992).

Edwardian materials were extravagant, such as lace, feathers, silk, satins, ribbons, flowers, feathers, and jewels (Stephens Frings, 1987). America, due to its colonial ties, closely followed European trends, with Paris having a large influence on American fashion. Rayon was the most popular material during the WWI period, and this popularity continued until the invention of nylon during the late 1930s in the US and late 1940s in the UK (Encyclopedia. com, 2018). The choice of colors for garments also widened, and there was an increase in fashion manufacturing. Thus, WWI was not a bad period for fashion. The mass production of military uniforms supported manufacturing, and the simplified fashion style of the WWI period resulted in a rise of semi-skilled and unskilled labor instead of skilled seamstresses, which meant that more was produced, and more jobs were offered to factory workers (Ewing, 1992). Rayon also had an impact on the mass production of stockings and accompanied a wider color palette; this resulted in stockings having the color of skin and achieving mass popularity. This popularity was supported by rayon, which does not crease and lasts longer. Stockings remain popular up to the present day, and this popularity was cemented with the introduction of nylon during the 1940s, which further extended their lifespan. The popularity of stockings was further exacerbated by the rise of working women who wore practical clothes and whose social status started to grow (Ewing, 1992; Encyclopedia.com, 2018).

The Roaring '20s: A Time of Flappers and Social Upheaval

The 1920s were a time of major social change, liberation, modernity, progress, and a decline in formality and traditional values, which resulted in cosmopolitan and open-minded outlooks on life, the rise of arts and technology, commercial culture, entertainment, and sports. The 1920s were shaped by WWI and the loss of a generation of men who had fought in the war, leading to social upheaval and the term 'the roaring twenties', as traditional class systems started to break down (Shrimpton, 2013). Inflation caused by the war further intensified these changes, as the middle classes became poorer, and there was mass unemployment (Fischenich et al., 2000). However, despite suffrage and despair, this decade was simultaneously prosperous because an aspiration was created, and some people started to live better than their ancestors due to new employment opportunities and industrialization, the rise of the entertainment industry, and media empires (Shrimpton, 2013). The 1920s are also known as a decade when people felt free from sexual restrictions and were able to live full lives and enjoy themselves (Fischenich et al., 2000).

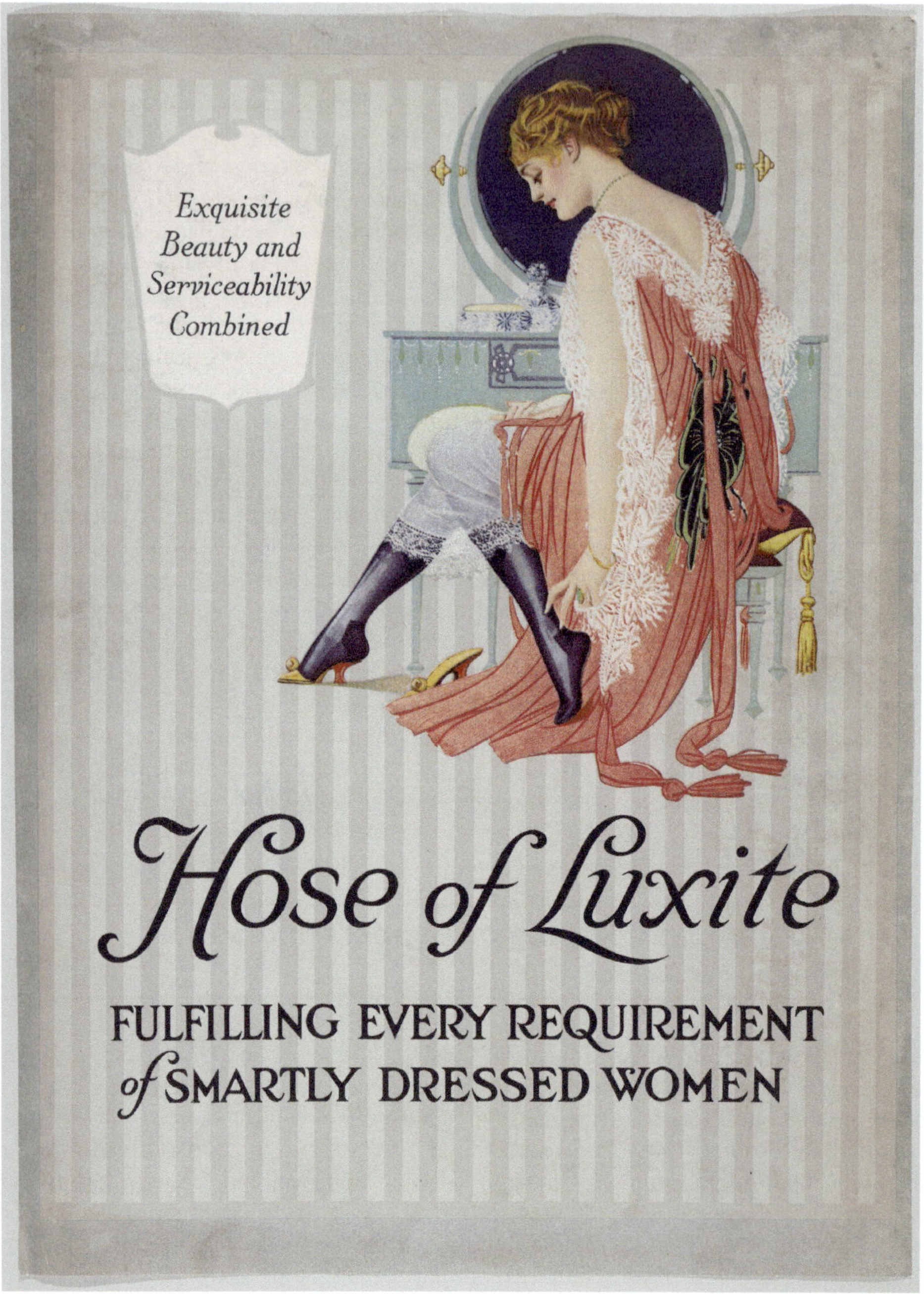

Figure 3.3 Hose of Luxite advert designed by Coles Phillips (1880–1927) featuring a woman wearing hosiery in 1918, on the eve of fashion revolution of the 'roaring' 1920s

Met Museum, Wikimedia Commons

OCTOBER 10, 1913. VOTES FOR WOMEN. 17

WILLIAM OWEN

WESTBOURNE GROVE, W.

SPECIAL PURCHASE

OF

WITNEY BLANKETS

bought previous to the great advance in price of wool, will be offered at the following reduced prices:—

LOT 1—250 pairs **Witney Blankets**, for single beds, size about 46ins. by 70ins. Usual price, 7/11. **Sale price, 5/11** per pair.

LOT 2—175 pairs **Witney Blankets**, for single beds, size about 54ins. by 80ins. Usual price, 10/11. **Sale price, 8/11** per pair.

LOT 3—143 pairs **Witney Blankets**, for single beds, size about 63ins. by 86ins. Usual price, 13/9. **Sale price, 10/11** per pair.

LOT 5—120 pairs **Witney Blankets**, for single beds, size about 64ins. by 88ins. Usual price, 16/9. **Sale price, 12/11** per pair.

LOT 6—225 pairs **Witney Blankets**, for single beds, size about 64ins. by 88ins. Usual price, 18/11. **Sale price, 15/11** per pair.

LOT 7—80 pairs **Witney Blankets**, for single beds, size about 66ins. by 88ins. Usual price, 23/6. **Sale price, 18/11** per pair.

LOT 8—75 pairs **Witney Blankets**, for single beds, size about 68ins. by 89ins. Usual price, 27/6. **Sale price, 21/6** per pair.

[illegible] **Witney Blankets**, for single beds, [illegible] per pair.

SALE PRICES.
3/11 4/11 5/11 6/11 8/11 10/6 each

LOT 16—140 pairs **Witney Blankets**, for double beds, size about 86ins. by 105ins. Usual price, 27/6. **Sale price, 21/6** per pair.

LOT 17—125 pairs **Witney Blankets**, for double beds, size about 86ins. to 105 ins. Usual price, 29/6. **Sale price, 23/6** per pair.

LOT 18—78 pairs **Witney Blankets**, for double beds, size about 88ins. by 105ins. Usual price, 33/6. **Sale price, 25/6** per pair.

LOT 19—54 pairs **Witney Blankets**, for double beds, size about 96ins. by 105ins. Usual price, 39/6. **Sale price, 29/6** per pair.

Manufacturer's Surplus Stock

OF

REAL DOWN QUILTS.

The designs and colours are excellent, and will be offered in many cases

AT NEARLY HALF-PRICE.

LOT 35—74 **Down Quilts**, for single beds, covered in good quality sateen, and well filled. Usual price, 23/6. **Sale price, 17/6.**

LOT 36—45 **Down Quilts**, for single beds, covered sateen, and extra well filled. Usual price, 29/6. **Sale price, 21/6.**

LOT 37—27 **Down Quilts**, for single beds, covered satin, artistic designs and colours. Usual price, 37/3. **Sale price, 25/6.**

LOT 38—39 **Down Quilts**, for double beds, covered sateen, exceptional value. Usual price, 2[illegible]/3. **Sale price, 21/6.**

LOT 39—25 **Down Quilts**, for double beds, covered satin and best French sateen. Usual price 37/6. **Sale price, 25/6.**

LOT 41—27 **Down Quilts**, for double beds, covered in satins and sateens, rich colours and designs. Usual price, 55/-. **Sale price, 39/6.**

LOT 42—33 **Down Quilts**, for double beds, good designs and colourings, extra well filled. Usual price, 69/6. **Sale price, 49/6.**

LOT 43—15 **Down Quilts**, for double beds, covered satin, with figured satin reverse, extra fine quality. Usual price, 84/-. **Sale price, 63/-.**

LOT 44—7 **Down Quilts**, for double beds, in best quality satin and silk. Usual price, £5/5/0. **Sale price, 75/-.**

WILLIAM OWEN

WESTBOURNE GROVE, LONDON, W.

THE COMPLETE REBEL.†

Many people have rebellious patches which give to their conduct a mottled and insecure look. As every dog may bite a citizen once, so a good man may feel that he has a right to his fling on one subject or on one occasion. But he soon hastens to sow over his patch with correct sentiments, and by a general lack of sympathy to earn the epithet of well-balanced. The enthusiast for reform in the East may be cold to the cause of outlawed women at home. The denouncer of foreign slavery may be fighting against Trade Unionism in his own country. The rebel of Ulster may be the reactionary of St. Stephen's. Some are even satisfied to have their fling over reformed-spelling or no-salt, and turn to the rest of life one vast blind spot. Indeed, the complete rebel, the man who keeps his consciousness always on the alert, and his sympathy and knowledge in the same pocket, is one of the rarest of beings.

Mr. Nevinson's rebelliousness, as expressed in his essays, is as thoroughgoing as cubism or post-impressionism. His heart is not held empty by traditions and conventions. His "bounty is as boundless as the sea." And yet this is how he sums up the secret of the untiring fighter:—

> Every rebel is a Quietist at heart, seeking peace and ensuing it, willing to let the stream of time glide past without his stir, dreading the onset of indignation's claws, stopping his ears to the trumpet-call of action, and always tempted to leave vengeance to Him who has promised to repay.

These words are profoundly true. The rebel knows that there is no use crying "Peace, Peace!" where there is no peace, and where there never can be peace till every battle is fought and every victory won. This is the "principle" that guides, or rather goads, the true rebel, a principle so deep and wide that critics cannot find it when they accuse the rebel of being "unbalanced," of tilting now at this, now at that, of being unstable, of having no rule of life. The restlessness that will not let the sword sleep in the hand, or the words remain silent on the lips, arises from the perpetual consciousness of "The Hound of Another's Hell."

But if the rebel is as haunted as Orestes, he is also the Happy Warrior:—

> If he wins, the more barbarous his suppression has been, so much the finer is his triumph, so much the sweeter the wild justice of his revenge. It is a high reward when the slow world comes swinging round to your despised and persecuted cause. . . . Whether he wins or loses, he will have enjoyed a comradeship such as is nowhere [illegible] to be found. . . . To him it has been granted to [illegible] and on the torch of that impassioned movement and change by which the soul of man appears slowly to be working out its transfiguration.

To the rebel also must belong the genius of perception. He must be able to see and hail Freedom's flag while it is still streaming against the wind; he must not wait to praise it when all the winds are changed. In the essay "Either Cowards or Unhappy," Mr. Nevinson finely illustrates some of the curiosities of that contemporary disdain which turns (with the wheel of Fortune) to retrospective adulation. The great instance is Swinburne, a passionate poet of Italy's past struggles, who had no sympathy or understanding for the Boer or the Irishman—a paper fighter to be abashed by the ghost of Byron, who was ready and glad to die for what he could praise.

The rebel then must be sorrowful, he must be full of joy, and he must see the vision.

Every Suffragist is aware of Mr. Nevinson's tireless championship of their cause and of the spirit of militancy. In essay after essay, often in the most unexpected places, he introduces the subject of the woman's fight. He generally brings it in quietly and naturally in a context in which the average reader is least prepared to find it, and where consequently it has most effect. There are still people who may give a start of surprise when they find the militancy of voteless women included among the great revolts of history, or when they read that if Joan of Arc were in England now the nation would treat her as it does the Suffragettes. But the qualities of dash and daring are always present in Mr. Nevinson's expressions of sympathy and appreciation. One can only wonder how he has had time to know and understand so many types of struggling human beings. Whether it is a fallen Sultan or a tormented peasant, the priest of Nemi, or the Maid of Orleans, the workhouse boy or the Hindoo, the Suffragists or the Corn Law fighters—they are all presented to us in the light of that particular kind of imagination which leads direct to the truth.

As a contrast to rebels of all kinds and colours, we welcome the serene presence of our old friend, Mr. Clarkson. Mr. Clarkson trying to "mind" an empty house and utterly defeated by the task of getting his own breakfast, or Mr. Clarkson at the beauty show, or as a juryman—he is always delightful. Does he appear in this volume as a warning of what a man may become if he does not take to rebellion? I hope Mr. Clarkson is still alive, he is such restful company. There are other detached essays, introduced as the author suggests, to help to keep us all sane.

But after all, nothing is so sane as anger and intolerance directed against every form of oppression and cruelty, and that splendid intolerance is generally found in those who have humour as well as indignation, who can laugh with mankind as well as pity him, enjoy a joke at his expense as well as fight for him. This happy combination keeps the complete rebel perpetually young, for with every new cause he and his enthusiasm are born again. All who care about the life of the world will thank Mr. Nevinson for giving them this book.

† "Essays in Rebellion." By Henry W. Nevinson. (London: James Nisbet and Co. Price 6s. net.)

D. H. EVANS & CO., LTD.

FASHIONABLE AUTUMN WEAR.

No. 51 VC.

WELL-CUT SUIT. In the new Basket Check Tweed; Coat fitting closely at Waist, with Black Satin Band from side Seams, fasten with Gilt Buckle in front. Embroidered Velvet Collar to tone. Corselet Skirt with Lap Seams, Plain Back. Coat lined Satin. In Grey, Brown, Blue, Mauve, etc. Price **73/6.**

Special Measures 4/6 extra.

No. 51 VC.

No. 60 VC.

ELEGANT EVENING GOWN in Black Charmeuse. Skirt cut with an over-drapery of [illegible] Jet Ornament. The b[illegible] is composed of Cream La[illegible] partly draped Black Ninon, which is edged with Diamante trimming. The folded waistbelt is finished with an Ornament to correspond with Skirt and a large Crimson Rose. Can be had in Ivory, Sky, Gold, Pink, Grey, and Sapphire. Price **5½gns.**

Special Measures 7/6 extra

No. 60 VC.

No. 56 VC.

HANDSOME COSTUME in Navy Blue Corded Cloth. Coat smartly cut with Revers and Strap of own material in the reverse way (as sketch). Waistcoat and Collar of the new Oriental Sponge Cloth. Skirt on Corselet, one-sided front, introducing Embroidery as on Coat, and slight fulness at back. Price **6½gns.**

Special measures 10/6 extra. Can be had in Black and Navy Coatings, or copied in New Autumn Shades.

Write for fully illustrated Catalogue of Autumn and Winter Fashions.

Carriage Paid throughout the United Kingdom.

No. 56 VC.

290 to 322, Oxford St., W.

Only One Address. No Branches Anywhere. Bond Street Nearest Tube Station.

Figure 3.4 Advert from *The Suffragette* newspaper featuring Sylvia Pankhurst during the period between 1913 and 1920, wearing slightly looser fashion of the time signaling shift towards fashion of the 1920s

UK's National Archives. Reprinted with permission

Illustration No. 11

Message.—(In figures 1, 2 and 3).

Heavy reinforcements for the enemy expected hourly.

(In signature in French shorthand)—

Before Arras.

Figure 3.5 The use of wartime morse code message hidden in fashion plate by Mary Helen Shaw, 1914–1918

UK's National Archives. Reprinted with permission

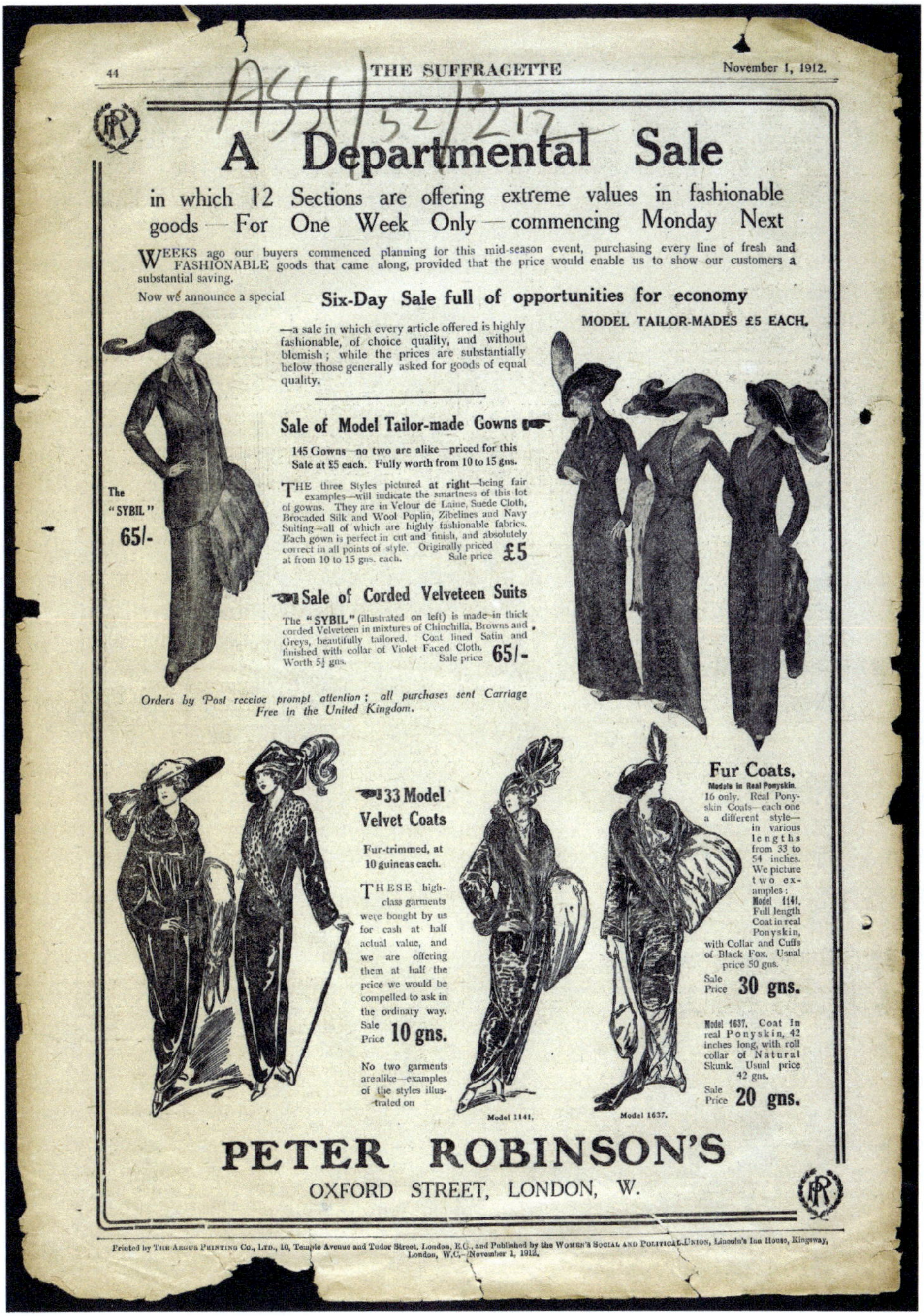

44 THE SUFFRAGETTE November 1, 1912.

A Departmental Sale

in which 12 Sections are offering extreme values in fashionable goods — For One Week Only — commencing Monday Next

WEEKS ago our buyers commenced planning for this mid-season event, purchasing every line of fresh and FASHIONABLE goods that came along, provided that the price would enable us to show our customers a substantial saving.

Now we announce a special **Six-Day Sale full of opportunities for economy**

—a sale in which every article offered is highly fashionable, of choice quality, and without blemish; while the prices are substantially below those generally asked for goods of equal quality.

MODEL TAILOR-MADES £5 EACH.

Sale of Model Tailor-made Gowns

145 Gowns—no two are alike—priced for this Sale at £5 each. Fully worth from 10 to 15 gns.

THE three Styles pictured **at right**—being fair examples—will indicate the smartness of this lot of gowns. They are in Velour de Laine, Suede Cloth, Brocaded Silk and Wool Poplin, Zibelines and Navy Suiting—all of which are highly fashionable fabrics. Each gown is perfect in cut and finish, and absolutely correct in all points of style. Originally priced at from 10 to 15 gns. each. Sale price **£5**

The "SYBIL" 65/-

Sale of Corded Velveteen Suits

The **"SYBIL"** (illustrated on left) is made in thick corded Velveteen in mixtures of Chinchilla, Browns and Greys, beautifully tailored. Coat lined Satin and finished with collar of Violet Faced Cloth. Worth 5½ gns. Sale price **65/-**

Orders by Post receive prompt attention; all purchases sent Carriage Free in the United Kingdom.

33 Model Velvet Coats

Fur-trimmed, at 10 guineas each.

THESE high-class garments were bought by us for cash at half actual value, and we are offering them at half the price we would be compelled to ask in the ordinary way. Sale Price **10 gns.**

No two garments arealike—examples of the styles illustrated on

Model 1141. Model 1637.

Fur Coats.

Models in Real Ponyskin.

16 only. Real Ponyskin Coats—each one a different style—in various lengths from 33 to 54 inches. We picture two examples:

Model 1141. Full length Coat in real Ponyskin, with Collar and Cuffs of Black Fox. Usual price 50 gns. Sale Price **30 gns.**

Model 1637. Coat in real Ponyskin, 42 inches long, with roll collar of Natural Skunk. Usual price 42 gns. Sale Price **20 gns.**

PETER ROBINSON'S

OXFORD STREET, LONDON, W.

Printed by The Argus Printing Co., Ltd., 10, Temple Avenue and Tudor Street, London, E.C., and Published by the Women's Social and Political Union, Lincoln's Inn House, Kingsway, London, W.C.—November 1, 1912.

Figure 3.6 An advert from *The Suffragette* newspaper featuring lady's fashion, November 1, 1912

UK's National Archives. Reprinted with permission

Social changes were followed by changes in fashion. In the US, this decade is known as the Decade of the Flappers (in the UK, the term was the Bright Young Things), for the explosion of color, energetic dancing, the rise of jazz music, and as a period of escapism as societal changes were embedded within a youthful reaction to the dark and serious clothes of the older generation and conservative Edwardian and Victorian values and behaviors. The youth rebelled against the pre-war fashion except for hats and veils, which took a new social role (Herald, 1991). Jazz had a particular role in the rebellious attitudes of youth because this was American music that broke racial and gendered barriers due to the prominence of women and Black singers. Dancing to jazz was seen as breaking the tradition by the youth, whereas the older generation still preferred foxtrot and saw jazz as immoral and a threat to existing values. Jazz then inspired fashion with flapper dresses, which were seen as bold fashion statements (Shrimper, 2013). The media age also began in this period, and people obtained ideas on how to live their lives from radio, cinema stars, and fashion magazines such as *Vogue* and *Vanity Fair.* Jean Patou, Madeleine Vionnet, and Coco Chanel were three designers who created the first modern styles of women's fashion that we know today. The fashion industry discovered the media potential and started to use it to appeal to mass consumers who were now dressing more fashionably than ever before and spending more money in bars, theaters, cabarets, etc. Film started to have a large influence on fashion with the prominence of Hollywood, which was reaching wider audiences. Many fashion designers worked for the cinema designing clothes and costumes or lending gowns for films, and since initial films were silent, visual effects were needed, which included stronger makeup and alluring outfits; this gave rise to the use of materials, such as the lams, sequins, and feathers (Shrimpton, 2013). The cinema influenced mainstream fashion as well as haute couture. Certain styles were named after Hollywood stars who wore them, and clean, simple lines with efficiency and fewer details in fashion became popular toward the end of the decade, also thanks to Coco Chanel and her revolutionary influence on fashion. Designers looked to improve their efficiency, such as Italian shoe designer Salvatore Ferragamo, who was producing handmade shoes but improved his production by assigning multiple people to produce different parts of his shoes (Herald, 1991; The Met, n.d.).

The fashion changes were preceded by major social changes, such as a rise in racing cars and, generally, increased road and air traffic. This resulted in travel-related fashion, such as leather jackets for bikers who formed their subculture and resisted mainstream fashion or early air hostesses who wore catsuits, hot pants, and miniskirts, which would today be considered sexist (Worsley, 2011), but it was liberation at the time it happened. Other social changes happened at this time, such as the rise of radio programs and the use of the gramophone. Rich people started to spend more time on expensive private yachts and ocean liners, the latter also giving rise to haute couture and cruise fashion collections (Herald, 1991) – the cruise collection began earlier but became popularized during the 1920s, with big designer names such as Coco Chanel designing cruise collections. Coco Chanel is often credited with the first cruise collection in 1919, designed for women who would visit Biarritz during holidays. Chanel also introduced and promoted a suntanned complexion during the 1920s (Vega, 2022). These changes in society and increased mobility also gave rise to consumerism, which boosted the fashion industry. However, while there was social progress, moralism and social tensions were still present underneath, and this was accompanied by, for example, prohibition laws in the US. The Federal Volstead Act of 1919 made it illegal to buy alcohol but not illegal to consume it; however, acceptance of certain types of illegal behavior rose during the 1920s, and 'this loosening of moral standards had a widespread impact on many people's approach to life' (Herald, 1991, p. 7). In terms of prohibition in the US, people attended the so-called speakeasies to drink (The Mob Museum, n.d.), and this also had an impact on fashion because speakeasies were places where modern women wore new fashions of the 1920s and expressed their new freedom.

It was during the 1920s that layers started to fall. The boyish silhouette was a style of the 1920s with baggy dresses, which were flat-chested beneath the new shapeless fit and revolutionary brassiere (Herald, 1991). The new slim line of the 1920s was modern, minimal, and geometric, and the surface of the body was broken by shapes of contrasting colors, and materials were dismantled and reassembled. By 1925, the dresses were the shortest than any other time in history, legs were given the impression of nudity with flesh-colored stockings made of artificial silk (Herald, 1991). Stockings were affordable to many women and, thus, widely popular. Therefore, while at the beginning of the decade the silhouette was barrel-shaped and a continuation of post-war modes with hemlines worn to calf length, the more the decade progressed the more the fashionable line grew narrower and straighter, and the female figure became more and more obscured, moving away from the initial girly and feminine view that was promoted by garment adverts at the beginning of the decade to a silhouette that emphasized hips (Shrimpton, 2013). By the mid-1920s, almost everyone was wearing boyish dresses with lower waists and short hems, except for older and traditional women who remained loyal to Edwardian fashion and wore long dark dresses covering legs, which sharpened the social and generational divide, visible through fashion styles (Shrimpton, 2013).

One of the features of the 1920s was also the cloche hat. This tight hat went around the head (this shape is sometimes called a head-hugging hat) and necessitated shorter hair,

Figure 3.7 Duncan sisters, cca. 1920 and cca. 1925. The sisters have short hair common for the 1920s. Published by Bain News Service

US Library of Congress

such as a bob, which became popular during the 1920s. The hat was bell-shaped and presented a change from gigantic Edwardian hats often decorated with feathers and birds. Due to the popularity of cloche hats, women cut their hair *en masse,* with 99 percent of the female population in the US and Europe having short hair (Herald, 1991, Shrimpton, 2013). Bobbed hair became popular because a short bob was a synonym with modernization and enlightenment, however, this was mainly popular with the younger generation during the 1920s while the older generation remained loyal to 'their long tresses, pinning the hair back; others cut only the side sections and wound these into a "kiss-curl" against the cheek, the back hair coiled into a tight chignon at the nape of the neck' (Shrimpton, 2013, p. 22). Other hats popular during this period included the asymmetrical shapes of the early 1920s and wartime hats, such as tricorne and bicorne, which became more extravagant with rich embroidery, feather, and tulle. Wide-brimmed hats were also popular for a romantic look, but the most iconic hat of the decade was the cloche hat, which by the end of the decade had been embraced by all social classes.

Figure 3.8 A cloche hat of the 1920s
Costume Institute, Wikimedia Commons

Key looks of the 1920s are summarized in Table 3.1 Despite social upheaval and revolutionary changes to fashion, Edwardian influences came back in the form of Edwardian-style blouses, which continued to appear in catalogs during the 1920s. This marked the beginning of the cyclical nature of fashion, a trend that was further developed during the 1930s.

The women's dress of the 1920s, the recognizable flapper dress with a low waist, was worn on its own or with a cardigan, and either in plain colors or in geometric

Table 3.1 Fashion Innovations of the 1920s

FASHION INNOVATIONS	DESCRIPTION
Silhouette	• Columnar silhouette • Belts, sashes, or ties worn around the hips • The waist disappeared and was loosely located around hips
The flapper dress	• Baggy, loose dresses seen as boyish or tomboy • Dropped waist dresses • The most distinctive feature of the 1920s
The sheath dress	• Slinky sheath dress made of chiffon, silk, or crepe de chine; it clung on the female form from shoulder straps
Beading and fringing	• Evening dresses with sequins and feathers, and fringed flapper dresses
La Garconne look	• Short hair and straight, looser dresses with bare arms • The lithe, athletic, modern form as a new sexy look
The little black dress (LBD)	• Coco Chanel introduces the LBD
Geometrics	• Bold, curved patterns in red, black, and blue; the popularity started in 1910
Edwardian blouses	• The blouse made of lace, with ruffles, or striped was seen as dual femininity because it was both demure and assertive
Style Russe	• Tunic shapes, fur trimmings, embroideries, influenced by Chanel's association with Grand Duke Dimitry and the influx of Russian immigrants to Paris after the Revolution
Hobble and kite dresses	• The period presents emancipation from Edwardian and *La Belle Époque* silhouette • Dresses become looser with hobble, and a narrow, shorter hemline, which started to appear in 1918

(*Continued*)

Table 3.1 Continued

FASHION INNOVATIONS	DESCRIPTION
Materials	• Fur coats and coats trimmed in fur • Knee length, wide cuffs, shawl collars, single large buttons • Velvet as a material for jackets, wraps, and dresses • Style and the luxury of Art Deco fashion (velvet) • Rayon – Quickly accepted by designers as a first man-made fabric for commercial use
Kimono style	• Japanese kimono-style dresses as a new form of beauty • Simplicity and oriental design • Tea gowns of 1925 were shaped like kimonos with square-cut sleeves
Bare backs and bias cuts	• Body-hugging dress had bare back and spiraled around the body and moved with the wearer; appeared late in the 1920s
Sweaters	• Silk or wool; striped, plain, or with various motifs • The flapper style of the 1920s
Trousers	• Bright young things of the 1920s style • Silken pajamas and sailor trousers for early evening
Hand-knitted garments	• Popular for winter • Came as a result of poverty during the war • Men, women, children • Knitted patterns mass produced and popularized
Bar shoes	• Popularized in the 1920s • Various heel heights, colors, and materials • New materials for this shoe – reptile leather, snake, lizard, or crocodile skin
Office clothes	• Women started to work in offices more; office work becomes a woman's profession and female typists replaced the male ones • Clothes become practical to enable free movement and showcase new self-confidence

(Continued)

Table 3.1 Continued

FASHION INNOVATIONS	DESCRIPTION
Social class recognition changed	• The silhouette no longer betrayed one's social status • Trained eye was needed to recognize materials and cuts and distinguish between cheap and expensive • Accessories and details also used to distinguish social class
Masculinity of women	• The new fashion labeled as masculine • Men started to see women as sexual and work competitors
Wedding dresses	• White becomes popularized as a color for the wedding dress
Bras	• Bras popularized as a fashion item • Bras were worn since the Edwardian time but during the 1920s, it became popular to use them to squash breasts in line with the boyish silhouette of the period
The cloche	• Bell shaped, head-hugging hats (the cloche hats) replaced large Edwardian hats
Hairstyle and makeup	• Short hair for women for the first time • The popularization of bob • Make-up shifted from a sign of loose morals to sign of social progress

Source: Author's work. Information adapted from Clarkson (2011, pp. 8–9), Shrimpton (2013, pp. 11, 18, 19, 25), Fischenich et al. (2000, pp. 21, 24), Worsley (2011, pp. 18, 21, 44), Ramzi (2024, n.p.), and Glassock (2004)

shapes, with geometric shapes being a sign of Art Deco (Clarkson, 2011). These dresses could have a straight line at the hemline or be irregular, and dresses often had V-necks. Eveningwear was centered on extravagance, such as floating panels, and Vionnet's bias-cut dresses, which followed the body shape while draperies from the hips gave an illusion of length and fullness. Attached panels and uneven hemlines added to the body movement (Clarkson, 2011).

Art Deco gained popularity during the 1920s. Art Deco introduced ethnic motifs and shapes from national traditions, folk art, and ancient civilizations, which were influenced by avant-garde art. One example of ethnic motifs is the Egyptian example, which coincided with the discovery of Tutankhamun's grave and instigated the so-called *Tutmania*

Figure 3.9 Detail of evening dresses designed by Dentelle Racine, Art-Goût-Beauté, June 1929

Wikimedia Commons

that translated into fashion (Herald, 1991, Shrimpton, 2013). The introduction of ethnic motifs into Western fashion also led to the invention of new colors such as Coptic, blue lotus, Sakkara, mummy brown, and carnelian (Herald, 1991) and, generally, rich fabrics and vibrant colors (Shrimpton, 2013). Ethnic motifs first appeared in the Edwardian period, but did not achieve wide popularity at the time (Clarkson, 2011).

The 1920s saw a rise in viscose rayon, which was used to make cheap dresses, linings, slips, underwear, and stockings (Worsley, 2011). In the US, the production of this material rose from eight million pounds (lb) in 1920 to 53 million in 1925 (Herald, 1991). Synthetic textiles gained popularity and, because of the simplicity of the new silhouette, enabled mass production, and while viscose rayon was previously seen as a vulgar material, it replaced pure silk. Other fashionable materials used for daywear were woolen fabrics, gabardine, velvet, crepe, cotton, georgette, silk, and taffeta (Shrimpton, 2013).

Despite social progress and changes during this decade, the upper classes still operated on their old, pre-war social calendar based on society events, and thus always needed clothes for the new season. The fashion industry, particularly high fashion, was built on these events and, as each new season required new designs, this gave rise to spring and summer collections of model clothes, the precursor to haute couture (Herald, 1991; Shrimper, 2013). Events encompassed grand balls, races, garden parties, and private exhibitions, and society in France, the UK, and the US operated under these calendars. By July each year, the society would move to the countryside, the French Riviera, or Palm Beach in Florida, which gave rise to the summer/cruise fashion we know today. In autumn each year, there was hunting and shooting in Scotland, New York, and London (Herald, 1991; Cady, 2019). The higher the social class, the more clothes were needed for each day, and, in England, upper-class women would receive an annual dress allowance as part of their dowry or jewelry (Herald, 1991; Golden, 2022). What is more, a wedding custom originally introduced by Queen Victoria and, thus, originating from the upper class, started to spread further. A wedding dress became white even though historically, working-class women wore black dresses, while ladies wore pink, blue, or their favorite color. The original idea was that the wedding dress needed to be practical; however, royals invented a custom of a dress that would seldom be worn again, which was then accepted by the upper classes, and then the masses (Worsley, 2011).

The haute couture business started to rise, particularly in France, the center of the world's fashion. Banks started to give loans to fashion businesses to revitalize the industry after the war, and this particularly benefited the haute couture business (Herald, 1991). This was also the period when the *Chambre Syndicale de la Haute Couture Française* gained prominence. The organization was created by Charles Worth in 1868 to safeguard high fashion (Harper's Bazaar, 2017). In 1927, there were 250,000 employees in the French fashion industry in Paris and, during this period, the main operating assumption of haute couture was established, meaning that each designer had one or two salons for showing the collections of model garments and live models were parading to clients in salons, with sewing being done per order and thus being expensive and out of reach to wider masses (Herald, 1991). Clients would be attended to by the same saleswoman, who developed a detailed understanding of each customer's taste and preferences. During fittings, clients would select the fit and color of model garments according to their wishes. Members of royalty had the privilege of choosing a design and having it withdrawn to prevent others from copying it (Herald, 1991).

While society started to develop its fashion and continued to operate under the pre-war calendar, the emancipation of women and consumerism were happening in wider society.

Figure 3.10 1920s dresses with vibrant colors and new patterns, 1926
Wikimedia Commons

Figure 3.11 Blue wedding dress, cca. 1856–1907, published by Currier & Ives
US Library of Congress

After WWI, women in Europe outnumbered men, and, in the UK in 1918, the Representation of the People Bill gave women the right to vote, albeit initially only to women over 30 years of age who met the property qualification (UK Parliament, n.d.). It was in 1928 that the Equal Franchise Act gave the right to vote to all women in the UK (UK Parliament, n.d._a). In 1920, the 19th Amendment to the US Constitution was ratified and increased women's rights (US Congress, n.d.). The role of women in society started to change substantially, particularly as women started to enter formerly male professions, and a battle for work equality started, along with changes to fashion as women needed clothes not just for staying at home and social events, but also for work. Male clerks were replaced by women typists and secretaries (Herald, 1991; Saval, 2015), and office work became a domain of women, moving them away from traditional female jobs of seamstresses, governesses, or home helpers (Fischenich et al., 2000). Working women wanted practical clothes that would also be economical and attractive, and this gave rise to abandoning complicated layers in favor of comfort and a lighter effect, which happened toward the end of the decade (Shrimpton, 2013).

While the masses did not have the money or the time required to attend the many fittings associated with haute couture, which was developing at the time, magazines promoted haute couture and created an aspiration. This, in turn, resulted in pirating, and the emergence of counterfeit fashion (Herald, 1991). One of the Parisian proponents of fighting the copying of Parisian fashion was Poiret, who travelled to the US to present his designs, only to later return to France, upset by American department stores copying his creations (Ewing, 1992). He then created *Le Syndicat de Dèfense de la Grande Couture Française*, an organization focused on finding copyright violations of French designs (Ewing, 1992).

The modernization and electrification of factories, combined with the simplified silhouettes of new women's fashion, facilitated the mass production of clothing. The loose, modern styles of the 1920s could be made in a range of standardized sizes, requiring minimal adjustments to the figure (Herald, 1991).This mass production made fashion more accessible to the masses and led to the rise of home dressmaking, a new profession for working-class women who knew how to sew. Home dressmaking was done by buying paper patterns and then making clothes at home (Shrimpton, 2013). In addition to that, department stores started offering multiple dressmaking alternatives in the 1920s. For example, in Liverpool (UK), a Bon Marche store offered three types of service: Model Gown Salon on the second floor where they offered bespoke dressmaking; the floor below had the cheaper dressmaking department where paper patterns were used with customers being able to buy material from the store, with sewing and one fitting offered by the department store; and finally, in the next department the customer would buy a pattern, materials and get the loosely cut garment to finish at home (Herald, 1991). These changes in fashion consumption led to changes in marketing and advertising, with new consumers buying more than ever before. It became relevant to understand who buys and what they buy which, in the US, resulted in promotional feature articles in women's magazines of the 1920s.

Consumerism was seen as increasing democracy and emancipation (Herald, 1991). The smoking campaign also targeted women, and it was during this period that the often credited, first public relations campaign was launched: The Torches of Freedom Campaign by Edward L. Bernays, often called the father of PR. This campaign heavily featured fashion and women's emancipation through fashion, with layers of clothes falling (Topić, 2021). The new consumerism and mass production also meant this period saw the rise of window shopping, with clothes in windows being promoted by dummies, which looked fresh and had a realistic haircut and makeup (Herald, 1991). The new sizing system helped support the mass market, especially because of standardization and uniformity, and this period gave rise to market segmentation, which became part of marketing and advertising work. For example, customer types were linked to their income, and there were six personality types in the Bullock's Department Store in LA: romantic, the statuesque, the artistic, the picturesque, the modern, and the conventional (Herald, 1991). Modern was, at the time, seen as fashionable and accepting of new trends, whereas artistic was enigmatic and with a suggestion of the foreign, which became popular, featuring, for example, dark hair and eyes, and this customer was seen eccentric and accepting of ethnic motifs, vivid colors and bizarre embroideries (Herald, 1991).

Another novelty of the 1920s is visible in the use of makeup, which was previously a sign of loose morals but in this decade became a sign of the emancipation of women who painted their faces, drank, and smoked. Plucked eyebrows, rouge, and lipstick were features of the decade, particularly black kohl-rimmed eyes and red lipstick (Herald, 1991; Shrimpton, 2013). Makeup was also seen as a feminist issue with Helena Rubenstein (1930) publishing *The Art of Feminine Beauty* and saying that women were entitled to good looks and independence. Herald (1991) argued that women in the US were spending USD 750 million on cosmetics before the Wall Street crash, and the UK spending was nearly the same. Census information from the US indeed shows an increased household spending on textiles and clothing as well as a rise in the manufacturing of these products (Census, n.d.; Bureau of Labor Statistics, 2006).

Some authors label the 1920s as the Age of the Flapper because flappers were, by 1924, known for their reckless behavior as well as their style, which means that they were smoking, putting on makeup, drinking and dancing in frenzy excitement, and 'taping up their breasts to get rid of unwanted curves, they looked youthful and boyish, and the new silhouette was slender, straight up and down like a board' (Clarkson, 2011, p. 11). The waistline dropped in 1925 to below the hip, and by 1927, it disappeared altogether with hemlines rising to 38 cm, which was a sign of progress and seen as scandalous in some circles. Flapper dresses were,

> straight, loose and sleeveless, revealing a new body awareness. Arms were bare, and legs and backs were exposed for the first time, becoming new erogenous zones .... The short, shift dress, which fell straight down from the shoulders and stopped above the knee, dominated the mid-to-late 1920s. Ornamented with geometric and abstract designs, the chemise was often beaded with bands of glittering sequins (Clarkson, 2011, p. 11).

The flapper dress often had an ethnic motif, visible seam decoration, and double seams, diagonal lines, asymmetric trimmed necklines, pockets, buttons, and belts, and narrow trailing scarves with uneven split hems and pleated panels on skirts and knife pleats (Clarkson, 2011). However, 'the flapper look was at its apogee and extremely short skirts were worn day and night. But hemlines crashed down along with Wall Street in 1928, just as waistlines and busts edged their way into fashion consciousness' (Clarkson, 2011, p. 11). During this period, Coco Chanel also introduced the little black dress (LBD) in 1926, which was seen as chic and suitable for both evening and day wear (Ramzi, 2024).

While the daywear became shorter, exposing legs and placing an emphasis on hips with dropped waists and the flapper dresses, eveningwear remained long, clinging, and feminine, low on the calf or ankle-length. Evening gowns were either sleeveless or short-sleeved, often shaped into a V-shape at the back or worn on one shoulder, fastened with shoulder straps or chains. Evening dresses were often clipped at the hip, had layers using lace, satin, net, chiffon, rich silk, or velvet, and started to come in many colors, or were black with colorful beads (Shrimpton, 2013). Eveningwear followed the same silhouette as daywear, the straight line, with the main difference being the exposure of skin, which was higher with eveningwear. Despite straight lines, eveningwear was glamorous because it was made of sheer and lavish fabrics, gold and silver embroidery, feathers, sequins, etc. (Fischenich et al., 2000). Eveningwear changed by the mid-1920s with the influence of Charleston, for which women wore short dresses with fringe edging and long necklaces, so evening dresses started to be shorter, slender, square-shaped, secured on the shoulder by straps, and some skirts were slit on the side to allow movement. Fashionable colors of the late 1920s for eveningwear ranged from 'black or white to Nile green, sky blue, orange and begonia, and extravagant feathers, long boas, layered skirts and swaying fringes all accentuated movement' (Shrimpton, 2013, p. 39; Fischenich et al., 2000). Eveningwear also came with coats, which changed in line with the 1920s changes to style and became loose, ample, and more fitted toward the middle of the decade, and it also became popular to wear shawls, which were inspired by the rise of the popularity of tango (Shrimpton, 2013, p. 39; Fischenich et al., 2000).

However, while the new fashion emancipated women, men's fashion remained somewhat conservative and men's outfits remained bulky, with the most used material being tweed, thick facecloth, or corduroy. Later in the decade, men started to wear more cotton rather than wool, which was softer on the skin (Herald, 1991). Thus, while men looked softer towards the end of the decade and moved towards pampering, women looked harsher as this was a sign of emancipation, particularly in progressive circles, such as literary ones, and 'by the end of the twenties it was clear that women's dress reform had revolutionized female roles in society' (Herald, 1991, p. 57). During the 1920s, men were also initially guided by conservative Edwardian rules, but as the decade progressed, old black or gray frock coats became outdated, and only older men wore them because, in Edwardian times, these outfits expressed tradition and authority. For most men,

> the suave morning coat with sloping front edges, teamed with a matching waistcoat and pinstriped trousers, was now considered correct for formal day or business wear by the social elite; morning suits also being favored for gala occasions and events such as garden parties, the races, and weddings. While these garments all had their place, the mainstay of the male wardrobe was the three-piece suit known as the lounge suit, but sometimes called the business suit when tailored in sober colors and conservatively styled (Shrimpton, 2013, p. 30).

In line with pre-war times, popular colors included black, gray, brown, and blue, while tweed remained popular in winter and flannel in the summer. Men's garments such as knitted cardigans also entered women's fashion for the first time, and Burberry designed their practical raincoat, which was globally accepted (Herald, 1991; Ewing, 1992). The decade also gave rise to leather helmets, jackets, coats, and sportswear. Racing in France coincided with the rise of haute couture and Coco Chanel, and this new racing fashion introduced revolutionary items such as translating men's fashion to women's fashion (Bott, 2007). Racing was popular and influential in fashion beyond France. In the UK, Ascot fashion emerged due to annual British horse race attended by the aristocracy, where new clothes were shown (Ramsay, 2024). The first solo, non-stop Atlantic flight of 1927 influenced fashion because it popularized leather jackets and coats for flying and driving, inspired by Charles Lindbergh, who flew over the Atlantic for the first time (Herald, 1991; Williams, 2010).

The jackets were hip-length, and trousers were tapered, high-waisted, and secured with braces or belts (Shrimpton, 2013). This fashion changed throughout the decade, and suits started to look 'snappier, with looser, knife-edge creased trousers and more shaped, double-breasted jackets with broader, sharper lapels' (Shrimpton, 2013, p. 32). In 1925, a radical change happened with longer, baggy trousers worn by men of all generations, and particularly by the working classes. These trousers were flared to 24 inches and were commonly known as 'Oxford bags' (Shrimpton, 2013) and constituted the first unusual element in men's fashion (Fischenich et al., 2000). For eveningwear, men's fashion remained relatively unchanged; a black coat, white waistcoat, white shirt, and a white bow tie were popular for evening functions, such as public dinners, dances, and assemblies. There was another option, popular in the US, consisting of a shorter black dinner jacket, white shirt, and black bow tie, and this became popular, particularly for private dinner parties and concerts (Shrimpton, 2013). For leisure or beach/country, a pullover inspired by tennis was worn under a jacket and white trousers (Fischenich et al., 2000).

REFLECT

Think about speakeasies of the 1920s that existed during the Prohibition in the US. How did these places, which violated laws, also serve as a place of resistance in fashion and societal expectations of women? Look for information and images on fashion in speakeasies of the 1920s, particularly the flapper dresses, and consider learning about women's roles in society. Consider Edwardian time vs the 1920s. What has changed, and how? Then, consider how women today express themselves with clothes. Look at examples, such as SlutWalks, and think about how fashion is used as a protest mechanism.

The 1930s: The Rise of Ready-to-Wear and Hollywood Glamor

The 1930s started with the Depression, following the Wall Street crash of 1929, and ended with WWII. This resulted in the loss of jobs, and the 1930s present a different sentiment than the roaring '20s, when there was widespread optimism and social progress. During the 1930s, unemployment rose, and purchasing power substantially decreased in many countries, including large fashion markets such as the UK, US, and Germany, which was linked to the Wall Street crash that happened on October 24, 1929. However, fashion and beauty were still important aspects of daily life (Constantino, 1994). Due to growing unemployment and economic hardship, designers had to cut prices and focus more on ready-to-wear clothes, and they started to produce more washable and economical clothes for practical use (Constantino, 1994). However, this decade is also known for

Hollywood glamour, which resulted in women being able to dress in both stylish and practical ways. Designers also had an opportunity to work with new fabrics, which enabled new designs, but the designers' focus remained on the silhouette.

Unlike the fashion style of the 1920s, which was boyish, the 1930s decade is known for a return to a more feminine style. Where in the 1920s the dresses were boxy and loose, in this decade,

> clothes were cut to follow the lines of the body, showing off the female figure in a more provocative manner than ever before. Shoulders were bared in the first halter neck and backless gowns, and the bias-cut dress pioneered by Parisian couturier Madeleine Vionnet – clung to every curve (Clarkson, 2011, p. 15).

Women's dresses and hair got longer again, which means that the fashion revolution of the 1920s was taken aback slightly, but fashion also took a new direction; the boyish silhouette of the 1920s was replaced with a return to femininity. Therefore, this decade is the first one that had a cyclical nature because some fashion of the 1930s was inspired by the Edwardian style, such as evening gowns. In other words,

> the angular shapes of the 1920s turned imperceptibly into flowing lines; short, straight hair became wavy and long enough to be put up; the waist was more emphasized; hats became more imaginative; in short, the whole silhouette changed, becoming less severe and less defined (Fischenich et al., 2000, p. 32).

Hemlines went back to ankle length, and waistlines moved back to their natural place, a change from the 1920s and baggy dresses with low waists. While the simplicity of the 1920s created a sack-like silhouette which did not show any curves, the early 1930s had simple lines that hugged curves, which created a soft, feminine silhouette (Reddy, 2020). At the same time, suits were neat-fitted with waist-length jackets, and skirts went to mid-calf. Coco Chanel, in this period, designed a wool jersey two-piece suit, which was labeled as a sporty look, and women wore it as day clothes (Clarkson, 2011). The style of the 1930s can be summarized as in Table 3.2.

The popularity of rayon continued throughout the decade until 1939, when nylon entered the fashion market. Silks, wools, and linens, cotton, tweed, and corduroy were also popular. The fabrics of the 1930s also included crepe de Chine, silk jersey, and new artificial fibers that started to appear in the market, such as the first stretch latex, later popularized further during the 1990s (Fischenich et al., 2000). Synthetic materials were introduced. Thus, mass production continued, including rayon being used for underwear, dresses, and stockings because it was washable and did not crease (Constantino, 1994). However, in 1939, stockings started to be made from nylon. Nylon stockings were the first fiber entirely produced in a laboratory, and nylon stockings were introduced to the public at the 1939 World's Fair, with sales starting on May 15, 1940. Prior to nylon, stockings were made of silk or rayon, but with the instant success of nylon stockings, sales were 20 percent of the stocking market by 1942. However, with the US entering WWII, nylon was declared a defense material and withdrawn from the civilian market to replace silk in the production of parachutes, ropes, netting, tire cord, and many other items. Some refer to this material as the 'fiber that won the war'. The fiber was reintroduced into fashion after the war (National Museum of American History, n.d.). The colors of the decade were black, navy, and gray for city wear and brown and green for autumn. Afternoon clothes

Figure 3.12 Zora Hurston playing drums in 1937 in a 1930s feminine dress
US Library of Congress

and evening dresses were black or pastel shades of peach, pink, green, maize, and blue, along with red (Constantino, 1994; Clarkson, 2011). This decade also saw a rise in flamboyant floral prints, and geometric prints remained popular, both for blouses and day dresses (Clarkson, 2011). White can also be seen as a popular color of the decade, because many clothes, particularly patterns, had a white color. There is a distinction between the time of year and the color worn, e.g., in spring and summer, women worn pastel colors such as

Table 3.2 The 1930s Fashion Innovations and Style Changes

FASHION INNOVATIONS	DESCRIPTIONS
Cyclical nature starts	• A boyish silhouette replaced with a more feminine, hourglass silhouette • An inspiration from Edwardian time
Silhouette	• The narrow waist, emphasized by a thin belt for everyday wear • More focus on the silhouette in the 1930s • Some women worn corsets again to achieve a slim figure
The princess line	• One-piece, narrow, calf-length dress with vertical seams, high at the neck • Decorated with a bow or a collar • Old-fashioned, conservative look • The same style for the evening with the exception of incorporating a small train to portray a majestic appearance
Bias-cut gowns	• Fabrics were cut diagonally so dresses clung naturally to the body • This dress style was introduced by Madeleine Vionnet
Skirts	• Skirts with wedge-cut pleats • Wedge-cut pleats, which gave fullness to hemlines ending at mid-calf • Skirts were fitted at the hip with yokes
Materials	• Fur – day and night clothes • Popular luxury items • Capes, coats, stoles, and wraps made using pelts of ermine, fox, mink, and chinchilla
Bell-shaped skirts	• Fit tightly over slim hips and then widening into a bell shape • Godets used to increase fullness of the skirt • Skirts covering knees or went down to calf
Jabot blouse	• A daywear style • Decorative frills cascaded from the collar down the front of the blouse
Sportswear influences	• Pioneered by Coco Chanel • Soft wool jersey fabric • Women engaged with outdoors activities more and needed comfortable and practical clothes

(Continued)

Table 3.2 Continued

FASHION INNOVATIONS	DESCRIPTIONS
Flared sleeves	• Narrow-fitting at the shoulder • Widened toward the wrist • Exaggerated on evening gowns
Costume jewelry	• Enamel and glass • Broaches, bracelets, beaded necklaces • The new look, affordable to many
Narrow suits worn with a hat and gloves	• Slim fitting • Tailored • A practical look for the day • Teamed with gloves and hats; various styles
Zips	• Slide fasteners • Replaced buttons • Schiaparelli made features of metal fastening
Halterneck backless evening gowns	• Back as the new erogenous zone • Draped fabric around the neck • Shoulders and back on show • Mid-1930s
Art Deco patterns	• Symmetrical geometric patterns • Art Deco prints as a left-over trend of the 1920s • Seen on dresses, blouses, and scarves
Bolero	• Introduced by Elsa Schiaparelli • Worn over suits and skirts and blouses • Office women accepted this style too as well as others
Two-piece suit	• Coco Chanel's design offering practical daywear to women in line with her fashion philosophy
Defined/padded shoulders	• End of the decade style change • Shoulders (padding, materials, or embellishments)
Trousers	• As the decade progressed, trousers became popular, particularly wide-legged ones • Vogue published an article and promoted these trousers on June 15, 1936 • Wide-leg trousers did not take off in this decade, but were introduced for the first time

Source: Author's work. Information adapted from Clarkson (2011, pp. 16–18), Fischenich et al. (2000, pp. 32, 34, 35), Worsley (2011), Reddy (2020, n.p.), Ramzi (2024a), and Ramzi (2024a, n.p.)

peach, rose pink, lilac, as well as yellow, light blue, and green while in winter the colors were chocolate brown, grey, tan, rust, burgundy, navy blue, and black. The colors also darkened during the decade, so lighter combinations were worn in the early 1930s, while in the late 1930s, the colors had heavier saturation, which made them bolder. For men, the colors of the 1930s were blue, tan, beige, cream, brown, and various shades of gray, which depended on the time of the year. Like with women, men wore different colors in fall and winter (e.g., navy blue, brown, and darker gray) than in summer and spring (lighter colors such as beige, cream, lighter and medium blue).

For women who could afford it, fashion was still stylish and elegant. The issue of the decade was that times were hard, and women could no longer afford as much as they could before; therefore, Hollywood glamour was just a dream and something to desire and aspire to, but it was not a reality for many (Clarkson, 2011). Working-class women had less purchasing power, so they had to add layers to clothes to make them look different and longer, which was often done by adding a contrasting fabric or fur to their hems; material was being added to collars and sleeves. Within a year, hemlines dropped further, becoming narrower and longer, and skirts, while longer, also started to gradually flare until they fell to the bottom of the calf (Constantino, 1994). Working women also took a hit in their empowerment because poverty and unemployment rose, which reversed earlier gains in women's empowerment, and instead of advancing in their careers, women were again expected to be more feminine and not compete with men, bear children, attend to the house, and get involved in social events (Fischenich et al., 2000).

Designers were still designing for the royalty and the rich, but had started to take notice of working women, whose days were spent working in offices, while the evenings were for cinema, theater, or dancing, and who therefore needed different styles of clothes. The wealthy looked to Paris for fashion, but others looked to the movies, which boosted the influence of Hollywood on fashion and resulted in Coco Chanel working in the film industry in 1929. Women copied the dress style and hair of movie stars such as Greta Garbo, with her bobbed hair being one of the mass influencers, along with Marlene Dietrich. Hollywood also contributed to innovations in the beauty industry with inventions such as false fingernails and eyelashes (Constantino, 1994). During the 1920s silent movies were focused on actresses wearing clothes they wore in everyday lives but with the introduction of sound and talk, costumes were developed to create stories and express behavior and emotions, and clothes provided meaning to movies because actresses no longer focused on exaggerated moves but also showcasing character personalities expressed with fashion (Fischenich et al., 2000).

The modern woman of the 1930s was coming in a different shape, with the flat-chested, boyish looks of the 1920s being a thing of the past; blossoms (flower patterns) were back as well as shoulders (Constantino, 1994). The biggest innovation of this period was a backless evening gown shaped to the body and with bias cut; this created layers, which were influenced by Hollywood movie stars (Constantino, 1994; Clarkson, 2011). However, there was a difference between daywear and eveningwear. Daywear before the 1930s was more grounded in decorative style than practicality, but due to the rise of women's position in society, with more women taking an active social role, which included women of all social origins, women started to lead busier lives, so clothes followed that. Eveningwear still had a hint of glamour and escape from daily life, but the daywear was practical and tidy. In 1939, with WWII, fashion designers and magazines started to emphasize economy, simplicity, and practicality, and make-do and mending became even more popular (Constantino, 1994). Mending had actually became popular even earlier than this because the 1930s was generally a decade when women faced more hardship and had to find innovative ways to look good while keeping a budget. This resulted in the rise of mending and accessorizing became important (Clarkson, 2011). Popular accessories included brooches, earrings, rings, and gloves (Clarkson, 2011).

Toward the end of the decade, function and practicality became even more important as the world approached WWII. By the start of the war in 1939, the fashion became more simplified, and focused on,

> simple clothes such as trousers, sweaters. Classic shirtwaisters and low-heeled shoes were the staples of most women's wardrobes. Designers began to adapt the mood of their collections to more military-inspired, square-shouldered clothing, with skirts that hung just below the knee and often slightly longer at the back (Clarkson, 2011, p. 18).

However, practicality did not necessarily mean a loss of femininity because the silhouette was an hourglass, and waistlines returned to the natural waist as opposed to the 1920s when they were loose, baggy, and on the hips. The waistlines were often made in a way that created more curvaceous figures, and necklines were lowered with scalloped edges and ruffled collars, with the jabot blouse also becoming highly fashionable along with the pussy-bow neckline (Clarkson, 2011). Working women wore a skirt and a blouse as standard daywear. This style became more functional by the end of the decade due to a shortage of materials and the influence of military uniforms on fashion (Fischenich et al., 2000). However, eveningwear of the 1930s remained glamorous and extravagant with 'long, wide skirts, narrow waists, and tightfitting tops', and this style can be seen as 'forerunners of the New Look launched by Christian Dior ten years later' (Fischenich et al., 2000, p. 35). By the end of the 1930s, a more angular line developed in women's fashion and this style carried on into the 1940s, particularly during WWII, due to its practicality. Skirts,

> had got shorter and now mostly just covered the knees. They were also narrower and tighter, sometimes pleated, and looked altogether more severe. The effect was heightened by the accompanying jackets and coats, which often had belts and padded shoulders, and with the addition of epaulettes even espoused a military style. Robust, warm fabrics such as tweed were very popular. Dresses were also shorter, tighter and plainer" (Fischenich et al., 2000, p. 41).

Not surprisingly, haute couture stagnated toward the end of the decade due to war efforts and many couturiers closing their businesses. Designers survived by making clothes as a variation of what they did before, as they could not engage fully with their work and set new trends. Paris was occupied by the Nazis and thus couturiers struggled, only surviving because Lucien Lelong, president of *Chambre Syndicale de la Haute Couture,* managed to preserve some fabric and prevent the Nazi plan to move haute couture to Berlin and Vienna (Fischenich et al., 2000).

The men's clothes of the 1930s were still conservative, with a business and social etiquette meaning heavy, dark suits, collars, ties, and hats (Constantino, 1994, p. 23). However, men also started to wear sporty jackets during the 1930s, which were worn with ties and had strong patterns. One of the popular fashion models for men was Cary Grant, who wore sporty jackets and suits with ties, while Fred Astaire was a model for eveningwear, with a white tie for dancing and a polo shirt with wide trousers for casual elegance

(Fischenich et al., 2000). Also, Clark Gable and his thin mustache, glossy, slick hair, and three-piece suits were popularized after Gable's appearance in the 1934 film *It Happened One Night*. The leading trend for men was still Savile Row tailoring and slimmed-down silhouettes, after looser, baggy fits of the 1920s. Thus, men's fashion trends somewhat followed women's trends. Men wore suits with semi-accentuated waists, which matched the shift of women's wear toward feminine silhouettes (Ramzi, 2024a). In the 1930s, popular hats among men were the Trilby (fur felt hat) or the Fedora hats. Fedora hats were similar to Trilby hats, the only difference being that Trilby hats had a slightly shorter crown. These hats were popularized by Hollywood stars and were worn by characters ranging from detectives to gangsters.

REFLECT

Watch Apple's New Look series and think about how Parisian couturiers survived WWII. Pay particular attention to the ethics of fashion designers and their discussions on the ethics of designing for the Nazis. Also consider the haute couture designs and compare them with the prêt-à-porter fashion of the time.

The 1940s: WWII and the Rise of Cheap Materials

The 1940s were the war years, a period when social influence was highly visible in fashion. This decade is usually divided into two parts: wartime fashion influenced by rationing and post-war fashion. *Vogue* wrote on February 1, 1943, 'By the time this issue of *Vogue* appears, a new type of currency will be coming into circulation in the United States. Not plastic pennies or a new series of banknotes, but rationing stamps' (Ramzi, 2024b, n.p.). Consumer goods were, in some cases, transformed into war goods, and fashion was heavily impacted due to some materials being particularly suitable to support the war effort. For example, even bathwater was limited in the UK in 1943, which increased adverts and sales of deodorants (Baker, 2002). Clothes rationing started in the UK on June 1, 1941, and people were given coupons for clothing items, which were progressively reduced as the war went on. The rationing scheme worked as an allocation program where each type of clothing item had a 'points' value, and this was determined based on how much material and labor went into manufacturing each item. The coupon allowance was at its lowest point between 1945 and 1946; for example, for the period between September 1, 1945 and April 30, 1946, only 24 coupons were issued, which meant each shopper had only three coupons per month. Special provisions were made for some people, such as manual workers, people wearing civilian uniforms, diplomats, theater performers, and new mothers and children (Imperial War Museum, n.d.). A public relations campaign was launched by the UK Government, encouraging people to mend clothes and be creative, which extensively used posters and government-published brochures. In the US, rationing was introduced through General Limitation Order L-85, known as Regulation L-85, which regulated that 'hems and belts could not exceed two inches in width, garments could not have more than one pocket, and ornamental sleeves, hoods, and scarves were banned' (Goles, 2023, n.p.). Nylon was also rationed because it was needed for military equipment, such as parachutes, and many American women struggled without stockings, which were originally made from silk and later replaced by nylon, so they turned to creativity and painted their legs to create an illusion of stockings (Goles, 2023). American rationing ended with VE Day on May 8, 1945, except for sugar, which continued until 1947; however, in the UK, which was directly affected by war, rationing continued until March 1949 for fashion and 1954 for all rationing.

What is central to this decade, when it comes to style, is the 'wide, padded shoulders, a narrow natural waistline, thin hips, skirts that fell just below the knee' (Baker, 2002, p. 5), which is similar to the 1930s. For men in this decade, 'the line fell in an inverted triangle from square shoulders down to the waist and hips' (Baker, 2002, p. 5). Both men and women wore heavy shoes, and accessories remained popular for women. Hats were tipped over foreheads or planted firmly on the back of the head; in this decade, however, when the war started, hats were replaced by fabric headscarves and turbans, particularly for women who worked in factories (Baker, 2002). Some authors call the war period non-fashion and argue that because of the war, conservative and military fashion styles also gained prominence, and tailoring had to be perfect because clothes had to last (Clarkson, 2011). During the 1940s, mending, making do, and restyling became popular, with women taking garments apart and fashion magazines giving tips on mending clothes. Main innovations and styles of the 1940s are summarized in Table 3.3.

Table 3.3 The Fashion Innovations and Style of the 1940s

FASHION INNOVATIONS	DESCRIPTIONS
Silhouette	• Wartime silhouette – tight, short-skirted at the start of the decade; sculptural and slim • The new, post-war feminine silhouette • Narrow, natural waistline
Slacks	• Women got used to wearing trousers at work and slacks became popular • The rise of pioneer pants • Trousers were worn with jackets
Sequins and beads	• Sequins and beads were not rationed and were used by designers to add sparkle to their clothes
Utility suit	• Blue, black, and brown • Military style boxy jackets and narrow, short skirts
Trench coats	• Military style
Gingham	• A very popular fabric in the US

(*Continued*)

Table 3.3 Continued

FASHION INNOVATIONS	DESCRIPTIONS
Couture eveningwear	• Couture gowns were made in satin and sewed in a structural way • Velvet, heavy satin, and faille
Monastic dress	• Loosely fitted and shaped like a voluminous tent • Soft shape when worn with a belt
Peasant dress	• Handwoven printed skirts with off-the-shoulder blouses • Drawstring necklines • Puffed sleeves
Bolero jacket	• Short, emphasizing the waist • Padded shoulders and shirring • Worn over strapless evening dresses
Jersey shift dress	• Synthetic jersey • Simple and elegant • Short unstructured design
Sportswear and beach	• Summer dresses and midriff-baring tops • Worn with matching shorts
Rayon print dress	• Daytime wear • Noncrease rayon fabric • Colorful prints with shirring and draping on the bodice or waist
The Kitty Foyle dress	• The shirtwaist dress with simple collar and caps on the sleeves • Approved by the War Production Board in the US • Named after Ginger Rogers who starred in the Kitty Foyle film and popularized the dress
Post-war: The New Look by Christian Dior	• The changed line • No more padded shoulders • Narrow, tiny waists, tightly fitting bodices • Ankle-length skirts or calf-length and very full • A vast amount of material; luxurious • Accentuating women's curves • The new femininity
Post-war eveningwear	• Luxurious and glamorous, strapless dresses, high-neck sleeveless dress as an innovation • The new, feminine silhouette

(Continued)

Table 3.3 Continued

FASHION INNOVATIONS	DESCRIPTIONS
Post-war everyday wear	• Suits still popular but adapted to the New Look with skirts that were tight, calf-length, jackets were hip-length and fitted with accentuated revers; sometimes buttoned asymmetrically • Wide, bell-shaped backs and small collars • Skirt and blouse as a combination; tight waists • Fine yarns, woolen materials for winter; cotton, silk, and synthetic for summer • The new feminine silhouette followed with everyday wear
Men's innovations	• The Zoot suit popularized in the US, particularly among Black and Hispanic men

Source: Author's work. Information adapted from Clarkson (2011, pp. 22–23), Fischenich et al. (2000, pp. 43, 44, 45), and Ramzi (2024b)

Wartime silhouette was tight, and short skirted at the start of the decade, and suddenly, 'the flirty fullness of the 1930s curvy female gave way to an angular, hard silhouette that, as *Vogue* declared in the same year, "would be brutally unbecoming unless women kept their figures"' (Clarkson, 2011, p. 24, emphasis in the original). This silhouette was driven by rationing, and thus it was sculptural and slim because 'the stiff tailoring, economy of cut, nipped-in-waist and narrow skirts produced a slim shape that de-emphasized the female curves and made the form appear slender yet mannish' (Clarkson, 2011, p. 24). However, this meant that beauty was not part of wartime silhouette but signaled competence, which was further exacerbated with the introduction of women's suits. The military-cut suit was central to wartime fashion, and women wore clothes that looked mannish because they were cut along the lines of male uniforms. These suits are sometimes called utility suits, and *Vogue* labeled them 'uniform suits' and 'tailored suits' in 1942 (Ramzi, 2024b). Monochrome colors were used, such as air-force blue and flag red, and military influence was everywhere. *Vogue* called this fashion 'couture austerity' because it was driven by necessity rather than desire, and the silhouette was refined and unadorned (Clarkson, 2011). This was also a decade when wide shoulders were used on women's suits with sharp and edgy shoulder pads, and this gave women, who were newly employed and supporting the war effort, a no-nonsense look. These suits were boxy, had wide shoulders, and were barely nipped in the waist, while jackets were short. The suits were tailored and well-made because they had to last several seasons due to the financial hardship many people were facing, restrictions, and rationing.

Another novelty in women's fashion during the early period of the 1940s was the so-called Kitty Foyle dress, popularized by Ginger Rogers. The item was a shirtwaist dress introduced before the end of the war and the New Look. The dress had a simple

Figure 3.13 Family strolling on Sunday in Greenbelt, Maryland, in 1942, wearing fashion of the 1940s period

US Library of Congress

A-line skirt, and the collar and caps on the sleeves added visual appeal without using too much material. It was a knee-length shirtwaist dress, which was both practical and looked good. In an article about the 'shirtwaist revival', *Vogue*, on March 15, 1943, wrote, 'The shirtwaist look is the right look for this spring' (Ramzi, 2024b, n.p.).

Because of the war, many governments introduced blackouts and required that people wear gas masks due to a fear of gassing as part of the attack. In the UK, London's Harvey Nichols advertised a special gas mask for women, stating, 'made of pure oiled silk ... in dawn, apricot, rose, amethyst, eau-de-nil green and pastel pink. The wearer can cover a distance of two hundred yards through mustard gas and the suit can be slipped over ordinary clothes in thirty-five seconds' (Baker, 2002, p. 7). British couture still existed because the country needed money, and since Paris was cut off, it gave rise to US and UK fashion with American and British designers leading new trends while France was occupied by the Nazis. Designers, during this time, tried to keep morale high (Baker, 2002). However, the

Figure 3.14 A woman wears simple fashion of the 1940s with an elegant hat, Washington DC, cca. 1943

US Library of Congress

war period gave rise to American functional and easy ready-to-wear clothes, and materials born out of this period were gingham, cotton, and denim (Clarkson, 2011). This was the time when New York found its place on the fashion map. Thus, the US looked inward for fashion as no new designs were coming from Paris. *Vogue* wrote on February 1, 1941,

> Since the fall of Paris, the influence of many of the last great French Collections which we saw has hung on. But in the past seven months, American designers—clothes, fabric, shoes, hat, jewelry designers—have come far; learned much; caught their breath … the most recent developments in fashion have stemmed from our own imaginations (Ramzi, 2024b, n.p.).

Hats were important during the war and sometimes seen as an act of resistance, along with accessories, which, due to rationing and mending of clothes, were particularly relevant because being fashionable was expressed through hats and accessories, which were not rationed. Women were joining the workforce more than ever, and gender roles collapsed with women also going to work on farms and in factories, not just in offices. Workwear during the war was centered on dungarees or blue denim trousers, general trousers, and one-piece coveralls for work (Baker, 2002). However, after the war ended, female

Figure 3.15 Yoshiye Abe makes an American flag in a Denver factory, between 1942 and 1945

US Library of Congress

workers were seen as not needed because men returning from the war needed jobs, and this resulted in attempts to put women back into the domestic sphere. For example, a UK magazine, *My Weekly,* on May 18, 1946, praised women for not needing men, saying the hero was no longer needed, but the UK government still tried to persuade women to go back home (Baker, 2002).

Men's fashion also changed during the war. At the start of the 1940s, men's clothes had a slim fit, which was linked to clothing rations, and double-breasted suits popular during the 1920s and 1930s became single-breasted, with no waistcoats. However, a somewhat contradictory novelty, due to the large use of material, was the introduction of the Zoot suit. These suits were particularly popular in the New York and Harlem area and worn by Black and Hispanic men, and afterwards, they spread to the West Coast. It was a 'knee-length draped jacket with 6″ shoulder pads, and eye-catching tie (bow or knotted), a long dangling keychain, very high-waisted trousers, fully and deeply pleated at the waist and generous in the leg but sharply tapered at the cuff" (Baker, 2002, p. 44). The look was accompanied by a 'long, greased hairstyle, combed back off the face, a broad brimmed hat and printed toe shoes (Baker, 2002, p. 44). After the war, men wore old uniforms altered to civilian clothes or sometimes unaltered. Men faced fewer social rules on appropriate dress, which resulted in combining trousers and jackets made of different but matching cloth. The new American V-line dominated with broad shoulders and narrow hips, which emphasized the male silhouette and gave a boost to men's fashion. However, practicality and durability were the emphasis of men's fashion (Fischenich et al., 2000). Eveningwear for men had more social rules, but these also loosened in comparison to previous times, and in the US, the popularity of ties with patterns emerged, and jackets became looser. Hats were worn with coats, and nylon became an important material because it was durable and easy to wash and dry.

In the US, after rationing, mass production quickly resumed, while Europe suffered destruction and took longer to rebuild. New optimism and mass production led some American designers to design more feminine clothes and again focus on luxury as well as draw from the Edwardian style with tight waistlines. Baker (2002) argued that 'the appearance of full skirts and narrow waists presages the coming to the New Look in 1947' (p. 21), which is commonly credited to Christian Dior. The New Look, centered on extravagance, with lots of fabric and a tiny, Edwardian waist, was supported by *Harper's Bazaar* and *Vogue* (Baker, 2002). It emphasized femininity and drew inspiration from Edwardian style and *La Belle Époque* in France, in a clear contrast to war fashion. Clarkson (2011), however, argued that the New Look started in the US by saying that 'the American softened silhouette presaged the dramatic New Look unveiled in 1947 by Christian Dior' (p. 21). However, regardless of its origin, while the New Look created excitement among fashion editors, it also attracted social criticism for fashion returning to the wealthy and ignoring working women, which is why some argued that the New Look was 'curtailing women's freedom' (Baker, 2002, p. 56).

The silhouette started to change after the war, and a softer line was added, which reduced the military style of clothes. On the eve of the New Look in 1947, Sears's catalog in 1946 featured Parisian suits, hip-draped skirts, coat frocks with stand-up collars, gathered sleeves, and curved-in waistlines (Clarkson, 2011). This new fashion, promoted by Parisian designers from the *Théâtre de la Mode* – a post-war exhibition of miniature wire mannequins dressed in real couture clothes, complete with miniature bags, shoes, jewelry, and hats – which caused a sensation in the US, was seen to leave war and rationing behind and give people hope, thus showing the influence of fashion in society. The exhibition opened in March 1945 and was a global success, and helped restore Paris's position as the center of haute couture. It also put Christian Dior, an unknown Parisian designer, in the spotlight, in large part because the American press later invented the term the New Look and credited Dior with bringing hope with his haute couture collection. The famous Bar suit from the New Look collection of 1947, echoed the miniature doll's suit he had created for the *Théâtre de la Mode of 1945*. After the *Théâtre de la Mode* show in Paris, visited by 100,000 visitors, the dolls were sent the next year for exhibition in New York and San Francisco to remind the American market that Paris is again leading in fashion (Fischenich et al., 2000). The dolls were lost for a long time but were found in 1980, which then instigated another exposure in Paris and New York.

The fashion line changed after the war, which was seen as the biggest change in fashion. Women's shoulders,

> became narrow and looked natural again, as shoulder pads were avoided. Compared to prewar fashion, the new style suggested gentleness and femininity: tightly fitting bodices, minuscule waists, with skirts that were ankle-length or calf-length and very full. Another line which accentuated the figure – helped once again by padding and corsets – had a very slim cut (Fischenich et al., 2000, p. 43)

Eveningwear became important again, and designers concentrated on creating glamour with 'immensely full skirts and low-cut bodices, often strapless and relying on a boned under structure, … made of the most luxurious fabrics, such as taffeta with good embroidery" (Fischenich et al., 2000, p. 44). A cheaper, off-the-rack version was made of cheaper, synthetic fabrics and printed materials. A cocktail dress also came into fashion; it was a less formal evening gown and shorter, never floor length. However, as time progressed, social events merged, and it became less relevant what type of clothes one wore. A feature of the New Look was also shoes and gloves, which were often matched to provide a full look; the influence of this look came from Christian Dior.

While there was a focus on the New Look in terms of luxury, the New Look influence was visible in everyday wear too. For example, while suits continued to be an everyday fashion, 'skirts were usually tight and calf-length, jackets were hip-length and fitted with relatively high, accentuated revers; sometimes jackets buttoned asymmetrically. Some designs had wide, bell-shaped backs and little collars' (Fischenich et al., 2000, p. 44–45). This fashion was made of fine yarn, woolen fabrics for winter, and cotton, silk, or new synthetic fibers for the summer. The everyday silhouette of the suit was the same as the glamorous New Look, with suits being calf-length, pencil-slim, or full and swirling skirts, which could have been gathered or pleated with tight-fitting tops defining the bust, and sleeves of the shirts were long or three-quarter (Fischenich et al., 2000). The *décolletée* became a thing again, but strapless dresses were for evening only; during the day, women covered their shoulders, – innovation happened with eveningwear. One example is a high-neck, sleeveless dress, which was an innovation of this period.

In terms of colors and materials, there was a change from the 1930s, which was largely influenced by the war. There was a move from pastel to bolder and stronger colors, and patterns also included stripes and checks. For women, materials in this period included rayon, wool, cotton, jersey, silk, velvet, net, and flannel. The use of materials was also influenced by rationing because materials were supporting the war effort. For men, materials included synthetic rayon blended with wool during wartime; otherwise, tweed and wool. Men's colors included blue and sand, and trousers had higher waists and cuffs during the 1940s, with a lesser focus on coats. Longer jackets returned during this period. While women expressed resistance with hats, men sometimes expressed patriotism with victory suits in navy, gray, and light brown. The suit style for men of the 1940s was, in style, similar to the 1930s, which presents another aspect of the cyclical nature of fashion. Casual wear for men started to gain popularity towards the end of the decade, which included more color and some patterns in jackets and trousers (Lehnert, 2000; Clarkson, 2011; Vintage Dancer, 2016).

REFLECT

Consumer behavior research developed as an area of marketing and advertising because of the economic situation in the 1940s and 1950s, which affected consumer spending. Read a paper by Ronald R. Fullerton analyzing the historical development of consumer behavior. Think of the fashion of the 1940s and consider how the war influenced fashion rationing and consumer spending. What does a situation of the 1940s tell us about consumers of the time?

Article to read: Fullerton, R.A. (2013), "The birth of consumer behavior: motivation research in the 1940s and 1950s", *Journal of Historical Research in Marketing*, Vol. 5 No. 2, pp. 212–222. https://doi.org/10.1108/17557501311316833

The 1950s: A Decade of Optimism and the Revival of Haute Couture

The 1950s were the decade of optimism and euphoria after the end of WWII. While rationing continued for a part of the 1950s in the UK (until 1954), this was not the case in the US, which also faced a new presidency and leadership of the country, with the election of Dwight Eisenhower as president in 1952. The year 1953 saw the coronation of Queen Elizabeth II in the UK, thus, both countries had new leadership and a new vision for life after WWII. There was new prosperity in the US because of the introduction of the credit card system, which created a new push towards consumerism in 1950 when the first credit cards entered mass use (Baker, 1991).

Dior's New Look was greeted with applause and global acclaim in 1947, and this look continued to be popular throughout the 1950s. Despite rationing that carried on, the UK Government promised to 'Make Britain great again' and organized the Festival of British exhibition in 1951, which had a positive outlook, and the general 1950s positive outlook included fashion (Clarkson, 2011). The new fashion found women working in factories, fields, and ambulances, and suddenly they were faced with new fashion femininity, including padded bosom and nipped-in waist, which offered a more romantic look. The fashion of this decade was centered on full skirts, stiff petticoats, pencil-slim skirts, and a sweater with all the trimmings, as well as tight-fitting pedal pushers or Capri and pirate trousers reaching the calf, while jeans became acceptable for leisure clothes. Informal school dances rose in popularity in the US, which gave rise to fashion, and girls wore full skirts with bright motifs and fitting blouses tucked into their skirts (Baker, 1991). Innovations and styles of the 1950s are summarized in Table 3.4.

Table 3.4 Fashion Innovations and Styles of the 1950s

FASHION INNOVATIONS	DESCRIPTIONS
Silhouette	• Hourglass, A-line, H-line, Y-line, the barrel line, and the balloon shape
Gloves	• Leather gloves for daywear • Long satin gloves as eveningwear worn with satin cocktail dresses • Big glitzy bracelets over the top
Slacks	• Ski-pant-style trousers made from synthetic stretch fabric, either plain or multicolored • Tailored to fit the body • Flat front waistband and side zip opening • Casual look; the growth of the American leisure market
Ballet shoes	• Popular in the US and Europe • Mass produced and worn with ankle socks and full skirts or with bare feet and capri trousers

(Continued)

Table 3.4 Continued

FASHION INNOVATIONS	DESCRIPTIONS
Net petticoats	• Petticoats were worn under skirts to give lift and movement • Stiffened with starch or a sugar solution to keep the form • Form and volume given to ballgowns • Nylon
Hats	• Pull-down bucket hats • Small lampshade-style hats • Coolie hats • Wide-brim picture hats • Black and white hats for special occasions • Black net veil for formal occasions
Pencil skirts	• A narrow, slim straight skirt (the hobble) • Restricted women's walking • Fell from a narrow waistband with little excess fabric, no gathers or pleats and with a small back split that allowed movement
Empire lines	• The straight empire-line shift dress, cut to the knee with narrow shoulders and a high boat neckline • Worn with big black sunglasses and pearls
Fur stoles	• Strapless eveningwear with a large fur stole wrapped around bare shoulders • Fastened with a large brooch for eveningwear
Oversized detailing	• Huge shawl collars, giant buttons, big turn-back cuffs on wide square-cut sleeves • Deep armholes (dolman sleeves)
Trapeze coats	• The loose, swing coat (tent) accommodated wide skirts of the time • Buttons on these coats emphasized the triangle shape of the cut
Sack dress	• The waistless sack dress by Givenchy • Freedom from hourglass figure • Audrey Hepburn popularized the dress
Sheath dress	• The fitted sheath clanging to woman's body shape • Satin or silk • Strapless • Required corseting

(*Continued*)

Table 3.4 Continued

FASHION INNOVATIONS	DESCRIPTIONS
Wide belts	• A big wide belt as a main fashion accessory • Worn with either full dirndl skirt or a straight pencil skirt
Pedal pushers and capris	• Calf-length trousers, cuffed or flounced at the hem or cut narrow • Capris had a small V at the hem to enable mobility
Full skirts	• Wide circular skirts for daywear (gingham or printed cottons) • Designs: poodle, American cowboy motifs • Eveningwear – full skirts made of frothy chiffon or rayon in vibrant colors (canary yellow, baby blue, or lime green)
Sweater dressing	• Short-sleeved turtleneck worn tight and fitted • Big bulky pastel sweater • Popular among teenagers and movie stars
Barbie doll	• Daily and eveningwear, teaching girls about fashion and consumerism
Celebrity influence	• Elvis Presley, James Dean (male) • Marilyn Monroe, Greta Garbo, Brigitte Bardot, Sophia Loren (female)
Jeans	• American influence portraying American lifestyle • A sign of youth protest
The return of Chanel	• Jersey suits for spring

Source: Author's work. Information adapted from Clarkson (2011, pp. 28–29), Fischenich et al. (2000, pp. 52, 53, 56), and Ramzi (2024c)

The 1950s were a period when Paris dominated the world of fashion, and Dior was unstoppable until his early death in 1957. But Dior was not the only influential Parisian designer. Cristóbal Balenciaga, Jacques Fath, and Hubert de Givenchy also worked in this period. However, despite the talent and prominence of these designers, haute couture was increasingly seen as elitist, and younger consumers, around 1956, started to identify as a separate consumer group (Clarkson, 2011). Young consumers rebelled against the older generation, whose traditional values were seen as based on the bourgeois worldview, whereas new consumers wanted more individualism in human life without tradition. This resulted in an existentialist approach to fashion, such as the focus on black in clothes, particularly black polo-neck sweaters (Fischenich et al., 2000). The youth were influenced by pop stars, such as Elvis Presley, whose fashion style enthused young consumers, while older consumers rejected his style. Rock and Roll also influenced fashion because the music movement was seen as the epitome of rebellion against traditional values, which also meant looking different. The colorful costumes were a stark contrast to the serious suits worn until the rise of rock'n'roll. This influence came from the US and spread around the world due to the rise of television and the American film industry, with films such as Rebel Without a Cause (starring James Dean) representing youth attitudes towards life. These films challenged the traditional values of the middle classes, increasingly seen as bourgeois and hypocritical (Fischenich et al., 2000). Female idols included Marilyn Monroe, Greta Garbo, Sophia Loren, and Brigitte Bardot. These female movie stars emphasized their sensuous lips and figures and were presented as confident, seductive, but also childlike women who do not want to grow up, mimicking male rebels such as Elvis Presley and James Dean, who were also seen as rebels who did not want to grow up and rejected their parents' work ethic and values. Not surprisingly, the protest of the young generation gave rise to jeans, which were an American influence portraying the American way of life and a rebellion from conventional fashion norms (Fischenich et al., 2000). This period also gave rise to the global popularity of the Barbie doll by the Mattel Corporation from the US. The doll was always criticized as unrealistic in terms of women's appearance, due to exaggerated bodily features such as an overly emphasized bosom, tiny waist, and long legs, which made Barbie look less like a real girl. However, Barbie was used to teach girls about different dressing styles since the doll came with a variety of clothes, so girls learnt the difference between daily and eveningwear and, accordingly, developed a taste in fashion and consumerism (Fischenich et al., 2000).

Two alternative shapes of the silhouette were prominent in the 1950s: 'the great full skirt that swirled and sashayed and the slim pencil tubular skirt that fell to the knee were quintessential silhouettes, and both placed great emphasis on the narrowness of the waist' (Clarkson, 2011, p. 30). This resulted in fashion dictating rigid and uncomfortable clothes, and women fell in line to appear sophisticated and have an allure. To be considered well-dressed in the 'fashion-conscious '50s', women also had to wear hats, gloves, matching shoes, and handbags. This was particularly relevant for eveningwear because while the daywear still retained some practicality, eveningwear was for showing, with long gloves, high heels, and earrings. However, while the hourglass silhouette was prominent in the 1950s, it was not the only silhouette of the 1950s, and Dior himself experimented with various shapes that differed from collection to collection. There was the princess line, the A-line, the H-line, and the S-line, and they all quickly followed one after another. Dior's introduction of the A-line,

> was quite simply a dress that fell from fitted shoulders outwards towards the hem and used stiffened fabric to create the shape. The A-line and the H-line were offering women even more choice and another set of vastly contrasting shapes were hailed as the latest look (Clarkson, 2011, p. 31).

The changes were difficult to follow, with shapes such as the Sack, the Princess, the Tulip, and the Trapeze quickly gaining popularity but also quickly disappearing. The Hourglass silhouette was seen as dominant during the 1950s due to Dior's New Look Corelle Line. *Vogue* wrote on March 1, 1952, 'It begins at the waistline. The waist is what catches the eye right away. It's newly high, it's newly low, or it's both… but it's always there, always stressed, and because that's the case, fashion looks more feminine than it has in years' (Ramzi, 2024c, n.p.).

Figure 3.16 A woman walks with a dog in New York City wearing a New Look-inspired dress of the 1950s

US Library of Congress

For men, shirts, ties, and carefully pressed trousers were the norm, but as men went back to work more, a business clothing culture emerged, and men started to wear dark, understated suits to fit into the new workplace. The only place to show some creativity was in leisure time, when they wore slightly lighter colors and looser clothes. The term 'corporation men' is a term associated with this period because men were doing white-collar jobs in companies, which resulted in grey flannel suits rising in popularity.

This look was popularized in popular culture, such as Alfred Hitchcock's film with Cary Grant as a Madison Avenue ad man in a flannel suit, or a novel by Sloan Wilson, *The Man in the Gray Flannel Suit*, which popularized the so-called uniform suit image: white shirts, silk ties, and carrying a briefcase. The 1950s also present a rise in ready-to-wear clothes and the mass production of shirts for department stores. Hats started to lose popularity, apart from older men who continued to wear them. The 1950s were also marked by a rebellion of young men from privileged backgrounds who protested the bourgeois style of their fathers by adopting a different style of clothing. This meant going back to Edwardian men's fashion with 'narrow trousers, frock coats and tailored jackets with velvet cuffs and lapels; these were complemented by a monocle, watch chain, and diamond tiepin' (Fischenich et al., 2000, p. 53). In the early 1950s, a new type of man suddenly emerged, with working-class men starting to wear Edwardian-style clothes while spending time on the streets, joining gangs, and becoming known as 'teddy boys'. They wore,

> draped, long, dark, single-breasted jackets, with long, narrow drainpipe trousers, and later tight jeans. They also wore a starched shirt, a vest, a narrow tie or bowtie, shoes with thick crepe soles or later, pointed winklepickers, and to crown it all their hair was brilliantined and shaped into a DA ('duck's ass') (Fischenich et al., 2000, p. 53, emphasis in the original).

Men also wore slim-fitting suits, skinny ties, letterman jackets, bowling shirts, saddle shoes, and chunky glasses. Frank Sinatra was a popular fashion influencer in this period, although he did not keep up with fashion trends and kept his hat and black and white shoes. This created a new popularity of hats among men, such as the Fedora, Panama, or boater hats. Other popular influencers for men, particularly on the rebellious side, include Elvis Presley and James Dean, who was wearing new suede footwear, a white t-shirt, and a leather jacket. Letterman jackets became popular paired with blue jeans and high tops, influenced by Dean. High-waisted trousers and pocket protectors were also present in this period for men (Lehnert, 2000; Clarkson, 2011). Suits in the 1950s were masculine silhouettes with a clear emphasis on the straight line, which started to change as the decade progressed. Later in the 1950s, the straight silhouette turned towards more form-fitting and slimmer shapes than in previous years; thus, shoulder pads were used to create a V-shaped torso (Fashion Beans, 2025). Men's fabrics were polyester, which gained popularity during the 1950s, and also wool, flannel, and mohair. The colors were dominated by gray, blue, and brown, but as the decade progressed, more vibrant colors were introduced.

For women, this was the period with the biggest push to go back home, and in the US, this resulted in the increased use of sedatives and anti-depressants, with the term trapped housewife emerging (Baker, 1991) – an issue tackled by the Mad Men series when portraying Betty, wife of the main protagonist Don Draper. However, the New Look continued to idealize the housewife, and magazines increasingly portrayed the home as a woman's place. This was the time when the ideal of beauty, nowadays widely criticized, emerged, with fashion magazines portraying women as tall, slender, corseted, in ballet positions with no emotions (Baker, 1991). Housewives were portrayed as wearing high stiletto shoes, full skirts, nipped waists, and narrow-fitting bodices, creating a doll-like impression, while working women, who were rarely portrayed, were seen through Grace Kelly as wearing tight-fitting suits looking almost like uniforms with high heels (Baker, 1991). This carried on until 1957, with most magazines focusing on housewives and very few showing working

Figure 3.17 Nina Stepyan wearing the New Look-inspired fashion of the 1950s, Fashion Theatre, 1951

UK's National Archives. Reprinted with permission.

women. From 1957, things slowly started to change, and loose-fitting styles of Yves Saint Laurent, Cristóbal Balenciaga, and Hubert de Givenchy started to emerge, which created the new look of the 1960s.

Rayons and quick-dry artificial fabrics were mass produced during the 1950s because these materials were easily washed, were shrink-proof, and dried quickly, so there was no need for mending clothes. Rayon was a low-cost fabric. Polyester fiber also became popular because it did not need ironing, and it had all the other benefits of nylon, such as drying quickly and being crease-resistant (Baker, 1991). The materials of the 1950s included cotton, denim, corduroy, silk, rayon, net, flannel, wool, and nylon. The reason for using some of these materials lies in their constitution, such as durability and easy washing, e.g., rayon. This can be seen as a move towards fast fashion because these materials were also historically always cheaper. Synthetic materials were also popularized during this period. Corduroy was popular among both men and women because women wore this material during the winter, and men generally favored it. Polka dots, plaid, gingham checks, floral, and abstract prints were popular patterns during the 1950s.

The 1950s were a time of consumerism and mass production, as well as the standardization of sizes; cutters were able to handle 200 layers of cloth at one time, producing more clothes than ever, while also improving quality and producing standard sizes (Baker, 1991). With the rise of mass production, designers began to distinguish themselves through annual collections organized around two seasons. This approach, based on the idea that old clothes should be replaced regularly, gave rise to the modern system of two seasonal shows each year – spring and autumn. French designers led the way in establishing this view of high fashion. Because of the rise of counterfeiting and copying in this period, French designers banned cameras and sketchbooks, and haute couture became more exclusive, while street fashion began to influence fashion styles (Baker, 1991). Haute couture tried to innovate and respond to the needs of women, and it made a comeback in US fashion magazines. Dior was seen as portraying the dream, because fashion was seen as a dream and a reality escape. Balenciaga introduced the tortoise shell-like jackets, ¾ sleeves, vertical side pockets in skirts, and patch pockets showing below the suit jacket, while Givenchy developed the chemise, a sack dress in 1957. The sack dress was popular in New York, with *Vogue* saying it is 'more than a fashion, it's actually a way of dressing' (Baker, 1991, p. 40). Around the same time, Chanel said that 'fashion fades, only style remains the same' (Baker, 1991, p. 41). However, in popular culture, women of the 1940s were portrayed negatively, and the girl next door image became popularly promoted. Therefore, working girls of the 1940s were seen as women a man would not take home because they were the girls who were wearing sweaters and were considered sexual in their appearance, wearing more fitting clothes with necklines exposed (Baker, 1991).

The beatniks were popular in this period. The beatniks were a non-conforming anti-fashion and anti-establishment group wearing black leotards, long heavy 'sloppy Joe' sweaters over a long black skirt worn with black tights, as well as tight-fitting straight-leg corduroy trousers and flat-heeled ballet pumps (Baker, 1991). The beatniks were involved in the culture of coffee houses with poetry readings, plays, and listening to what was perceived as cool music or, in the UK, local skiffle groups. Yves Saint Laurent took inspiration from this movement and created his beatnik-inspired collection in 1960, which gave rise to his fashion style.

The period of the 1950s is sometimes seen as the golden age of couture due to this period also coinciding with Dior's New Look popularity. Dior revived French couture with his extravagant designs, which were historically a hallmark of French fashion. However, this period is also known for the return of Coco Chanel, who, according to some records, returned to designing because she objected to the femininity of Dior's designs and the step back this has made for women (Fischenich et al., 2000; Clarkson, 2011). While Dior himself experimented with several silhouettes, hourglass, *H*-lines, and *Y*-lines, the decade also progressed to introduce a trapeze shape and A-line silhouette. By 1958, hemlines were being reduced, and skirts were flaring out, which paved the way for miniskirts, but designers mainly focused on refined, linear silhouettes, which de-emphasized the waist. The latter was pushed by Chanel, who made a big return to fashion on February 5, 1954. Her 1954 collection featured jersey suits using straight lines (Ramzi, 2024c).

REFLECT

The Good Wife's Guide was published in May 1955 in *Housekeeping Monthly*. The article featured what a good wife should do for her husband. The original article is not available online, but more recent articles have published rules and illustrations from the original article. Read articles listed in this box, analyze illustrations, and consider the role of beauty and fashion in a good housewife's life. Then, consider the issues with depression and anxiety of women during the 1950s discussed in the previous chapter. What was the role of fashion in this period, and how was fashion used to keep housewives happy?

Articles to read:

https://medium.com/@twoguyswhoblog/the-good-wifes-guide-dfcba00e778c
https://retrohousewifegoesgreen.com/the-good-housewifes-guide/

The 'Swinging '60s': The Rise of Hippies and Anti-Fashion Movement

The 1960s, or the 'Swinging '60s', were an extraordinary decade because of the austerity and post-war rebuilding that happened during the 1950s. However, in fashion, many different styles were popularized. There was Jackie Kennedy, the US First Lady, wearing simplistic silhouettes and pastel colors, giving a presidential and refined look. Then, there was Mary Quant and the introduction of the miniskirt and trimmed hair, accepted by mods. There was Space Race fashion. Then, hippie fashion influenced the development of the boho style forever.

A novelty in the fashion industry was the decreased influence of Parisian haute couture and the rise of London in fashion. The demise of the domination of the Parisian fashion industry is sometimes attributed to Yves Saint Laurent, who designed his last collection for Dior in 1960, centered on 'a cool Beat collection of black leather suits and knitted caps to an astonished and slightly bewildered audience' (Clarkson, 2011, p. 33). This beatnik-inspired collection launched Yves Saint Laurent and gave him popularity among rebellious youth, but it nearly destroyed the House of Dior. The beatnik look remained popular in this period, and it was promoted as an outsider and bohemian image that combined elements of popular culture and high art. It featured handmade sandals, black turtleneck sweaters, black berets, and tight black trousers, and this look was particularly popular in California and New York (Connikie, 1990). Long hair and ethnic wear, which were on the margins before, became almost mainstream and another way of dressing up. The Hippie Dream and the Hippie Look, by the end of the decade, entered high fashion even though this was a contradiction in terms because hippies rejected the work ethic of Western society and conformism and engaged in practices that shocked the world, such as drugs, free love, and communal life, dreaming also of creating alternative societies with flowers as symbols of peace (Connikie, 1990).

This decade was, therefore, marked by youth culture and the post-war industrial boom when young people were refashioning themselves, and the youth market resulted in a new generation of designers catering to a new generation of fashion consumers. An important influence in this decade was The Beatles, who influenced young people with their distinctive hairstyle and clothing and presented a symbol of the youth culture. Bob Dylan and Mick Jagger were also symbols of this decade and presented a rebellious look. Dylan particularly went from the 'Beatnik to hippie to suede-jacketed country rocker' (Connikie, 1990, p. 7). The Rolling Stones also had their influence with a threatening and deliberately unkempt appearance. The Supremes influenced youth with gloves, satins, and feather boas (Connikie, 1990; Clarkson, 2011). This new influence happened around 1963, and it coincides not just with the rise of youth culture influenced by the music industry, but the rise of Yves Saint Laurent, who started his label in 1962 and took a youthful approach to fashion – initially designing for the wealthy which is typical for French designers but then also moving towards ready-to-wear fashion. The focus on youth was also present because, in the US, there was the Vietnam War and student protests, which put young people in the spotlight. The hippies were sometimes seen as a direct result of compulsory military service and the war (Connikie, 1990). This set the tone for fashion during the 1960s, and fashion was also influenced by the decade's anything-goes attitude.

An important invention of the Swinging Sixties was the miniskirt introduced by Mary Quant. This skirt was eight or nine inches above the knee and stayed there while women who embraced this look wore tights instead of stockings (Connikie, 1990). Maxi and midi lengths of skirts came in a period between 1969 and 1970. However, a hippie woman did not wear a mini skirt, but long floor-length skirts often accessorized with love beads and bells, thus presenting a different outlook on the fashion of the 1960s, which needs to be understood in the context of the division between mainstream and hippie society. Women and men 'went barefoot, had long hair, and wore jewelry, jeans, and shirts in colorful flowery patterns. The women also often wore long, flowing, flowery dresses' (Fischenich et al., 2000, p. 59). This was an anti-fashion statement similar to beatniks, who were protesting ambition and who wore messy, 'beat', clothes. However, contrary to their anti-establishment and anti-fashion philosophy, the hippie style soon became mainstream and 'floor-length skirts, fluttering scarves and bandanas, old-fashioned lacy blouses, and similarly nostalgic clothing quickly appeared in department stores, being cheaply mass-produced and proving highly popular' (Fischenich et al., 2000, p. 59). The hippie look eventually influenced the decade and despite a conflict in values, entered the mainstream, particularly with the rise of the popularity of midi and maxi skirts. Rich young people started to show contempt for work because they could afford it. Designers also embraced this style, and the final collections of the decade embraced all skirts, mini, maxi, and midi (Connikie, 1990).

In the 1960s, if the hippie style and Mary Quant's miniskirt were subcultures, Jackie Kennedy's style was the culture, which developed the so-called *Jackie Look* and kept couture going. Yves Saint Laurent also designed the *Le Smoking* suit for women. Another novelty of the 1960s was a diminished line between formal and casual wear, which stopped having meaning. The latest looks were delivered weekly, and fashion during the 1960s became central to the youth identity. The 1960s youth was the first post-war generation that reached adulthood, and since their social ideas changed, this had a radical impact on all areas of life, reaching the status of a cult (Fischenich et al., 2000). One of the central features of the young generation was a rejection of haute couture and a demand for fashion that would be affordable and match their spirit; thus, fashion also started to be used to express political identities and rebellion against elitism (Fischenich et al., 2000). Innovations and styles of the 1960s are summarized in the Table 3.5.

Table 3.5 Fashion Innovations and Styles of the 1960s

FASHION INNOVATIONS	DESCRIPTIONS
Silhouette	• Sheath and A-line dressed without defined waist
Space-age looks	• Moon girl collection of 1964 • Space-inspired helmets in wool or white leather • An opposition to the hippie fashion
Miniskirts	• Skirts shorter and shorter as the decade progressed • Mary Quant • Worn with big belt hung loosely over the hips • Women of all ages, not just young
Hosiery	• All-in-one nylon tights • Emphasis on legs • Strong colors with thick stripes, printed patterns, diamonds and plaid for winter • Lacy versions for summer dresses
Graphic lines	• Op Art look to mini skirts, shift dresses, and short A-line coats • Optical illusions in fashion • Strong graphic impact
Materials	• Synthetics – polyester, nylon, other man-made fabrics as helpful for movement; dresses made in special stretch nylon • Plastics – shiny PVC used for everything, clothing and boots, etc.
Boots	• Various shapes and styles • Black, white, and silver • Over-the-knee boots worn with mini skirts • Mid-calf Parisian boots, white kidskin, pointy toe and no heel, with a flat ribbon bow around the top
Chainmail	• Plastic chainmail and aluminum appearing in silver, black, and white • Futuristic image • Trend for transparency
Psychedelia	• Emphasis shifting from London to the US by mid-1960s • Flower children of San Francisco, anti-Vietnam chants, long hair, and ragbag of utilitarian and ethnic garments • Brocade jeans, frilly shirts, flower-print tunics, Mao jackets, Indian scarves • European designers started to copy the hippie style

(Continued)

Table 3.5 Continued

FASHION INNOVATIONS	DESCRIPTIONS
Sheer and transparent	• Transparent panels of clear plastic or mesh like netting • See-through clothes becoming more daring with Yves Saint Laurent leading the way • Saint Laurent sheer black chiffon blouse
Oversized sunglasses	• Op art and space-age styles • Round and goggle-like • Celebrity accessory
Maxi and midi lengths	• Long coats, skirts, and dresses as an antidote to mini • The maxi went to the ankle • The midi was cut to mid-calf • A choice for women to decide • Many women chose midi knit cardigans over short skirts with boots to show a fleeting glimpse of leg
Cut-outs	• Shapes cut out of dresses • Revealing midsection
Shift dresses	• A-line shift falling in a clean triangular line from shoulder to mid-thigh • Big, circular pockets • Cutaway armholes and contrast edging around the neck, hem, and armholes • Some worn over a skinny rib sweater and ribbed thighs for daywear or with heels for eveningwear
Sex liberation and fashion	• Transparent blouses and ultrashort skirts
Trapeze line	• Yves Saint Laurent introduced in 1958; gained popularity during the 1960s
Tent dresses	• Cut in straight or A-line shapes, synthetic fabrics • Inspired by the 1920s
The hippie look	• Flowery, colorful patterns; women wore long, flowing, flowery dresses • Men and women had long hair and went barefoot • Jeans
Yves Saint Laurent	• Le Smoking tuxedo for women
The Jackie Look	• A presidential look of Jackie Kennedy, with pastel colors and refined elegance • Served as an opposition to the influence of sub-cultures such as Saint Laurent, beatniks, and hippies

Source: Author's work. Information adapted from Clarkson (2011, pp. 34–35), Fischenich et al. (2000, pp. 56, 57, 58, 59, 68), and Ramzi (2024d)

One of the fashion features of the 1960s was a trapeze line, which Yves Saint Laurent showed in 1958; these were 'tent dresses or coats without a waist, narrow at the top, widening toward the bottom, and usually ending just above the knee' (Fischenich et al., 2000, p. 56). Therefore, unlike in the 1950s when the balloon and the A-line, the barrel line, and the *Y*-shape were introduced, the trapeze gained popularity in the 1960s. Dresses were elegant and ladylike, shaped like sacks or flowing around the body, made of delicate fabrics such as lace and silks, special occasion dresses often had gold and sequin embroidery (Fischenich et al., 2000). Tent dresses were particularly popular, clearly inspired by the 1920s because they were often cut in 'straight or A-line shapes from stiff (synthetic) fabrics .... They were much shorter than the dresses of the 1920s and generally made a pretty loud impression. They challenged the idea of traditional, ladylike elegance, and that was indeed the intention' (Fischenich et al., 2000, p. 57).

The 1960s saw success for women in business and politics, and increased women's rights due to a general view of the decade that anything was possible. This was accompanied by a 'dumb blond' image, which was linked to fashion because 'a pretty girl in a mini skirt wasn't expected to say anything intelligent' (Connikie, 1990, p. 16). However, the demographic changed in this decade and there were more men than women, thus women no longer had to be pretty to find a man and started to dress more simply, for example, in practical pantsuits and jeans (Connikie, 1990). An inspiration was drawn from a skirt suit popularized from the time of Queen Alexandra, wife of King Edward VII of Britain, who wore sleek travel suits made by a tailor John Redfern, and popularized them among feminists who saw them as resistance to femininity (Worsley, 2011). These suits came into prominence again during the 1980s, after a break during the 1970s, when they became part of a working woman's power suit consisting of tight skirts and jackets with wide masculine shoulders, which was also a feature of the 1980s. Men's style was influenced by Italian designers and consisted of short suit jackets, tailored with narrow lapels, worn over narrow-collar shirts and slender ties with narrower trousers (Connikie, 1990).

The feature of the 1960s was sex liberation, with books on sex education and movies booming with this theme. Anti-pregnancy pills also removed the fear of pregnancy and social disapproval that came along with out-of-marriage pregnancy, with young consumers also rebelling against the moral standards of earlier generations. Being sexually liberal meant being modern, and this fed into fashion with transparent blouses and ultrashort skirts (Fischenich et al., 2000). Twiggy was the feature of the decade with her androgynous look and no visible feminine features, that young consumers liked while the older ones were scandalized. These changes in social views of sex also had an impact on male fashion, with differences between male and female clothing becoming blurred. Men during the 1960s also had long hair and wore clothes that emphasized the body, while women hid their bodies and had a sexless outlook, with short trousers and short hair becoming popular but contributing towards a child-like and androgynous look. The decade has similarities with the 1920s because during the 1920s men started to have a softer outlook whereas women started to look harsher and had a nickname *garçonnes* (mannish women); similarly, in the 1960s, women's fashion took inspiration from the 1920s and women appeared boyish with the term androgynous starting to gain wider use (Fischenich et al., 2000). This boyish look was also followed by hairstyles with hair backcombed using a huge amount of hairspray, and the outlook was child-like. However, men's hair became longer, in contrast to women's, thus changing gender roles. Haircuts by Beatles members became popular with their hair longer than was previously common for men, and this further exacerbated the change from Parisian designers influencing fashion to fashion influence moving to pop stars. Other than this, men's fashion was centered on suits, which during the mid-1960s moved to tighter and closer-fitted cuts, which also applied to coats, which often came with belts, e.g., trench coats. Instead of a shirt with a tie, it started to be possible to wear turtleneck sweaters, which were seen not just as fashionable but also practical (Fischenich et al., 2000). Apart from tweed and fine wool, corduroy became popular and came into mass use. Trousers were tighter than in the 1950s, but this started to change towards the end of the decade with the rise of the 1970s flares. Jeans became a common leisurewear that continued in popularity from the 1950s, and jeans were accompanied by polo shirts (Fischenich et al., 2000).

The 1960s witnessed a further rise in the popularity of television, which resulted in global lifestyles and the sharing of knowledge, including fashion trendsetting. More people started to dress fashionably regardless of income because fashion was now available at decreased prices. This gave rise to an attitude that clothes are for temporary use, one season, purchased quickly and discarded even quicker. This naturally impacted the quality of clothes, but it also gave rise to department stores and boutiques. Big fashion houses started to feel the impact of this trend and focused more than before on ready-to-wear fashion, with haute couture still being an important feature of couture houses, but it no longer generated the largest income; thus, by the mid-1960s, every fashion house offered prêt-à-porter (Fischenich et al., 2000). Prêt-à-porter collections started to be shown twice a year, in Paris and Milan. This helped meet the demand for more affordable fashion, but it also took some fashion designers out of business, such as Cristóbal Balenciaga, who closed his fashion house because he believed that fashion could only be art (Fischenich et al., 2000). This changing trend also meant that fashion trends were not always dictated by haute couture. To some extent, haute couture set trends, but haute couture was also influenced by youth culture. Hippie and street/youth influence was countered by futuristic fashion, which was embraced by French designers. In its ideology, it was the direct opposite of flowery hippie fashion. This was not the first time there was an attempt to introduce this theme to fashion; an attempt was made during the popularity of the beatniks, who were fascinated by sci-fi literature and film, as well as traveling to the Moon (Fischenich et al., 2000).

Colors of the 1960s were centered on soft pastels on one side, and the vivid, bright, and neutral earth tones on the other side; thus, colors in this period included a wider range than in other decades. The decade is known for new colors such as lime green, magenta, lemon, mimosa, jade, hot pink, and tangerine, which were not present in other decades. These were then also mixed with flowery patterns by hippies, which added the psychedelic prints that hippies are known for. Mature women favored plaid and polka dots, which were stocked by the department stores and dominated department catalogues. The 1960s also saw a further rise in polyester, nylon, and rayon, accompanied by acrylic, which was also widely in use during this period. Perspex, PVC, and Spandex were also popular in this period and celebrated as innovations. Ready-to-wear labels adopted new materials, trying to cater to young consumers or households who wanted to wash-and-wear clothes that did not need ironing. In this period, the fashion industry started to list its fiber contents, mandated by the Textile Fiber Products Identification Act in the US. *Vogue* wrote on April 15, 1965,

> What's the Hot Ticket? ... It's tied or sewed onto every dress made in America, and it tells you exactly what the dress is made of—down to the last fibre. Percentages are given, names spelled out; and some names that used to sound like

Figure 3.18 Ann Bonfoey Taylor walking in Colorado in 1967 wearing bright colors of the 1960s

US Library of Congress

1984 or Dr. No's laboratory—names like polyester, acrylic, triacetate—now have a familiar, trusted ring. (We may still not know what they mean, actually, but we know how they perform: brilliantly.)... Some fabrics are all natural fibres, some all synthetic; the great majority are mixtures, with a spectrum of strengths and capabilities. (Ramzi, 2024d, n.p.).

REFLECT

Find 1960s coverage of a fashion magazine, and collect adverts published during the decade. Consider the following questions: Who is the target audience? What fashion trends are being promoted (bohemian, space-age, etc.)? How are gender roles and ideals portrayed in the clothing and language? What social values or norms does the ad reflect or challenge? How do advertisements connect to broader cultural shifts (e.g., the youth movement)? How did fashion in the 1960s become a form of rebellion or expression? What role did advertising play in reinforcing or challenging societal norms?

The Crazy '70s: Flares and Political Upheaval

The 1970s, popularly also known as the 'Crazy '70s', were sometimes labeled as a me-decade. This was a period of political upheaval marked by unemployment, energy crisis, recession, civil and gay rights protests, environmental protests, and anti-nuclear protests but also innovation in technology, such as the introduction of a computer microchip, and the general rise of globalization – which resulted in the global spread of food chains such as McDonald's and Kentucky Fried Chicken for example (Herald, 1992). This period saw a rise in feminist writing and an increased importance of all social movements campaigning during this period. In feminism, Germaine Greer wrote *The Female Eunuch*, challenging a traditional perception of femininity and patriarchal expectations of women (Greer, 1970). A women's strike for equality in New York City was held in August 1970 when thousands of women marched demanding equal rights, better childcare, and abortion rights, which is why this event is sometimes known as the Women's Liberation March. Women also embraced their bodies, which were at the center of fashion.

Clothes of the 1970s were clingy and soft, and embraced the figure in its natural form with little structure from undergarments. The sense was that women were liberated, and this also gave rise to wearing trousers, including a further popularization of jeans. Designer denim became a thing for any occasion. It was a decade of 'anything goes'. *Vogue* wrote in the January 1970 issue, 'Shawls, capes, ponchos—anything that can be wrapped, strapped, or rolled around the body is home free in every way.' (Ramzi, 2024e, n.p.). The social unrest and student protests from the 1960s were still felt in society, now divided over the way of living too, with attempts from the youth to find alternative ways of living, including a focus on drugs, free love, and living in communes, and the women's movement was a part of this social struggle (Fischenich et al., 2000).

Figure 3.19 A poster invite for a protest of women workers, minority women, and lesbians, 1976

US Library of Congress

The 1970s were a decade when there was a sense of nostalgia for previous decades and an interest in traditional cultures, which created a retro style that was promoted by popular culture. For example, *The Great Gatsby* from 1974 was set in the 1920s with Mia Farrow and Robert Redford wearing creations of that period, labeled as retro. Other popular culture influenced this style too, such as the American TV series *Happy Days* and the *American Graffiti* film, which portrayed teenagers from the 1950s (Herald, 1992). Retro culture also included ethnic, natural, and rootsy styles, which were popular in the first few years of the 1970s (Clarkson, 2011). Nostalgia styles included grandma shirts, long peasant skirts, gypsy skirts, ethnic clothes such as inspired by Bedouin and Afghan ethnic clothes, etc. All these clothes reminded people of 19th- and 20th-century clothes, which is another cyclical aspect of fashion that returned to the 1970s and gained popularity. Trends from the 1960s were also popular and returned to the 1970s, but fashion became more casual, with a distinction between daywear and eveningwear hardly distinguishable anymore (Fischenich et al., 2000). The 1940s style was also popular for a while, noticed by *Vogue*, which wrote, in the June 1972 issue, 'The Sweeping Comeback of Dark Nails,' declared, 'Ultraviolet, another classic '40s shade, looking better than ever on '70s nails.' (Ramzi, 2024e).

The 1970s dress style was marked by dressing as a system of signs that signaled one's lifestyle and aspirations. American psychologists wrote articles about the power of dressing and its social and political implications, and magazines wrote about language and status symbols referencing designers that fit certain symbols and clothes, and seeing women as not just fashion consumers but also career women (Herald, 1992). UK and US *Cosmopolitan* editions started to offer sex advice, taking the initiative with men, makeup, and body, and there was a sense of social change. This was also influenced by the rise of radical feminism that opposed fashion and was faced with stereotypes of radical feminists always wearing T-shirts with slogans, baggy jeans, practical carry-all bags, buttons in place of jewelry, flat shoes, and hair with minimal maintenance, either long or short (Herald, 1992). However, this gave rise to more freedom for women in terms of fashion, so career women started to cross-dress for professional purposes, and while previously women were trying to fit into men's world, now skirts and high heels were discarded in favor of heavy boots and jeans (Herald, 1992). Women's executive dress was still inspired by male suits, but now these outfits were accompanied by trousers, not skirts anymore, which was a novelty and presented progress. Radical feminists also influenced the start of power dressing, which started around 1978 (Herald, 1992) and spilled over into the 1980s. Power dressing was linked to padded shoulders and tailored coats. Youth fashion was marked by the rise of skinheads in the UK, who grew out of the mods movement of the 1960s, which faded in popularity after becoming mainstream. The youth fashion was a working-class reaction to middle-class hippies, since the hippie movement had become mainstream by the end of the 1960s, and the lifestyle was embraced by the rich, including fashion, which led to the rise of punk, a direct opposite of peaceful hippies with its confrontational style. Up to this day, the hippie movement serves as an inspiration for designers due to the focus on floral designs, long, flowing silhouettes, and prints and details (Worsley, 2011). Skinheads wore tight short trousers, often bleached, Crombie coats, suspenders, shirts with button-down collars, and big boots, often Doc Martens (Herald, 1992), which became a symbol of the skinhead movement. There was a revival of the mod movement in the 1970s UK, but it did not last long because the original mods grew up, got married, and became disillusioned with the movement (Worsley, 2011). Mods were not a good fit for protest and street culture because their movement was about having money to spend and liberating themselves by wearing slick hair and miniskirts until this became mainstream.

Second-hand clothes grew in popularity, with new clothes also being made from old clothes. Some declared that 'fashion as a dictatorship of the elite is dead' (Herald, 1992, p. 15). The rise of the environmentalist and animal rights movements also meant that women stopped wearing fur, with UK *Vogue* declaring that 'no woman with her eyes open would walk about now in the skins of a rare animal and be the butt of raised eyebrows and uncomplimentary remarks' (Herald, 1992, p. 15). Haute couture also got criticized in this period, with Kennedy Fraser saying in 1975 that haute couture is 'a degenerate institution propped up by a sycophanting press' (Herald, 1992, p. 24). This prompted haute couture companies to focus more on ready-to-wear clothes that were also casual and practical. The rich remained loyal to Paris, but there was also a rise of anti-establishment brands, such as Vivienne Westwood, who infamously created a T-shirt defacing the Queen during the Jubilee celebrations of 1977. Fashion in this period was based on the 1920s, 1930s, and 1940s particularly in France where designers drew inspiration from these decades using tweeds, crepes, gabardines, and gauzier silks for formal daytime designs and romantic eveningwear, despite clothes being every day and practical, it remained haute couture with finishes and cuts of high quality (Herald, 1992).

One of the most distinguished features of 1970s fashion was flared trousers, with jeans being particularly popular. However, while flares are one of the most distinguished symbols of the 1970s, their history is longer. Flares are also known as bell-bottoms because of their shape, and they originated in the early 19th century when some sailors from the US Navy wore them before they had official uniforms. The style was later adopted by the British Royal Navy in the mid-19th century. In the 1970s, flares were popularized by Sonny Bono and Cher, who appeared in flares on TV. While the popularity of flares diminished during the 1980s, they returned to fashion in the 1990s, the second half, and their new name was boot-cut; this is because the flare was not as wide as in the 1970s. Flares keep coming back to fashion, but they also present a standard shape of jeans for many designers and retailers, particularly high street brands who stock them regularly (European Fashion Heritage Association, 2018). In 2015, the *Guardian* published a history of flares in pictures, labeling these trousers as a symbol of the 1970s and showing their different shapes and styles (Whitmore, 2015). Fashion innovations and styles of the 1970s are summarized in Table 3.6.

Table 3.6 Fashion Innovations and Styles of the 1970s

FASHION INNOVATIONS	DESCRIPTIONS
Silhouette	• Tight on top and loose on bottom
Bodystockings	• Made of elastic material • A one-piece close fitting • Enveloping the whole body • Inspiration from the 1930s Hollywood glamour • Popular on the dance and disco scene
Midi skirts	• A response to initially very short mini skirts • Calf-length • A-line • Made of four stripes of fabric
Maxi skirts	• Ankle or floor length • A counter to the 1960s mini skirt • Maxi skirts were often worn in dress form with a choker and crochet shawl • A-line skirt with a fitted bodice
Diana decollete	• An asymmetric neckline • One bare shoulder • Inspiration from the second half of the 19th century and first used by Elsa Schiaparelli in the 1930s and Madame Grès in the 1950s
Jumpsuits	• Charlie's Angels pantsuits • One-piece • Usually with short legs • Jersey

(*Continued*)

Table 3.6 Continued

FASHION INNOVATIONS	DESCRIPTIONS
Unisex	• Identical clothing on hairless male and female models • Rudi Gernreich • The androgynous look of Diane Keaton in Annie Hall
Carmen and gypsy looks	• A flamenco style • Ethnic fashion trend • Narrow at the hips, thighs, and knees and ending in a wide skirt, with lace or frills at the off-the-shoulder neckline • Gypsy look – frilled or unevenly hemmed skirts worn with blouses tied above the waist
Wraparound	• Wrap dress and wrap skirts • Knit jersey wrap launched in 1972
Parkas	• Long outer garment • Large pockets • Tough cotton fabric with removable lining • Young people's fashion
Gauchos, knickerbockers and jodhpurs	• Mid-length trousers • Calf-length wide-bottomed gauchos • South American cowboys inspiration • Full breeches gathered below the knee
Kaftans	• Eveningwear • Exotic fabrics • Edged in metallic trims
Folkloric	• Tibetan and Chinese quilted jackets • Ethnic influence from Africa and India
Flares and trouser suits	• A major trend of the 1970s • Began gently flared then reached wide bell-bottom by 1975 • Heavy crepes, wool jersey knits, Courtelle jersey, and woven polyester suiting (Trevira)
Patterns, prints, and colors	• Floral motifs • Nature patterns • Geometrics and stripes continued from the 1960s • African and Native American textiles and prints • Earth tones (white, black, beige, and olive) contrasted with mustard, brick red, and dark orange

(*Continued*)

Table 3.6 Continued

FASHION INNOVATIONS	DESCRIPTIONS
Eastern influences	• Kenzo, Yuki, and Zoran labels • Yohji Yamamoto • Eastern minimalism • Refined clothes, fluid and sculptural
Hotpants	• Extremely brief shorts • Velvet or lurex for eveningwear • Worn under a maxi or midi skirt with the front open to reveal legs
Granny dresses	• Empire waistlines • Ornate fabric bodice and exotic sleeves • Earth Mother style • Granny dresses with a high frilled or lace neckline and floral prints on brushed fabric • Romantic floral prints and old-fashioned dresses of the Victorian era
Punk	• Malcolm McLaren and Vivienne Westwood • Anti-establishment • Bondage, safety pins, ripped edges, and irregular stitching resembling chaos
Disco fashion	• 1977's Saturday Night Fever • Shiny, metallic, and glittery materials (sequins, Spandex, Lurex) • Bandeau tops and stretch skirts • Dancewear adapted to disco • Gold lamé, leopard skin, and glowing white clothes
Anti-fashion	• Back to nature – knitting and crocheting
Pleated skirts	• Knee length • Took over from miniskirts towards the 1975 when miniskirts lost popularity • Made of jersey, tweed, or check woolen fabrics
Shirt dresses	• Popular for a short period of time, later replaced with jersey
Nostalgia	• Big fashion cycles with popularization of the 1920s, 1940s, 1950s, and 1960s styles • Old styles labeled as retro

Source: Author's work. Information adapted from Clarkson (2011, pp. 40–41), Fischenich et al. (2000, pp. 72, 74, 75), and Ramzi (2024e)

Figure 3.20 Red and cream loafers designed by Pierre Cardin, late 20th century
Collection of the Smithsonian National Museum of African American History and Culture, Gift of Antoine 'Fats' Domino

Fashion in this period was seen as a way of expressing an opinion and while there was still a focus on anti-fashion, some new haute couture houses and designers started to operate in this period, such as Kenzo, Issey Miyake, Vivienne Westwood, and Ralph Lauren. The hippie movement still defined this era and continued its influence into the 1980s. The high fashion took an inspiration from the hippie movement and created an idyllic look, which resembled the hippie style but not in an earthy way. The look is sometimes described as romantic, and it was championed by British designers such as Zandra Rhodes, Ossie Clark, and Laura Ashley. In the US, this style was embraced by Jessica McClintock and Giorgio di Sant' Angelo (Ramzi, 2024e). *Vogue*, from January 1970 instructed its readers to embrace this sensual and free-spirited style, 'All languorously falling things—and with lots and lots of long, dangling fringe to keep the languor lingering … anything that makes you dream a little bit about yourself.' In the spread: an image of film star Natalie Wood wearing a couple of Zandra Rhodes looks described as 'yards and yards of purest fantasy—designs that summon the delectable world of Russian fairy tales and English storybook pantomimes' (Ramzi, 2024e, n.p.).

A back-to-nature view of fashion was a feature of the younger generation, who preferred knitting or crocheting and making clothes such as cardigans, woolly hats, giant shawls, and floor-length dresses, as well as furnishings such as blankets, cushions, and curtains (Fischenich et al., 2000). This focus on knitting and crocheting left a mark on haute couture, which continued to draw inspiration from the street, and thus, Sonia Rykiel became famous for her knitwear, which was feminine and sophisticated. Knitted clothes spread to everything, including suits, trousers, coats, etc. (Fischenich et al., 2000). Patchwork

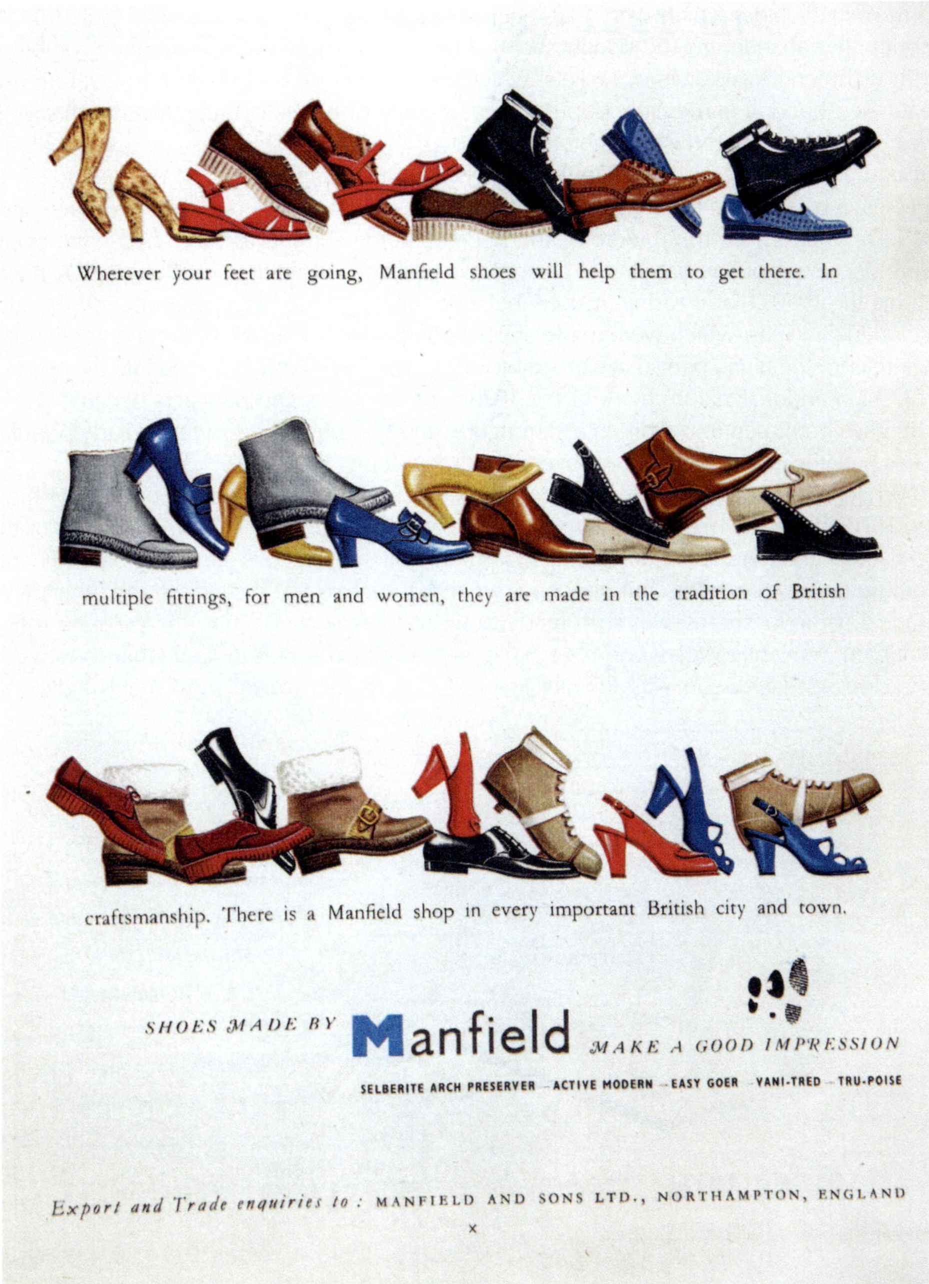

Figure 3.21 An advert for Manfield shoes, Northampton, England

UK's National Archives. Reprinted with permission

also became popular because of its improvised, rural outlook, and since dressing up was frowned upon, this gave rise to the popularity of patchwork. Skirts and blouses were casual during the 1970s, and skirts became very short, which resulted in a counter-fashion in the form of midi skirts, which were calf-length, usually made in A-line, and of four strips or fabrics, thus abandoning the straight shape of the 1960s. These skirts 'were often combined with waist-length sweaters or jackets, which were sometimes lined with artificial fur and featured a hood, a particularly popular type or collar or head-covering taken from sportswear and leisurewear' (Fischenich et al., 2000, p. 74). Pleated skirts also gained popularity around 1975 as a response to miniskirts, which lost popularity around this period. With dresses, a particularly popular style was a shirtdress with a belt, but these were replaced by jersey dresses by the middle of the decade. Some summer dresses had wrap-overs, were sleeveless, or had batwing or crescent-shaped sleeves (Fischenich et al., 2000). It was during the 1970s that wearing trousers became fully acceptable for women, and this also included pantsuits, which were made of corduroy, tweed, or velvet, or knitted, for the day, whereas for the night, pantsuits were made of georgette or silk. This turned into the essence of fashion and a signature mark of the 1970s once trousers and pantsuits became flared. This gave both men and women a slim figure, and flared jeans were particularly popular. Jeans became an essential part of every wardrobe during the 1970s.

While haute couture existed with Yves Saint Laurent making a mark on high fashion, the 1970s were not marked by haute couture and its influence. This was because of the casualness and the social questioning of fashion, which resulted in some established haute couture houses retreating, but new ones emerged, such as Karl Lagerfeld and others who made a name for themselves with ready-to-wear collections. Because of the anti-fashion sentiment, Vivienne Westwood rose in the ranks during this period, and while Westwood is a designer label, she was initially associated with the protest movement and punk.

Figure 3.22 A photo showing a shopping area in London, Carnaby Street, 1960
UK's National Archives. Reprinted with permission

Figure 3.23 A cover page photo showing a shopping area in London, Carnaby Street 1969 with people wearing fashion that will become a hallmark of the 1970s

UK's National Archives. Reprinted with permission

Figure 3.24 Girls shopping in the King's Road area wearing fashionable clothes, West London, 1969

UK's National Archives. Reprinted with permission

Westwood claimed that punk was never a street movement but fashion right from the start and that she played a significant part in this form of anti-fashion with her partner Malcolm McLaren (Fischenich et al., 2000). Because of the anti-fashion sentiment, youth fashion rose in popularity during this period, which shifted fashion taste away from the wealthy, mature elite. While haute couture continued, particularly due to the popularity of the little black dress, popularized by *Breakfast at Tiffany's* film, young people were more likely to follow the beatniks and the mods (modernists), particularly at the beginning of this decade. Mods inspired the looks of bands such as The Who, The Small Faces, and The Beatles. However, youth fashion was not initially easily found, and thus new shops were needed, which gave rise to boutiques; small, self-service shops set up in London by designers who were offering a more affordable fashion for younger consumers, and they offered a better customer experience by being able to get to know their customers better. Boutiques soon gained mass popularity, particularly because they catered to the mods, and thus shops were opened on London's King's Road and Carnaby Street. These new shops also gave rise to internationally popular, slim-fitting outfits using bright colors, because of which London got a nickname, Swinging London, and this gave rise to this style's popularity in the US.

Colors changed throughout the 1970s, with colors of the 1960s being first popular, then replaced by darker, muted colors such as browns of all shades being combined with orange and moss green, and aubergine and purple gained popularity too. The materials of this decade also included Perspex, PVC, polyester, acrylic, nylon, rayon, and Spandex. Often, the whole outfit was in the same color, at least in different shades, and the look was accompanied by platform shoes. Initially, at the beginning of the decade, shoes were broad and squarish and had clumpy heels, but towards the end of the decade, shoes became narrower and heels narrower and slimmer, with platform shoes disappearing (Fischenich et al., 2000). Space age style became more popular during this decade, popularized by André Courrèges, who created modern couture clothes. His angular mini-dresses and trouser suits were white and silver, worn with astronaut-style accessories (flat boots, goggles, and helmets), and thus this style became known as the 'space-age' style (V&A, n.d.).

Designer denim and the rise of leisurewear mark this period. Calvin Klein joined Levi's, Lee, and Wrangler. *Vogue* wrote in 1978,

> The lowly blue jean was apparently not worthy of a Name Designer logo. Until now, that is. Just when skeptics were saying that the blue-jean market was saturated and there was talk of the demise of denim; just when the sales of Levis were falling and many stores were reducing their markup on jeans, the Calvin Kleins and Geoffrey Beenes and Ralph Laurens and Oscar de la Rentas begin branding blue jeans with their celebrated names and initials .... Calvin Klein, who introduced his first denim jeans earlier this year ... insists that 'jeans are not dead: they're hot and sexy and still great.' He claims he waited to get into the jeans scene until he could get a licensee (Puritan Industries) to make them 'at a reasonable price. I want the girls who can't afford to wear my clothes to wear my jeans' (Ramzi, 2024e, n.p.).

The rise of denim further exacerbated the domination of New York as a fashion capital. Manhattan became home to designers who were setting directions in fashion, such as Calvin Klein, Ralph Lauren, Bill Blass, Stephen Burrows, Oscar de la Renta, Halston, and Anne Klein. Eleanor Lambert, a publicist who created the New York Fashion Week

(Berkeley, n.d.) and the International Best Dressed List, organized a string of events in 1973 that further put American fashion in the spotlight. By helping organize fashion shows featuring French and American designers, she achieved global publicity and further promoted American fashion. The final event Lambert organized was held in Versailles and was sometimes dubbed the Battle of Versailles. The *International Herald Tribune* wrote on November 30, 1973, that 'the real surprise was that American fashion has come of age. The French can no longer ignore it' (Ramzi, 2024e, n.p.).

REFLECT

Find an advert from the 1970s from one big brand published in a fashion magazine. Consider why you selected that advert. What appeals to you? What visual elements stand out (colors, poses, styles, setting)? What fashion trends are visible (e.g., flares, glam rock, disco, denim)? What does the tone of the ad suggest about societal attitudes (e.g., liberation, consumerism, individualism)? How does this reflect broader movements like feminism, the sexual revolution, environmentalism, or Black movement?

The 1980s: Power Suits and the Political Backlash

The 1980s present a backlash after the Swinging Sixties, the Crazy 70s, and the 1970s punk rock. The 1980s mindset was focused on being serious, grown-up, and hard-working at its heart, which created a cult of success (Carnegy, 1990; Fischenich et al., 2000). The yuppies (young upwardly mobile professionals) were a feature of the decade and presented the spirit of hard work and individual responsibility (Carnegy, 1990, p. 6). This style featured a well-dressed young executive. It was a widespread social trend to be fashionable, well-dressed, and make money (Carnegy, 1990). This group was the focus of the decade, because there were fewer young people due to the rise of birth control, and these professionals were increasing in numbers and had extra money to spend, which also gave rise to business meeting clothes (Carnegy, 1990).

Calvin Klein and Ralph Lauren grew their business in the US and targeted this group, thus becoming the most successful designers of the decade because they were producing everything a working woman needed (Carnegy, 1990). This was particularly the case because these two brands focused on the working woman's style, which became known as the trademark of the American fashion culture. Because of the focus on the working woman, Donna Karan rose in recognition and obtained a nickname, the Queen of 7th Avenue, due to her 'toned-down, working women's high style, yet comfortable, clothing and accessories' (Carnegy, 1990, p. 12). The rise of focus on the American working woman also led to the rise of department stores, which no longer had everything but were composed of boutiques of various designers. This resulted in a trend of putting designer labels on everything because a designer label must have been seen on everything one wore in this period. *Vogue* was not in favor of yuppies and their dressing style that centered on skirt suits, pussy-bow blouses, and running shoes instead of pumps, and the yuppies' promotion of brands such as Ralph Lauren and Coach. For men, the yuppie style meant a three-piece suit, a Rolex, a Burberry trench, and a squash racquet; thus, for both men and women, yuppie style was seen as overly capitalist and pretentious. At the end of the decade, *Vogue*, in an article published in 1989 said,

> The horrifying little yuppie suit (which, with its copycat male pinstripes and flop-doodle little-girl bow tie, did more for making women look stuffy and drab than, as intended, male and 'powerful') is now, thank the gods of Seventh Avenue, on the endangered species list (Ramzi, 2024f, n.p.).

However, *Vogue* celebrated Ralph Lauren's Americana collection inspired by American southwestern culture, along with the tradition of the English gentry (Ramzi, 2024f).

The 1980s were also a time of economic hardship, with policies introduced by Ronald Reagan in the US and Margaret Thatcher in the UK to increase youth employment (Topić, 2021), which meant that the working classes could not afford a lot, and fashion was affected. This was the reason why street fashion emerged. The wealthy wore designer brands, such as Chanel and Versace, but these styles remained detached from the main societal trend until Jean Paul Gaultier picked up the street style and introduced it to his new collection. However, this changed during the middle part of the decade, and things started to look up, which gave rise to interest in designer shoes, bags, and accessories, with New York becoming the center of fashion due to Donna Karan, Calvin Klein, and Ralph Lauren working in New York and producing everything (Clarkson, 2011). American women turned against simply copying the Parisian style and embraced American designers, which created a new American style with its emphasis on the casual and practical, easily introduced due to rising manufacturing (Worsley, 2011).

Haute couture further lost its global domination, with many countries developing their own styles, which were now crossing national borders. Countries such as the UK, Germany, Japan, and the US had a large influence on fashion. Fashion became playful and was affected by postmodernism. There were elements of previous fashion periods, but these were mainly a reference, not similar to the nostalgia of the 1970s. For example, there were frilly blouses and long skirts as reminders of 19th-century dress, and the main reminders of the fashion past were haute couture and ready-to-wear designer collections. While fashion always had a cyclical nature and a historical quote of previous styles, in the 1980s, there was a mix of old styles that were put together randomly and made into something new (Fischenich et al., 2000). There was a tendency towards simple, functional elegance while fashion indulgence remained in the realm of haute couture. The 1980s were mainly known for abandoning styles and trends and developing and putting together different styles (Fischenich et al., 2000). However, not everything was lost for couture, thanks to Karl Lagerfeld. Lagerfeld was appointed to revive the House of Chanel in 1983, which was an instant success. *Vogue*'s June 1983 issue praised Lagerfeld's collection for Chanel: 'Suddenly, everyone is talking about Chanel. One of the reasons—Karl Lagerfeld, now the designer for Chanel Couture' (Ramzi, 2024f, n.p.).

The male look in this period drew from the dandies of the 19th century and focused on silk and velvet because men in the 1980s wanted to look softer, which ran in opposition to women who wanted to look tougher since the 1970s and the rise of women's consciousness about their position in the world. The rise of the yuppie look turned male fashion toward more conservative suits and ties, which was high fashion for all generations (Carnegy, 1990). The new woman of this period was still borrowing from the male wardrobe, and there was a rise of the female executive of the 1980s who were wearing

Figure 3.25 Chanel No.5 advert, 1927
Musée Carnavalet, Histoire de Paris

skirts of various styles, jackets as standard wear, and shoulder pads that signaled authority and gave an aura of success (Carnegy, 1990). These shoulder pads were popular during the 1920s and 1930s, too; thus, this form of fashion is cyclical and frequently featured in various fashion periods.

The 1980s also gave rise to powerful women who climbed to high positions of power for the first time, such as Margaret Thatcher, who became the first female Prime Minister of the UK, and Geraldine Ford, a vice-presidential candidate in the US in 1984. Dress for success became a mantra during the 1980s because women were not only present in the world of work but also started to climb the ladder, which was expressed by the clothes they wore. These clothes were meant to stress competence rather than draw attention to the body, which resulted in women preferring suits such as,

> a long, wide blazer with broadly cut shoulders emphasized by pads, worn with a slimline knee-length skirt or a pleated skirt and high-heeled, simple yet elegant pumps. Now and again, the skirt could be substituted by fine and modestly wide pleated pants (Fischenich et al., 2000, p. 87).

Dresses were made in soft fabrics and with wide shoulders and covered knees (Fischenich et al., 2000). The shoulder pads became a distinctive feature of the 1980s, and the decade is generally known through these power suits for women. *Vogue*'s October 1985 issue, had a title 'power dressing' and portrayed women hovering above men, the accompanying text stating,

> A different way of looking at fashion—as entertainment, as fantasy, as a provocative element. And men looking differently at women. Women at men. The women dressing to be noticed ... and gain the upper hand. Men can fuel fantasy. But women set the direction ... and the tone. You get the sense that things are changing (Ramzi, 2024f, n.p.).

The power suits had exaggerated and padded shoulders, 'a double-breasted silhouette made a figure loom larger and peplums made women look more imposing. The power suits were not masculine or looked like traditional men's suits, they roared femininity rather than whisper it' (Ramzi, 2024f, n.p.).

Popular culture featured and popularized this style, such as the American shows *Dynasty* and *Dallas,* where characters such as Alexis in *Dynasty* (Joan Collins) wore tight skirts, tailored jackets with a sharp appearance, broad shoulders, and a narrow waist to emphasize the bosom. Colors were strong and vibrant, and high heels were an essential part of the outfit. Women followed the fashion from *Dynasty* and *Dallas,* and the impact of *Dynasty* is so strong that Netflix made a new version of the show in 2017. Eveningwear was centered on skintight dresses with slits, dark curls, and appropriate hairstyles, which gave a *femme fatale* outlook. This was often the portrayal of bad characters in the soap operas such as *Dynasty,* whereas more feminine (and often portrayed more positively) characters wore modest colors, emphasized the figure less, and were often blonde, like Crystal in the original *Dynasty* (Linda Evans). However, while padded shoulders were popularized during the 1980s and became a mark of this period, the inspiration for this style derived from Elsa Schiaparelli's designs during the 1930s (Fischenich et al., 2000).

Colors of the 1980s introduced crazy neon colors, which were popular in this decade, along with pink, black, white, indigo, green, burgundy, and various shades of orange, tan, and brown. Fun, party costumes were a hallmark of the 1980s, too, as well as leggings. Other popular items included windbreaker jackets, oversized sweaters, white sneakers, prom dress culture in the US, and high-waist jeans, then later also crossing over to the 1990s. Fabrics of the 1980s included polyester, velour, velvet, cotton, jersey, and Lycra. The latter was particularly popular for leggings, an aerobic style associated with the 1980s. Fitness fashion, such as vibrant colors, leggings, Lycra bodysuits, sweatbands, and the popularity of workout videos emerged (Ramzi, 2024f). Jane Fonda's workout video of 1982 became one of the best-selling videotapes of all time. Disco and its fashion continued its popularity that started to develop during the 1970s because of American films such as *Grease* and *Saturday Night Fever.* This resulted in clothes being,

> designed with artificial disco lighting in mind; made from fabrics such as satin or threaded through with Lurex, they would glint and sparkle to great effect. There was a specific disco style for women, but strangely not for men, even though John Travolta's white suit and black shirt with outward-turned collar in *Saturday Night Fever* had caused great uproar (Fischenich et al., 2000, p. 91).

Japan started to grow economically during the 1970s. During the 1980s, Japanese designers started to innovate. For example, Rei Kawakubo designed a new dress with Yohji Yamamoto. This new dress disguised the shape of the body beneath layers of clothing, often geometric and asymmetric in shape, thus challenging the ideas of femininity, but still rooted in Japanese tradition, however radical in the Western world. These dresses drew from kimonos or karate jackets and had carefully contrasted shapes (Carnegy, 1990). The 1980s were generally a period when Japanese designers rose to recognition, such as Issey Miyake, Comme des Garçons' Rei Kawakubo, and Yohji Yamamoto. These designers changed fashion by focusing on concepts and technology and throwing conventions away (Ramzi, 2024f). Some of these designers started their work in the 1970s, but they achieved impact during the 1980s. Some highlights include Issey Miyake's red plastic bustier and Yohji Yamamoto's red-tulle bustle coat (Ramzi, 2024f). Towards the end of the decade, there was a relaxation in all areas of fashion, which was an introduction to the 1990s, where the view was 'anything goes', and individualism was at the center of society and consequently fashion. Yuppies also started to fade in influence towards the end of the decade, when nostalgia emerged, with designers transforming fashion so that collections in 1988 and 1989 were full of fringes, beads, and flowers (Carnegy, 1990), which drew inspiration from the 1960s.

In the period between 1982 and 1983, 'short black studded leather jackets or denims mixed with spray-on trousers for the girls, cut-off shorts, baggy drawstring shorts … for the boys' were popular (Carnegy, 1990, p. 44). Generally speaking, the 1980s can be seen as a retreat to the past, with old wardrobes coming into style, sometimes 10 years old, drawing from previous decades (Carnegy, 1990). For example, Yohji Yamamoto's autumn 1989 collection was inspired by the America of the 1950s (Carnegy, 1990). In men's fashion, the American TV show *Miami Vice* was a particular influence. This series popularized suits in lighter colors and Versace labels, as well as a novelty of men wearing a T-shirt underneath a suit, which now appeared, not just appropriately dressed but also sexy (Fischenich et al., 2000).

The silhouette of the 1980s was aggressive and based on the male silhouette with wide shoulders and pads, with suits being essential for both men and women. Male suits were double-breasted with front-pleated trousers, creating a broad and powerful image, which was accompanied by female suits with jackets worn over narrow, knee-length skirts (Carnegy, 1990). The classic Armani jacket was popularized during this period; 'the classic Armani jacket, hanging loosely from wide shoulders, disguised the waist and narrowed the hips leaving hair, makeup and legs to proclaim femininity' (Carnegy, 1990, p. 32). Fashion innovations and styles of the 1980s are summarized in Table 3.7.

Table 3.7 Fashion Innovations and Styles of the 1980s

FASHION INNOVATIONS	DESCRIPTIONS
Silhouette	• Aggressive and based on male silhouette
Androgyny	• Men's suits, ties, and close-cropped hair (masculinity) • Red lips, corset-style basque (femininity) • Two styles combined for an androgynous look
Streetwear	• Letters, numbers, and graphics • Oversized T-shirt
White prairie skirts	• White lace and broderie anglaise skirts and dresses • Full-tiered skirts with peasant tops • Accessories (brown leather belts and purses)
Stripes and tartan	• Bulky, multi-colored tweeds • Short kilts • Traditional clothing
Full skirts and layering	• Multilayered full skirts and sweaters worn with bras over the top • Chunky boots • Street look • Vivienne Westwood
Wide clinch belts	• Cinched-in waist • A curvaceous silhouette • Belts
Suits and shoulders	• Dynasty • Power suit • Couture: black and white dogtooth pencil skirts with nipped-in jackets • Armani's Donna campaign 1984–85 • Padded shoulders inspired by E. Schiaparelli's style of the 1930s
Oversized	• Oversized dresses and shirts worn with big belts
Puffball skirts	• 1986 • Christian Lacroix

(Continued)

Table 3.7 Continued

FASHION INNOVATIONS	DESCRIPTIONS
Asymmetrics	• Slashed shoulders and halfway hems • One-sleeve wonders • Black Lycra • Cut-outs
Laura Ashley dresses	• A sweet femininity • A counter to power suits • Neo-Victorian, old romanticism • Conservative taste
American fashion	• The rise of American functional approach to fashion
Fitness fashion	• Lycra body suits • Leggings • Punchy colors • Leg warmers • Sweatbands • Workout videos

Source: Author's work. Information adapted from Clarkson (2011, pp. 48–49), Fischenich et al. (2000, p. 91), and Ramzi (2024f)

In advertising, it became popular for designers to have advertising campaigns and no longer rely solely on fashion editors to promote them. Designers were not just selling clothes but also an image, with successes of the decade being Calvin Klein and Ralph Lauren in the US and Giorgio Armani in Italy. In Japan, Kawakubo and Yamamoto also became popular and claimed they were making functional clothes for a working woman, which became popular among younger consumers due to the focus on black color and unusual shapes (Carnegy, 1990). Yamamoto's label was saying 'there is nothing so boring as a neat and tidy look', thus promoting the minimalist look of fashion boutiques, which ran in opposition to other designers and department stores full of clothes (Carnegy, 1990).

REFLECT

Find fashion adverts from the 1980s. 1980s advertising emphasized style, power, and aspiration. How do you think this shaped people's sense of identity during that time? Looking at the ads, what values do they promote? Do you see any similarities or differences with advertising today?

The 1990s: The Fall of the Berlin Wall and the Globalization of Fashion

The year 1989 was the year of the stock market crash, which created a recession in 1990. This had a profound influence on fashion because the notion of *more is more* present during the 1980s disappeared. At the time of the economic downturn, designers had to adapt to a changed social sentiment and deliver a minimalist look, which gave a further boost to Calvin Klein, Jil Sander, and Helmut Lang. However, despite the economic downturn, fashion carried on, particularly for the rich, and the 1990s present one of the decades that were marked by some prominent top models, such as Kate Moss, Linda Evangelista, Naomi Campbell, Claudia Schiffer, Elle MacPherson, and Cindy Crawford, among others. This was also the start of the celebrity culture. Vicki Woods, in *Vogue's* July 1991 issue, asked,

> Why are these girls so famous? Why are they personalities in their own right? Why are they known from one side of the globe to the other? How come I can turn on the TV in Scotland and watch Christy Turlington washing her little face with three kinds of Camay soap? How come a Japanese news crew flies to Paris to ask Linda Evangelista—in English— what her hobbies are? … How come these girls are paid so much? Photographed so much? In such demand? Where has the extraordinary phenomenon of the supermodel come from? (Ramzi, 2024g, n.p.).

Fashion brands sought to work with these top models due to the exposure it provided, and this rise of supermodels coincided with the rise of individuality in fashion, a hallmark of the 1990s.

The 1990s also presented the global wind of change with the fall of the Berlin Wall, followed by the fall of Communism across Europe. This led to a new fashion market because Germany united, and other European communist countries shifted towards globalized, free-market policies. This gave rise to the importance and growth of the EU as new democracies in Europe set a goal of joining the European club. In Latin America, there were changes in government and policies, Nelson Mandela was released from prison in South Africa, and George Bush became the president of the US, focusing on the new patriotism, which influenced fashion as people started to also wear patriotic apparel (Feldman, 1992). Due to a more connected world, fashion started to cross borders, and this also gave rise to the 'American look', such as those designed by Calvin Klein, Ralph Lauren, Bill Blass, and Donna Karan. Younger US designers also gained recognition, such as Michael Kors, Isaac Mizrahi, Gordon Henderson, Carmelo Pomodoro, and Norma Kamali. American designers focused on the European ready-to-wear market worth USD 50 billion and started to open stores in Europe, which was followed by retailers such as Gap (Feldman, 1992). In 1992, the United States Commerce Department sponsored national participation at many Asian and European fashion trade shows, which resulted in the American Designer Pavilion in Paris in 1992, which was the first time that American designers presented their clothes at *Prêt-à-Porter Féminin* (Feldman, 1992). The US embassy also supported designers who were not big enough to enter the European market themselves, and the American mail-order merchants entered the Japanese market with catalog fashion (Feldman, 1992).

The American look was promoted in Japan, such as denim, accessories, cowboy boots, and blazers (Feldman, 1992).

Patterned and colored prints returned from the 1960s, presenting a retro style (Feldman, 1992). There was a further fall of the yuppies, and as recession and unemployment hit, there was less dining out, more at-home video rentals, and an increased sale of books on crafts (Feldman, 1992). This resulted in decreased sales of department stores and retail, and manufacturers were particularly hit, which gave rise to the fashion discount culture, and designers started to launch less expensive lines. For example, in the UK, John Galliano, in 1991, created the Galliano Girl with clothes trying to attract younger buyers due to being half price, which were sold through the so-called 'diffusion collections' (Feldman, 1992, p. 21). In Italy, Moschino created the 'cheap and chic' collection of cream-colored fabrics to avoid the glare of the white, signature question mark prints, hot pants, and pop art-inspired fabrics. In the US, Donna Karan and Calvin Klein also created cheaper items with Ungaro, Gaultier, and Armani from Europe, following the trend. Donna Karan was particularly successful with the DKNY line of apparel, which was cheaper than her other designs. Michael Kors stated that 'just because a woman doesn't have the pocketbook, doesn't mean she doesn't have style' (Feldman, 1992, p. 23).

Men's fashion of the period was an interpretation of classic themes, with 'solid and pinstriped suiting's, subdued checks and plaids, and ties and other accessories similar to those worn by 1980s men' (Feldman, 1992, p. 23). Men also started to wear brighter vests and T-shirts under jackets. Rebecca Moses, a US designer, described the 1990s as a decade of femininity, saying, 'casualness that *is* American sportswear with a ladylike edge' (Feldman, 1992, p. 25, emphasis in the original). The decade indeed gave rise to the image of the working woman and leisure clothes, such as jeans, leggings, tracksuits, and longer-lived clothes. There was also a comeback of the 1960s and 1970s fashion (Feldman, 1992) along with 1990s-specific popular items such as wide headbands, Lycra and spandex instead of nylon and polyester as relevant materials, A-line dresses, baby doll dresses over tight leggings, often in stretch velvet or with denim cut-offs (Feldman, 1992). Denim and cotton remained popular, along with retro looks, and new microfiber materials were introduced in sportswear. Office wear during the 1990s meant that many styles for working women were different from the 'dress for success' style, and this resulted in more expression in the 1990s. It was not just one or two colors or a strict design of clothes specific to each decade. There were more feminine outfits for executive women, not just copycat male-female suits of the previous decade.

The colors of the 1990s were both bold and subtle but started to move away slowly from the neon colors of the 1980s. Neon green stayed, and electric blue emerged, but other colors became popular, such as teal and magenta. This was particularly the case in the early 1990s when there was a focus on minimalism and neutral colors such as navy and gray, while in the mid-1990s, bolder and more vibrant colors started to emerge, with teal being particularly popular in the US. Neon, however, returned as the decade progressed, particularly neon green, electric blue, and magenta. Fitted and loose garments both were popular. The 1990s version of male outfits featured masculine cut pant suits, worn with vividly patterned ties, outsized men's watches, and sensible flat-heeled shoes. Yohji Yamamoto designed oversized menswear-style suit jackets and coordinated trousers. Fashion innovations and styles of the 1990s are summarized in Table 3.8.

Table 3.8 Fashion Innovations and Styles of the 1990s

FASHION INNOVATIONS	DESCRIPTIONS
Silhouette	• Body-fitting chemise dresses, loose and fluid, floating styles, ultra-full skirts buttressed by petticoats • The decade of personal freedom, casual clothing, easy fitting, comfortable, jeans and workout clothes, T-shirts or sweatshirts, and more relaxed attires for men
Yves Saint Laurent	• Rive Gauche collection (a striped black and white cotton blend jacket with black silk trousers)
Long suit jackets	• Early in the decade • Worn with mini skirts with matching and contrasting fabrics and colors • Unmatched skirt and a jacket
Plaids	• Grunge revival of plaid flannel shirts
Classic handbags	• The 1950s Grace Kelly bag
A social change	• A more personal style • Society and fashion alike changed since the Edwardian style, completing societal transformation
Ecology and the criticism of fashion	• Rejection of fur due to the rise of animal rights organizations • Protests against fur and animal testing • Small eco-stores open in the US and Europe selling 100% cotton and linen
Materials	• Shiny satins, velvets, slinky metallic-hued lamés, laces, solid and patterned silks, and airy chiffons, embellishments
Fashion add-ons	• Jewels, accessories, variety of shoes
A change from elitism	• Fashion started to be influenced not just by elites and fashion designers, but from all societal groups
Style	• Sheer, see-through fabrics, blouses and dress tops, visible bra beneath
Individualism	• Anything-goes attitude in fashion
Grunge fashion	• The rise of Nirvana, Soundgarden, and Pearl Jam influenced alternative fashion

Source: Author's work. Information adapted from Feldman (1992), Ramzi (2024g), and Vargas (2025)

Designers started to focus on expressing individuality through apparel; thus, fashion became an inner identity. Melissa Sones wrote in the *Mirabella* magazine,

> Fashion used to filter down from the aristocracy to the average woman ... but today the so-called aristocracy has changed ... while fashion still comes from the runways, we also have other influences: from the streets, from MTV, from rock and roll music, from films and from a multitude of things going on around us... (Feldman, 1992, p. 56).

The 1990s were the decade of individualism, but also a further rise of feminism, which in the 1990s focused on criticizing the beauty and fashion industries. For example, in 1991, Naomi Wolf (1991) published a book called *The Beauty Myth*, criticizing the female beauty concept, or more precisely the lack of perceived beauty, as a political weapon against women's advancement. In this period, a fight started against weight and age discrimination (Feldman, 1992), which disproportionately affected women. This then also spilled over to the criticism of advertising portraying women as youthful, with flawless skin and super slim bodies, and wearing expensive clothes (Feldman, 1992). The criticism of fashion and beauty standards and the advertising portrayal of women have also led some women to argue against this criticism. For example, Camille Paglia, professor at the University of Arts in Philadelphia, said that 'women enjoy color and fabric and fashion and we should not have to apologize for that' (Feldman, 1992, p. 45). In other words, feminists again expressed criticism of the fashion and beauty industry, mirroring historical hostilities, and while things have not escalated to the point where they were before, the publicity surrounding the negative impact of fashion, beauty, and advertising industries on women was more profound than during the 1980s.

What also needs to be mentioned for the 1990s is the grunge style influenced by grunge bands from Seattle, such as Nirvana, Pearl Jam, and Soundgarden. This gave rise to thrift fashion such as flannel shirts, vintage tees, baggy, aged jeans, sneakers, and day-old hair, and this style was more widely adopted than the Punk fashion of the 1970s because it was less shocking (Ramzi, 2024g). The look influenced teenagers and then eventually made it into mainstream fashion and on catwalks. Marc Jacobs created the now-famous Grunge collection for Spring/Summer 1993, albeit he was fired by Perry Ellis for that collection; this firing is nowadays known as the most infamous firing in the fashion industry. Suzy Menkes wrote for *Vogue*'s January 1993 issue,

> I told Marc Jacobs that his Perry Ellis show—all floppy coats worn with crochet vests and hot pants or ombre chiffon tunics and pajamas—looked like hippies with attitude. 'I don't like labels. It's how you wear clothes today. It's how the girls look when they come in here,' he said. How grunge is that? (Ramzi, 2024g, n.p.).

Towards the end of the decade, nostalgia emerged, and designers created collections with sleeves from the 1880s and bias cuts from the 1930s and used couture craftsmanship from the 1950s (Ramzi, 2024g). The cycle emerged again, even in an individualistic decade. Ethnic motifs and folklore also came back into fashion. John Galliano was a proponent of this look, launching his label in 1986. By 1995, he was a head designer for Givenchy, and in 1997, he was appointed as a designer for Dior. Alexander McQueen launched his label in 1992 and used natural history in his fashion, and Vivienne Westwood celebrated

Victorian culture in her Anglomania collection. Designers also started to license their names more than ever before, continuing a trend that started in the 1970s. Marc Jacobs was appointed as the creative director of Louis Vuitton in 1998 and introduced their first-ever ready-to-wear collection, which was also followed by Prada.

REFLECT

Look at adverts from the 1990s and consider how a shift to individualism affected advertising. What is different? Is there a similarity between the 1990s fashion and fashion advertising, and today's fashion and fashion advertising?

Fashion Cycles and Forecasting

Fashion cycle is usually depicted as a bell-shaped curve that encompasses five stages: introduction, rise in popularity, peak of popularity, decline in popularity, and rejection. The cycle can encompass a single style or a single item, such as a designer's style or a particular type of dress (e.g., a shirtwaist dress) (Stephens Frings, 1987). The way the fashion cycle works is portrayed in Table 3.9.

There are differences between fashion cycles, with some cycles lasting longer than others; thus, we speak of classics, fads, cycles within cycles, interrupted cycles, recurring cycles, and reverse adoption, and all cycles are linked to taste (Table 3.10). The fashion cycle process differs between countries and cultures (Spell, 2001).

Table 3.9 Fashion Cycle Stages

FASHION CYCLE STAGES	FASHION CYCLE DESCRIPTIONS
Introduction	• A designer creates something new, and the manufacturer offers a new style to the public. • A terminology often heard is 'the latest fashions' but this does not mean this new style has yet been accepted. This first cycle stage implies only style and newness.
Increase in popularity	• More and more people wear a certain style. Designers will never sell in mass numbers, but some items remain the most popular from their collections or in new fashions. • Copying and adaptation happens in this stage. Some manufacturers will buy line-for-line copies of the original style sold at a reduced price whereas others will copy styles using cheaper fabric and less detail and sell at lower prices.

(*Continued*)

Table 3.9 Continued

FASHION CYCLE STAGES	FASHION CYCLE DESCRIPTIONS
Peak of popularity	• When a style peaks in popularity, manufacturers produce many variations of a certain style, and there is a range of prices.
Decline of popularity	• So many copies of a style are produced that fashion-conscious consumers get tired of a style and look for something new. • The style goes into sales and the price is reduced significantly.
Rejection of a style	• New looks already emerged and a new cycle begins for a new style.

Source: Author's work. Adapted from Stephens Frings (1987, pp. 47–48)

Table 3.10 Length of Fashion Cycles

LENGTH OF CYCLES	DESCRIPTIONS
Classics	• Some styles remain and never become old-fashioned or obsolete. • A classic is usually characterized by the simplicity of design, which prevents the style being easily dated. • Chanel suit is an example of a classic, which peaked in the 1950s and enjoyed popularity again in the 1970s but the style remains a classic for businesswomen.
Fads	• Short-lived fashion or fads, which come and go in a single season. • These styles lack a designer's introduction and/or character to keep consumers engaged. • These styles are usually cheaper and flood the market fast, which causes saturation and consumers tiring out quickly. • An example of fad was a punk look popular in England during the 1980s.
Cycles within cycles	• This is linked to design elements such as silhouette, texture, color, or details. These details may change while the style remains popular. • Jeans are an example of this because they gained popularity during the 1960s but continued throughout the 1970s. Their fashion cycle was very long but various shapes were invented such as bell, cigarette, baggy, and skinny legs that keep coming and going out of fashion.

(*Continued*)

Table 3.10 Continued

LENGTH OF CYCLES	DESCRIPTIONS
Interrupted cycles	• Buying summer clothes in August is an example of an interrupted cycle. This is when manufacturers stop producing or stocking clothing because they fear a decline in popularity. • A social upheaval or depression can also interrupt a cycle.
Recurring cycles	• After a style dies, it may also later resurface, which is why in fashion industry, we speak of cycles. • When a style reappears, it is often re-interpreted with a change in fabric and detail.
Reverse adoption	• Fashion occasionally begins with consumers. • An example are street fashions and young consumer's fashion style of the 1960s and 1970s.
Taste	• Fashion is also often linked to taste. • Taste is individual's preference towards a certain style. • Good taste in fashion often implies sensitivity to beauty and appropriateness, and people can be identified within various stages of a fashion cycle. • Fashion leaders often buy something at the beginning of a cycle while others imitate them.

Source: Author's work. Information adapted from Stephens Frings (1987, pp. 48–49, 51–52)

Fashion Forecasting

Fashion reflects life, and thus, people are important in determining what fashion is and what the fashion industry needs to produce. Designers have understood this for a long time; for example, Bill Blass stated that 'you have to understand people to make clothes for them' (Waltz, 1978, p. 47). Because of the importance of understanding consumers, forecasting is also an important aspect of fashion work.

Forecasting is linked to trends, styling, and the direction of fashion. Fashion forecasters exist because merchandizers must work ahead of a season to prepare stock for selling, and thus, they have to identify signs indicating change and estimate what consumers will accept. The forecasting judgment is based on 'experience, awareness of trendsetting designers, fashion cycles, and economic, social and technological influences on both the garment industry and the consumer' (Stephens Frings, 1987, p. 56). Fashion forecasters make decisions on which fashions are prophetic, which segment of the market will accept certain fashion styles, and decide on the time when a certain fashion will be acceptable to certain consumers (Stephens Frings, 1987). The prophetic style comes from designer collections, and these are fresh ideas that express the mood of the times. Often, designers use a similar silhouette or color because these elements are based on current interests or events, and if several designers respond to a similar stimulus, that signals a fashion trend (Stephens Frings, 1987). The way consumers are targeted depends on their income, education, lifestyle, age, and fashion preferences.

There is a delay in accepting new styles and trends, which forecasters take into consideration. For example, fashion from Italy and France quickly spreads to other European countries, while it can take a while for the American public to accept these styles due to the process of adapting styles and silhouettes. Equally, styles coming from New York, the fashion capital of the US – and lately also the world – get more easily accepted in the US because they are designed for the American market. Historically, fashion styles were accepted by the more affluent consumer group because those who lived in urban areas and earned more tended to accept fashion more quickly. Fashion forecasters consider all these elements, as well as the origin of fashion and the timeline of acceptance, adaptations to style, and consumer target groups. Forecasters also rely on other sources of information in their work, such as market research. Forecasters conduct market studies to determine the consumer base, their needs and interests, and factors influencing their decisions. This process later works together with advertising because it is advertising that always creates a desire for a certain product, including fashion. Market information collected by forecasters includes analyses of new collections, sales records, and surveys with consumers (Stephens Frings, 1987).

Paris still has a leading role in evaluating new collections and emerging trends and styles, and thus, retail buyers will attend Parisian fashion shows, both haute couture and prêt-à-porter. They also attend fashion shows in Milan, London, New York, and Tokyo. Apart from market research on consumers and fashion show attendance, fashion forecasters also analyze trade publications.

DISCUSSION QUESTIONS

- Discuss the change in societal views of fashion, from haute couture to ready-to-wear. How have societies changed, and how was this reflected in haute couture and ready-to-wear?
- What made Paris the center of the fashion world?
- Discuss the growth of mass production in the West and how it affected fashion. What happened because of industrialization? How did mass production emerge?
- Discuss the development of haute couture vs. ready-to-wear. What influenced this change in fashion?
- Discuss fashion styles and how they changed through the decades. What societal changes influenced fashion changes? How does each decade differ from the preceding one? How does each preceding decade differ from the following one? How is women's societal position reflected in fashion styles in different decades?
- How do trend forecasters gather and interpret information? What are the most influential sources today?
- How can PR and marketing professionals use fashion forecasts to craft more effective campaigns or brand strategies?
- What skills do future PR and marketing professionals need to interpret and act on fashion forecasts effectively?

References

Baker, P. (2002). *Fashion of a Decade: The 1940s.* New York: Facts on File.

Baker, P. (1991). *Fashion of a Decade: The 1950s.* New York: Facts on File.

Berkeley, B. (n.d.). Eleanor Lambert: American Fashion's Pioneer. *W magazine.* Retrieved from https://www.thewonline.com/article/eleanor-lambert-american-fashions-pioneer?utm_source=chatgpt.com

Bott, D. (2007). *Chanel: Collections and Creations.* London: Thames & Hudson.

Bureau of Labor Statistics. (2006). *100 Years of U.S. Consumer Spending Data for the Nation, New York City, and Boston.* Washington, DC: US Department of Labor. Retrieved from https://www.bls.gov/opub/100-years-of-u-s-consumer-spending.pdf

Cady, K. (2019). Dressed to Kill: A History of British Sporting Fashion. *The Frick Pittsburgh Museums and Gardens,* September 26. Retrieved from https://www.thefrickpittsburgh.org/Story-Dressed-to-Kill-A-History-of-British-Sporting-Fashion

Carnegy, V. (1990). *Fashions of a Decade: The 1980s.* New York: Facts on File.

Census. (n.d.). *Census of Manufacturers: 1921.* Retrieved from https://www2.census.gov/prod2/decennial/documents/05459821ch1.pdf

Clarkson, K. (2011). *Vintage Fashion Sourcebook.* London: Carlton Books Limited.

Connikie, Y. (1990). *Fashions of a Decade: The 1960s.* New York: Facts on File.

Constantino, M. (1994). *Fashions of a Decade: The 1930s.* New York: Facts on File.

Encyclopedia.com. (2018). Rayon. Update June 11, 2018. Retrieved from https://www.encyclopedia.com/sports-and-everyday-life/fashion-and-clothing/textiles-and-weaving/rayon

European Fashion Heritage Association. (2018). *The History of Symbols: Flares.* July, 14. Retrieved from https://fashionheritage.eu/the-history-of-symbols-flares/

Ewing, E. (1992). *History of 20th Century Fashion.* London: B.T. Batsford Ltd.

Fashion Beans. (2025). Men's Fashion Guides – 1950s Men's Fashion – Timeless Mid Century Style. By Fashion Beans editors, February 25. Retrieved from https://www.fashionbeans.com/article/1950s-mens-fashion/

Feldman, E. (1992). *Fashions of a Decade: The 1990s.* New York: Facts on File.

Fischenich, S., Horbas, C., Kaiser, A., Kothe, R., Meisner, J., Roth, A., Willemsen, C., Wolter, G., & Zipperer, A. (2000). *A History of Fashion in the 20th Century.* Cologne: Konemann Verlagsgesellschaft.

Fullerton, R.A. (2013). The birth of consumer behavior: Motivation research in the 1940s and 1950s. *Journal of Historical Research in Marketing, 5*(2), 212–222. https://doi.org/10.1108/17557501311316833

Glassock, J. (2004). Twentieth-Century Silhouette and Support. *The Met,* October 1. Retrieved from https://www.metmuseum.org/essays/twentieth-century-silhouette-and-support

Golden, P. (2022). *Marriage Settlements of the Georgian Era: Land, Money, or Love.* Retrieved from https://www.paullettgolden.com/post/marriage-settlements

Goles, K. (2023). What Not to Wear: Clothing Rationing During World War II. *Library of Congress Blogs,* January 19. Retrieved from https://blogs.loc.gov/law/2023/01/what-not-to-wear-clothing-rationing-during-world-war-ii/#:~:text=Better%20known%20as%20Regulation%20L,measurements%20for%20feminine%20apparel%20items

Greer, G. (1970). *The Female Eunuch.* London: MacGibbon & Kee.

Harper's Bazaar. (2017). The history of haute couture: From humble beginnings to present day. *Harper's Bazaar,* January 19. Retrieved from https://www.harpersbazaar.com/uk/fashion/a31123/the-history-of-haute-couture/

Herald, J. (1992). *Fashions of a Decade: The 1970s.* New York: Facts on File.

Herald, J. (1991). *Fashions of a Decade: The 1920s.* New York: Facts on File.

Imperial War Museum. (n.d.). *8 Facts about Clothes Rationing in Britain During the*

Second World War. Retrieved from https://www.iwm.org.uk/history/8-facts-about-clothes-rationing-in-britain-during-the-second-world-war

Lehnert, G. (2000). *A History of Fashion in the 20th Century.* Cologne: Konemann.

National Museum of American History. (n.d.). *Experimental stockings.* Retrieved from https://americanhistory.si.edu/collections/object/nmah_1200996#:~:text=It%20was%20the%20first%20fiber,made%20of%20silk%20or%20rayon

Pearce Rotondi, J. (2025). *How World War I Helped Women Ditch the Corset.* History.com. Published March 10, 2021. Updated, June 30, 2025. Retrieved from https://www.history.com/articles/world-war-i-women-corset

Poiret, P. (1934). *My First Fifty Years.* Gollancz: Unknown Binding.

Ramsay, L. (2024). The History of Ascot Fashion from 1711–2024. *Hello! Fashion,* June 24. Retrieved from https://www.hellomagazine.com/hfm/495370/history-of-ascot-fashion/

Ramzi, L. (2024). A 1920s Fashion History Lesson: Flappers, the Bob, and More Trends That Made the Roaring Twenties Roar. *Vogue,* April 1, 2020. Retrieved from https://www.vogue.com/article/1920s-fashion-history-lesson#:~:text=Top%20Designers%20of%20the%20Era,%2C%20Jeanne%20Paquin%2C%20and%20Premet

Ramzi, L. (2024a). A 1930s Fashion History Lesson: Goddess Gowns, Surrealism, and More Trends of the Escapist Era. *Vogue,* April 5. Retrieved from https://www.vogue.com/article/1930s-fashion-history-lesson

Ramzi, L. (2024b). A 1940s Fashion History Lesson: Wartime Utility Suits, the New Look, and More Trends of the Decade. *Vogue*, April, 19. Retrieved from https://www.vogue.com/article/1940s-fashion-history-lesson#:~:text=Designers%20like%20Norman%20Norell%2C%20Bonnie,Claire%20McCardell%20rose%20in%20profile

Ramzi, L. (2024c). A 1950s Fashion History Lesson: Dior's New Look, Hollywood Bombshells, and The Golden Era of Couture. *Vogue*, April 27. Retrieved from https://www.vogue.com/article/1950s-fashion-history-lesson#:~:text=The%20aesthetic%20is%20famously%20considered,for%20most%20of%20the%20decade

Ramzi, L. (2024d). A 1960s Fashion History Lesson: Mini Skirts, Mods, and The Birth of Boho. *Vogue*, May 1. Retrieved from https://www.vogue.com/article/1960s-fashion-history-lesson

Ramzi, L. (2024e). A 1970s Fashion History Lesson: Disco, Designer Denim, and the Liberated Woman. *Vogue*, May 15. Retrieved from https://www.vogue.com/article/1970s-fashion-history-lesson

Ramzi, L. (2024f). A 1980s Fashion History Lesson: Lycra, Power Suits, and Clothing as Concept. *Vogue*, May 20. Retrieved from https://www.vogue.com/article/1980s-fashion-history-lesson#:~:text=Responding%20to%20the%20times%2C%20designers,peplums%20made%20the%20wearer%20even

Ramzi, L. (2024g). A 1990s Fashion History Lesson: Supermodels, Grunge, and the Dawn of the Digital Age. *Vogue*, May 30. Retrieved from https://www.vogue.com/article/90s-fashion-history

Reddy, K. (2020). 1930–1939. *Fashion History Timeline,* last update August 18, 2020. Retrieved from https://fashionhistory.fitnyc.edu/1930-1939/

Rubenstein, H. (1930). *The Art of Feminine Beauty.* London: V. Gollancz.

Saval, N. (2015). *Cubed: A Secret History of the Workplace*. New York: Anchor Books.

Shrimpton, J. (2013). *Fashion in the 1920s.* Oxford: Bloomsbury Publishing Plc.

Spell, C. (2001). Management fashions: Where do they come from: and are they old wine in a new bottle? *Journal of Management Inquiry,* 10, 358–373.

Stephens Frings, G. (1987). *Fashion: From Concept to Consumer,* 2nd edition. Englewood Cliffs, New Jersey: Prentice-Hall, Inc.

The Met. (n.d.). Shoes. Retrieved from https://www.metmuseum.org/art/collection/search/158861

The Mob Museum. (n.d.). *The Speakeasies of the 1920s.* Retrieved from https://prohibition.themobmuseum.org/the-history/the-prohibition-underworld/the-speakeasies-of-the-1920s/

Topić, M. (2021). *Corporate Social Responsibility and Environmental Affairs in the British Press: An Ecofeminist Critique of Neoliberalism.* London: Routledge.

UK Parliament. (n.d.). *1918 Representation of the People Act.* Retrieved from https://www.parliament.uk/about/living-heritage/transformingsociety/electionsvoting/womenvote/case-study-the-right-to-vote/the-right-to-vote/birmingham-and-the-equal-franchise/1918-representation-of-the-people-act/

UK Parliament. (n.d._a). *Women Get the Vote.* Retrieved from https://www.parliament.uk/about/living-heritage/transformingsociety/electionsvoting/womenvote/overview/thevote/

US Congress. (n.d.). *Amdt19.1 Overview of the Nineteenth Amendment, Women's Suffrage.* Retrieved from https://constitution.congress.gov/browse/essay/amdt19-1/ALDE_00013822/#:~:text=Nineteenth%20Amendment%3A,State%20on%20account%20of%20sex

V&A. (n.d.). *An Introduction to 1960s Fashion.* Retrieved from https://www.vam.ac.uk/articles/an-introduction-to-1960s-fashion?srsltid=AfmBOorNQEs2MeHoABUFTxWJ18yjaJkFx1xwjNclCUFas29UoUQ0-Gyg

Vargas, M. (2025). 5 Ways To Wear The '90s Grunge Plaid Skirt This Summer. *Vogue*, June 23. Retrieved from https://www.vogue.co.uk/article/grunge-plaid-skirt

Vega, M. (2022). A Sail Through the History of Cruise Collections. Get on Board!. *L'Officiel,* June 27. Retrieved from https://www.lofficielmonaco.com/art-and-culture/a-sail-through-the-history-of-cruise-collections-get-on-board

Vintage Dancer. (2016). 1940s Men's Suit History and Styling Tips [blog]. *Vintage Dancer,* September 29. Retrieved from https://vintagedancer.com/1940s/1940s-mens-suit-history/

Waltz, B. (1978). *The Fashion Makers.* New York: Random House.

Whitmore, G. (2015). The history of flares – in pictures. *The Guardian*, January 24. Retrieved from https://www.theguardian.com/fashion/gallery/2015/jan/24/the-history-of-flares-in-pictures

Williams, C. (2010). Lindbergh Flight a Marketing Windfall. *WWD*, April 21. Retrieved from https://wwd.com/fashion-news/fashion-features/back-in-time-lindbergh-flight-3044640/

Wolf, N. (1991). *The Beauty Myth: How Images of Beauty Are Used Against Women.* New York: William Morrow and Co.

Worsley, H. (2011). *100 Ideas That Changed Fashion.* London: Laurence King Publishing Ltd.

CHAPTER 4

Haute Couture vs. Prêt-à-Porter

Learning Objectives

- Distinguish between haute couture and prêt-à-porter (ready-to-wear) fashion.
- Examine the development of the fashion industry within the broader context of societal change and industrialization.

The Size of the Fashion Industry

Fashion is one of the biggest industries driving a significant part of the global economy (Fashion United, n.d.). If fashion were ranked against national GDPs, it would be the seventh-largest economy in the world (McKinsey, 2017). According to McKinsey's state of the arts report, the fashion industry continues to grow, even though there is a slower pace of growth due to global challenges, the post-COVID-19 pandemic effects, and changes in consumer behavior. The highest growth is expected to be in Europe (due to the rise in tourism), the US (due to the resilience of wealthy individuals), and Asian markets, such as Japan and Korea, which continue to be lucrative for the fashion industry (McKinsey, 2024).

According to the market forecast by Statista (2024), the fashion market is expected to grow annually by 7.54 percent, which will result in a projected market volume of USD 1.18tn by 2029. The number of users in the fashion market is expected to amount to 2.8bn users by 2029, and the average revenue per user is expected to amount to USD 392.11 (Statista, 2024). According to Business Research Insights (2025), the global haute couture market is predicted to reach USD 15.44bn by 2033, which is a rise from USD 12.56bn in 2024. The global ready-to-wear market is predicted to reach USD 296.6bn by 2033, a rise from USD 112.3bn in 2023, which presents a growth of 10.2 percent (Market US, 2024).

Spending on marketing and advertising among luxury brands is growing after a slowdown caused by the COVID-19 pandemic. For example, LVMH Group, known for its ownership of luxury house, Louis Vuitton, has increased its spending on marketing and advertising by over 30 percent in 2022. Capri Holdings, which owns brands such as Versace, Michael Kors, and Jimmy Choo, has spent over USD 320m in 2022 (Statista, n.d.). Social media remains a valuable way of promoting luxury fashion brands; for example, six out of 10 affluent consumers aged between 18 and 39 follow a luxury brand on

DOI: 10.4324/9781003515043-6

social media, and big brands, which hold haute couture status, have millions of followers (Statista, n.d.). However, while ready-to-wear fashion is a main income for fashion brands nowadays, historically, haute couture was the most popular aspect of fashion, and the fashion industry, as we know it today, developed from this form of high-quality craftsmanship and artistry.

REFLECT

Conduct a social media use analysis segmented by generation. Consider how generational differences influence consumer behavior and advertising and PR strategies. How does your favorite brand communicate with its audiences? Is this appealing to you? If yes, does data show that the brand is particularly oriented toward your generation, or do they use different communication strategies to appeal to many different consumers?

Haute Couture

In 1961, Audrey Hepburn starred in *Breakfast at Tiffany's,* portraying a troubled call girl, Holly Golightly. In the opening scene of the film, Hepburn appears on a deserted Fifth Avenue in New York, leaving a taxi outside upmarket jewelry store Tiffany's, dressed in a slinky black satin gown, long satin gloves, and large tortoiseshell sunglasses, accompanied by pearls around her neck and a diamond ornament in her hair. She drinks her coffee, eats a pastry outside the store, and looks at the jewelry store's window. This short scene was a defining moment in fashion because Hepburn promoted the little black dress (LBD). The dress was designed by Hubert de Givenchy, the head designer for the film, and was supported by costume designer Edith Head, known for sophistication and glamor. The LBD was originally popularized by Gabrielle Coco Chanel in 1926, and while Givenchy's black dress is long, Chanel's original design was knee-length. Chanel turned the dress into haute couture and promoted it as elegant and economical. *Breakfast at Tiffany's* cemented the position of a black dress as a foundation of style, and this invention came from an haute couture brand, which then made a lasting mark on fashion and style as we know it today.

Haute couture is a luxury, high-end fashion. Each garment costs thousands of dollars. This is because haute couture is hand-crafted and made to measure, and each clothing piece is a one-of-a-kind item in terms of sizing and fit. Haute couture is sometimes seen as a form of art because designers communicate their ideas about the human body (Fischenich et al., 2000), and haute couture items are known as fine craftsmanship and artistry. Haute couture means high fashion and the 'high art of sewing', which started in the 19th century. For a long time, haute couture was a synonym for fashion. While haute couture is no longer the only source of income for fashion houses, it remains important for advertising and continuing designer legacies. Therefore, haute couture houses have ready-to-wear collections and sell licenses, but haute couture remains their core business. Haute couture provides a fashion house with a legacy and ensures attention and spotlight on these fashion houses that have historically influenced fashion with their designs.

The reason for the prestige of haute couture lies in their formal recognition awarded by the French organization, *La Fédération de la Haute Couture et de la Mode* (FHCM) (The Federation of Haute Couture Fashion),

> which brings together the most emblematic French and international design Houses with a focus on creativity and a unique and innovative know-how. The FHCM is both a Professional Organization dedicated to its Members and an Event Organization that coordinates the Paris Fashion Week® and Haute Couture Week (Fédération de la Haute Couture et de la Mode, n.d.).

The federation is composed of three *Chambres Syndicales* (trade unions), *Chambre Syndicale de la Haute Couture* (Trade Union of High Fashion), *Chambre Syndicale de la Mode Féminine* (Trade Union of Women's Fashion), and *Chambre Syndicale de la Mode Masculine* (Trade Union of Men's Fashion).

The *Chambre Syndicale de la Haute Couture* was founded in 1911 following the first Chamber created by Charles Frederick Worth in 1868 (Fédération de la Haute Couture et de la Mode, n.d.). The haute couture denomination,

> is legally protected and is granted by the Commission responsible for the Control and Classification of Couture Creation, sitting at the Ministry of Industry. The Member Houses of the Chambre Syndicale de la Haute Couture thus meet relating to the "intelligence de la main", personalization, rhythm of the collections, know-how displayed in ateliers which must be located in Paris, and the highest level of creativity. The *Chambre Syndicale de la Haute Couture* also has corresponding Members whose ateliers are not based in Paris but whose activities are similar to those of the great couturiers (Fédération de la Haute Couture et de la Mode, n.d., emphasis in the original).

The *Chambre Syndicale de la Mode Féminine* was,

> founded in 1973 after the great couturiers and fashion designers decided to unify their respective approach by presenting their ready-to-wear collections together; This Chambre Syndicale brings together Fashion Houses from all horizons which are most recognized for their creativity and know-how in womenswear (Fédération de la Haute Couture et de la Mode, n.d.).

Finally, the *Chambre Syndicale de la Mode Masculine,*

> also founded in 1973 is identically selective. This Chambre Syndicale brings together Fashion Houses from all horizons which are most recognized for their creativity and know-how in menswear (Fédération de la Haute Couture et de la Mode, n.d.).

The first organization to be founded was thus the *Chambre Syndicale de la Haute Couture,* founded in 1911 and focused on women's fashion, which was initially only haute couture. Men's fashion started to gain attention in 1973 when an additional chamber was formed for men's fashion, but historically, women's fashion was high fashion, and couturiers were showcasing women's garments sewn to perfection and tailored-made to each female client.

According to haute couture rules, to become haute couture, a fashion designer must employ 20 artisan seamstresses, 20 technical staff members, and show two collections a year, in January and July. The haute couture show must be shown in Paris. Haute couture houses can show haute couture collections elsewhere, but the first showing is done in Paris, which is a condition to maintain haute couture status. The haute couture creations must be handmade by artisan seamstresses and to a client's measure, thus tailored-made, which has historically distinguished haute couture from other forms of fashion. As recognized by *Vogue*, 'there are few things grander in fashion than haute couture' (Bala, 2020, n.p.). Haute couture has a small clientele of approximately a few thousand people worldwide (*Vogue* estimated approximately 4000 in 2020; Bala, 2020). Invitations to runway shows for haute couture are prestigious, and a brand can only become haute couture by invitation from the *Fédération de la Haute Couture et de la Mode,* which controls brands and ensures that rules of craftsmanship and exclusivity are always upheld. Members also receive support from the federation and a place on the haute couture fashion runway calendar, which gives them exposure and prestige. Paris Haute Couture Week is a most sought-after fashion show, with people who attend events often purchasing fashion items as a form of art collection (Explore France, 2021). There is often confusion about who is recognized by the French federation because many brands label themselves as couture. However, the difference is that haute couture is a brand that has been formally invited to become a member of the French federation, while couture is anyone who produces fashion items that are handmade and one-of-a-kind, but being couture does not mean one is also haute couture. The federation makes annual decisions on who should be invited to membership in haute couture, and they feature haute couture brands on their website: https://www.fhcm.paris/en/maisons?status=1

Paris is the historical home of haute couture. The influence of Parisian haute couture was popularized outside of France through local designers who were influenced by Parisian haute couture and who implemented those practices in their countries. The influence of Parisian haute couture was also supported by the popularity of Parisian haute couture in the United States. Already in 1893, the Chicago Fair featured Parisian designers, and American *Vogue* followed this interest in French fashion since its foundation. For many decades, its fashion views were aligned with Parisian fashion (Ewing, 1992). American high society was a fan of haute couture. For example, in a Pulitzer Prize-winning novel describing the life of New York society of the late 19th and early 20th century, Edith Wharton in the *Age of Innocence* describes dresses being sent to Paris for Worth to re-do it; it was customary at the time to repurpose wedding dresses and a sign of poor taste to always be in the latest fashion. Ladies ordered new dresses and kept them for two years before wearing them, which was seen as fashionable and in good taste, up until the 'roaring '20s', when society started to change (Wharton, 1920).

Haute couture went through a dark period during WWII, with the Nazi occupation that cut off Paris from the rest of the world. However, couturiers continued their work, led by Lucien Lelong, who was the head of the *Chambre Syndicale de la Haute Couture* and who prevented a relocation of fashion from Paris to Berlin during WWII. Only 20 couturiers remained in Paris during the occupation, including Chanel, who was accused of collaborating with the Nazis, and Lelong recruited younger designers, such as Pierre Balmain and Christian Dior, and helped them develop their style so they could help rebuild Parisian fashion (Croll, 2014). Both designers soon developed their own houses and gained success, particularly Dior with his New Look. While Chanel had masculinity as her muse and promoted a view that clothes should be comfortable, thus also promoting practicality and comfort (Bott, 2007), Dior took fashion to a more feminine direction and was criticized by Chanel, who saw it as a step back (Miller, 2024). Therefore, haute couture went through cyclical changes from feminine, extravagant, and rebellious, then Chanel with a more masculine and mannish style during Chanel's popularity peak, then back to feminine with Dior, and then later again to revolutionary and cool with Yves Saint Laurent (Croll, 2014; Miller, 2024). Haute couture was, thanks to the popularity of Dior's New Look, revived during the late 1940s and 1950s, but this changed during the 1960s with a focus on affordability, which gave rise to ready-to-wear clothes, popularized in the US (Croll, 2014). This also meant that while there were 106 haute couture houses during the 1950s, during the 1970s, there were only 19 (Croll, 2014). Thus, during the 1970s, haute couture houses and ready-to-wear houses joined forces and founded an organization called the *Fédération Française de la Couture de prêt-à-porter des Couturiers and Créateurs de Mode* to help them fight the declining market. However, during the 1980s and the 1990s, the commercialization of haute couture happened with a conglomerate, LVMH, from France, which purchased a large portfolio of fashion brands such as Dior, Givenchy, Celine, and Kenzo, making LVMH an haute couture empire. In the late 1990s, another conglomerate, Kering (originally PPR), acquired Alexander McQueen, Gucci, Balenciaga, and other companies, thus further commercializing haute couture (Croll, 2014). Despite commercialization, some haute couture companies resist takeovers and trade publicly, such as Hermès, which is buying back shares (Hermès, n.d.).

While haute couture was developed in France and its influence spread around the world, in England, haute couture was not initially a term used for high fashion. The high-class designers were called court dressmakers. Court dressmakers were firms that started as private dressmakers and had a distinguished clientele. The standards of clothes made by court dressmakers were suitable for court circles but not necessarily for royal occasions. The court dressmakers did not always design their clothes; many purchased models in Paris and adapted and copied them (Ewing, 1992). In France, dressmakers were known as couturiers, which is where the term widely used up to the present day comes from. The identities of personal couturiers were kept secret because the wealthy did not want everyone to know who created their garments. The first couturier was Rose Bertin, a dressmaker to Queen Marie Antoinette, who created a role for her as the court's official minister of fashion (Stephens Frings, 1987). In contrast to the wealthy, the poor were making their clothes and sewing for themselves, often passing special occasion garments through generations. This contrast was one of the reasons for the 18th-century French Revolution, which began in 1789 and prompted the fashion industry that was developing in France at the time to switch to simpler garments from elaborately decorated costumes of the wealthy (Stephens Frings, 1987). This also prompted changes in haute couture, where clients started to rely on couturiers and their judgments on styles and fabrics, which gave rise to the haute couture business. It can be argued that 'the independent modern couture is a bridge between the class-structured fashion of the past and the democratization of fashion today' (Stephens Frings, 1987, p. 6).

Haute couture is linked to European royalty, who are known for high fashion, with some haute couture houses historically giving royals a chance to choose certain designs and colors which were then not available to anyone else (Herald, 1992). While today's royals try to look like everyone else, such as Catherine, the Princess of Wales, who is known for high-street fashion choices, historically, royals were the envy of the masses. The first queen of style was Elizabeth I, who crafted her look to promote the identity of a 'Virgin Queen', thus focusing on youthful innocence in her style when she first ascended to the throne, only to change this style later to something with deeper decolletage and hoop skirts emphasizing her hips (Croll, 2014). The popularity of royal fashion was also historically visible in France with Louis XIV's focus on shoes with red heels as a sign of an upper-class status for men, and Marie Antoinette's horse-riding fashion and frequent visits to Paris to debut fashion and introduce her style to the public, who copied her (Croll, 2014).

For couturiers, the image has always been important. Ever since the concept of fashion was invented, fashion items have been linked to their creator. Fashion houses need to create an image, and designer names attached to fashion help in creating labels, which create lifestyles. This is also how fashion houses advertise in fashion magazines and how they conduct advertising and PR; they present their house as an epitome of elegance and promote the good quality of their clothing (Fischenich et al., 2000).

REFLECT

In what ways does haute couture function as a PR tool? Reflect on how brands generate press coverage, social media buzz, and influencer engagement through couture shows, red carpet placements, or editorial features.

Prêt-à-Porter / Ready-to-Wear

Haute couture was popular among elites, but by the 1960s it was no longer in high demand, which opened the way for prêt-à-porter, inspired by the American ready-to-wear fashion that gained popularity during the 1940s (Fischenich et al., 2000). While prêt-à-porter was popularized after WWII, it had existed since the 18th century when manufacturers started to make various capes, coats, and other items that did not have to be made to fit. Department stores were the main source of expanding fashion and making it more available to the masses, and the growth of department stores went along with the growth of the middle class. These department stores emerged from smaller shops, some originating as early as the 18th century, such as Fortnum and Mason (1707), Browns and Chester (1780), Dickins and Smith (1790, later Dickins and Jones), Clark and Debenham (1791, later Debenham and Freebody), Swan and Edgar (1812), Peter Robinson's (1833), Marshall and Wilson (1837, later Marshall and Snelgrove), Harrods (1849). Fortnum and Mason, and Harrods started as grocers and later switched to fashion (Ewing, 1992). In the US, many well-known American department stores started in the 19th century (Bittman, 2019). The crucial years for the emergence of department stores in the UK and the US were the period between 1850 and 1875 (Jefferys, 2011[1954]). Department stores became popular in the first decade of the 1900s, and apart from growing, also became places of luxury (Croll, 2014).

Prêt-à-porter is today one of the most important aspects of a fashion business. Prêt-à-porter clothes comprise designs created by fashion designers but produced industrially and in large numbers, which then reduced the price of these clothes and reached a wider audience. Many big fashion designers have very successful ready-to-wear collections, such as Chanel and Dior, for example, and some big designer labels produce only prêt-à-porter clothes, such as Ralph Lauren, Calvin Klein, and Donna Karan. Unlike traditional, mass-produced fast fashion, prêt-à-porter is a luxury end of ready-to-wear fashion. However, prêt-à-porter can also include clothes sold in department stores, usually termed off-the-rack clothes (Fischenich et al., 2000).

Prêt-à-porter clothes are more focused on wearable and practical, and it is no surprise that these clothes were popularized by American designers who have historically always focused on a working woman. When one looks at prêt-à-porter collections of haute couture designers, the distinction between the glamour and extravagance of haute couture and the practicality of prêt-à-porter is significant, albeit haute couture, in recent years, has had a lot of practical designs going in line with a wider focus on women's empowerment and the fact that many women hold senior CEO roles and can afford haute couture but cannot wear extravagant and glamorous clothes at work.

Perfumes also became part of a wider label offer and were often attached to designer's names, such as Chanel No. 5 (nowadays also new perfumes such as Mademoiselle, Gabrielle, etc.), and many labels up to this day have their perfume, which supports business goals of fashion labels as perfumes are more accessible to wide population than fashion. However, Pierre Cardin was the first couturier to start taking prêt-à-porter more seriously than other couturiers, such as Paul Poiret, doing it when business was struggling and out of desperation (Croll, 2014). Due to his focus on prêt-à-porter (his first collection was presented in 1959 after starting his couture business in 1950), Cardin was removed from *Chambre Syndicale de la Haute Couture* but he carried on and launched men's prêt-à-porter in 1961 and while the *Chambre* re-instated him into membership later, he withdrew his membership out of protest in 1966 (Croll, 2014).

The fashion focus on designers eventually fed into advertising and PR, which increasingly centered on designer creations, such as Yves Saint Laurent's perfume YSL, where the designer himself posed naked for an advert in 1971. This campaign forever changed fashion advertising, shifting it away from promoting only the product and toward promoting the designer as an icon. This can also be seen as the start of fashion PR, as focusing on the fashion label and designer to build a story and create a legacy is part of PR work. Other designers followed up and used this approach, such as Calvin Klein. What is more, this type of promoting fashion labels changed the image of fashion artists and designers, who started to become seen as an integral part of their label's communication as they became symbols of their products (Fischenich et al., 2000). Image formation became important for communication, which brought relevance to PR activities in building the company and the designer's image. Prêt-à-porter saw a further rise during the 1980s and 1990s when licensing deals were also introduced, with designers giving their names to producers making T-shirts, watches, luggage, etc. Pierre Cardin was a leader in this area and licensed his name to products such as handbags, home décor, watches, etc. However, this also cheapened his brand, and Cardin's brand became associated with cheap products (Croll, 2014).

An argument can be made that prêt-à-porter democratized fashion because it made fashion more widely available to all; however, there are still dress codes that operate at societal levels, for example, corporate dress codes or job interviewing dress codes. Haute couture is still popular among designers and an essential part of their work for those who have a haute couture status because haute couture 'displays clothes that are generally considered to be unwearable and that are intended only to create an image that serves the marketing of prêt-à-porter or licensed articles' (Fischenich et al., 2000, p. 97). The reason for this is also to create an emotional attachment and a positive and artistic association with the fashion brand, which is also why haute couture shows are elaborate, with a lot of artistic creations that draw attention to the brand.

REFLECT

Choose one ready-to-wear campaign from a major fashion house (e.g., Chanel, Dior). In small groups, review the visual and textual messaging. What narrative is being told? Who is the target demographic? How is accessibility, affordability, or lifestyle emphasized? How does this differ from haute couture campaigns by the same brand? What communication techniques are used to balance luxury with wearability? In what ways does prêt-à-porter serve as a brand gateway for wider audiences?

DISCUSSION QUESTIONS

- What is the difference between haute couture and prêt-à-porter?
- Why is haute couture still prestigious despite the rise of the prêt-à-porter market?
- What is the role of syndicates in the fashion industry?
- What role does haute couture play in shaping brand identity and storytelling?
- How do fashion houses use couture to generate cultural capital, prestige, or media attention?
- Can haute couture be considered a form of strategic communication?

References

Bala, D. (2020). Everything You Need To Know About The Inner Workings Of Haute Couture. *Vogue,* July 6. Retrieved from https://www.vogue.co.uk/fashion/article/behind-the-scenes-at-haute-couture

Bittman, L. (2019). *Compartment Couture: New York City Department Stores 1850–1930*. Fashion History Timeline, last updated February 22. Retrieved from https://fashionhistory.fitnyc.edu/compartment-couture/

Bott, D. (2007). *Chanel: Collections and Creations*. London: Thames & Hudson.

Business Research Insights. (2025). *Haute Couture Market Report Overview*. An update from February 10. Retrieved from https://www.businessresearchinsights.com/market-reports/haute-couture-market-108326#:~:text=Global%20haute%20couture%20market%20size,meticulously%20crafted%20clothing%20and%20accessories.

Croll, J. (2014). *Fashion that Changed the World*. Munich: Prestel Verlag.

Ewing, E. (1992). *History of 20th Century Fashion*. London: B.T. Batsford Ltd.

Explore France. (2021). *Everything You Need To Know About Haute-Couture.* January 11, 2021. Retrieved from https://www.france.fr/en/article/everything-you-need-to-know-about-haute-couture/

Fashion United. (n.d.). *Global Fashion Industry Statistics*. Retrieved from https://fashionunited.com/statistics/global-fashion-industry-statistics

Fédération de la Haute Couture et de la Mode (n.d.). *The Federation.* Retrieved from https://www.fhcm.paris/en/federation-de-la-haute-couture-et-de-la-mode

Fischenich, S., Horbas, C., Kaiser, A., Kothe, R., Meisner, J., Roth, A., Willemsen, C., Wolter, G., & Zipperer, A. (2000). *A History of Fashion in the 20th Century.* Cologne: Konemann Verlagsgesellschaft.

Herald, J. (1992). *Fashions of a Decade: The 1970s.* New York: Facts on File.

Hermès. (n.d.). *Glossary.* Retrieved from: https://finance.hermes.com/en/glossary/

Jefferys, J.B. (2011[1954]). *Retail Trading in Britain 1850–1950: A Study of Trends in Retailing with Special Reference to the Development of Co-operative, Multiple Shop and Department Store Methods of Training.* Cambridge: Cambridge University Press.

Market US. (2024). *Global Ready-to-Wear Market by Type.* A report, last update November 2024. Retrieved from https://market.us/report/ready-to-wear-market/

McKinsey. (2024). *The State of Fashion 2025: Challenges at Every Turn.* November 11. Retrieved from https://www.mckinsey.com/industries/retail/our-insights/state-of-fashion

McKinsey. (2017). *The State of Fashion 2017.* Retrieved from https://www.mckinsey.com/~/media/McKinsey/Industries/Retail/Our%20Insights/The%20state%20of%20fashion/The-state-of-fashion-2017-McK-BoF-report.pdf

Miller, J. (2024). The New Look Revisits Coco Chanel's Nazi Ties and Feud with Christian Dior. *Vanity Fair,* February 6. Retrieved from https://www.vanityfair.com/hollywood/the-new-look-coco-chanel-christian-dior?srsltid=AfmBOoooU8XJhJsV1BMwDBoNudVhs5HlxFTRACISsOwLRn7O8st_64OE

Statista. (2024). *Fashion Worldwide* (May 2024 update). Retrieved from https://www.statista.com/outlook/emo/fashion/worldwide

Statista. (n.d.). Luxury advertising and marketing. Retrieved from https://www.statista.com/topics/4149/luxury-advertising-and-marketing/#editorsPicks

Stephens Frings, G. (1987). *Fashion: From Concept to Consumer,* 2nd edition. Englewood Cliffs, New Jersey: Prentice-Hall, Inc.

Wharton, E. (1920). *The Age of Innocence.* New York: Scribner Books.

PART 2
ADVERTISING AND PR PRACTICE IN THE FASHION INDUSTRY

CHAPTER

5 Digital Fashion Advertising and PR

Learning Objectives

- Identify key digital developments shaping contemporary fashion advertising and public relations.
- Develop strategies for writing SEO-optimized content tailored to fashion communication.
- Analyze the evolution of fashion advertising and PR within a digital media landscape.
- Evaluate the impact of emerging technologies – such as the metaverse, artificial intelligence (AI), and augmented reality (AR) – on fashion communication and events.

A New, Digital World

In 2011, Swedish retailer H&M announced a fashion capsule collection designed by fashion blogger Elin Kling called *The Elin Kling Collection*, with 10 percent of proceeds going to UNICEF. This was a change from previous collaborations H&M had had with celebrities, such as Madonna. The move was cheered by fashion enthusiasts (Fashion Network, 2011). This is not the only collaboration of bloggers and social media influencers with the fashion industry. While historically celebrities had the most power in endorsing fashion brands and creating a following, this is nowadays no longer the case, and many people take fashion advice from social media influencers and bloggers.

Apart from always reflecting societal progress and change, fashion has also consistently adapted to technological changes. For example, in the 1930s, the rise of cinematography caused collaborations with Hollywood, with many designers working for films to promote their designs (Constantino, 1994). During the 1970s, lifestyle magazines grew in popularity, which also increased the popularity of individual styles and not just following trends from major fashion houses, and this resulted in a simultaneous popularity of haute couture, prêt-à-porter, and vintage fashion. During the 1980s and the 1990s, with the start of the digital revolution, fashion quickly jumped aboard and engaged with fashion e-commerce, which initially struggled due to constraints of dial-up speeds, limited stock, and a lack of funding and a vision on how to trade online (Crewe, 2013). However, these issues were the beginning, and the fashion industry quickly recovered and developed e-commerce

DOI: 10.4324/9781003515043-8

infrastructure, online marketing and advertising tools, and direct-to-consumer models, which digitalized fashion into the industry we know today (Boughlala & Smelik, 2024).

As part of relationship-building efforts, apart from online selling and social media communication, fashion communications practitioners nowadays also offer virtual fitting, virtual closet apps that allow wearing clothes in augmented reality through a smartphone app, as well as apps such as *Whering,* which scans all clothes in the wardrobe and then displays various styles. These apps have contributed toward relationship building with consumers and also became part of corporate social responsibility (CSR) efforts by helping prevent the waste caused by ill-fitting online purchases. Consumers have been increasingly sensitive to the waste and environmental damage that the fashion industry causes, and these apps are reducing the environmental impact and providing credibility to the fashion industry by showing they are listening to consumer concerns.

With the rise of digital communication and consumer engagement on social media, including with bloggers and vloggers, the fashion industry turned towards promoting its works online, largely because eWOM (electronic word-of-mouth) became important for fashion. eWOM is generally defined as 'any positive or negative statement made by potential, actual or former customers about a product or company which is made available to a multitude of people and institutions via Internet' (Hennig-Thurau et al., 2004, p. 39). Since many consumers have social media accounts and participate in social media communities, communicating on social media has become important for the fashion industry to advertise their products and new collections, but also to build relationships with publics. Building relationships with publics is linked to the co-creation of meaning and socially constructing reality (Botan & Taylor, 2004). In fashion, co-creation is seen as a collaboration between bloggers, social media influencers, and celebrities on one side and the fashion brand on the other side. With this, stakeholders and organizations are similarly interpreting events and situations (Heath & Coombs, 2006).

REFLECT

Select two magazine and two digital fashion campaigns. Consider how these campaigns were presented, what the message was, and who the target audience for the campaigns was. Has messaging changed with time? If so, how? Which type of messaging do you prefer (if different)? Consider yourself as an audience and how brands could effectively target you. Then consider generational differences and discuss how the two selected brands you brought to class could target multiple generations.

Using Social Media in Fashion Advertising and PR

Traditionally, advertising and PR worked with mass communication through advertising campaigns (advertising) or working with journalists, doing product placements, and signing celebrities for endorsements, to maintain a positive image of a fashion brand with the publics (public relations). A large part of this effort was building relationships with fashion journalists and magazine editors; however, with the rise of social media, many fashion brands turned toward more personal and direct digital communication with publics. Some fashion brands, such as Calvin Klein in 2019, stopped traditional campaigns and focused exclusively on digital campaigns and working with consumers directly. This also impacted advertising as advertising messages were replaced with direct communication, focusing on niche publics of each brand through targeted messages and getting the right messages to the right people at the right time (Scott, 2007). Using social media helps fashion advertising and PR professionals build strategic messages and contributes toward creating social capital, because they can establish a virtual relationship with followers on social media.

Fashion brands promote their products on many social media platforms. According to some data, Instagram tends to be the most popular platform for building a following in fashion, and many fashion influencers use it. Instagram has been called the visual *Vogue* and a cornerstone of fashion digital advertising and public relations because 'Its visually driven interface is a perfect match for the aesthetic-centric fashion industry, allowing brands and fashion designers to showcase their work through high-quality images and videos' (Uphance, n.d.). Two other platforms important for fashion are Pinterest and TikTok. Pinterest serves as a digital fashion archive, and it provides a meaningful tool for fashion forecasting and influencing trends and personal styles. TikTok is seen as a trendsetting platform because of short videos anyone can post that encourage creativity and spontaneity, including DIY styling tips, and trend transformations (Uphance, n.d.). Since social media influencers have a mass following on Instagram, fashion PR professionals work on building relationships with them to achieve earned media or publicity, and recognition from publics that follow social media influencers. Some fashion PR professionals stress the importance of having an online presence because brands that are not on social media risk being left behind. However, social media complicates traditional models of top-down communication, so fashion PR professionals are adapting their communication strategies across platforms to maintain exclusivity and diversify content (Cassidy & Fitch, 2013).

There is sometimes contention between celebrities and social media influencers. Celebrities have historically benefited from large media exposure but the rise of social media influencers and bloggers has endangered them in terms of self-promotion and fan engagement. Social media influencers who became famous are often described as micro-celebrities who 'deploy and maintain their online identity as if it were a branded good' (Senft, 2013, p. 346). In fashion public relations, celebrities and micro-celebrities act as third-party endorsers of the fashion brand and create meaning for consumers. There are four types of endorsements that celebrities can give: explicit (endorsing the product), implicit (asserting that they use the product), imperative (asserting that followers should buy the product), and co-presentational endorsement that creates a relationship between the fashion brand, celebrity, and a consumer (Seno & Lukas, 2007). The fashion industry mainly uses co-presentational endorsement to create a relationship between the brand, celebrity, and publics. The product becomes difficult to imitate by competitors, and since engagement with celebrities and bloggers is a two-way process based on interaction and two-way communication, this presents the essence of fashion PR activities. However, fashion PR professionals need to work with all stakeholders, such as celebrities, bloggers, and social media influencers, as well as traditional fashion magazines.

REFLECT

How is your personal aesthetic part of your 'brand'?
What aspects feel authentic, and which are strategically constructed for engagement?
How do you curate your online persona differently across platforms (Instagram, TikTok, YouTube, LinkedIn)?
What does this reveal about the field of fashion influence?
To what extent do you feel pressure to maintain consistency?
Does this pressure shape your creativity, mental well-being, or authenticity?

Working with Fashion Bloggers

Blogs are important for fashion advertising and public relations professionals. Blogs can be used both as advertising venues (e.g., placing digital adverts using Google AdSense) and as a PR opportunity. Bloggers are popular among fashion enthusiasts, particularly from younger consumer groups who prefer to consume content by bloggers and social media influencers they can identify with. One of the reasons some consumers like blogs is because of the interactive approach of bloggers and differences in their writing style, which tends to be more personal, and the content is based on personal experiences (Lichtenstein, 2009). Fashion blogs are sometimes perceived as street fashion (Bollier & Racine, 2005) and can assist in understanding public opinion. According to Statista, in 2022, blogs were read across all generations of Americans: 21 percent of 18- to 29-year-olds, 26 percent of 30- to 49-year-olds, and 17 percent of 50- to 64-year-olds (Statista, 2022). This statistic is only for the US and for computer use; however, according to some other industry data, 85 percent of people reported reading blogs, translating to 4.44 billion global blog readers (Singla, 2024). Global readership of blogs shows that blogs are generally popular, with worldwide visits to Blogger.com for a period between October 2023 and March 2024 showing that the platform had 35.9 million visits in only the first three months of 2024 (Statista, 2024), while some industry publications reported that more than 409 million people read blogs on the WordPress platform every month, viewing over 20 billion pages each month (Taheer, 2024). These numbers show the importance of bloggers for advertising and PR practitioners but also signal a generational change of habits because while bloggers were initially popular among younger generations, statistics now show an increase in readership across generations (Statista, 2022).

Nardi et al. (2004) argued that people blog to document their lives, express emotions, form communities, provide comments and personal opinions, and articulate their ideas through writing. Boram et al. (2010) added that people blog because of self-reflection, self-actualization, and self-satisfaction, to meet their own needs. However, as a blogger grows their audience, these motives move toward digital engagement and e-shopping, including brand endorsements and product placements, which is where collaboration with fashion advertisers and PRs often emerges. In addition to that, it is easier to interact with bloggers than with mainstream journalists.

Working with bloggers is linked to the co-creation of meaning. Fashion brands need to select bloggers, social media influencers, and celebrities carefully because, through co-creation of meaning, they influence each other. Bloggers provide meaning to fashion brands by endorsing products, and the type of products bloggers endorse creates a meaning for the blog (Escalas & Bettman, 2015). Building relationships with bloggers is also relevant for fashion PR professionals because the field depends on synergy between owned and earned media. Fashion PR professionals combine owned media (websites, blogs, and social media platforms) in collaboration with bloggers, social media influencers, and celebrities who endorse fashion brands through their channels and thus earn the brand eWOM.

Fashion PR practitioners have reported an increased workload and pressure because of working with bloggers. They said they do not have the time to work with every blogger because they cannot talk to everyone. As a result, they look to work with those who have credibility and where there is also a possibility to build a relationship as a practitioner normally does with journalists (Cassidy & Fitch, 2013). Credibility is thus an important concept for fashion PR practitioners because publics also look for credibility when deciding who to follow. Credibility for fashion can be based on the usual credibility concepts such as source credibility, message credibility, and site credibility (Esteban-Santos et al., 2018). In fashion, the source credibility is linked to connections and a sense of having an interpersonal relationship between a blogger and a follower, which is often superficial or illusory, but it is important for gaining followers. Message credibility is often measured by the number of visits, likes, and shares. The site credibility is linked to the specialism of the content a blogger shares, and bloggers specializing in a certain content will likely achieve more following the more they publish and interact with their followers.

REFLECT

You are part of the PR team for a fashion brand preparing to launch a new eco-conscious clothing line. The campaign focuses on sustainability, affordability, and style. Your task is to identify and propose a collaboration with one or more fashion bloggers who align with the brand's values and target audience.

Blogger research – Find 2–3 fashion bloggers or micro-influencers (via Instagram, TikTok, YouTube, or personal blogs) who emphasize sustainability or conscious consumerism, have an engaged, style-conscious audience, and produce visually compelling content.

For each blogger, evaluate:

Content tone and aesthetic (does it match your brand?)

Audience engagement (likes/comments, not just follower count)

Any past brand collaborations (are they selective or oversaturated?)

Search Engine Optimization (SEO) and Corporate Blogs

Apart from working with bloggers and influencers, and organizing digital and in-person events, since the rise of digital communication, fashion communicators have engaged with corporate blogging to create meaningful content and communicate with audiences such as consumers, media, and fashion buyers. Before the rise of AI, many professionals used tools such as search engine optimization (SEO) for blog writing and focused on appearing high in Google searches. With the rise of AI, many are considering changes to SEO writing for Google and whether it is going to be relevant in the future. However, AI uses online sources in giving answers to users, and thus, corporate blogging is still relevant, and optimizing content through keywords still has value even if the focus is changing from communicating with Google to communicating with AI.

SEO writing is supported by tools that help communicators find keywords people use in searches. While some advanced tools require a subscription, there are also free tools such as https://www.keyword.io/ and https://answerthepublic.com/. These tools are useful in finding ideas for corporate blogging and content creation, and understanding consumers and what information they look for. In addition, with the rise of AI there are new tools that help communicators understand what information people search for on AI. Tools like social listening platforms, such as YouScan, prompt analytics tools such as PromptAid, and platforms like Team-GPT, LowFruits, and Semrush offer generative AI features for keyword and topic clustering. Also, SEO keyword tools such as SpyFy and Semrush monitor AI queries.

SEO Tools for Content Creation

The keyword.io helps communicators find keywords people use in searches and websites, including Google, KWFinder, YouTube, Amazon, Bing, Yandex, Wikipedia, eBay, Alibaba, Fiverr, and Fotolia. Communicators can suggest a desired keyword and see what kind of information people are looking for, which then helps them create content that uses those keywords and statements to direct individuals to their website. Equally, the AnswerThePublic tool helps communicators see what kind of questions individuals ask online, and these questions can be answered in blogs and website content, directing traffic to the corporate website and/or social media accounts of the company. As an example, on April 29, 2025, the author of this textbook input the keyword *fashion* into keyword.io, which resulted in 704 individual keywords that appeared in search. These 704 keywords are terms used by individuals to look for information on fashion on Google. While some keywords are generic and difficult to use in writing, many could have been used for creating meaningful content, such as 'best fashion sneakers', 'boho fashion', and 'best fashion magazines'. Fashion communicators could have easily turned these keywords into corporate blogs by writing a text on why their sneakers are 'the best fashion sneakers' in the market or writing about 'boho fashion' if this is the collection they have or giving some advice to readers on the 'best fashion magazines' (note the use of the same keyword consumers used). By doing this, fashion communicators give information to consumers that is useful and relevant to them, which increases the credibility of communication messages, and at the same time, they direct traffic to their websites. Equally, AnswerThePublic search using the same *fashion* keyword revealed 142 questions consumers asked, many of which could be converted to online content. For example, blogs could be easily written answering consumer questions such as 'why fashion matters', 'why is fashion important', and 'will fashion designers be replaced by AI'. It is important to always use the same terms as consumers do, because this helps with the content being offered in consumer searches.

Corporate blogging is an excellent tool for practitioners because it can be used to provide industry and company news. Journalists read corporate blogs, which sometimes earns coverage for organizations. Producing a lot of online content, including blogs and social media posts, is relevant not just for relationship building but also for SEO, which was a large part of advertising and marketing work. SEO, in basic terms, means communicating with Google effectively to be positioned higher in search rankings, which makes content visible to individuals when looking for information and/or products. Practitioners have to consistently produce content, and over a long period, this eventually results in Google recognition. Google recognition does not depend only on the amount of content or keywords. Google indexes hyperlinks (this forever transformed search engines, which previously cheated on consumers by packing texts with keywords even though texts had nothing to do with what individuals were looking for). Hyperlinks count how many links point toward each page, and then each page gets attributed a numerical value, which corresponds to the value of those numbered links. Google's algorithm is a secret and complicated. After the initial counting of hyperlinks, bounce rate, and keywords started to get counted, too. Google also takes into consideration metatags attached to the content, but basic primacy is given to links and the number of links. A whole industry has emerged trying to trick Google, including by falsely exchanging links; however, if discovered, the website can get removed from searches, thus, it is essential to act ethically and be credible in providing online information.

REFLECT

Choose a keyword and use keyword.io and AnswerThePublic tools and explore what information consumers are looking for. Come up with several blog topics and then discuss with your peers which content could be seen as more credible by consumers and why.

Tools for Analyzing AI Prompt Trends

Since 2022, there has also been a notable rise in artificial intelligence (AI), which has changed the way SEO works. AI has risen in prominence in the fashion industry, with AI tools being used to create personalized fashion retail experiences and user-generated garments, which has led to the invention of the term cyborg designer, someone who is a human enmeshed with technologies and human networks (Särmäkari & Vänskä, 2022). This also created new opportunities for fashion advertisers because now they can create virtual worlds and avatars to interact with consumers and communicate with them, as well as create video games and provide them to consumers to engage them with an organization.

Advertising and PR professionals can use social listening tools to understand how audiences use AI, which offers them an insight into emerging trends, concerns, and information needs. Platforms like YouScan, Brandwatch, Meltwater, and SproutSocial enable communicators to monitor keywords and hashtags users use. These tools collect data from social media platforms, forums, blogs, and news sources so that a sentiment analysis can be done, and recurring questions and influential voices can be identified. Using these tools enables tracking how people discuss AI on social media and understanding what kind of information people seek on AI, how they phrase it, and whether they are satisfied with the results.

While tools like Keyword.io and AnswerThePublic do not track AI prompt usage, they show what people want to know, and thus, it is likely they will ask the same question from AI tools, such as ChatGPT or Gemini. Platforms like PromptBase, FlowGPT, and AIRPRM have user-shared prompts for ChatGPT and other AI tools, which help communicators understand how people structure their queries, what the popular topics are, and what formats are effective.

REFLECT

Search for a social listening platform, such as YouScan, Brandwatch, or Meltwater. Search for terms and hashtags about AI styling or AI in fashion. Review the results and note: What are the dominant themes or questions people have about AI in fashion? Are audiences expressing excitement, skepticism, or concern? Which influencers, brands, or media outlets are driving the conversation? Are there noticeable differences between luxury and retail fashion audiences? How could a fashion brand use these insights to shape its PR or influencer strategy? What risks or opportunities do you see in how AI is being discussed in the fashion space? How can social listening help a PR communicator respond quickly to shifts in public perception of AI technologies in fashion?

Fashion in the Metaverse and the Rise of AR and AI in Fashion Shows

In 2022, on the last day of the London Fashion Week, Doddz presented the UK's first Augmented Reality (AR) Screensaver collection, in partnership with Snapchat. The event, DEFY – A Digital Fashion Show, was held by the iconic Shoreditch Kachette, and was the first digital fashion show in the world. Doddz was nominated for the 15th Annual Shorty Award for this collection (Shorty Awards, n.d.). Caroline Rush from the British Fashion Council predicted that 10–15 percent of our wardrobe will soon be made up of digital items (Shorty Awards, n.d.). This statement was linked to the environmental problem and pollution because textile production contributes to global carbon dioxide emissions (Shorty Awards, n.d.), and washing and discarding clothes further adds to the environmental issue. The fashion industry thus became determined, in part also due to increased consumer activism and the rise of corporate social responsibility (CSR) policies, to reduce its environmental impact. Digital fashion and AR are seen as potential solutions to the environmental problem. In Doddz's show, the audience was invited to interact with artworks by holding their phone up to canvases and watch them come to life, as well as taking part in an educational experience about AR, and virtually try garments in front of large screens (Shorty Awards, n.d.). Models at Doddz' show walked in a vest and cycling shorts, while the full collection was only visible on phones.

Doddz's event was not an isolated one. Digital Fashion Weeks started due to the COVID-19 pandemic in 2020. British Fashion Week was the first one to announce a digital format. In Italy, Prada headed the first digital Milan Fashion Week. The collection was presented with videos and under the headline 'The show that never happened'. Prada showcased their collection via five video chapters by international artists. The focus of the digital show shifted from the silhouette to details, with blurred transitions and contrasted floral colors with black and white, which contributed toward creating a film style of the collections' presentation (Elan, 2020). In Paris, the entire couture and menswear was presented on video platforms (Browchuk, 2020). The first metaverse Fashion Week took place in 2022 on Decentraland, a virtual 3D world led by users who can register as organizers of events, attend shows, shop using cryptocurrency, buy land to construct buildings, areas, and streets (Pozzo, 2024). Brands are embracing the metaverse because it helps them launch creative campaigns and retail media networks to remain competitive and build relationships with consumers.

Metaverse is a new form of fashion experience, which contributes to consumer experience and enables communication professionals to build relationships with consumers by creating communities and brand experiences. Metaverse in fashion works in many ways: video games where consumers can purchase outfits for an avatar and customize it, applications with built-in augmented reality (AR), which help in visualizing products, and non-fungible tokens or NFTs, which are digital assets representing real-world objects (Ruiz Viñals et al., 2024). Metaverse is used for analyzing consumer behavior because fashion advertisers and PRs look for a relationship between metaverse experiences and purchase behavior.

AI came to prominence in 2023 with the first digital fashion collection utilizing AI being the Fabricant's Deep Collection, designed by Amber Jae Slooten in 2017 and then re-released in 2023. This collection 'used images from Paris Fashion Week to algorithmically generate designs that were then translated into 3D animations. The collection features seven designs, showing "hyperreal visualizations of a complete fashion collection, without the collection ever existing in real life"' (Boughlala & Smelik, 2024, p. 11, emphasis in the original). In 2023, the first AI Fashion Week also took place, as a global event featuring over 400 submissions of algorithmically generated fashion collections (AI Fashion Week, 2023). Google created an AI model to allow shoppers to virtually try clothes by looking at how clothes look on a variety of models of different sizes, body shapes, ethnicities, hair styles, skin tones, etc. (Scott, 2024). Levi Strauss & Co. did a similar thing as Google, which created a backlash about a prospect for AI models replacing human models, particularly models of color to promote diversity (the original intention of the initiative, as argued by Levi Strauss & Co.), which opened ethical questions about using AI in fashion. This resulted in a public apology from Levi Strauss & Co. (Levi Strauss & Co., 2023).

REFLECT

Interview a few family members of different generations. Ask them how they shopped throughout their lifetimes and what changes they witnessed. Ask them how they feel about it. Then ask how they consume news and information and compare findings across generations. Reflect on your own experiences with shopping and what changes you witnessed in your lifetime.

Table 5.1 summarizes strategies for digital communication in fashion, with a distinction between luxury and retail fashion.

Table 5.1 Digital Communication Strategies in Fashion

TACTIC	TECHNIQUES – LUXURY FASHION	TECHNIQUES – RETAIL FASHION
Brand image	• Aspirational • Exclusive • Heritage • Craftsmanship	• Accessible • Relatable • Trend-led • Value-focused
Website	• Polished • Minimalist • Emphasizing design	• Functional • Optimized for conversion, promotional
Social media communication	• Curated posts • Controlled release of content	• Frequent posting • User posts
Email marketing	• Personalized, VIP invites • Seasonal lookbooks	• Discounts • Flash sales • Back-in-stock alerts
Collaborations	• Celebrity ambassadors • Fashion icons aligned with brand values	• Influencers with high engagement and large reach
E-commerce	• Focus on exclusivity, limited availability	• Focus on convenience, speed, and mass appeal
SEO	• Brand storytelling • Long-form editorials • Blogs with advice • Social listening tools	• Trend-based content • FAQs • SEO-optimized product descriptions • Social listening tools
AI	• AI use for sentiment analysis and trend forecasting • Social listening tools	• AI use for sentiment analysis and trend forecasting • Social listening tools

(Continued)

Table 5.1 Continued

TACTIC	TECHNIQUES – LUXURY FASHION	TECHNIQUES – RETAIL FASHION
Campaigns	• Seasonal, linked to runway collections and fashion weeks	• Continuous, aligned with sales calendars
Content	• Editorial content focused on storytelling	• Product-driven, practical, user-generated
Voice	• Formal, curated	• Conversational, friendly, playful
Campaign examples	**Chanel – See you at 5 – A rendez-vous (2023/2024)** Short film by Luca Guadagnino starring Margot Robbie and Jacob Elordi. Music by Daft Punk, 'Veridis Quo' Cinematic storytelling, exclusivity, high-production quality https://www.youtube.com/watch?v=fo4LLux-tfM&t=3s	**ASOS TikTok #AsSeenOnMe Campaign** User-generated content and influencer collaboration, hashtag campaign encouraging customers to share outfits https://www.tiktok.com/tag/asseenonme

Source: Author's work based on SEO training and running two websites, and observations of the fashion industry on social media and subscriptions to fashion magazines (*Vogue*, *Cosmopolitan*)

DISCUSSION QUESTIONS

- How did the rise of digital platforms (websites, blogs, social media) transform the way fashion brands communicate with audiences?
- In what ways did fashion journalism and traditional media lose or retain influence in the digital age?
- How has the role of fashion influencers and content creators changed the fashion PR landscape?
- What are the benefits and risks of fashion brands relying on platforms like Instagram for campaign visibility?
- How has digital communication made fashion more participatory for consumers?
- Can user-generated content be as valuable as professionally produced campaigns for a brand?
- What role do AI, virtual influencers, and the metaverse play in fashion communication?
- How can fashion PR professionals prepare for evolving digital trends while maintaining brand consistency?
- Why is SEO important for fashion brands, especially those operating online?

References

AI Fashion Week. (2023). AI Fashion Week. Season 1 Summary at Spring (NYC), April 20–21. Retrieved from https://fashionweek.ai/season-1/#:~:text=With%20over%20350%20submissions%20to,submissions%20from%20around%20the%20world

Bollier, L., & Racine, D. (2005). *Ready to Share: Creativity in Fashion and Digital Culture*. Ready to Share Conference. A Norman Lear Center Conference, Annenberg Auditorium, USC Annenberg School of Communication. January 29. Retrieved from: https://archive.learcenter.org/wp-content/uploads/1969/12/RTSBollierRacine.pdf

Boram, P., Sookyoung A., & HaeJung, K. (2010). Blogging: Mediated impacts of flow on motivational behavior. *Journal of Research and Interactive Marketing, 4*(1), 6–29.

Botan, C.H., & Taylor, M. (2004). Public relations: State of the field. *Journal of Communication, 54*(4), 645–661.

Boughlala, A., & Smelik, A. (2024). Tracing the History of Digital Fashion. *Clothing and Textiles Research Journal, 43*(3), 1–16. https://doi.org/10.1177/0887302X2412835

Browchuk, E. (2020). Digital Fashion Weeks and Virtual Shows: A Rundown of Fashion's New Rhythm. *Vogue,* June 29. Retrieved from https://www.vogue.com/article/digital-fashion-weeks-2020

Cassidy, L., & Fitch, K. (2013). Beyond the Catwalk: Fashion Public Relations and Social Media in Australia. *Asia Pacific Public Relations Journal, 14*(1–2), 5–19.

Constantino, M. (1994). *Fashions of a Decade: The 1930s.* New York: Facts on File.

Crewe, L. (2013). When virtual and material worlds collide: Democratic fashion in the digital age. *Environment and Planning A: Economy and Space, 45*(4), 760–780. https://doi.org/10.1068/a4546

Elan, P. (2020). 'Show that never happened': Prada's digital hangover in Milan. *The Guardian,* July 14. Retrieved from https://www.theguardian.com/ fashion/2020/jul/14/show-that-never-happened-pradas-digital-hangover-in-milan

Escalas, J.E., & Bettman, J.R. (2015). Managing Brand Meaning through Celebrity Endorsement. Brand Meaning Management. *Review of Marketing Research,* 12, 29–52.

Esteban-Santos, L., Garcia Medina, I., Carey, L., & Bellido-Perez, E. (2018). Fashion bloggers: Communication tools for the fashion industry. *Journal of Fashion Marketing and Management: An International Journal, 22*(3), 420–437.

Fashion Network. (2011). Fashion blogger designs first collection for H&M. *Fashion Network,* January 10. Retrieved from https://ww.fashionnetwork.com/news/Fashion-blogger-designs-first-collection-for-h-m,143763.html

Heath, R.L., & Coombs, W.T. (2006). *Today's Public Relations.* London: SAGE.

Hennig-Thurau, T., Gwinner, K.P., Walsh, G., & Gremler, D.D. (2004). Electronic word-of-mouth via consumer-opinion platforms: What motivates consumers to articulate themselves on the internet? *Journal of Interactive Marketing, 18*(1), 38–52.

Levi Strauss & Co. (2023). LS&Co. *Partners with Lalaland.ai.* Press release, March 22. Retrieved from https://www.levistrauss.com/2023/03/22/lsco-partners-with-lalaland-ai/

Lichtenstein, S. (2009). The Decline of Experts in the Age of Web 2.0: Lay Blogger Perceptions of Experts. *ACIS 2009 Proceedings.* Paper 5, 1034 –1044. Retrieved from https://core.ac.uk/download/pdf/301348857.pdf

Nardi, B.A., Schiano, D.J., Gumbrecht, M., & Swartz, L. (2004). Why we blog. *Communications of the ACM, 47*(12), 41–46. Retrieved from https://dl.acm.org/doi/10.1145/1035134.1035163

Pozzo, B. (2024). Fashion in the metaverse. In DiMatteo, D.A., & Cannarsa, M. (eds), *Research Handbook on the Metaverse and Law.* London: Edward Elgar (pp. 217–228). https://doi.org/10.4337/9781035324866.00021

Ruiz Viñals, C., Gil Ibáñez, M., & Del Olmo Arriaga, J. L. (2024). Metaverse and Fashion: An Analysis of Consumer Online Interest.

Future Internet, 16, 1–15. https://www.mdpi.com/1999-5903/16/6/199

Särmäkari, N., & Vänskä, A. (2022). 'Just hit a button!' – fashion 4.0 designers as cyborgs, experimenting and designing with generative algorithms. *International Journal of Fashion Design, Technology and Education, 15*(2), 211–220. https://doi.org/10.1080/17543266.2021.1991005

Scott, D. (2007). *The New Rules of Marketing and PR: How to Use News Releases, Blogs, Podcasting, Viral Marketing, & Online Media to Reach Buyers Directly.* New York: John Wiley & Sons, Inc.

Scott, S. (2024). *Google Shopping's Getting a Big Transformation.* Retrieved from https://blog.google/products/shopping/google-shopping-ai-update-october-2024/

Senft, T.M. (2013). Microcelebrity and the Branded Self. In Hartley, J., Burgess, J., & Bruns, A. (ed), *A Companion to New Media Dynamics*. Chichester: Wiley (pp. 346–354).

Seno, D., & Lukas, B.A. (2007). The equity effect of product endorsement by celebrities: A conceptual framework from a co-branding perspective. *European Journal of Marketing, 41*(1–2), 121–134.

Shorty Awards. (n.d.). From the 15th Annual Shorty Awards. DEFY – the world's first digital fashion show. Retrieved from https://shortyawards.com/15th/defy-the-worlds-first-digital-fashion-show

Singla, A. (2024). How Many People Read Blogs? (2025 Readership Stats). Retrieved from https://masterblogging.com/blog-readership-statistics/#:~:text=past%20the%20headline-,How%20often%20do%20people%20read%20blogs%3F,users%20read%20blogs%20every%20day

Statista. (2024). *Worldwide visits to Blogger.com from October 2023 to March 2024.* Retrieved from https://www.statista.com/statistics/187276/bloggercom-monthly-visits/

Statista. (2022). *Share of internet users who read blogs on a computer in the United States in 2022, by age*. Retrieved from https://www.statista.com/statistics/479180/internet-users-who-engaged-with-blogs-on-computer-within-the-last-month-usa/

Taheer, F. (2024). *Ultimate List of Blogging Statistics and Facts* (Updated for 2025). Retrieved from https://optinmonster.com/blogging-statistics/

Uphance. (n.d.). The Ultimate Guide to Social Media in Fashion: Everything You Need to Know. Retrieved from https://www.uphance.com/insights/guide-to-social-media-in-fashion/#:~:text=Instagram%20is%20the%20cornerstone%20of,high%2Dquality%20images%20and%20videos

CHAPTER 6 CSR Communication for the Fashion Industry

Learning Objectives

- Define corporate social responsibility (CSR) and explain key debates and interpretations related to the concept.
- Analyze the historical and sociological development of CSR communication within the fashion industry.
- Evaluate current practices and strategies of CSR communication in the contemporary fashion industry.

Growing Importance of CSR

In 2022, Pretty Little Thing (PLT), a fast fashion company, organized a runway show to increase its visibility and recognition, only to find protesters in front of the Londoner Hotel. The protesters were holding signs alleging that PLT and their parent company, Boohoo, committed a 'wage theft' by paying their workers around GBP 7K annually, while their CEO is worth GBP 1.42 billion, and their creative director is earning GBP 4.8 million per year (Davidson, 2022). This protest presented a PR nightmare for the PTL stemming from growing consumer and activist focus on the fashion industry and its environmental impact, as well as the fashion industry and its human and working rights violations.

Allegations of workers' rights violations and environmental criticism aimed at the fashion industry have resulted in an increased focus on corporate social responsibility (CSR) policies, which are particularly relevant due to global supply chains, resource-intensive production (environmental destruction), labor practices (sweatshop allegations), and consumer-facing brand images. Allegations have resulted in negative industry and brand images and many corporate scandals. However, CSR is becoming more important for the fashion industry because of growing consumer awareness and demand for transparency and sustainable practices, and fashion companies are tied to ethical and environmental considerations. Because of that, and the media and activist spotlight on the fashion industry, CSR implementation and communication have become an increasingly important aspect of fashion advertising and PR work.

DOI: 10.4324/9781003515043-9

Corporate Social Responsibility: Definitions and Issues

CSR has affected corporations since the 1970s and 1980s, when the wider use of this concept started in the US and the UK. CSR policies came as a direct result of youth unemployment and social unrest, and thus, two conservative politicians, Ronald Reagan in the US and Margaret Thatcher in the UK, pushed for CSR policies to tackle anti-corporate protests and social unrest (Pillay, 2015). This CSR push was part of the open market agenda centered on weakening the role of the government in the economy by calling for corporations to be socially responsible and self-regulate. In the UK, this meant calling on corporations to help tackle youth unemployment, which gave rise to various employment programs and apprenticeships (Moon, 2004, 2005), which signalled a wider pressure on corporations to engage in socially responsible behavior and move away from shareholder orientation. These new policies and a call for corporations to provide social support originate from a debate that had already started in academic literature during the 1960s.

American economist Milton Friedman criticized advocates of the social responsibility concept, which he called an attempt to dominate society without armed revolution (Friedman, 1962, 1970). Friedman's view is commonly known as the *shareholder approach* because he believed corporations must only pay taxes and report to shareholders, which constitutes a neoliberal approach to the economy and society. At the opposite side of this view is the so-called *stakeholder approach*, whose proponents originally advocated for environmental protection, which was the initial focus of social responsibility efforts, that eventually gave rise to CSR as we know it today. The stakeholder approach expects corporations to consider the interests of all stakeholders and not just shareholders, which means they need to look after the interests of shareholders, customers, suppliers, and employees to be considered socially responsible (Freeman, 2010; Freeman & Hassnaoui, 2011). This debate is often known as the Friedman–Freeman debate and presents a cornerstone of discussion on CSR, which up to this day, causes disagreements between academics and activists. However, these two perspectives are not the only ones. While both Friedman and Freeman were liberals with different perspectives on how to socially manage corporations, some researchers reject the CSR concept as a whole. These authors argued that both Freeman and Friedman are liberals who are trying to save capitalism and improve corporate performance, but using different means, with which consumerism and environmental damage continue (Ireland & Pillay, 2009; Sheehy, 2014). CSR can also be seen as a smokescreen for capitalism, perpetuated by liberal media who saturate coverage on CSR and environmental degradation while also advocating for economic growth and further depletion of resources, with which nothing ever changes (Topić, 2021).

CSR presents a rich area of scholarship with hundreds of studies tackling this concept from various viewpoints and using case studies from different industries. The general agreement is that having good CSR policies improves corporate performance because consumers are more likely to support organizations with robust CSR policies (Brammer & Millington, 2008). However, some authors argued that corporations change their CSR policies as consumers' focus changes, thus accusing corporations of 'mirroring the zeitgeist' (Topić et al., 2020) and greenwashing. Greenwashing is particularly linked to marketing, advertising, and PR because of corporate attempts to do green marketing while not meaningfully changing policies on depleting resources. Critics argue that corporations embrace green marketing or general CSR policies because of branding and PR rather than genuine interest in society or the environment (Alves, 2009). Greenwashing practices include falsely promoting products as environmentally friendly (Lyon & Montgomery, 2015), collaborations with NGOs to improve reputation (Holzer, 2008; Rohwer & Topić, 2018), which are not always genuine, and responding to external pressures and negative media coverage (Carroll & McCombs, 2003; Kowalczyk & Kucharska, 2020; Yu & Choi, 2016; Story & Neves, 2015).

REFLECT

Do you feel personally responsible for the labor and environmental impact of your clothing choices?

What kind of CSR communication would most influence your fashion purchasing decisions?

Are ethical fashion campaigns reaching all socioeconomic groups, or only affluent consumers?

Think about a fashion brand you regularly purchase from. What CSR policy do they have (if any)? Where can these messages be found (e.g., website, social media)? Have you seen these messages before reading this chapter? Do you believe in the authenticity of the CSR message of your favourite brand?

The Evolution of Fashion CSR and Fashion CSR Communication in Advertising and PR

CSR in fashion and the way it evolved for advertising and PR practitioners can be divided into several periods, with the debate on CSR starting in the 1970s, around the same time when the social unrest and the academic debate between Freeman and Friedman started in the US.

Early Foundations of CSR in Fashion (pre–1970s)

In the period before the 1970s, industrialization and early labor conditions affected the fashion industry; however, there was limited public scrutiny of corporations and thus less formal CSR at the time, which led to the already-mentioned social unrest against corporations. In the 1960s, the early labor movement emerged and started to call for ethical reform, which also had an impact on the fashion industry. In fashion, textile mills were a focus of the struggle because these factories segregated workers based on their race, thus prompting protests from Black American workers. This fight continued into the 1970s when a lawsuit was filed in the US by Shirley Lea, Romona Pinnix, and Annie Tinnin, three Black women who successfully argued that Cone Mills denied them employment based on their race and gender (see Lea vs. Cone Mills, 1970). Advertisers during the 1960s started a Creative Revolution, which meant increased reliance on visual communication and not heavy text, and boosted fashion advertising. The message of the new advertising was to buy new goods to escape consumerism, and models in ads became younger, had longer hair, and wore 'rebel' garb and serious expressions. The ads of the 1950s, when families were portrayed through doting wives with children, were gone. The Creative Revolution introduced a rebellion against conformity and a hyper-state of individualism, which was presented as addressing the real problems of society. This shift led to greater use of emotional appeal in advertising, further perpetuating individualism (Frank, 1997; Fox, 1984; Reading, 2013). In public relations, this was a period of publicity work, and many publicists supported fashion designers by creating publicity around their salons or couture collections.

The Rise of Ethical Awareness (1970s–1990s)

As a result of the activism of the early labor movement, environmental and consumer activism started to grow during the 1970s, which paved the way for the rise of CSR due to the rise of feminist and workers' rights activism. Sociologists also analyzed issues such as a growing middle-class consciousness and a shift to individualism, which corresponds with the rise of yuppies in fashion during the 1980s (Carnegy, 1990). Nike had a sweatshop scandal in the 1990s, and anti-fur campaigns started. As a result of these scandals and increased consumer awareness, fashion communicators turned towards defensive and reactive PR strategies and corporate silence. Nike initially did not respond to allegations of sweatshops and its chairman has stated that their sales have not been impacted, but as criticism and backlash grew, the company was forced to make changes such as monitoring supply chains, auditing and monitoring their production facilities to 'root out underage workers and require overseas manufacturers of its wares to meet strict United States health and safety standards' (Conway, 2019, n.p.). This scandal happened before the rise of social media, and it caused damage to Nike, which spent a decade cleaning up its reputation and winning back consumers.

PR efforts in this period were focused on reacting and repairing reputation when something happens, rather than brands having meaningful strategies on CSR or crisis management. In advertising, mass advertising and marketing started promoting designer labels to middle-class consumers, which created a mass market of the 1970s (History.com, 2025). However, 1989 saw the creation of the World Fair Trade Organization (https://wfto.com/) to improve the livelihoods of communities, which started ethical consciousness and affected fashion, giving a foundation for CSR campaigning. The Clean Clothes Campaign (https://cleanclothes.org/) also started in 1989, in the Netherlands. This organization argues that everyone who works in the global fashion industry should have protection of their human rights, which also impacts fashion PR and advertising. The year 1997 saw a rise of the Global Reporting Initiative (GRI) (https://www.globalreporting.org/), which prompted organizations to start publishing social responsibility statements on their websites, making CSR part of their PR because the GRI advocated for transparency in work, including social, environmental, and economic transparency and benefits for everyone. Sustainability reporting came about because of this advocacy, and this practice continues up until the present day.

The Transparency Crisis (2000s)

During the period between the 1990s and 2000s, there was a rise of globalization, which particularly affected, and to some extent empowered, the fashion industry because supply chains and factories moved offshore; however, this opened new issues with labor rights, wages, and working conditions, continuing scandals with sweatshops. In this period, there was also an increased global media scrutiny. Due to the rise of digital communication, it became easier to expose bad practices and raise consumer awareness due to easier access to global information. In public relations, strategies for managing CSR included sustainability reporting, ethical sourcing campaigns, and CSR sections on websites. All these practices are still present today, most notably in fashion companies that report on their sustainability, eco-friendly materials, tackling plastic packaging, etc. The period of the 2000s presents a rise in fashion advertising because image management became a focus of fashion designers, including collaborations with the most sought-after professionals from the fashion industry (Giambelli, 2023).

Image Management and Authenticity (2010s–present)

With the further rise of digital communication, as well as social media networks, ethical consumerism rose, which drove a change in the corporate world that started to focus on purpose-driven branding. Social media contributed to the democratization of CSR narratives and increased consumer awareness about brand violations of labor rights and environmental degradation. CSR communication became embedded into storytelling, brand activism, and sustainability policies were strengthened, along with the rising focus on diversity, which also became part of CSR.

However, increased brand focus on CSR, which was then also heavily communicated via advertising and social media campaigns, also resulted in corporate image and reputation crises because of accusations of greenwashing and woke-washing. Sociological research focused on looking at generational differences in approaching and understanding CSR, identity politics, and climate change. Some brands responded by launching sustainable collections, such as Swedish retailer H&M, which launched Conscious Collection worldwide to promote a sustainable future for fashion. The press release from H&M's website depicts the collection in the following way,

> The collection unites modern romantic designs and every piece in the collection is made from a sustainably-sourced material, such as 100% organic cotton, Tencel or recycled polyester. From the floral-printed coordinated separates to the floaty dresses, all in a colour palette of earthy tones, blush pink and white, this is a statement of intent to take responsibility and lead the change towards a more sustainable fashion industry. The campaign features thirteen inspirational women from all around the world, including Naomi Harris and Rosario Dawson. The H&M Conscious Collection for Spring 2019 launches in the beginning of April and will be available worldwide, in store and online (H&M, 2019, n.p.).

In this period, heavier regulation was introduced to address working conditions, such as the California Transparency in Supply Chains Act of 2012 or the Modern Slavery Act of 2015 in the UK. The UK's Modern Slavery Act requires all companies with a global turnover above GBP 36 million to publicly file an annual slavery and trafficking statement, explaining what steps were taken to combat these issues in operations and supply chains (Modern Slavery Act, 2015). In California, retailers and manufacturers with global revenue over USD 100 million that work in California must publicly disclose to what degree they are addressing forced labor and human trafficking in their manufacturing networks

(California Transparency in Supply Chains Act, 2012). Also, the Federal Business Supply Chain Transparency on Trafficking and Slavery Bill (2020) was introduced to the House of Representatives in the US. The bill was meant to mandate disclosing what measures companies with profits exceeding USD 100 million are taking to address forced labor, slavery, human trafficking, and child labor within their global supply chains. The bill did not pass, but it was evidence of the growing debate on CSR issues. However, later on, the Trafficking Victims Protection Reauthorization Act came into effect (approved in 2022, became public law in 2023, US Congress, 2023), mandating at the federal level civil liability for companies that have known or should have known about modern slavery in their manufacturing chains. This act had several updates and reiterations following the situation as human rights abuses evolve (US Department of Justice, n.d.). As a result of these legislations or legislative attempts, many fashion companies now have public CSR policies, particularly focusing on sustainability, and recently also on diversity.

Apart from state legislation, non-governmental organizations (NGO) watchdogs emerged in this period, such as Fashion Revolution, which was formed as a response to the Rana Plaza disaster of 2013, when a building housing a large fashion production company collapsed, killing 1,134 workers and injuring thousands more, with some people reporting having to self-amputate themselves to get out of the rubble. The investigation revealed that factory owners knew the building was damaged but had taken no action; instead, they pressured workers to return to the factory a day after an inspection of cracks in the walls was conducted (Clean Clothes Campaign, n.d.).

The Fashion Revolution organization was founded by Carry Somers and Orsola de Castro, and has since grown into a global fashion activism movement, which mobilizes citizens, brands, and policymakers (Fashion Revolution, n.d.). The organization states that its aims are,

> an end to human and environmental exploitation in the global fashion industry; Safe, dignified working conditions and living wages for all people in the supply chain; Redistributed and more equal balance of power across the global fashion industry; A bigger and stronger labour movement in the global fashion industry; A global fashion industry that works to conserve precious resources and regenerate ecosystems; A culture of transparency and accountability across the value chain; An end to throwaway culture and shift to a system where materials are used for much longer and nothing goes to waste; Heritage, craftsmanship and local wisdom are recognised and valued" (Fashion Revolution, n.d., n.p.).

The organization, among other things, such as research and education, also organizes protests and raises awareness on social media, which presents challenges to advertising and PR professionals; however, this practice also reduces greenwashing in fashion, as, owing to social media, malpractice can nowadays be easily exposed and spiral into a scandal.

Many other organizations promote sustainable and ethical fashion, such as the Cascale Sustainable Apparel Coalition (https://cascale.org), The Fashion Pact (https://www.thefashionpact.org), Ethical Trade Initiative (https://www.ethicaltrade.org), and the Institute of Positive Fashion (https://instituteofpositivefashion.com). Many major brands are members of these initiatives, and their logos are displayed on the initiatives' webpages. Participating brands state their membership on their official websites, usually in corporate mission statements, which presents a form of fashion PR work. However, some companies also feed this information into their advertising efforts, such as, for example, Patagonia, a brand that incorporates CSR into its work and received international recognition for its efforts from UNEP (UN Environmental Program) in 2019 (UNEP, 2019).

REFLECT

Find two brands, one luxury and one retail. Analyze their CSR communication strategies using their corporate websites. Discuss with peers how retail and luxury fashion brands differ in their CSR communication strategies. What were the key messages the two brands used in communicating their CSR policies? Which channels do they mainly use to communicate their policies? Are CSR strategies linked to issues identified in the fashion industry, such as labor and human rights protections, and the environment?

Table 6.1 summarizes strategies for digital communication in fashion, with a distinction between luxury and retail fashion.

Table 6.1 CSR Communication Strategies in Fashion

TACTIC	TECHNIQUES – LUXURY FASHION	TECHNIQUES – RETAIL FASHION
Message	• Craftsmanship • Longevity • Ethical luxury	• Affordable • 'Doing good'
Sustainability & CSR messages	• Durability • Heritage • Timelessness • Fair labor • Regenerative agriculture • Carbon footprint	• Recycled materials • Conscious collections • Transparency in sourcing • Circular fashion • Factory safety
Engagement	• Elite participation (celebrity, expert ambassadors, curated editorials)	• Community-focused (repair programs, recycling incentives)
Transparency and traceability	• Impact reports • Certifications	• Dashboard style metrics and reporting • Supply chain communication (source location, factory conditions, labor policies) • Apps like Open Supply Hub that visualizes production steps

(*Continued*)

Table 6.1 Continued

TACTIC	TECHNIQUES – LUXURY FASHION	TECHNIQUES – RETAIL FASHION
Platforms and campaigns	• Brand-owned platforms • Instagram • Seasonal narratives linked to brand legacy	• Social media campaigns, influencer campaigns • Reactive campaigns linked to big events (Earth Day)
Voice	• Authoritative • Legacy-driven • Minimalistic	• Friendly • Educational
Visual style	• Cinematic • Refined • Emotional storytelling	• Infographics • Action-driven • Direct messaging to consumers
Campaign example	Chloé – B Corp Certification (2021) included public announcement and social media storytelling about ethical sourcing and inclusion. Press release announcement: https://www.chloe.com/experience/us/news/chloe-just-achieved-b-corp-certification/	H&M Conscious Collection focused on using organic and recycled materials, eco-labels. Press release announcement: https://about.hm.com/news/general-news-2019/h-m-s-conscious-collection-launches-worldwide-with-a-sustainable.html

Source: Author's work based on this chapter, observing various fashion brands on social media (both luxury and retail), and studying and teaching brand campaigns in the undergraduate fashion PR course

DISCUSSION QUESTIONS

- How have historical labor movements and global trade patterns shaped modern CSR communication in fashion?
- In what ways do consumers influence how brands communicate their CSR efforts?
- What makes CSR communication credible? What distinguishes effective CSR messaging from greenwashing?
- When a brand faces a labor or environmental scandal, what kind of response is most ethical?
- How should brands balance positive storytelling with acknowledgment of ongoing challenges?
- What role does transparency play in consumer trust, and how much transparency is too much or too little?
- How could emerging technologies (e.g., AI) improve or complicate CSR communication in fashion?
- What will CSR communication in fashion look like in 10 years?

References

Alves, I.M. (2009). Green spin everywhere: How greenwashing reveals the limits of the CSR paradigm. *Journal of Global Change and Governance, II*(1), 1–26.

Brammer, S., & Millington, A. (2008). Does it pay to be different? An analysis of the relationship between corporate social and financial performance. *Strategic Management Journal*, 29, 1325–1343.

California Transparency in Supply Chains Act. (2012). Retrieved from the Government of California: https://oag.ca.gov/SB657

Carnegy, V. (1990). *Fashions of a Decade: The 1980s*. New York: Facts on File.

Carroll, C.E., & McCombs, M. (2003). Agenda-setting Effects of Business News on the Public's Images and Opinions about Major Corporations. *Corporate Reputation Review, 6*(1), 36–46.

Clean Clothes Campaign. (n.d.). *Rana Plaza.* Retrieved from https://cleanclothes.org/campaigns/past/rana-plaza

Conway, N. (2019). Sweatshops Almost Killed Nike in the 1990s, Now There are Modern Slavery Laws. *TFL,* September 27. Retrieved from https://www.thefashionlaw.com/visibility-is-central-to-a-successful-supply-chain-heres-what-brands-need-to-know/

Davidson, E.E. (2022). Protesters assemble outside Molly-Mae's not so pretty little runway show. *Dazed,* February 17. Retrieved from https://www.dazeddigital.com/fashion/article/55489/1/protesters-molly-mae-hague-pretty-little-thing-runway-show-boohoo-fast-fashion

Fashion Revolution. (n.d.). *About.* Retrieved from https://www.fashionrevolution.org/about/

Federal Business Supply Chain Transparency on Trafficking and Slavery Bill. (2020). Retrieved from the website of the US Congress: https://www.congress.gov/bill/116th-congress/house-bill/6279#:~:text=This%20bill%20requires%20certain%20issuers,labor%20in%20their%20supply%20chains

Fox, S. (1984). *The Mirror Makers: A History of American Advertising and Its Creators.* New York: William Morrow and Company.

Frank, T. (1997). *The Conquest of Cool: Business Culture, Counterculture, and the Rise of Hip Consumerism.* Chicago: The University of Chicago Press.

Freeman, I., & Hasnaoui, A. (2011). The Meaning of Corporate Social Responsibility: The Vision of Four Nations. *Journal of Business Ethics,* 100, 419–443.

Freeman, R.E. (2010). *Strategic Management: A Stakeholder Approach.* Cambridge: Cambridge University Press.

Friedman, M. (1970). The Social Responsibility of Business is to Increase its Profits. *New York Times Magazine*, September 13. Retrieved from http://www.colorado.edu/studentgroups/libertarians/issues/friedman-soc-resp-business.html

Friedman, M. (1962). *Capitalism and Freedom.* Chicago: University of Chicago Press.

Giambelli, A. (2023). Y2K fashion campaigns to live a nostalgic summer. *G-Club,* July 24. Retrieved from https://www.nssgclub.com/en/fashion/33875/campaign-fashion-2000s

History.com. (2025). The 1970s. *History.com,* first published July 30, 2010; updated April 15, 2025. Retrieved from https://www.history.com/articles/1970s

Holzer, B. (2008). Turning Stakeseekers into Stakeholders a Political Coalition Perspective on the Politics of Stakeholder Influence. *Business and Society,* 47, 50–67.

H&M. (2019). *H&M's Conscious Collection launches worldwide with a sustainable fashion future in mind,* April 8. Retrieved from https://about.hm.com/news/general-news-2019/h-m-s-conscious-collection-launches-worldwide-with-a-sustainable.html

Ireland, P., & Pillay, R. (2009). Corporate social responsibility in a Neoliberal age. In Utting, P., & Marques, J. C. (eds.), *Corporate social responsibility and regulatory governance: Towards inclusive development?* New York: Palgrave-Macmillan (pp. 77–104).

Kowalczyk, R., & Kucharska, W. (2020). Corporate social responsibility practices incomes and outcomes: Stakeholders' pressure, culture, employee commitment, corporate reputation, and brand performance. A Polish–German cross-country study. *Corporate Social Responsibility and Environmental Management, 27*(2), 595–615.

Lea vs. Cone Mills (1970). Retrieved from https://openjurist.org/438/f2d/86/lea-v-cone-mills-corporation-lea

Lyon, T.P., & Montgomery, A.W. (2015). The Means and End of Greenwash. *Organization & Environment, 28*(2), 223–249.

Modern Slavery Act (2015). Retrieved from the website of the UK Government: https://www.legislation.gov.uk/ukpga/2015/30/contents

Moon, J. (2005). An Explicit Model of Business-Society Relations. In Habisch, A., Jonker, J., Wegner, M., & Schmidpeter, R. (eds.), *Corporate Social Responsibility Across Europe. Berlin*: Springer.

Moon, J. (2004). Government as a Driver of Corporate Social Responsibility. No. 20–2004 *ICCSR Research Paper Series,* ISSN 1479–5214, 1–27.

Pillay, R. (2015). *The Changing Nature of Corporate Social Responsibility: CSR and Development – The Case of Mauritius.* New York: Taylor & Francis.

Reading, T.A. (2013). Hip Versus Square: 1960s Advertising and Clothing Industries and the Counterculture. Research Papers. Paper 396. Retrieved from http://opensiuc.lib.siu.edu/gs_rp/396

Rohwer, L., & Topić, M. (2018). The Communication of Corporate-NGO Partnerships: Analysis of Sainsbury's Collaboration with Comic Relief. *Journal of Brand Management, 26*(1), 35–48. DOI: https://doi.org/10.1057/s41262-018-0111-7

Sheehy, B. (2014). Defining CSR: Problems and Solutions. *Journal of Business Ethics*, 131, 625–648.

Story, J., & Neves, P. (2015). When corporate social responsibility (CSR) increases performance: Exploring the role of intrinsic and extrinsic CSR attribution. *Business Ethics: A European Review, 24*(2), 111–124.

Topić, M. (2021). *Corporate Social Responsibility and Environmental Affairs in the British Press: An Ecofeminist Critique of Neoliberalism.* London: Routledge.

Topić, M., Bridge, G., & Tench, R. (2020). Mirroring the Zeitgeist: An Analysis of CSR Policies in the UK's Food, Soft Drink and Packaging Industries. *Journal of Global Responsibility, 12*(1), 62–75.

UNEP. (2019). *US outdoor clothing brand Patagonia wins UN Champions of the Earth award*, 24 September. Retrieved from https://www.unep.org/news-and-stories/press-release/us-outdoor-clothing-brand-patagonia-wins-un-champions-earth-award

US Department of Justice. (n.d.). *Key Legislation.* Retrieved from https://www.justice.gov/humantrafficking/key-legislation

US Congress. (2023). *S.3949- Trafficking Victims Prevention and Protection Reauthorization Act of 2022.* Retrieved from https://www.congress.gov/bill/117th-congress/senate-bill/3949

Yu, Y., & Choi, Y. (2016). Stakeholder pressure and CSR adoption: The mediating role of organizational culture for Chinese companies. *The Social Science Journal,* 53, 226–235.

CHAPTER 7 Working with Fashion Magazines for Advertising and PR

Learning Objectives

- Analyze how fashion magazines act as gatekeepers within the fashion-media ecosystem.
- Evaluate the agenda-setting power of fashion magazine editors in shaping industry priorities and public taste.
- Assess how digital platforms have transformed traditional magazine gatekeeping and redefined editorial influence.
- Apply a strategic framework for partnering with fashion magazines across both print and digital channels.

Fashion Magazines: Setting the Fashion Agenda

In January 1990, the cover page of the British *Vogue*, shot by Peter Lindbergh, featured five new models, Naomi Campbell, Cindy Crawford, Linda Evangelista, Christy Turlington, and Tatjana Patitz (see cover page in an article by Crawford, 2016). These models were not styled extravagantly. Instead, the cover showed them in simple, everyday clothes, photographed in black and white. The cover was raw, modern, and broke away from the high-glamour and over-styled norms of the 1980s. This was a moment when a fashion magazine did not just dictate fashion trends but also created celebrities out of top models, which signalled a cultural shift where the face of fashion was no longer just a fashion garment, but a woman with a name, personality, and a voice. Fashion thus became more about who wears it than what is being worn. This cover page launched the supermodel era, which blended fashion, celebrity, and commerce, and redefined relationships between readers and fashion icons, while also showing the power of fashion magazines in constructing identities, not just reflecting them. Cindy Crawford reflected on the importance of the 1990 *Vogue* cover in a *Vogue* edition from 2016, saying,

> At the time I had no idea it was going to be so legendary. *Vogue*'s editor Liz Tilberis, had asked Peter Lindbergh to photograph the new woman of the Nineties; Peter's reply was that he couldn't do it with just one woman. The idea of beauty had broadened; it could not be summed up with either a blonde, blue-eyed girl or a

DOI: 10.4324/9781003515043-10

> sexy brunette, he told her. There was change in the air and Peter and Liz picked up on that. We weren't photographed with a ton of hair and make-up; we were quite undone. Coming out of the Eighties, which was all big hair and boobs pushed up, it felt refreshing and new (Crawford, 2016, n.p.).

Fashion magazines have historically curated fashion trends, created editorial content, and influenced consumer taste in fashion, with which they set the fashion agenda. Fashion magazines have a unique role as cultural intermediaries (Bourdieu, 2010), such as shaping and reflecting fashion trends, beauty standards, and lifestyle aspirations. Magazines have a social role in creating cultural capital and forming identities, which gives magazines social relevance. Magazines also had an important role in forming the taste of young consumers of the future, particularly teen magazines. In a study of teen magazines and their social significance, Greenwood (2013) quoted a participant who reflected on her experience of reading teen magazines when she was between 11 and 13 years old saying,

> As I moved from a child to a 'teen' and began to be interested in appearance, fashion and beauty, I liked the fact that these magazines had hints and tips about topics relevant to my age group. I felt 'educated' by them. Everyone my age was reading these magazines, and I was strongly influenced by my peers (p. 38, emphasis in the original).

Many different forms of magazines are relevant for fashion advertisers and PRs, such as teen, young adult, bridal, homes and gardens, parent and child, family lifestyle, and hobby magazines. Along with fashion magazines, this market forms an opportunity for advertisers and PRs to place products and promote their brands. The main leaders in the fashion magazine market are *Vogue* and *Harper's Bazaar,* which were the first fashion magazines in the world; however, many other fashion magazines are relevant for the fashion industry and thus, also advertisers and PR professionals. Magazines are published all over the world and have an international audience, with some magazines being published in several countries (e.g., *Vogue*, *Elle*, etc.). Most adults read magazines in some form, either print or digital, and thus magazines cumulatively reach a larger audience than a prime-time TV program (Kim et al., 2015). Therefore, magazines are also a fertile ground for advertising and PR professionals. The value of magazine advertising is in being able to communicate to a wide variety of demographic groups and effectively target desired audiences, because magazines operate in a niche market and people buy them because they are interested in the topics they cover and the products they advertise.

REFLECT

Select one recent issue of a fashion magazine of your choice. Analyze the editorial–advertising ratio. Count total pages; then count full-page ads, partial ads, branded content, and editorial. Compare how much space is devoted to advertising versus editorial. Consider brands that buy the most space, and sections with the heaviest ad clustering (e.g., front-of-book, back cover). Articulate the magazine's personality (e.g., authority-driven, guidance, advice) by reviewing content. Cross-check whether advertisers in the issue match that portrait.

Fashion Magazines as Cultural Products and Commodities

Fashion magazines can be seen as cultural products and commodities. As cultural products, fashion magazines circulate in a cultural economy of collective meanings by providing how-to recipes, illustrated stories, and narratives, which allow readers to reflect and find an identity by seeing various models and fashion and beauty items (Moeran, 2006). As commodities, magazines are publishing products, whether digital or print, and are important places for advertisers, particularly advertisers promoting cosmetics, clothing, fragrances, and personal care (Moeran, 2006). Therefore, like women's general magazines, fashion magazines are a part of capitalist production and consumption (Beetham, 1996). Because magazines are produced for multiple audiences (readers and advertisers), editors work to communicate to two audiences (Marchand, 1985), which means that magazine content is a mix of cultural and sales pitches (Moeran, 2006). Like with other publishing industries, particularly newspapers and general magazines, there is a tension between fashion magazine editors and advertisers because editors like to praise their sales, communicating that it is the cultural side that sells, but the reality is that advertising income is essential for the survival of fashion magazines (McKay, 2000). However, fashion, like fashion magazines, is also a cultural product and commodity because fashion also communicates to multiple audiences, those who buy clothes, create buzz around clothes, or show off clothes (Moeran, 2006).

Fashion magazines closely follow seasonal calendars and are often prepared six months in advance. The March and September issues are important editions because they feature the latest spring/summer and fall/winter collections shown in major fashion weeks, London, New York, Paris, Milan, and recently also Tokyo – some seasonal adjustments are made for Tokyo due to differences in timelines. Seasonal editions of fashion magazines are important milestones for advertisers and PR professionals working with fashion magazines, because most fashion and beauty companies aim to feature in these important editions, and advertisers will try to place ads in these issues. Placing stories and adverts requires careful planning, as well as relationship-building for earned coverage (e.g., editorials). Magazine editors usually pick one or two trends to focus on in the seasonal coverage for each seasonal issue, which means that advertisers and PR professionals should work in advance to promote their innovation and new collections to magazine editors for a potential feature and a recommendation, or a mention in the coverage. Other than these two important seasonal issues, other issues will cover various aspects of fashion, such as holiday fashion, swimwear for summer, and gifts in December (Moeran, 2006). While there has been more fluidity in coverage recently due to digital editions and the need to create extra content, which increased writing about collections, these two seasonal editions are still important for advertisers and PR professionals. Many fashion magazines now also have websites with blogs and/or LinkedIn blogs, and they have newsletters sent to readers with new content. Some magazines also have popular podcasts, which are available on their websites and podcast platforms, such as Apple and Spotify.

Magazine editors obtain clothes for photo shoots from brands, which may be very cooperative or fussy. This depends on whether the magazine is large and established, and whether it is relevant for the brand's consumer base. Magazines will focus on preferred fashion names, taking into consideration advertising, which creates the notion of power and a tension between editors and advertisers. In a study by Moeran (2006), a fashion magazine editor illustrated the dynamic by saying,

> When it comes to fashion and beauty, we have to cooperate with advertisers subtly. We borrow different clothes for our fashion pages and have to choose our brands very carefully. We try to balance the interests of both readers and advertisers by representing everything. We can't publish whole product ranges, so we take turns among different products put out by different fashion and beauty companies (p. 734).

Magazines were historically gatekeepers of information and fashion trends and had a hegemonic position in deciding on what should be endorsed in fashion, which impacted designers and brands, but also society. Bourdieu's cultural capital theory (Bourdieu, 1986) explains how magazines conferred status on certain trends and dismissed others, which means that to work in a fashion magazine, one had to possess a certain knowledge and a viewpoint on fashion and trends, which for the field of fashion magazines constitutes cultural and social capital. This is largely still true because aspiring fashion journalists need to have a good knowledge of fashion styles, and main brands and their distinctive history, including haute couture.

Fashion magazines have an important role in shaping fashion discourses. In a study of the editorials in *Vogue*'s Style Ethics section in the period between 2009 and 2013, Baker Jones and Hawley (2017) argued that *Vogue* incorporated sustainable fashion discourse, which has the potential to shape or alter perceptions on sustainable fashion. The authors argued that *Vogue* has cultural capital, which puts them in a position of power in constructing meaning for the industry. Bourdieu (2010) indeed saw magazines as cultural intermediaries, with fashion media existing between the production and consumption of fashionable goods. Therefore, publications like *Vogue* – which developed cultural capital over the time – are in a unique position to connect fashion consumers and producers, which means that fashion magazines play an important role, along with blogs, newspapers, television, and movies in changing power relations around issues such as gender, sexuality, social class, race and ethnicity, colonialism, and sustainability (Baker Jones & Hawley, 2017; Lister & Wells, 2001).

REFLECT

Anatole France, a French writer (1844–1924), said, 'If I were allowed to choose from the pile of books which will be published 100 years after my death, do you know which one I would take? ... I would simply take a fashion magazine so that I could see how women dress one century after my departure. And these rags would tell me more about the humanity of the future than all the philosophers, prophets, and scholars' (cited from Stephens Frings, 1987, p. 4). Find a historical fashion magazine and look at how women dressed at the time. Discuss what dress styles can tell you about humanity and the social position of women. Look also at the adverts of the time. What do they say? How do they try to appeal to consumers? What is the message? Is the message linked to social events of the time? If so, what was it? You can find this information by creating a free account at Mary Evans Images Library and/or the UK National Archives. Readers from other countries can look at their national archives and/or national libraries to find images that paint a societal story through fashion. Pinterest also has a lot of adverts and magazine pages, and many magazines allow trial access to their historical online archives.

History of Fashion Magazines and the Evolution of Practice in Working with Fashion Magazines for Advertisers and PR Professionals

Magazines started to rise in prominence during the 19th century. The pioneering titles in fashion magazines were *Harper's Bazaar*, founded in 1867, and *Vogue*, founded in 1892. These magazines began as high society-focused or literary periodicals, gradually incorporating fashion illustrations, sketches, and style advice. For example, *Vogue* started as a weekly high-society journal covering news about the New York social elite, local social scene, traditions of high society, social etiquette, and reviews of books, plays, and music. After the magazine was purchased by Condé Nast Publications in 1909, the magazine was transformed into a women's fashion magazine focusing on beauty, composure, and etiquette (Britannica, n.d.). In this period, the first notable editors emerged. Edna Woolman Chase at *Vogue* shaped editorial direction, forging close links with prominent designers of the era, such as French couturiers Worth and Poiret, as well as adapting to societal changes and endorsing American fashion and ready-to-wear clothes as American tastes and needs evolved. Woolman Chase was *Vogue*'s editor-in-chief from 1914 to 1952. A special article about Woolman Chase published in October 1954 issue of *Vogue* stated about her editorial style, 'Who can say how strong a part *Vogue* has taken in changes; taken, without itself changing its original purpose – to report fashion with authority; to have, and to create, respect for taste' (*Vogue*, 1954, p. 77).

The 20th century saw a rise in photography and fashion editorial. In this period, photographic editorials (e.g., by photographers like Cecil Beaton, Irving Penn, Richard Avedon) changed how magazines presented clothing and models. This shift made fashion imagery more aspirational and visually impactful, which became a key to both selling garments and constructing ideals of beauty, which was later re-invented with the rise of the supermodels, and Lindbergh's supermodel cover page of January 1990. The 20th century was a golden period of fashion magazines, particularly when it came to gatekeeping and the influence of editors and photographers.

The Editor as an Agenda-Setter

Fashion editors, particularly editors-in-chief, historically held a major influence over the editorial policy of the magazine, and thus their editorship directly influenced brands. Editors shaped the cultural conversation around fashion and had the power to decide which designers and trends earned coverage. *Vogue* is a particularly good case for understanding the importance of fashion magazine editors.

Diana Vreeland

As the editor-in-chief of *Harper's Bazaar* and *Vogue*, Diana Vreeland was known for supporting glamorous fashion, discovering models based on their personalities, and championing unconventional beauty. In 1936, she started writing a popular column entitled 'Why Don't You?', where she offered extravagant advice to readers, such as wearing hats with fruits (*Harper's Bazaar*, 2014). In 1939, she joined *Harper's Bazaar* full-time and shortly after obtained the role of editor-in-chief. She held that job for 23 years, which made her one of the most influential magazine personalities. In 1962, she left Bazaar to join the staff at *Vogue*, becoming the editor-in-chief in 1963. As editor of *Vogue*, she transformed fashion publishing into imagination, provocation, boosting *Vogue*'s global influence. *Vogue* started to reflect her taste for the novel, bizarre, and outrageous, which matched her personality, widely considered to be eccentric and dramatic (Britannica, n.d._b). *Vogue*'s photography and design, under her leadership, showcased youth culture, rock music, and a rejection of traditional standards (Britannica, n.d._b). She is credited for introducing ideas such as featuring models in exotic and international locations, embracing the so-called imperfect beauty, and blurring lines between fashion, art, and fantasy with surrealist spreads and theatrical styling. She also had a voice as an editor and would command trends, for example, by writing 'Pink is the navy blue of India' (Britannica, n.d._b). Her editorial style turned fashion editors into cultural curators and elevated *Vogue* from a style guide to a cultural institution, a role *Vogue* still has today. Vreeland re-imagined *Vogue* in the 1960s and did more than dress women; she gave them a vision. She created the notion of 'beautiful people', which was a 'subclass of youthful, wealthy, and footloose members of the less-exclusive international set who were supposed to set the tone of fashion, art, and society' (Britannica, n.d._b, n.p.). In her biography, her successor Grace Mirabella (1995) wrote that Vreeland was initially difficult to work with because she did not have clear guidance and standards; she was driven by her dreams and wanted *Vogue* to give people something they did not know they needed.

Grace Mirabella

Grace Mirabella, upon taking over editorship of *Vogue* from Vreeland, changed its focus to working-class women and lifestyle and appealed to women who were interested in everything. One of her famous statements includes, 'We live in an age when everyone is obsessed with what's trendy … Style is the antidote to trendiness' (Meltzer, 2022, n.p.). Mirabella's shift to working-class women further confirms the powerful role fashion magazines have in creating cultural trends and movements. Her editorial philosophy can be described as practical elegance for a modern woman.

Mirabella became a *Vogue* editor in 1971 and inherited a magazine focused on unconventional beauty, but still a glamorous, glossy magazine. She initially worked in a variety of roles at *Vogue*, then as the associate editor-in-chief of *Vogue* under the editorship of Diana Vreeland (Mirabella, 1995). Mirabella said that she admired Vreeland because of 'all of her style and know-how, which she was about' (Banks & Hess, 2021, n.p.). Mirabella became an editor when the world was changing and operated during the rise of the second wave of feminism of the 1970s, when fashion stopped being just a fantasy and art to admire, but moved into something that had to be used in everyday life; it had to be practical and suitable for working women. Mirabella responded to the societal change, and her editorial style emphasized wearable fashion, health and fitness, career and lifestyle coverage, and neutral palettes and clean photography. This philosophy came from her working-class and first-generation American background, which informed the political shift of her editorship. Mirabella was not a bohemian socialite like Vreeland; she was a member of the new generation of working American women who were taught to be financially independent (Banks & Hess, 2021; Mirabella, 1995), which influenced her editorship. Mirabella famously repainted *Vogue*'s office beige, which was a shift from Vreeland's avant-garde red and leopard office (Mirabella, 1995). Her editorship supported American designers who traditionally focused on a working woman's style, thus also showing the influence of the magazine editor. While Vreeland gave readers dreams, Mirabella provided guidance and made *Vogue* more accessible to a wider readership, while not losing its aspirational focus. Mirabella expanded the magazine's relevance during the 1970s and 1980s and helped shape the image of independent, career women, bridging the gap between fashion fantasy and functional lifestyle media. Mirabella's tenure at *Vogue* created a turn from the theatrical excess of Vreeland, who was known as eccentric, to a pragmatic sophistication. Her editorial style was focused on women of the 1970s who were ambitious, active, and self-aware. *Vogue*, under Mirabella, became a companion to women navigating modern life. Mirabella said about her philosophy, 'I'm a firm believer that the key to dressing well, the key to style, is that you don't have to reinvent yourself every day' (Banks & Hess, 2021, n.p.). Soon after leaving *Vogue*, Mirabella founded a magazine, *Mirabella,* in 1989, which she edited until 1994.

Anna Wintour

Anna Wintour started editing *Vogue* in 1988, replacing Mirabella, who was perceived as out of touch due to her refusal to make *Vogue* more like Elle, a new competitor in the magazine market (Mirabella, 1995). Mirabella argued in her memoir that she could not stand the glitz of the 1980s and the 40,000-dollar ball gowns, crinolines, or hats (Mirabella, 1995). Wintour was first an editor of a series of New York magazines, British *Vogue* (1986), and *House & Garden* (1987). She changed Mirabella's strategy to a high/low style of dressing and started to combine her support and endorsement of both couture and prêt-à-porter. She started to put celebrities on the cover page, not just models (Britannica, n.d.), which increased the audience appeal. Wintour's first *Vogue* cover (November 1988) broke a convention because it featured a model in jeans, a couture top, and windswept hair (Vogue, 1988). This cover page also signaled a shift in *Vogue*'s photography direction under Wintour, which focused on featuring women's bodies on cover pages, rather than just faces, as was the case before her tenure. The November 1988 cover page merged high fashion with mass appeal, resulting in further covers featuring Hollywood stars, athletes, and cultural icons, and paving the way for this practice to become conventional. She famously said, 'Mass with class—that's my mantra' (Britannica, n.d._a). Wintour is also known for editorial precision because she is focused on emerging designers, trend forecasting, the global fashion economy, and controlled, polished, and forward-looking content. Wintour is known for being a visual communicator and very skilled in leading fashion editorials (Oppenheimer, 2005). Wintour globalized *Vogue* and turned it into a global brand, increasing its influence across platforms, countries, and media. She launched the careers of many designers, including John Galliano, Marc Jacobs, and Alexander McQueen (Britannica, n.d._a). She also increased *Vogue*'s charity engagement by transforming the Met Gala, the annual fundraising event for the Costume Institute of the Metropolitan Museum of Art. This event is an elite gathering of Manhattan socialites, and it became an internationally chronicled celebrity-dominated red-carpet event known as the 'East Coast's answer to the Oscars' (Britannica, n.d._a, n.p.). Wintour redefined the editing of a fashion magazine and positioned the editor not just as an agenda-setter but also as a cultural executive with institutional influence. In June 2025, Wintour announced her decision to step down as the editor-in-chief of *Vogue* and focus on her second role, the content director of the Condé Nast corporation that owns *Vogue* (Gasthalter, 2025).

REFLECT

Choose a fashion magazine and look at its historical cover pages. Choose a cover that stood out to you, either because it made an impression on you visually, emotionally, or ideologically. Consider the following questions,

What drew your attention to this issue?
What messages did the issue convey about fashion and/or society?
How did it influence, if in any way, your view of fashion, gender, race, body image, or aspiration?
Did the editorial challenge or reinforce societal norms?
What role did the editor play in shaping the narrative of the issue?

The Digital Era and the Shifting Power Dynamics

The rise of fashion websites, blogs, and social media (e.g., Instagram, TikTok) disrupted the traditional gatekeeping role of print magazines. Digital platforms require constant, shorter content cycles, contrasting with monthly or quarterly print schedules. The emergence of bloggers and social media influencers created a competition between influencers and magazines for brand partnerships and audience attention. Magazines, once the primary gatekeepers, now share the stage with decentralized voices – some of whom command larger followings than established editorial staff. For example, some influencers have over 10 million followers on Instagram and collaborate with many brands, such as Caroline Simpson, with 10.2 million followers and brand collaborations with Everlane and Reformation (Influencity, 2024). Many iconic print magazines have reduced frequency or ceased operations entirely; others pivot to digital-first strategies or incorporate subscription-based content. Sociologically, this shift reflects changing reading habits, the democratization of fashion commentary, and the fragmentation of audiences into niche communities.

Magazine circulation has been in decline since the rise of digital communication. Statista projected that the worldwide revenue of magazines will reach USD 32.72 billion in 2025, with a revenue change of -2 percent (Statista, 2025). According to the same source, revenue is expected to show an annual growth rate of -2.35 percent and reach a total value of USD 29.76 billion by 2029 (Statista, 2025), which presents a decline. Statista also predicted that the number of magazine readers worldwide is expected to amount to 817.8 million users by 2029 (Statista, 2025). The decline is linked mainly to traditional, print magazines due to the rise of digital consumption, which is why many magazines are going digital to engage younger audiences. However, many luxury consumers, in a study conducted by *Vogue* Business and Statista in 2022, said that magazines and newspapers are an important source of information about fashion, with the number going as high as 73 percent of respondents from the UK (Statista, 2024).

Fashion magazines face a challenge from bloggers because they are no longer the gatekeepers of fashion-related information (Rocamora, 2012). Fashion blogs have become an important source of fashion news, commentary, and trend forecasting, and many PR professionals and advertisers also work with fashion bloggers. Fashion bloggers have a seat in fashion runways, along with fashion editors (Titton, 2015), and brands increasingly collaborate with bloggers due to their large audiences, sometimes larger than some magazines. These changes have impacted fashion journalism, including fashion magazines, despite scholarly criticism about bloggers' fashion knowledge and critical thinking skills being dubious (Rocamora, 2012). What is more, some fashion journalists became bloggers themselves (Fulton, 2015), and influencer marketing has seen a rise due to brand collaborations with bloggers (Luvaas, 2017). Even though bloggers are not trying to compete with fashion magazines, and mainly focus on self-expression or showcasing their passion (Dufy & Hund, 2015), they have still impacted fashion magazines because readers see blogs as democratic spaces (Marwick, 2013) and as places where fashion is worn by the real people who do not enforce standards of beauty, as fashion magazines have historically done, e.g., thinness and beauty standards (Rocamora, 2012). Bloggers are seen by readers as relatable and friendly, while magazines have always been seen as untouchable and disconnected from their readers (Marwick, 2013; Colliander & Dahlén, 2011). This is why many fashion magazines incorporated blogs into their online publication strategy, which is true for both print and digital magazines. Magazines also increased their social media presence and content creation and promotion, which gave rise to editor influencers, or magazine editors who also have a large following on social media (Fernandez, 2018). These editors and fashion magazines generally now also use Instagram as a platform focused on creating visual content, which was initially a domain of social media influencers. However, it is visible that while fashion bloggers initially did not compete with magazines, nowadays some incorporate photos similar to magazine photo shoots, which comes in response to magazines going to social media and adopting influencer-style content and promotion strategies.

In a study of major fashion magazines, Cheng and Tandoc (2022) analyzed 'about' pages of fashion magazines and argued that fashion magazines position themselves in terms of audiences they try to 'appeal to, the topics they cover, and the theme of the magazine itself' (p. 1220). This appeal also includes being specific about who their readers are and distinguishing themselves based on the topics they emphasize. For example, their study showed that '*InStyle*, for example, focuses on "celebrity style", *Grazia UK* covers "smart, shoppable fashion", and *Vogue* "places fashion in the context of culture"' (p. 1221). Equally, magazines tend to place bloggers or influencers outside of journalism and see them as someone to write about, and they particularly emphasize their authority, status, and exclusivity as opposed to blogs, which are more focused on personal experience and validation (Cheng & Tandoc, 2022).

REFLECT

Choose a fashion magazine brand. Scroll through that brand's Instagram Stories. Answer the following questions,

What kinds of content appear most frequently (runway clips, shoppable links, memes, backstage selfies)?
Which editorial tone dominates (exclusive authority, advice, guidance, etc.)?
How does the format invite or discourage audience interaction (polls, swipe-ups, comments)?

Table 7.1 summarizes strategies for digital communication in fashion, with a distinction between luxury and retail fashion.

Table 7.1 Strategies for Working with Magazines for Advertisers and PR Professionals

KEY STRATEGIES	TECHNIQUES – LUXURY FASHION	TECHNIQUES – RETAIL FASHION
Defining strategic objectives	• Reinforcing brand prestige, cultural capital, and exclusivity • **Goal:** curated editorial features in high-status fashion magazines that align with brand's aesthetic and heritage (*Vogue*, *Harper's Bazaar*) • Align strategy with strategy of the magazine and editor-in-chief (e.g., couture vs. ready-to-wear collections)	• Increasing brand visibility, consumer trust, and purchase intentions • **Goal:** securing broad editorial coverage across print and digital editions, magazine mentions across social media channels to drive engagement, traffic, and sales
Research-informed selection of magazines	• Identifying brand alignment, tone, aesthetic, values, past covers, featured designers • Magazine's editorial boards (fashion directors and editors), research coverage of luxury fashion, explore recurring contributors (stylists, writers, photographers) and networking for future collaborations, analyze the quality of readership and influence over mass exposure	• Focusing on audience fit and engagement using digital tools (e.g., media kits) to research magazine's digital traffic, reader demographics, and engagement rates • Finding out which magazines ideal consumers of the retail brand read • Identifying magazines that run product roundups, shoppable guides, and influencer features • Researching recent brand collaborations, and prices

(*Continued*)

Table 7.1 Continued

KEY STRATEGIES	TECHNIQUES – LUXURY FASHION	TECHNIQUES – RETAIL FASHION
		• Using social media and media kits to find contact people and design outreach strategy based on audience alignment and recent content. Focus on mass reach
Building relationships with editorial staff	• Cultivating close and long-term relationships with senior and fashion editors • Personalized invitations and preview access are essential	• Working with fashion assistants, stylists, and junior editors • Sending visually engaging press kits, which can be easily edited and repurposed
Editorial placement	• Long-lead features in legacy magazines (*Vogue*, *Harper's Bazaar*) • Prioritize exclusivity, high-art imagery, and focus on emphasizing heritage, craftsmanship and the designer's creative vision • Use aspirational narratives	• Target both legacy magazines and online magazines • Aim for a broader reach. Highlight value, trend responsiveness, and customer lifestyle fit • Use relatable narratives over aspirational
Collaborations	• Co-host invite-only events or dinners with editors and high-profile guests during fashion week or product launches	• Partner for accessible activations, pop-ups, or giveaways promoted through magazine's digital platforms
Campaign integration	• Coordinate magazine features with high-production brand campaigns, launches, or fashion weeks	• Use magazine features to support short-term sales or promotions • Coordinate with influencer campaigns
Paid media strategies	• High-profile placements reinforcing exclusivity and status • Focus on impact and legacy	• Lower cost, high-frequency adverts • Focus on sales
Visual communication	• High-resolution, art-directed images that align with magazine aesthetic • Offer exclusive image rights • Digital features targeting magazine-branded podcasts, virtual panels, or metaverse experiences. Positioning as innovation leaders	• Flexible image sets and product shots usable across print, web, and social media formats • Digital features prioritize shoppable content, product roundups, and editor picks, suitable for magazine websites or social media accounts

Source: Author's work based on observing various fashion brands on social media (both luxury and retail), subscription to *Vogue* and *Cosmopolitan*, and studying and teaching brand campaigns in the undergraduate fashion PR course, as well as reading various biographies and academic and popular books

DISCUSSION QUESTIONS

- How does understanding an editor's vision – like Vreeland's fantasy, Mirabella's realism, or Wintour's power precision – help advertising and PR professionals craft pitches that are more likely to be accepted?
- How have the relationships between fashion magazines and advertising/PR professionals changed from the 1960s to today's digital landscape?
- What factors should a brand or PR team consider when selecting a magazine to approach for editorial or advertorial placement?
- In what ways do editors like Wintour or Vreeland shape not just trends, but public perception of brands? Can a single editorial placement redefine a brand's image?
- Who holds more power in the relationship between fashion editors and PR professionals today – and how can this affect what stories are told and which brands are spotlighted?
- Can a brand's placement in a major magazine (e.g., *Vogue*) create long-term value?
- How do influencers, online publications, and social media blur or challenge the traditional PR–editorial–advertising model of working with fashion magazines?

References

Baker Jones, K., & Hawley, J.M. (2017). "Chic but Scrupulous, Down to the Very Last Stitch": "Style Ethics" in American *Vogue*. *Fashion Practice, 9*(2), 280–302, 10.1080/17569370.2016.1220137

Banks, L., & Hess, L. (2021). Grace Mirabella, former Editor-in-Chief of *Vogue*, Dies at 92. *Vogue,* December 23. Retrieved from https://www.vogue.com/article/grace-mirabella-obituary

Beetham, M. (1996). *A Magazine of Her Own*. London: Routledge.

Bourdieu, P. (2010). *Distinction: A Social Critique of the Judgment of Taste*. London: Routledge.

Bourdieu, P. (1986). The Forms of Capital. In Richardson, J.G. (ed), *Handbook of Theory and Research for the Sociology of Education*. New York: Greenwood Press (pp. 241–258).

Britannica. (n.d.). *Vogue: American magazine*. Written and fact-checked by the Editors of Encyclopaedia Britannica. Last Updated: May 22, 2025. Retrieved from https://www.britannica.com/topic/Vogue-American-magazine

Britannica. (n.d._a). *Anna Wintour: British editor*. Written and fact-checked by the Editors of Encyclopaedia Britannica. Last Updated: May 31, 2025. Retrieved from https://www.britannica.com/biography/Anna-Wintour

Britannica. (n.d._b). *Diana Vreeland: American editor and fashion expert*. Written and fact-checked by the Editors of Encyclopaedia Britannica. Retrieved from https://www.britannica.com/biography/Diana-Vreeland

Cheng, L., & Tandoc, E.C., Jr. (2022). From magazines to blogs: The shifting boundaries of fashion journalism. *Journalism, 23*(6), 1213–1232.

Colliander, J., & Dahlén, M. (2011). Following the fashionable friend: The power of social media: Weighing publicity effectiveness of blogs versus online magazines. *Journal of Advertising Research, 51*(1), 313–320.

Crawford, C. (2016). The Inside Story: The Vogue Supermodel Cover. *Vogue*, September 13. Retrieved from https://www.vogue.co.uk/article/peter-lindbergh-vogue-supermodel-cover-story

Duffy, B.E., & Hund, E. (2015). 'Having it all' on social media: Entrepreneurial femininity and self-branding among fashion bloggers. *Social Media+ Society, 1*(2), 1–11.

Fernandez, C. (2018). Fashion Editors or Influencers? Sometimes It's Hard to Tell. *Business of Fashion,* May 31. Retrieved from https://www.businessoffashion.com/articles/news-analysis/fashion-editors-or-influencers-sometimes-its-hard-to-tell/

Fulton, J. (2015). Are you a journalist? New media entrepreneurs and journalists in the digital space. *Javnost – The Public, 22*(4), 362–374.

Gasthalter, C. (2025). As Anna Wintour Shifts Her Focus at Condé Nast, *Vogue* US Will Seek a New Editorial Lead. *Vogue*, June 26. Retrieved from https://www.vogue.com/article/anna-wintour-vogue-new-head-of-editorial-content?utm_source=nl&utm_brand=vogue&utm_mailing=VOG_Daily_AW_062625&utm_campaign=aud-dev&utm_medium=email&bxid=65eb403ba868be363810bebd&cndid=76550460&hasha=525b17ec13603e303a27f4fa76148468&hashb=4c8bd12fda1cc3a6d206d62722a87d84fef81b8e&hashc=916199e54142fe98ec7d94bd41bf8f7f319c5b198d8b930648ae3b2bca0a5451&esrc=JOURNEY_PAYWALL&utm_term=VOG_Daily

Greenwood, G.L. (2013). *Fashion Marketing Communications.* London: Wiley.

Harper's Bazaar. (2014). Diana Vreeland Asks, Why Don't You... *Harper's Bazaar,* Harper's Bazaar staff, June 20. Retrieved from https://www.harpersbazaar.com/culture/features/a2620/diana-vreeland-why-dont-you/

Influencity. (2024). *Top 10 Fashion Influencers to Watch in the USA.* October 21. Retrieved from https://influencity.com/blog/en/top-10-fashion-influencers

Kim, J., Lee, J., Jo, S., Jung, J., & Kang, J. (2015). Magazine Reading Experience and Advertising Engagement: A Uses and Gratifications Perspective. *Journalism & Mass Communication Quarterly, 92*(1), 179–198.

Lister, M., & Wells, L. (2001). Seeing beyond Belief: Cultural Studies as an Approach to Analysing the Visual. In van Leeuwen, T., & Jewitt, C. (eds.), *Handbook of Visual Analysis.* London: Sage (pp. 61–91).

Luvaas, B. (2017). What does a fashion influencer look like? Portraits of the Instafamous. *Fashion, Style, & Popular Culture, 4*(3), 341–364.

Marchand, R. (1985). *Advertising the American Dream.* Berkeley and LA: University of California Press.

Marwick, A. (2013). 'They're really profound women, they're entrepreneurs': Conceptions of authenticity in fashion blogging. In *7th international conference on weblogs and social media*, Boston, MA, 8–11 July 2013. LA, CA: Association for the Advancement of Artificial Intelligence. Retrieved from https://tiara.org/wp-content/uploads/2018/05/amarwick_fashionblogs_ICWSM_2013.pdf

McKay, J. (2000). *The Magazines Handbook.* London: Routledge.

Meltzer, M. (2022). Remembering Grace Mirabella and Her Inventive Magazine. *New York Times,* February 9. Retrieved from https://www.nytimes.com/2022/02/09/style/grace-mirabella.html

Mirabella, G. (1995). *In and Out of Vogue.* New York: Doubleday.

Moeran, B. (2006). More Than Just a Fashion Magazine. *Current Sociology,* 54, 725–744.

Oppenheimer, J. (2005). *Front Row – Anna Wintour: The Cool Life and Hot Times of Vogue's Editor in Chief.* New York: St Martin's Press.

Rocamora, A. (2012). Hypertextuality and remediation in the fashion media: The case of fashion blogs. *Journalism Practice, 6*(1), 92–106.

Statista. (2025). *Magazine – Worldwide.* Retrieved from https://www.statista.com/outlook/amo/media/newspapers-magazines/print-newspapers-magazines/magazine/worldwide

Statista. (2024). *Importance of magazine and newspaper articles as a fashion information source for luxury consumers in selected countries/regions worldwide as of May 2022.* Retrieved from https://www.statista.com/statistics/1325798/print-media-fashion-luxury-consumers/

Stephens Frings, G. (1987). *Fashion: From Concept to Consumer*, 2nd edition. Englewood Cliffs, New Jersey: Prentice-Hall, Inc.

Titton, M. (2015). Fashionable personae: Self-identity and enactments of fashion narratives in fashion blogs. *Fashion Theory, 19*(2), 201–220.

Vogue. (1988). *November edition cover page.* Retrieved from https://archive.vogue.com/issues/1988

Vogue. (1954). We celebrate Edna Woolman Chase's 60 years at Vogue. *Vogue,* October 15. Retrieved from https://archive.vogue.com/article/1954/10/15/we-celebrate-edna-woolman-chases-60-years-at-vogue

CHAPTER

8 Press Releases and Event Management in the Fashion Industry

Learning Objectives

- Identify the historical development of press releases within the fashion industry.
- Examine the evolution of fashion events and their relationship with media and publicity.
- Analyze the role of early couturiers in shaping both fashion events and the practice of issuing press releases.
- Apply Goffman's dramaturgical theory to analyze how fashion events function as staged performances.
- Evaluate fashion events as sites for the display and exchange of cultural capital within the fashion industry.

Press Releases: A Historical Conversation Starter

In 2018, Rihanna launched a collection with Fenty, *Rihanna Savage x Fenty*. The collection promoted body positivity and inclusive prices, which were in line with Rihanna's values and public advocacy. Rihanna said to *Vogue*, 'I can only hope to encourage confidence and strength by showing lingerie in another light. You don't have to stick to one personality with lingerie; it's fun to play around. You can be cute and playful one week and a black widow next week. You can take risks with lingerie. I want people to wear Savage x Fenty and think, I'm a bad bitch. I want women to own their beauty' (Yotka, 2018, n.p.). The campaign was launched with a powerful press release promoting inclusivity and positive body image, thus achieving earned coverage by many fashion and cultural magazines such as *Vogue, Teen Vogue, Vanity Fair, Time magazine, Glamour,* etc. This shows the power of press releases to start a conversation and earn media coverage.

Fashion events and press releases have a distinctive purpose in the fashion industry. Press releases are a form of formal, written communication used to convey news, announcements, and brand perspectives to media and broader audiences. Events management, on the other hand, is a large part of the job due to increased reliance on organizing joint events with magazines and influencers, which fashion advertising and PR professionals have always done, but increasingly so since the rise of digital communication. Events

DOI: 10.4324/9781003515043-11

management includes coordinating and executing runway shows, product launches, and pop-ups, which showcase the brand's identity and create consumer engagement.

The high-visibility nature of the fashion industry means that events and press coverage can determine the brand's prestige and increase market success. The evolution of event management and press release strategies is linked to changes in media technologies, globalization of fashion markets, and changed social expectations. Fashion events and press releases are not just advertising or PR tools but also a cultural artifact that reflects broader social values, such as norms around beauty, luxury, and aspiration. Press releases were often, throughout history, handed out to journalists and editors as part of a press kit, a practice that continues up to this day, albeit in a multimedia format. In addition, press releases are inextricably linked to events where they have been historically used as a form of publicity.

THE INVERTED PYRAMID WRITING STYLE

The inverted pyramid is a foundational structure in news writing, also used for writing press releases to make PR content more appealing to journalists. The writing style focuses on providing the most essential information (who, what, when, where, why, and how), followed by background and additional details. This writing style ensures the reader receives the most relevant information even if they do not read the entire article (Scanlan, 2003). In the case of PR professionals, this writing style makes press releases publishable with minimum editing, and the inverted pyramid style draws attention from journalists, helping them quickly decide whether to pursue the story. From a sociological perspective, the inverted pyramid reflects broader institutional constraints in news production, which impede the work of journalists, such as tight deadlines, limited space, objectivity, efficiency (Tuchman, 1978), and, since digitalization, the lack of time for attention to details.

PRESS RELEASE WRITING FRAMEWORK

1. **Headline**
    - Catchy but clear: combine creativity with clarity.
    - Include brand name and core announcement (e.g., launch, collaboration, campaign).
    - Add context and value: one or two sentences expanding on the headline with a unique hook or angle.
2. **Dateline**
    - Format: CITY, COUNTRY – [Month, Day, Year]
3. **Lead Paragraph**
    - Core announcement: who, what, when, where, and why (the inverted pyramid)
    - Newsworthiness: focus on what's new, timely, or exclusive.

4. **Second Paragraph**
   - Brand mission and relevance: tie the news to brand values (e.g., sustainability, innovation, inclusivity).
   - Contextualize within industry trends: show why these matter in fashion now.
   - Fashion-specific knowledge (e.g., style, historical trend returning, brand innovation, etc.)
5. **Supporting Details**
   - Collection inspiration: theme, season, design notes, color palette.
   - Materials and process: sustainability or craftsmanship claims.
   - Designer/Founder Quotes
6. **Call to Action**
   - Where to find or purchase: Website, retail partners, event dates.
   - Launch timeline: include embargoes or preview access if needed.
7. **Boilerplate**
   - About the brand: 2–3 sentence summary of brand identity, founding date, key achievements, mission.
8. **Contact Information**
   - Media Contact Name
   - Email Address
   - Phone Number
   - Social Media Handles

Source: Authors' work. Adapted from PR Newswire (n.d.) and Merritt (2020)

Press Releases in the Fashion Industry

Before formal press releases, designers would privately share sketches or hold press previews, which were linked to early publications relying on personal relationships and the creation of an exclusive pipeline for brand information. Pre-1900s couture salons shared illustrated cards, fabric swatches, and handwritten show notes. For example, the House of Worth was showing designs on live models (Krick, 2000), which can be seen as a precursor to fashion shows. The House of Worth is also credited with being the first couture house to use living women as fashion models, which changed the practice from using mannequins – wooden dummies showcasing clothing (Evans, 2011). Worth produced drawings, photographs, and papers and gave them to the press, including lookbooks or photograph albums, along with press and textile samples, sketches of designs, and photograph packaging, precursors to press releases and press kits (Jisc Archives, n.d.). British designer Lucile, on the other hand, is credited with setting up 'mannequin parades', precursors to catwalks (Lawford, n.d.; ASU FIDM Museum, n.d.). Grand London ladies were invited to these shows, served tea, and a list of models and dresses that looked like a theater program (Lawford, n.d.), or a precursor to what later became a press kit.

In 1906, when Ivy Lee wrote a press release after a Pennsylvania railroad accident, which is commonly seen as the first press release (Seitel, 2017; Theaker & Yaxley, 2013; News Museum, n.d.), albeit some authors dispute this claim and argue that press releases existed earlier (Wilcox et al., 2015; Page et al., 2023), a modern press release as we know today was born. Lee's press release followed a nowadays commonly used template (headline, dateline, boilerplate), And this form of writing quickly became popular in the fashion industry. Press releases in the early fashion industry were typewritten, mailed, or telegraphed to news desks. For example, a New York-based publicist, Eleanor Lambert, was handing out press releases attached to the back of a photograph, and these documents outlined garment descriptions and seasons. The Hunt Museum has a photograph and a press release from Lambert. The black and white photograph features a model on Upper Mount Street, Dublin, and a handwritten press release statement is attached to the back of the photograph, written by Lambert. The description describes the clothes as 'Check-mate – low-placed, oversize patch pockets on a three-quarter coat in Irish hand-woven tweed is twinned with a black and white checked dress of Welsh fabric, casual costume designed by Sybil Connolly for Fall and Winter 1961' (Hunt Museum, n.d.). This is an early example of a press release, specific to the fashion industry and thus focusing on writing knowledgeable fashion content, which is a difference between conventional press release writing and press release writing in fashion. As the fashion industry grew, so did its publicity needs, which opened opportunities for PR practitioners. Already in the 1910s and 1920s, early couture publicity activities were visible, with designers such as Lucile courting American newspapers with descriptive line sheets and model photographs, and mannequin parades organized on an elevated stage, presented by young women selected by Lucile (Lawford, n.d.). With her publicity efforts, Lucile expanded her influence beyond Paris and London and elevated her designs to popularity in the US, thus becoming one of the first couturiers to become an international brand (Lawford, n.d.). She was also the first couturier to engage with media to promote her fashion, by writing weekly and monthly columns for *Harper's Bazaar* and *Good Housekeeping*, which started around 1910 (Lawford, n.d.). These media-related activities started to be used by designers generally, with a peak in popularity happening during the 1920s when designers started to court journalists and invite them to show, along with trying to give them materials that carefully crafted the image of the brand. However, putting on shows as a theatrical performance was central to gaining publicity while keeping the artistic component. This created a dual meaning to fashion events. Troy (2003) argued that events became 'a theatrical performance and a real-life event, an aestheticized production with aspirations to high culture on one hand and an opportunity for fashion marketing on the other' (p. 209).

Typed press-photo captions and one-page releases were common during the period from the 1930s to the 1960s. For example, Lambert's original press releases were single-spaced, typed, and stamped 'FOR IMMEDIATE RELEASE', with her New York mailing address (Tiffany, 2011). It was also common to send multi-page, posted press kits to foreign editors. This was done via cable/telegraph bulletins. A significant milestone in fashion press releases and events happened during the 1940s, when press weeks emerged. Publicist Eleanor Lambert gathered editors in New York for a press week while Paris was blocked because of the war in Europe. This activity institutionalized front-row seat assignments in fashion weeks and press kits. The press week later became the New York Fashion

Week (Berkeley, n.d.), and Lambert is known as a doyenne of fashion PR in the US. Lambert also helped establish the Council of Fashion Designers of America, for which she wrote press releases, as well as establishing many other fashion events that promoted the American fashion industry (Fine Collins, 2004; Mears, 2023).

Things changed in the late 20th century with the rise of globalization and the 24-hour news cycle, leading to the expansion of fashion weeks, which started to be hosted by many cities, increasing competition for media coverage. Press releases became polished and started to include professional photography, style guides, and brand statements. The 1980s and 1990s saw a rise in professionalizing PR, and established PR agencies started to offer fashion PR services more than ever (EPR Staff, 2025). In this period, press releases were also telegraphed. For example, Women's Wear Daily (WWD) cable bulletin sheets were typeset in New York right after show reports were cabled from Paris, and this was then rushed to US retailers and editors (for samples see Idea, n.d.).

Then came the digital era, which transformed press releases via email distribution, online pressrooms, and real-time social media announcements. This created a shift from purely text-based press releases to multimedia press kits containing images, videos, and behind-the-scenes footage. For example, during the first decade of the new millennium, 2000–2010, fashion houses launched lookbooks and shifted to storytelling using emails and sending the press file via email communication. From the 2010s onwards, an emphasis has been on livestreams and social media, which blurred lines because press releases are now part of a larger media kit that also includes embedded videos, shareable GIFs, hashtag schedules, and simultaneous global communication. Burberry became the first luxury brand to livestream a runway show in 2010 (Sullivan, 2010), and in 2020, they started to issue interactive Twitch press releases, merging traditional PR press releases with real-life videos (Burberry, 2020). From the 2020s onwards, digital showrooms became popular, along with lookbooks and 3-D garment files, pre-written social media copies, and content is now optimized for multimedia communication by media organizations, such as TikTok captions and Reels, because earned media is nowadays also influencer-driven.

Technology has driven changes in fashion PR and advertising, and while press releases and event management remain core aspects of fashion PR work, changes throughout the decades coincide with technological advancements. The fashion PR work thus went from PRs working with early 20th-century society editors, to mid-century glossy magazines, 1990s super-bloggers and trend sites, to today's micro-influencers. All these activities nowadays run concurrently, increasing workloads and skill demands on fashion PRs. Press releases remain important aspects of PR work, but they have moved ever more into storytelling. They keep the cultural role in telling a story, and not just what is new. They remain essential for fashion PR work, but now they are part of the PR kit bundles, which allow journalists and influencers to choose what they wish to use in their writing. Press releases shaped fashion history; looking at historical press releases paints a story of fashion and fashion PR developments.

Sociologically, press releases can be seen as an agenda-setting and framing aspect of fashion PR work because press releases shape how both journalists and audiences perceive brands, new collections, collaborations, and brand values. The reason fashion PR professionals can build an agenda with press releases is that press releases are generally used by powerful institutions to shape or build the media agenda, not just respond to it (Reese, 1991; Shoemaker & Reese, 1996). Editors and influencers who share this content and images shape and reshape these messages, which can reinforce brand narratives. Press releases are a good tool for articulating a designer's vision and reinforcing a brand's heritage and history. They can also be used for ethical and sustainable communication about brand strategies, which has become increasingly relevant. Press releases contribute to brand storytelling and image creation, particularly about craftsmanship, luxury, or innovation, which some brands romanticize, such as big designer brands with a long history (Chanel, Dior, etc.).

REFLECT

Drawing from figures like Eleanor Lambert, who helped professionalize American fashion PR in the mid-20th century, consider how press releases evolved from tightly controlled, typewritten statements sent to editors into today's fluid, multimedia announcements distributed across social platforms. How have these changes impacted the tone, format, and strategic purpose of press releases? Consider how publicists once controlled narratives through selective access, and how digital media has either democratized or diluted this process. You may compare a historical press release with a contemporary one, analyze how press releases have shaped public perception of fashion's role in society, or imagine how you would craft a campaign today using insights from PR history.

Fashion Events

The early 20th century saw the birth of fashion shows as we know them today. Before that, early 1900s Parisian couture houses (e.g., Worth) held private, invitation-only fashion showings of their latest collections to wealthy clients (Skov et al., 2009). The popularization of fashion shows was also exacerbated by the rise of department stores in the US and the UK, which started to host fashion shows to attract everyday customers, making fashion more accessible; however, these shows were not exclusive or intimate; instead, they were focused on entertainment and spectacle (Leach, 1984). During the mid-20th century, runway shows were popularized and professionalized, particularly after WWII and in fashion capitals such as Paris, Milan, London, and New York. New York Fashion Week, which started during the 1940s, was the first fashion week emerging from Lambert's press weeks (Berkeley, n.d.), but it gained popularity and influence during the 1970s. In the late 20th century, particularly during the 1980s and 1990s, there was a rise of supermodels, such as Naomi Campbell, Linda Evangelista, Cindy Crawford, and others, popularized by British *Vogue*'s iconic cover page (Crawford, 2016), which turned runway shows into media events, gaining global traction. Corporate sponsorships and big budgets followed and turned runway shows into spectacles. The period of the late 20th century also saw an expansion of fashion events to Asia, with major fashion brands hosting shows in cities including Tokyo, Hong Kong, and Shanghai.

In the 21st century, a digital revolution happened, which led to live streaming of runway shows and the rise of social media for engaging with the fashion industry, expanding the need for PR professionals. Fashion shows are nowadays often live-streamed, which gives immediate access to the runway show to global audiences. Beyond the traditional runway, brands now also engage with VR/AR, pop-up stories, and experiential marketing events (Boughlala & Smelik, 2024; AI Fashion Week, 2023), which contribute to the creativity of fashion PR work.

Sociologically speaking, events such as runway shows can be seen as cultural rituals where insiders, such as designers, editors, and influencers, and outsiders (audiences) construct trends and status. Goffman's ideas about performance can be applied here; events are staged, showcasing brand narratives and creating aspirations toward presented lifestyles. Goffman (1959) argued that social interaction is a form of dramaturgical performance with individuals managing their impressions to others, much like actors on a stage. Goffman's (1959) framework introduced the front stage concept that refers to the public space where individuals perform socially expected roles. The back stage is a private space where individuals step out of their roles and prepare for performance. In the context of fashion, the front stage would be a fashion show where models showcase collections and designers create a performance asserting their legacy and fashion as art, while the back stage would be what happens behind the scenes when events are planned. Therefore, in Goffman's terms, fashion events become a form of impression management where designers use clothing, models, and setting to shape perceptions of their brands.

Attendance at high-profile events, such as fashion week in a major fashion city, can also be seen as a marker of cultural capital (Bourdieu, 1986) because this showcases one's status and social networks. Cultural capital can be seen as embodied, knowledge, practices, and affiliations that present a social advantage within a given field (Bourdieu, 1984), in this case, fashion, because having an invitation to attend a prestigious fashion event turns into symbolic capital for influence, relevance, as well as career progression in fashion. Equally, having access to invite-only events or major fashion weeks, beyond access, signals also cultivated taste, which increases the social legitimacy of the attendee. Entwistle and Rocamora (2006) thus described fashion events as places where industry professionals perform and exchange cultural capital through theatrical representation and appearance, which articulates fashion capital, position, and status in the field.

REFLECT

Choose a fashion campaign and analyze it through Goffman's lens. Answer the following questions: What is the front stage in this campaign? Where and how is the performance happening (ad visuals, press events, social media)? What could the back stage look like? Consider production choices, team roles, model preparation, or strategy meetings. How is the brand or individual practicing impression management? Think about clothing, posture, slogans, tone, or curated environments. What identity or role is being performed? How does it align with or challenge audience expectations?

DISCUSSION QUESTIONS

Press Releases

- What role did press releases play in reinforcing gatekeeping structures in the mid-20th-century fashion industry? How did they shape which designers, trends, or models received media attention?
- How have press releases evolved from tools of institutional communication to instruments of brand storytelling in the digital era?
- How do fashion press releases contribute to the construction of identity, aspiration, and taste? Can they be analyzed as texts of symbolic consumption?

Fashion Event Management

- Fashion shows were once exclusive industry events. With the rise of livestreaming and social media, how has the meaning and purpose of these events shifted?
- How do fashion events reproduce or challenge social hierarchies? Who is given visibility or access, and how are audiences curated?
- How could Bourdieu's concept of cultural capital help us understand who gets invited to fashion events, or how fashion PR manages associations with taste, status, and distinction?
- In what ways do high-profile fashion events like the Met Gala or Paris Fashion Week serve as sites for the accumulation and display of cultural capital?
- How do invitations, guest lists, and seating arrangements at fashion events reflect and reinforce social hierarchies within the fashion industry?
- How did Eleanor Lambert's founding of New York Fashion Week in 1943 transform the fashion industry's relationship with the media and the public?
- In what ways did this event shift fashion from an elite, closed-door practice to a more organized and public-facing industry? What parallels can be drawn between Lambert's early shows and today's global fashion weeks?

Press Releases and Fashion Events Management

- How do press releases shape media narratives before, during, and after fashion events?
- In what ways do press releases and fashion events function as complementary tools for brand storytelling?
- How do they each contribute differently to the construction of brand identity and audience engagement?
- Can a fashion event be successful without a press release?
- How does the press release act as a form of narrative control over unpredictable or chaotic elements of live fashion events?
- With the rise of digital platforms, do press releases still matter in the context of fashion events?
- Are influencer posts, live tweets, and visual media replacing traditional press releases, or simply reshaping them?
- How can the relationship between press releases and fashion events be understood through a sociological lens? What social meanings are constructed or reinforced through their coordination?

References

AI Fashion Week. (2023). *AI Fashion Week.* Season 1 Summary at Spring (NYC), 20–21 April. Retrieved from https://fashionweek.ai/season-1/#:~:text=With%20over%20350%20submissions%20to,submissions%20from%20around%20the%20world

ASU FIDM Museum. (n.d.). *Lucile.* Arizona State University, Herberger Institute for Design and Arts, ASU FIDM Museum. Retrieved from https://asufidmmuseum.asu.edu/learn/articles/lucile

Berkeley, B. (n.d.). Eleanor Lambert: American Fashion's Pioneer. *W magazine.* Retrieved from https://www.thewonline.com/article/eleanor-lambert-american-fashions-pioneer?

Boughlala, A., & Smelik, A. (2024). Tracing the History of Digital Fashion. *Clothing and Textiles Research Journal, 43*(3), 1–16. https://doi.org/10.1177/0887302X241283504

Bourdieu, P. (1984). *Distinction: A Social Critique of the Judgement of Taste.* Cambridge, MA: Harvard University Press.

Bourdieu, P. (1986). The Forms of Capital. In Richardson, J.G. (ed), *Handbook of Theory and Research for the Sociology of Education.* New York: Greenwood Press (pp. 241–258).

Burberry. (2020). *Burberry is the first luxury brand to partner with Twitch to livestream its fashion show.* Burberry corporate website, September 14. Retrieved from https://www.burberryplc.com/news/corporate/2020/burberry-is-first-luxury-brand-to-partner-with-twitch-to-livestr?

Crawford, C. (2016). The Inside Story: The Vogue Supermodel Cover. *Vogue*, September 13. Retrieved from https://www.vogue.co.uk/article/peter-lindbergh-vogue-supermodel-cover-story

Entwistle, J., & Rocamora, A. (2006). The field of fashion materialized: A study of London Fashion Week. *Sociology, 40*(4), 735–751. https://doi.org/10.1177/0038038506065158

EPR Staff (2025). The Evolution of Apparel Public Relations: Crafting Stories Beyond the Fabric. *Everything PR News,* May 24. Retrieved from https://everything-pr.com/the-evolution-of-apparel-public-relations-crafting-stories-beyond-the-fabric/?

Evans, C. (2011). The Ontology of the Fashion Model. *AA Files*, 63. Retrieved from https://www.readingdesign.org/fashion-model

Fine Collins, A. (2004). The Lady, the List, the Legacy. *Vanity Fair,* May 1. Retrieved from https://www.vanityfair.com/news/2004/04/eleanor-lambert200404?srsltid=AfmBOooJO4B8pZAPrJ4yV3QGUvUtoW4oXb51Wq61jvBaUYPBf0GcATJe&

Goffman, I. (1959). *The Presentation of Self in Everyday Life.* Harpswell, ME: Anchor.

Hunt Museum. (n.d.). *Black and White Photograph, Checkmate.* Retrieved from https://www.huntmuseum.com/explore/item/fc675a6d-a209-33b0-9d69-ff28d076b637/?pos=2408&s%3D%26filter%5Bmultimedia.%40type%5D%5B%5D%3Dimage=

Idea. (n.d.). *Four issues of WWD cable bulletins.* Retrieved from https://www.ideanow.online/wwd.html?

Jisc Archives. (n.d.). *House of Worth (1825–1952).* Retrieved from https://archiveshub.jisc.ac.uk/search/archives/86e442ee-7044-3acb-b33b-176b170d6f04

Krick, J. (2000). Charles Frederick Worth (1825–1895) and the House of Worth. *Heilbrunn Timeline of Art History.* New York: The Metropolitan Museum of Art. Retrieved from http://www.metmuseum.org/toah/hd/wrth/hd_wrth.htm

Lawford, C. (n.d.). *Lucile, the first international couturier.* Fashion Tours London. Retrieved from https://fashiontourslondon.co.uk/kate-reily-bodices/

Leach, W. R. (1984). Transformations in a Culture of Consumption: Women and Department Stores, 1890–1925. *The Journal of American History,* 71, 319–342.

Mears, P. (2023). *The CFDA 1962–2012.* January 1. Retrieved from https://cfda.com/news-insight/the-cfda-1962-2012/?

Merritt, T. (2020). *Press Release Writing 101.* Public Relations Society of America (PRSA), January 13. Retrieved from https://progressions.prsa.org/index.php/2020/01/13/press-release-writing/

News Museum. (n.d.). *The First Press Release.* Retrieved from https://www.newsmuseum.pt/en/spin-wall/first-press-release?

Page, T.G., Wilson, C., & Adams, E.E. (2023). Rethinking the start date for media relations and press releases: The peace movement of the 1800s. *Public Relations Review,* 50, 102409.

PR Newswire. (n.d.). How to Write a Press Release: Tips and Best Practices. Retrieved from https://www.prnewswire.com/resources/articles/how-to-write-a-press-release-tips-and-best-practices/

Reese, S.D. (1991). Setting the Media's Agenda: A Power Balance Perspective. *Communication Yearbook*, 14, 309–340.

Scanlan, C. (2003). Writing from the Top Down: Pros and Cons of the Inverted Pyramid. *Poynter,* June 20. Retrieved from https://www.poynter.org/reporting-editing/2003/writing-from-the-top-down-pros-and-cons-of-the-inverted-pyramid/

Seitel, F.P. (2017). *Practice of Public Relations.* Longman: Pearson Education.

Shoemaker, P., & Reese, S. (1996). *Mediating the Message in the 21st Century: A Media Sociology Perspective.* New York: Routledge.

Skov, L., Skjold, E., Moeran, B., Larsen, F., & Csaba, F. (2009). *The Fashion Show as an Art Form.* Copenhagen: Department of Intercultural Communication and Management, Copenhagen Business School. Retrieved from https://research.cbs.dk/en/publications/the-fashion-show-as-an-art-form

Sullivan, R. (2010). Walk Boldly Into the Future: Burberry Streams Show Tomorrow Live In 3D. *Vogue,* February 22. Retrieved from https://www.vogue.com/article/vd-walk-boldly-into-the-future-burberry-streams-show-tomorrow-live-in-3d?

Theaker, A. & Yaxley, H. (2013). *The Public Relations Strategic Toolkit: An Essential Guide to Successful Public Relations Practice* (1st ed.). London: Routledge.

Tiffany, J. (2011). *Eleanor Lambert: Still Here.* New York: Pointed Leaf Press.

Troy, N.J. (2003). *Couture Culture: A Study in Modern Art and Fashion.* Cambridge, MA: MIT Press.

Tuchman, G. (1978). *Making News: A Study in the Construction of Reality.* Los Angeles, California: Free Press.

Wilcox, D.L., Cameron, G.T., & Reber, B. (2015). *Public Relations Strategies and Tactics* (11th ed.). Pearson.

Yotka, S. (2018). Everything You Need to Know About Rihanna's Savage x Fenty Launch. *Vogue*, May 9. Retrieved from https://www.vogue.com/article/rihanna-savage-x-fenty-lingerie-launch-details?

PART 3
ADVERTISING AND PR IN HAUTE COUTURE AND LUXURY READY-TO-WEAR

CHAPTER 9

Spotlight on Style and Influence: A Look at Histories and Campaigns Shaping Legacies of Haute Couture and Luxury Ready-to-Wear Houses

Learning Objectives

- Analyze the historical milestones of haute couture and luxury ready-to-wear fashion designers and understand how their personal philosophies and cultural contexts influenced their brand identity.
- Identify major advertising campaigns and PR strategies used by iconic designers and assess their impact on brand perception and consumer behavior.
- Compare and contrast the promotional approaches of different designers across time.
- Interpret fashion advertising and media coverage as cultural texts that reflect and construct notions of identity, status, and style.
- Apply concepts of brand storytelling and image management to case studies of designer-led fashion houses.
- Critically assess earned, paid, and owned media strategies employed by fashion designers to build cultural capital and maintain relevance.

The Cultural Capital of Luxury Fashion and the Distinctiveness of Its Advertising and PR

In Apple's series The New Look, Lucien Lelong (played by John Malkovich), head of the Lelong haute couture house and the president of the trade union of haute couture (*Chambre Syndicale de la Haute Couture*), presents Christian Dior (played by Ben Mendelsohn), at the time a designer in the House of Lelong holding a doll constructed of bent wire. Lelong says, 'It's the future of French fashion'. *Théâtre de la Mode* (Theater of Fashion), presented in spring 1945 after the end of WWII and the liberation of Paris, was an extraordinary moment because French designers presented French designs on dolls to account for the lack of materials after WWII, while showcasing that the French fashion industry was not dead. Over 60 designers, including Balenciaga, Schiaparelli, and Dior, created miniature haute couture outfits for 27-inch wire mannequins. These dolls were displayed in a theatrical set in Paris and then sent on tour across Europe and the US (Fischenich et al., 2000; Clarkson, 2011). *Théâtre de la Mode* was a powerful act of cultural diplomacy. It showed the resilience of French fashion and restored its prestige by reminding

DOI: 10.4324/9781003515043-13

the world of the ability of haute couture to delight audiences. The event also showed how storytelling, artisanry, and the spectacle of haute couture are central to haute couture's public image, and how fashion's survival depends on the use of excellent public relations.

Advertising and public relations in haute couture and luxury ready-to-wear are not focused on product promotion, like retailer fashion. Instead, haute couture and luxury ready-to-wear brands focus on strategic advertising and PR to build and reinforce the brand's cultural capital. These brands are focused on creating lifestyle, aspiration, and exclusivity, and they do so by creating an image of heritage, legacy, rarity, artisanry, and prestige. Unlike retail fashion brands, haute couture and luxury ready-to-wear sell identity, status, and emotion, not products focused on practical use. As a result, communication of haute couture and ready-to-wear brands is often highly curated, and every runway show, campaign, or editorial contributes toward creating long-term narratives about craftsmanship, heritage, legacy, and aesthetic vision. To achieve this, many luxury brands engage in a variety of communication strategies such as documentary films and film-like campaigns, usually of high-quality production, behind-the-scenes content, spectacular runway shows, and various collaborations with carefully selected celebrities who serve not just as promoters of the brand but also as brand ambassadors. At the same time, many big designer houses create mystique by limiting accessibility, inviting only selected journalists and editors to runway shows, and controlling brand image. This chapter explores how haute couture and luxury ready-to-wear brands balance visibility and exclusivity, and how their advertising and PR strategies historically evolved to account for the rise in digital communication.

Understanding the haute couture and luxury ready-to-wear designers and their approach to advertising and PR is essential for anyone wanting to enter the fashion industry. To work in the fashion industry, one needs to have an understanding and appreciation of the deeper cultural meanings behind luxury brands' advertising and PR strategies, not just grasp the mechanics of promotion. Understanding cultural meanings behind luxury brands' communication helps in understanding how luxury brands accumulate and sustain cultural capital, and how they position themselves as leaders in the fashion industry. A designer's personal history, aesthetic vision, and values are often an essential part of the brand's identity and storytelling, and designers influence how collections are presented, who represents the brand, and how the public perceives the brand. For fashion communicators, recognizing the interplay between personal narratives, heritage branding, and aspirational communication is essential to craft campaigns that resonate with both elite and aspirational customers.

The House of Chanel

The House of Chanel was founded by Gabrielle Coco Chanel, a French designer born in 1883, who revolutionized global fashion and turned it into the fashion we know today. Chanel's vision for fashion and some of her contributions to fashion innovations stem from her background of growing up in an orphanage in France. Her first fashion decisions were influenced by the gowns nuns were wearing, which translated to popularizing the color black in her fashion, and contrasting black with white (Shipton, 2011; Chanel.com, n.d.-). Previously, black was only the color of grief. Other colors of Chanel include gold, beige, and red (Inside Chanel – The Colors of Chanel). Chanel is also credited with introducing the little black dress (LBD) in 1926 (DiDonato, 2015), which was labeled as the Ford of dresses (Bott, 2007), and popularizing women's trousers in the 1920s. Her tweed and jersey suits are often seen as iconic and timeless, and forever associated with Chanel, who created the suit and wore it as early as 1913. She called the suit 'a fashion statement of the century' (Bott, 2007, p. 12). The iconic suit has a jacket and a skirt always cut from the same fabric to avoid differences in material, and it is a symbol of French elegance (Bott, 2007). The suit is,

> constructed according to a precise code: strict lines, a fitted cut articulated at exactly the right place to allow ease of movement; braid trimming on the jacket; sleeves fitted precisely at shoulder level; real pockets; an enduring range of colours – being, navy blue, black, as well as pink, cherry red or pale green; a consistent choice of fabrics – jersey and tweeds or daring combinations (Bott, 2007, p. 12).

Coco Chanel took inspiration from masculine clothes, which resulted in the popularization of trousers (Bott, 2007). She also popularized fake pearls, jewelry, and suntan, the latter normally being a class issue. In Edwardian times, ladies were wearing umbrellas to protect their skin from the sun, while working-class women had a suntan, but Chanel changed that. Chanel's focus on fashion was simplicity, and she also introduced this philosophy into design in Chanel No.5, a signature perfume of the House of Chanel up to the present day. She started her work in horse races in France, which was the beginning of the trend-setting practice in French fashion. She opened her first shop in Paris in 1910 on Rue Cambon, and in 1913, a second shop was opened in Deauville, a horse racing area. In 1915, she opened a shop in Biarritz, also a horse racing area (Inside Chanel – Biarritz). Indeed, a lot of haute couture fashion origins lie within horse racing and the aristocracy that attended those races. It was only in the 20th century that fashion democratized and became available to all, in large part thanks to Chanel and the rise of the department stores in the US.

La Belle Époque in France was, like Edwardian fashion, centered on big dresses, complicated designs, corsets, and big hats. Chanel was on the other side of that, focusing on a new, simple, and practical style, which changed fashion forever. Chanel famously said, 'nothing is more beautiful than freedom of the body' (Bott, 2007, p. 28) and 'simplicity is the keynote of all true elegance' (Samaha & Hyde, 2021, n.p.). Chanel also briefly designed for Hollywood films and lived in England during the late 1920s, but neither relocation lasted long, and she returned to Paris, where she lived in the Hotel Ritz (Bott, 2007). Camelia was one of her favorite flowers, and this features in Chanel fashion. For example, when one orders an haute couture item from Chanel, they will receive the item in a box, which is black and white, the signature colors of Chanel, along with a certificate of authenticity and camelia flowers (Inside Chanel – The Camelia; Inside Chanel – Haute Couture). Tweed and jersey suits, camelias, pearls, jewelry, a color palette contrasting black and white along with gold, beige, and red, are the signature of the House of Chanel up to the present day.

During WWII, Chanel, like other designers in France, had to close her shops, but she managed to save Chanel No. 5 production, which continued during the war years. After the war, she retired but then came out of retirement because of Dior's New Look, which she saw as a step back from women's empowerment that her simple, practical, and masculine-inspired fashion achieved (Miller, 2024). She returned with a new collection in 1955, which was a success, particularly Chanel's iconic 2.55 bag (Forsberg, 2024), which

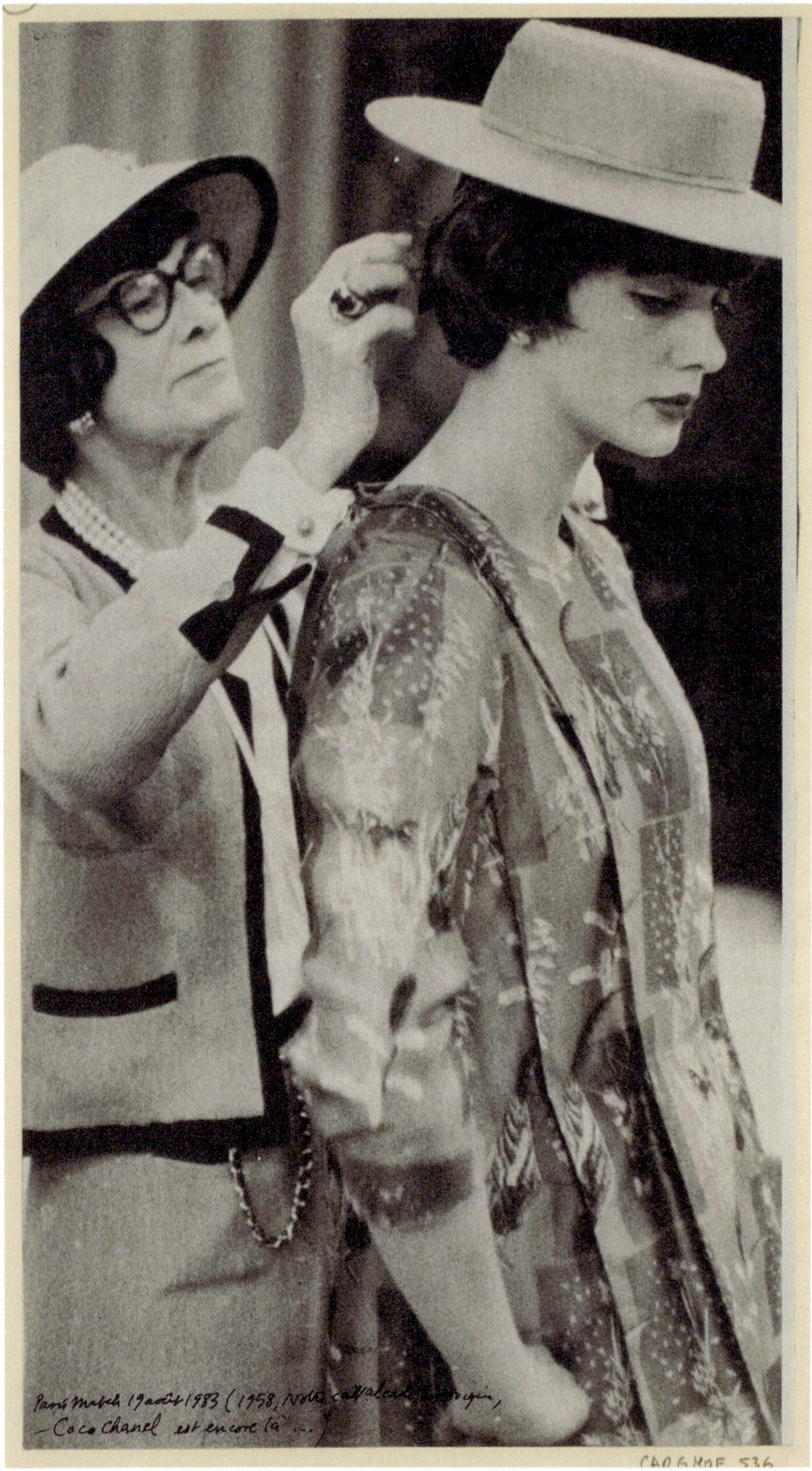

Figure 9.1 Coco Chanel in 1983 wearing iconic Chanel tweed suit
Musée Carnavalet, Histoire de Paris

to this day is copied by many designers. Chanel's philosophy can be summarized through her famous statement, 'Fashion changes but style endures' (Samaha & Hyde, 2021, n.p.). Chanel's silhouette was fluid and androgynous (Pike, 2020).

She died in 1971 and was succeeded by Karl Lagerfeld, who had served as a creative director for 36 years, alongside establishing and managing his label. *Vogue* said about his work for Chanel,

> Upon assuming the reins in 1983, Lagerfeld swiftly revived Chanel, reinterpreting the house founder's iconic tweed skirt suits, little black dresses, and quilted handbags. He did it via the lens of hip-hop one season and California surfer chicks the next—he was a pop culture savant—without ever forgetting what the revolutionary Coco stood for: independence, freedom, and modernity (Phelps, 2019, n.p.).

The style of the House of Chanel remains focused on suits (tweed and jersey), colors of Chanel, LBDs, jewelry, and camelia flowers, and the dominant silhouette is still masculine-inspired and focused on comfort and practicality. With this, the brand celebrates and continues the legacy of their founder, and uses this legacy and heritage in their advertising and PR.

REFLECT

Watch Chanel runways, specifically the latest haute couture fall/winter and the latest ready-to-wear fall/winter. You can find these runways on Chanel's YouTube channel. When watching shows, pay attention to the colors of the collection, tweed jackets, women's suits, and black dresses. Analyze shows and new collections in line with what you know about the legacy of Chanel and their contributions to innovations in fashion. Consider how new collections draw from Chanel's legacy designs, to what extent collections also draw from styles from various decades, and what innovative items you can recognize in a new collection.

Chanel's Advertising and PR

Chanel's advertising and PR efforts are centered on narrative-driven campaigns, which can be visual, such as The One That I Want, Chanel No. 5 campaign, or with a voiceover, such as the Inside Chanel campaign. Chanel focuses on narrative-driven campaigns because they do not sell products directly. Instead, they focus on building a legacy through narratives, visual communication, and emotional stories that reinforce brand identity. Campaigns like The One That I Want are produced as short films rather than standard adverts, and use cinematography to explore themes connected to Chanel's legacy and the brand's understanding and vision of silhouette and femininity. In the Inside Chanel campaign, most chapters go back to Gabrielle Coco Chanel and focus on the storytelling of her legacy through the life, style, vision, and work of their founder. This emphasizes the legacy and history of the brand. Chanel uses an emotional approach to advertising and PR by appealing to feelings over function, attempting to emotionally connect audiences

Figure 9.2 An advert for Chanel No.5 from 1923

Musée Carnavalet, Histoire de Paris

Figure 9.3 A black and white advert of iconic Chanel suits
Musée Carnavalet, Histoire de Paris

with the brand before the product; therefore, the brand is at the center stage, product is backstage. Celebrities are used as a muse and embodiment of a brand rather than for mere endorsement. Nicole Kidman, Audrey Tautou, Gisele Bündchen, and Kristen Stewart are the embodiment of the brand, not just consumers. This is also reinforced through fashion shows, interviews, and behind-the-scenes content, which is often published on the brand's YouTube channel.

Finally, luxury is emphasized, but not in a way that could be perceived as overly communicated or vulgar. Chanel avoids overexposure and focuses on high-profile, high-production campaigns, released selectively. For example, the Inside Chanel campaign started in 2012, and it is still ongoing. Therefore, there is no saturation with communication content from Chanel, which preserves the cultural capital and mystique of the brand. Chanel can be seen as a master of advertising and PR, particularly the iconic Inside Chanel campaign. The brand blends cinematographic storytelling, emotional symbolism, and founder's history, heritage, and legacy to transform Chanel products into cultural artifacts through minimal but powerful advertising and PR campaigns, which craft the image of the brand as exclusive, elegant, timeless, and rooted in emotion, legacy, and rebellion that transformed fashion into the industry we know today. Chanel uses high-art collaborations, high-quality films, selective media partnerships, and narrative-focused campaigns to preserve its status as an haute couture legacy brand.

Table 9.1 provides an analysis of Chanel's notable advertising and PR campaigns, starting from the 1920s when Chanel No. 5 was launched.

Table 9.1 Chanel's Advertising and PR: A Historical Summary and Analysis of Notable Campaigns and Initiatives

PERIOD	NOTABLE CAMPAIGNS	MEDIUM	STRATEGY AND MESSAGES	SOURCES
1920s	Launch of Chanel No. 5 in 1921	Chanel hosted a party and sprayed perfume around the table Boutique on the Rue Cambon launch and in-store promotion	• Positioning designer and her products through exclusivity and luxury	History.com (2021)
1930s	Print ads in the *New York Times* (1924) *Vogue* and *Harper's Bazaar*'s features from 1920s and beyond	Print advertising	• Elegant minimalism • Subtle expansion into mass advertising	*New York Times* print adverts, 16 Dec 1924, 10 June 1934 *Vogue* historical archive *Harper's Bazaar* historical archive
1940s	WWII gifting perfumes to US soldiers	Word-of-mouth	• Resilience and loyalty prestige	The Land of Desire (2020)
1950s	Marilyn Monroe's Chanel quote (1952) in *Life* magazine	Earned media coverage	• Celebrity endorsement • Earned publicity and media coverage	Shapouri (2008) Anbouba (2024) Inside Chanel – chapter 2 – Marilyn and No.5
1950s–1960s	'Every Woman Alive Wants Chanel No.5' print adverts	Magazine adverts	• Luxury • Femininity • Prestige • Legacy and heritage assertation	The Last Fashion Bible (2021)

(*Continued*)

Table 9.1 Continued

PERIOD	NOTABLE CAMPAIGNS	MEDIUM	STRATEGY AND MESSAGES	SOURCES
1970s–1980s	TV adverts directed by Ridley Scott Adverts by Catherine Deneueve	TV adverts	• Surreal visuals • Perfume as high art	La Piscine / Share the Fantasy (1979)
				Chanel N°5, the 1982 Film by Ridley Scott: L'invitation au Rêve, le Jardin – Chanel Fragrance(1982) The Last Fashion Bible (2021)
1990	Egoiste perfume launch	TV adverts and event promotion	• Daring, avant-garde • Masculinity	AdLand TV advert (1990)
1990s	Andy Warhol No.5 pop art – Chanel purchased rights to use as adverts	Art campaigns, high-fashion print	• Heritage merged with pop art	The Last Fashion Bible (2021)
1998	No.5 film starring Estella Warren	Digital films Now also on YouTube	• Hollywood style • Luxury romance • High-quality production	Chanel N°5, the 1998 film by Luc Besson, with Estella Warren: Le Loup – Chanel Fragrance (1998)
2004	No.5 film starring Nicole Kidman	Cinema, TV, digital	• Hollywood style • Luxury romance • Largest fragrance advertising budget • High-quality production	Chanel N°5, the film with Nicole Kidman – Chanel Fragrance (2004)

(Continued)

Table 9.1 Continued

PERIOD	NOTABLE CAMPAIGNS	MEDIUM	STRATEGY AND MESSAGES	SOURCES
2011	No.5 film starring Audrey Tautou	Digital films Global print	• Intimate storytelling, modern identity • Cinematographic approach to filming	Chanel N°5, the film Train de Nuit with Audrey Tautou – Chanel Fragrance (2011)
2012	No. 5 film starring Brad Pitt	Digital films	• Modern identity • Cinematographic approach to filming • Celebrity endorsement	Chanel N°5, the film with Brad Pitt: There You Are – Chanel Fragrance (2012)
2012	Inside Chanel Campaign (2012-)	Digital films, (YouTube, website)	• Intimate storytelling • Founder legacy • Heritage • Symbolic visuals • Dramatic narratives	Inside Chanel (2012–) Chanel.com (n.d.)
2014	No. 5 film starring Gisele Bündchen	Digital films (YouTube)	• Hollywood style • High-quality production • Luxury romance • Introducing a new Chanel woman who works, had a child, and a relationship • Child features in the campaign	Chanel N°5, the film with Gisele Bündchen, Michiel Huisman, and Lo-Fang – Chanel Fragrance (2014)
2014	L'Instant Chanel film	Digital films (YouTube)	• Hollywood style • High-production • Luxury storytelling	L'instant Chanel, The Chanel Moment: Film 5 – Chanel Watches (2014)
2021	Chanel Connects	Podcast (website and YouTube)	• Interviews and storytelling • Promoting culture and arts	Chanel Connects (2021–) – Chanel YouTube channel

(Continued)

Table 9.1 Continued

PERIOD	NOTABLE CAMPAIGNS	MEDIUM	STRATEGY AND MESSAGES	SOURCES
2021	The Chanel Culture Fund	Digital videos, YouTube	• Storytelling, promotion of arts and culture • Global partnership program promoting and awarding arts and culture organizations (museums, curators, artists and cultural institutions)	The Chanel Culture Fund (2021–) – Chanel YouTube channel
2024	No. 5 See You at 5 film	Digital video, YouTube	• Symbolic visuals • Artistic, high-production film • Cinematographic approach to filming	A rendez-vous (2024)
2024	Bleu de Chanel film	Digital video, YouTube	• Modern identity • Expansion to men's fragnance	Bleu De Chanel, the Martin Scorsese film starring Timothée Chalamet (2024)
2024	Chanel and Literature	Digital video, YouTube, interviews and endorsements	Storytelling, brand ambassador endorsement, writers' endorsements/ collaboration High-production videos, interviews	Chanel and Literature (2024–) – Chanel YouTube channel

Source: Author's work

DISCUSSION QUESTIONS

- In what ways does Chanel's founder, Gabrielle Coco Chanel, continue to shape the brand's image today?

- What does timelessness mean in the context of Chanel, and how is it constructed through their advertising and PR?
- Chanel campaigns are often cinematic and narrative-driven (e.g., The One That I Want or No. 5 The Film). How does this differ from conventional fashion advertising?
- What are the emotional themes Chanel frequently explores in its campaigns?
- What does Chanel's preference for short films and symbolic storytelling reveal about its brand values?
- How does Chanel use celebrities in comparison to other brands?
- How does Chanel's use of famous figures like Marilyn Monroe contribute to legacy building?
- How does the Inside Chanel video series function as both PR and brand education?
- In what ways does Chanel use visual codes (color, symbols, clothing items) to reinforce identity without using direct advertising language?

The House of Dior

The House of Dior was founded by Christian Dior, a French designer who created the 1947 New Look. Dior, in some ways, can be seen as a direct opposite to Chanel's masculine-inspired, practical fashion. Dior was always focused on femininity, which was an initial inspiration for the much-celebrated New Look of 1947, which forever placed Dior on the fashion map. The New Look was inspired by *La Belle Époque*, a more conservative fashion of the 1900s focused on emphasizing a nipped-in waist, which appears in tiny, bell-shaped, full, voluminous skirts that communicate soft femininity and emphasize the feminine hourglass silhouette (Sinclair, 2012; Fischenich et al., 2000; Lehnert, 2000; Clarkson, 2011). The 1947 New Look was a stark contrast to the practical, Chanel-inspired fashion of the 1940s period, when there was also a lack of materials due to war rationing, and when there was less emphasis on women's silhouette due to Chanel's influence. Dior's collection was seen as,

> truly feminine, lavish and extremely luxurious fashion accentuated women's curves …. The new line was very different from the severity of prewar and wartime fashion. Full, calf-length skirts, wasp waists, tight tops, padded hips, and a gently sloping shoulder line were characteristic of the new femininity that was reminiscent of the 19-century role models: delicate women who did not have to work (or at least did not look as if they did), who spent their days at leisure making themselves look beautiful, and who indulged themselves and lived a life of luxury (Fischenich et al., 2000, p. 43).

Fischenich et al. (2000) argued that the new focus on fashion and femininity was not a coincidence because people wanted to push war memories aside, and Dior's haute couture stood for something new and represented a life people wanted after the misery of war, which also included a 'revival of traditional, bourgeois values and gender images which suddenly seemed to promise security after all the destruction' (Fischenich et al., p. 43). However, apart from feminists and Chanel, who criticized Dior's New Look, Texan

Mrs. Warren J. Woodward formed the Little-Above-the-Knee Club to express dissatisfaction with Dior's wasteful skirt styles, which used a lot of material. This group did not gain mass popularity, but they presented important grassroots opposition to the mainstream fashion because they organized protests. Woodward said, in 1947,

> I didn't feel like throwing away an entire wardrobe .... I thought a lot of women might feel the same way and now I know they do .... We are going to wear the clothes that look best on us – styles we have a right to choose. Why should a girl cover up her legs – they may be her best selling point (*The Courier Mail*, 1947).

Figure 9.4 Christian Dior making haute couture
Musée Carnavalet, Histoire de Paris

Figure 9.5 The Bar suit, a hallmark of Christian Dior's New Look
©Adrien Dirand, reprinted with permission

Figure 9.6 La Gallerie Dior, an exhibition portraying iconic interpretations of the New Look

©Adrien Dirand, reprinted with permission

However, Dior was the most influential designer during the 1940s and 1950s because the popularity of the New Look (Heyl, 2016) spilled over to the 1950s. This look became a central aesthetic feature of the House of Dior and a historical legacy. The House of Dior is still focused on femininity and at least slightly emphasizing waist, something that commonly features in Dior designs regardless of who the head designer is.

Dior was born in 1905 in Normandy, France. He moved to Paris in 1911, where he worked in diplomacy and as an art gallery owner. However, while he initially had support from his father in owning an art gallery, the sudden death of his mother and brother led to a family collapse, resulting in a gallery closure. This prompted Dior to start selling sketches to couturiers, and he landed a first job as an assistant couturier, a career which was interrupted with the onset of WWII (Pochna, 1994). During the occupation of Paris, Dior started to work for couturier Lucien Lelong, who was also the president of the *Chambre Syndicale de la Haute Couture* (Pochna, 1994). After the war, Dior was invited to revive the Philippe et Gaston clothing company, which became the House of Dior. The House of Dior was decorated in white and grey, Dior's favorite colors, and these colors are to this day colors of Dior along with soft pink. Dior wrote about colors in his biography, saying these colors and his affection toward them are linked to his mother's decorations from their childhood home, *Les Rhumbs,* soft pink and grey gravel (Dior, 1957[1956]).

The iconic New Look was influenced by Dior's favorite colors and *La Belle Époque* ideal of long skirts, tiny waist, and beautiful fabrics, presenting a fashion cycle with Edwardian/*La Belle Époque* style returning in the late 1940s. This style is known to be influenced by the memory of Dior's mother and the period of the 1900s, where New Look-like fashion was promoted and regularly worn. The New Look was seen as a symbol of youth, hope, and the future, albeit some criticized it as a return to conservatism, which prompted Chanel to return from retirement (Miller, 2024; Baker, 2002). However, like Chanel, Dior's designs and styles are also marked by early influence, in this case from his mother, showing how fashion, even as artistic as haute couture, is fundamentally influenced by designers' personal stories, thus warranting studying designers and their histories, along with histories of their most notable designs. Dior justified his feminine and lavish designs, also criticized because of excessive use of materials by saying, 'Temperamentally, I am reactionary … we were just emerging from poverty-stricken, parsimonious era, obsessed with ration books and clothes coupons: it was only natural that my creations should take the form of a reaction against this' (cited from Sinclair, 2012, p. 28). *Harper's Bazaar*'s legendary editor-in-chief, Carmel Snow, named his first big collection the New Look by saying, 'My dear Christian, your dresses have such a New Look!' (Dior La Galerie, n.d./n.p.).

Christian Dior had famous assistants, such as Pierre Cardin, Yves Saint Laurent, John Galliano, and Raf Simons, who all also created their own successful labels and made a name for themselves. In 2016, Maria Grazia Chiuri was appointed as the first woman creative director of the House of Dior. In 2025, Jonathan Anderson was named as the new creative director of Dior, which presents a turning point in the House of Dior because this is also the first time since Christian Dior that one person is in charge of all House collections – women's, men's, and haute couture (Dior La Galerie, n.d.). All Dior designers followed the style of the House of Dior, apart from Beatnik-influenced

Yves Saint Laurent, who almost destroyed Dior in 1960 (Clarkson, 2011). Chiuri also followed Dior's design while also introducing feminist slogan shirts into collections, which resulted in successful advertising and PR. Christian Dior prematurely died in 1957, leaving forever open the question of the further fashion impact the House of Dior could have made on the fashion industry had Dior lived longer and further developed the New Look. In 1997, a Christian Dior Museum was opened in his childhood home, *Les Rhumbs,* Granville, Normandy.

REFLECT

Watch Dior runways, specifically the latest haute couture fall/winter and the latest ready-to-wear fall/winter. You can find these runways on Dior's YouTube channel. When watching shows, pay attention to the colors of the collection, waistlines on dresses, silhouette shapes, and luxury skirts. Analyze shows and new collections in line with what you know about the legacy of Dior and his contributions to innovations in fashion. Consider how new collections draw from Dior's legacy designs, to what extent collections also draw from styles from various decades, and what innovative items you can recognize in a new collection.

Dior's Advertising and PR

Dior is an haute couture fashion house and uses similar advertising and PR strategies consistent with other haute couture and luxury brands. Dior focuses on cinematographic storytelling and luxury fantasy (e.g., Lady Dior short films, J'adore Dior fragrance adverts as driven by narratives, not product promotion), often using high-production cinematographic films. Celebrity endorsements and ambassadorships are carefully selected to align with the brand, e.g., Charlize Theron, Natalie Portman, and Robert Pattinson, to enhance brand recognition and loyalty. Dior is also at the forefront of digital PR using AR try-ons, virtual runway shows, immersive online experiences, interactive quizzes, and storytelling on mobile apps and websites.

Dior has often drawn inspiration from global crafts and traditions, such as Mexican *escaramuzas,* Native American embroidery, and Chinese folk costumes; however, this has sometimes drawn criticism for cultural appropriation (Singh, 2019). Finally, Dior also focuses on values-based messages, such as feminist messaging embraced by Maria Grazia Chiuri (We Should All Be Feminists), artisanal craftsmanship, women-centered narratives, and asserting heritage and legacy through documentaries. By blending various messages, brand history, and modern activism and appeal, the brand has shifted toward traditional luxury advertising to values-led branding, particularly through runway PR stunts and social media campaigns.

Table 9.2 provides a historical summary of advertising and PR by the House of Dior starting with the iconic New Look of 1947, which has been forever associated with Christian Dior and femininity.

Table 9.2 Dior's Advertising and PR: A Historical Summary and Analysis of Notable Campaigns and Initiatives

PERIOD	NOTABLE CAMPAIGNS	MEDIUM	STRATEGY AND MESSAGES	SOURCES
1947	The New Look Launch, February 12, 1947, Dior's Avenue Montaigne salon, Paris	Fashion show Magazines (*Vogue, Harper's Bazaar*)	• Establishing Dior as post-war fashion visionary • Emphasizes femininity and luxury	History.com (2024) du Plessix Gray (1996) *Vogue* April 1, 1947 cover page Dior La Galerie (n.d.)
1947	Miss Dior fragrance launch	An exclusive launch event in Dior's salon; invitation cards sent to selected guests and the press	• Emphasizing exclusivity and luxury • Establishing Dior as couturier and perfumer • Asserting the vision of femininity as central to Dior (feminine New Look style and a perfume that smells like love, according to Dior)	Dior.com (n.d.) Dior La Galerie (n.d.)
1950s	Couture and Miss Dior campaigns	Magazine adverts, fashion editorials and cover pages (*Vogue, Harper's Bazaar*)	• Exclusivity and luxury emphasized • Asserting image of Dior as couturier and perfumer • Asserting brand vision of femininity	*Vogue* historical archive: June 1949, April, July 1950, August 1950 *Harper's Bazaar* historical archive: March 1950, April 1950, August 1951, November 1952
1967	Miss Dior Fragrance campaign	Magazine and print adverts, in-store promotions	• Repackaging and remarketing Miss Dior to appeal to a more liberated and modern consumer	Dior La Galerie (n.d.) Les Archives de la Mode (n.d.)
1970s	Advertising campaigns	Print and magazine adverts	• Expanding Dior's positioning and asserting luxury and femininity • Blending art and fashion in illustrated poster adverts	Les Archives de la Mode (n.d.)

1980s	Advertising campaigns	TV adverts	• Expanding Dior to mass market, by particularly focusing on perfumes • Movie-like advert for appeal and effect	Fahrenheit Dior advert (1988) Eau Sauvage 1980s TV advert
1999	J'adore Dior	TV, cinema, digital, magazines	• Charlize Theron embodies elegance and sensuality • Emphasizing timelessness of Dior's glamour	Dior J'Adore (1999)
2009	Lady Dior campaigns	Short, high-quality films, magazines, digital	• Merging cinematic storytelling with luxury branding • Showcasing Lady Dior bag through noir films	The Lady Noir Affair / By Lady Dior / Chapter One / Directed by Olivier Dahan Feat. Marion Cotillard (2009) Lady Dior campaigns video list, (2009–2016)
2011	Miss Dior Chérie	TV, digital, magazines	• Romanticizing French femininity with youthfulness • Using film aesthetics and Sofia Coppola's features in the campaign	Miss Dior Chérie (2011)
2014	Lady Dior web documentary series	Short web documentaries, high-quality production	• Narrating lady Dior campaigns • Asserting legacy and celebrity endorsements	Lady Dior Web Documentary Series 2014
2014–2015	Dior and I	Documentary film Cinematographic style Released at the Tribeca Film Festival US release by The Orchard France release by Dissidenz Films Further releases in 2015 (Japan, Australia, UK)	• Behind-the-scenes look at Raf Simons' first haute couture collection for Dior • Weaves past and present through excerpts from Christian Dior' autobiography read by a poet Omar Berrada	Dior and I documentary (2014–2015)

(Continued)

Table 9.2 Continued

PERIOD	NOTABLE CAMPAIGNS	MEDIUM	STRATEGY AND MESSAGES	SOURCES
2017	We Should All Be Feminists	Runway, social media, PR stunts	• Leveraging feminist messaging • Embedding cultural relevance into fashion products	Munzenrieder (2016) La Galerie Dior (n.d.)
2017	Inside Dior	Documentary YouTube	• The show presents a story of a new creative director Maria Grazia Chiuri	Inside Dior (2017)
2018–present	Dior Men / Dior Icons	Magazines, digital, social media, video	• Highlighting minimalist menswear with modern elegance • Featuring celebrities such as Robert Pattinson	Dior ambassador Robert Pattinson stays sharp in Dior Icons #shorts
2020–present	Fashion documentaries	YouTube brand channel	• High-quality fashion documentaries about the history of the House of Dior • A mix of old and new documentaries A mix of legacy and heritage documentaries, and behind-the-scenes documentaries	Dior documentaries 1 Dior documentaries 2
2020	Made public a documentary Haute Couture from 1949 directed by Henri A. Lavorel	YouTube brand channel	Historical fashion documentary promoting haute couture collection Fall/Winter 1949	The world of Monsieur Dior in his own words 2020

2020	Christian Dior: Designer of Dreams exhibition turned into campaign	Documentary film, YouTube	• Exhibition was on display in Paris until 2018 • Virtual exhibition reminded audiences about legacy of Christian Dior • High-quality documentary film • Presenting brand's legacy and history through modern means of communication	'Christian Dior, Designer of Dreams' at the Musée des Arts Décoratifs (2020)
2020	Fall/Winter Haute Couture campaign	Documentary, YouTube	• Presenting brand's legacy and history, and promoting current creative designer and her vision • High-quality production film • Asserting legacy and heritage	Dior Autumn/Winter 2020–2021 Haute Couture 2020
2021–2023	Dior x PSG Partnership	Sponsorships, press events, social media	• Fusing sports and luxury fashion by dressing Paris Saint-Germain players in Dior	The Paris Saint-Germain get dressed up in Dior (2023)
2021	Podcast launch	YouTube brand channel	• Narrating and asserting Dior's historical legacy and craftsmanship	The A.B.C. Dior Podcast Series Illustrated (2021)
2023	Book club initiative	YouTube brand channel	• Celebrating reading • Celebrity endorsement	The Dior Book Tote Club (2023)
2023	Dior Beauty AR Tools	Digital (app, web), interactive media	• Launching augmented reality try-ons and quizzes • Personalizing beauty experience	Dior.com (n.d._a)

(*Continued*)

Table 9.2 Continued

PERIOD	NOTABLE CAMPAIGNS	MEDIUM	STRATEGY AND MESSAGES	SOURCES
2023	Mini documentary on Dior Autumn/Winter 2023	Documentary, YouTube	• The making of a collection • Asserting legacy and heritage through archival materials and brand history • Luxury fashion, high-quality craftsmanship and artisanry, creative vision behind designs	The making of Dior Autumn/Winter 2023–2024
2024	Documentary on Cruise 2024 collection	Documentary, YouTube	• The making of a collection • Asserting legacy and heritage through archival materials and brand history • Luxury fashion, high-quality craftsmanship and artisanry, creative vision behind designs	'Dior Metamorphosis': The Making of Dior Cruise (2024)
2024	Mini documentary on men's Summer 2024 collection	Documentary, YouTube	• The making of collection • Asserting legacy and heritage through archival materials and brand history • Luxury fashion, high-quality craftsmanship and artisanry, creative vision behind designs	The Making of the Dior Men's Summer 2024 Show

Source: Author's work

DISCUSSION QUESTIONS

- How did Christian Dior's 1947 'New Look' reflect postwar social and cultural shifts in femininity and fashion?
- In what ways did Dior's approach to silhouette, volume, and structure redefine the ideal of elegance in the mid-20th century?
- Why was the New Look both celebrated and criticized when it was first introduced?
- What elements of Christian Dior's aesthetic legacy remain visible in today's Dior collections?
- To what extent should a modern fashion house adhere to the founder's original vision?
- Is Christian Dior's legacy primarily about fashion design, or is it also about branding, storytelling, and identity?
- How has Dior used cinematic storytelling in its advertising campaigns (e.g., Lady Dior short films, J'adore perfume ads), and how does this differ from traditional fashion advertising?
- What role do celebrity ambassadors play in shaping Dior's brand image and consumer appeal?
- How does Dior's advertising balance fantasy and reality, and what emotional or aspirational messages are being communicated?
- How has Dior's advertising under Maria Grazia Chiuri integrated feminist messaging (e.g., We Should All Be Feminists runway moment)? Is this an example of authentic activism or brand opportunism?
- In your opinion, which Dior campaign (past or present) has been the most effective in shaping brand perception?

Maison Schiaparelli

Maison Schiaparelli was a historical name of the designer house founded by Elsa Schiaparelli, an Italian-French fashion designer popular during the 1920s and 1930s period. Elsa Schiaparelli's vision for fashion can be seen as centered on artistic collaboration and surrealism. Schiaparelli is best known as an innovator and for merging metaphysical and artistic themes. She is credited with the wrap dress and zippers and is also famous for collaborating with artists such as Salvador Dali, Man Ray, Jean-Michel Frank, and Giacometti (Kotsoni, 2025; Thurman, 2003). The *New Yorker* magazine labelled Elsa Schiaparelli as the Mother of Invention, praising her approach to fashion, which Schiaparelli herself called 'shocking' in her biography. Shocking is a reference to a violent magenta she introduced to her designs, which became her signature color. She introduced this color in 1937 (Schiaparelli, 2007[1954]; Schiaparelli.com, n.d._b). Sometimes known as the 'Queen of Fashion' and a headline attraction in international glamorous societies of the 1920s and 1930s, Schiaparelli was someone who knew everyone who was always 'there', and she became one of those who were always 'there' herself (Secrest, 2014).

Schiaparelli is often compared with Coco Chanel due to the two designers being contemporaries; however, Schiaparelli is seen as a homely and aristocratic couture poet of the interwar period, while Chanel is seen as a prose stylist who designed clothes for an emboldened new woman (Thurman, 2003). Schiaparelli is also seen as connected to the

Figure 9.7 An illustration of Schiaparelli's fashion show
Musée Carnavalet, Histoire de Paris

avant-garde. An exhibition at the Philadelphia Museum of Art, and an accompanying publication with teaching guidance, was titled 'Shocking! The Art and Fashion of Elsa Schiaparelli' (Philadelphia Museum of Art, 2003). Innovations Schiaparelli introduced include graphic knitwear, evening gowns with plastic, wrap dress, mix-and-match separates and svelte culottes, wedgie, the jumpsuit, the overall, paper clothes, transparent raincoats, folding eyeglasses, fun furs, the scarf dress, colored hosiery, athletic wear, the shirtwaist jacket, ethnic-themes collections, and the ready-to-wear boutique (Thurman, 2003). The Wooden Soldier Silhouette, as Schiaparelli titled her fashion in the 1930s, was centered on power suits and the so-called 'hard chic' style. Her suits had linebacker shoulders and an inverted trapezoid shape, and were worn by stars such as Marlene Dietrich, Greta Garbo, Katherine Hepburn, and Joan Crawford (Thurman, 2003). Despite her avant-garde image and experimentation with colors (magenta pink) and materials (rayon, cellophane, early plastics), she also focused on practical wear and introduced knitwear and sportswear early on, such as the already mentioned wrapped dress, but also swimsuits (Schiaparelli.com, n.d._a).

Elsa Schiaparelli was born in Rome, Italy, in 1890. She grew up in a family of aristocrats and intellectuals and studied philosophy even though she wanted to be an actress. In 1911, she published a collection of poems, *Arethusa*, which were seen as overly sensual and, once her parents found out about the poems, landed her a place in covenant in Switzerland. She left the covenant after a hunger strike and moved to London in 1913 (Schiaparelli.com, n.d.). She married in 1914 (to count Wilhelm Wendt de Kerlor) and moved to New York in 1916, which was a transformative event because on the liner to New York, Elsa met Gabrielle Picabia, the wife of Dada painter, who introduced Elsa to avant-garde artists (Schiaparelli.com, n.d.; Papalas, 2017), later resulting in fashion collaborations. Elsa and her husband lived on her dowry, which resulted in her working a part-time job and leading a Bohemian life while her husband was absent; thus, she asked for a divorce and moved to Paris in 1922. Elsa initially worked at an antique dealer's while frequenting famous restaurants on evenings, which grew her artist circle (Schiaparelli.com, n.d.; Papalas, 2017).

A transformative experience, which led to developing a career in fashion design, was accompanying a friend to a fitting at Paul Poiret, a popular couturier of the time, where she tried various designs despite not being able to afford them. Poiret thought Elsa would be a good model for his designs and offered to loan her his clothes. This 'experience of a couture house, luxury, quality, design, colors, materials, embroidery and shapes lit a spark in Elsa that would prove to be the one of the turning points in her life' (Schiaparelli.com, n.d., n.p.). Therefore, in the mid-1920s, Elsa became a freelance designer, and her first design was a hand-knit pullover with a black and white trompe-l'oeil motif, which was declared a masterpiece by American *Vogue* (Schiaparelli.com, n.d._a). In 1928, her business grew, and she designed a new collection, Schiaparelli-Pour le Sport (Schiaparelli-Sportswear), which included knitwear, swimsuits, beach pajamas, and accessories, with varied motifs and colors. This collection gained popularity in the US, landing her first licensing agreements (Schiaparelli.com, n.d._a). From 1929, Schiaparelli introduced further innovations in materials, cuts, details, and accessories such as,

> a raincoat in rubberised wool and silk, jumpsuits with visible zips (which would later be followed by colored zips and then multi-colored versions), the first evening dress (a wrap dress with a plunging neckline), culottes (which would cause a scandal in England), strong-shouldered suits (the ancestor of the power suit), reversible black and white evening dresses, aerodynamic cuts created by skilfully placed flounces, eccentric hats (such as the Mad Cap, which was copied to such an extent that Elsa would almost regret having designed it), and a licence in the United States for metal mesh bags (Schiaparelli.com, n.d._a, n.p.).

After an initial success in the US, Schiaparelli introduced her famous artistic collaborations and new materials (Schiaparelli.com, n.d._a), and her reputation grew to the point that she became the first designer to feature on the cover page of *Time Magazine* in 1934. Her customer base started to include the biggest celebrities of the time, such as Wallis Simpson, Marlene Dietrich, Katharine Hepburn, Greta Garbo, Lauren Bacall, Gene Tierney, Gala Dali, Marie-Laure de Noailles, Daisy Fellowes, Nusch Eluard, Arletty, Vivien Leigh, Ginger Rogers, Juliette Gréco, and Mae West (Schiaparelli.com, n.d._b).In 1932, her couture house expanded to city and evening wear, and in 1933, she opened stores in London and New York. In 1934, she presented a collection of three perfumes, not just the initial fragrance 'S' launched in 1928, but also Soucis, Salut, and Schiap (Schiaparelli.com, n.d._b). Her most memorable piece from the 1930s was a collaboration with Salvador Dali,

> with whom she created now-legendary pieces (suits with bureau-drawer pockets, a shoe-hat, a lobster-printed dress, a skeleton dress, the tear dress, Le Roy soleil perfume bottle, etc.), and Jean Cocteau, whose drawings featured on coats, evening

> ensembles, and jewellery. The surrealist and artistic spirit took hold of leather ankle boots with toes represented by topstitching, along with the men's fragrance bottle in the shape of a pipe (in a nod to Magritte), gloves with red python nails, ankle boots fringed with long monkey fur, a Rhodoid necklace incrusted with insects, and handbags with luminous (battery-powered) decorations (Schiaparelli.com, n.d._b, n.p.).

In 1937, she launched her most famous perfume, Shocking, and the color shocking pink (Schiaparelli.com, n.d.). WWII put her work at risk, as with other Parisian designers, and she tried to save her business in 1940, with a new perfume, Sleeping. She also created new and radical clothing, suitable for war and air raids, such as 'zippered jumpsuits with maxi pockets intended to hold the equivalent of a handbag, a coat with an integrated bag, transformable dresses, etc.' (Schiaparelli.com, n.d._c, n.p.). Soon after, she left Paris for the US, where she gave lectures on the theme of 'Clothes and the Woman', which were widely attended, including one lecture attracting 36,000 visitors (Schiaparelli.com, n.d._c). After the war, she returned to Paris and presented a collection in September 1945 and took part in the traveling exhibition *Théâtre de la Mode* in the US (Schiaparelli.com, n.d._d). In 1946, she launched,

> *the Constellation* wardrobe: six dresses, one reversible coat, and three folding hats, all under 12 lbs. Despite the strike of part of her Haute-Couture ateliers, Elsa presented her collection in August 1949. The pieces were not finished. You could still see pins, fabric swatches, and no buttonholes. However, the youthful style, evident daring, and the evening dress with a visible bra led the *New York Times* to describe the collection as 'Striking'. Newsweek devoted its front page to Elsa (Schiaparelli.com, n.d._d, n.p., emphasis in the original).

She decided to close her couture house in 1954, realizing that haute couture had changed, and she wrote her biography, also published in 1954. She died in 1973, and Schiaparelli ceased to exist until Diego Della Valle acquired the rights to the Schiaparelli brand in 2007, including perfume and fashion legacy. In 2014, with designer Marco Zanini as creative director, Schiaparelli officially relaunched its couture line.

REFLECT

Watch Schiaparelli runways, specifically the latest haute couture fall/winter and the latest ready-to-wear fall/winter. You can find these runways on Schiaparelli's YouTube channel. When watching shows, pay attention to the colors of the collection, iconic designs previously introduced by Elsa Schiaparelli (e.g., re-interpretation of wrapped dress, the Lobster dress, etc.). Analyze shows and new collections in line with what you know about the legacy of Schiaparelli and Elsa's contributions to innovations in fashion. Consider how new collections draw from Schiaparelli's legacy designs, to what extent collections also draw from styles from various decades, and what innovative items you can recognize in a new collection.

Schiaparelli's Advertising and PR

Schiaparelli's approach to advertising and PR has historically been linked to Elsa's personality and fashion, thus bold, surrealist, and avant-garde. Instead of relying on conventional advertising methods, Schiaparelli embraced theatrical collaborations with artists and emphasized publicity stunts to craft her designer and brand persona. Since the Maison Schiaparelli ceased to exist in the 1950s when Elsa retired and closed the house, until 2007 when her brand was revived again, the advertising and PR strategy changed from personalized style centered on Elsa's personality, to a brand legacy celebrating her life and approach to fashion. Therefore, nowadays the brand is to an extent aligned with other haute couture houses such as Chanel and Dior, which celebrate the legacies of their founders. However, celebrating the legacy of Elsa Schiaparelli means also extensive red carpet and celebrity collaborations, which fit Elsa's personality and personal strategies of always knowing people and being part of society. Therefore, the brand continues with earned media and celebrity endorsements and, just as historically, Hollywood stars (e.g., Katharine Hepburn) and socialites (e.g., Wallis Simpson) wore Schiaparelli's designs and promoted her work, nowadays socialites and pop stars such as Beyonce and Kardashians also promote Schiaparelli's fashion, signaling brand legacy and continuity not just in new fashion designs, but also advertising and PR strategies.

Table 9.3 provides a summary of advertising and PR efforts of Schiaparelli, starting from 1927. These communication efforts are different from other designers in the sense that they focus more on society and publicity, as Elsa did in the past. However, they are consistent with what other haute couture brands do because of their focus on designer persona and brand history and legacy.

Table 9.3 Schiaparelli's Advertising and PR: A Historical Summary and Analysis of Notable Campaigns and Initiatives

PERIOD	NOTABLE CAMPAIGNS	MEDIUM	STRATEGY AND MESSAGES	SOURCES
1927–1928	Knitwear launch	Magazines, in-store events	• Introducing knit sweaters, sporty chic and zippers as novelty • Positioning the designer as modern and playful	Borrelli-Persson (2022)
1928	Perfume S launch	Innovative packaging, press releases	• Design by Jean-Michel Frank (black and white bottle) • The first unisex scent • Challenged gender norms	Kim (2015), Schiaparelli (n.d.)

(Continued)

Table 9.3 Continued

PERIOD	NOTABLE CAMPAIGNS	MEDIUM	STRATEGY AND MESSAGES	SOURCES
1930s	Surrealist jewelry and novelty hats	Fashion press, live events, magazine features	• Collaboration with surrealists • Presentation of sculptural hats • Jewelry as theatrical spectacle	Dscene (2021)
1934	*Time Magazine* cover	*Time Magazine*	• First female designer to feature in *Time* • Photographed by Man Ray for Vogue	Schiaparelli (n.d.) *Time Magazine*, August 13, 1934
1935	Move to Place Vendome & Themed shows	Events, press invitations	• Fashion presentations with theatrical staging and choreography • Grand opening at Place Vendome	Schiaparelli (n.d.)
1935–1938	Surrealist couture collections	Press	• Structured dresses, lobster brooch, tears dress, drawer-suit, circus themes, craft	Schiaparelli (n.d.) Reeder (2011)
1937	Shocking perfume campaign	Print, bottles as sculptural objects, posters	• Debut of Shocking perfume with pink brand color • Vibrant visuals and feminist allure in packaging	Les Archives de la Mode (n.d._a)
1940s	Clothes and the Woman US lecture series Spring 1940 collection, military theme with trench brown and camouflage print taffetas	Magazines, fashion shows, invitations to lectures	• Continued surrealist couture and war-conscious themes • Publicity and advocacy for French couture	Philadelphia Museum of Art (2003)

(*Continued*)

Table 9.3 Continued

PERIOD	NOTABLE CAMPAIGNS	MEDIUM	STRATEGY AND MESSAGES	SOURCES
1950s	Final collection and brand closure (1954)	Press features, farewell runway shows	• Emphasized Elsa's legacy and final thematic collections • Farewell to fashion	Philadelphia Museum of Art (2003)
2007	Brand acquisition and archival exhibits	Museum exhibits, fashion retrospectives	• Public interest revived through museum showcases	Williams, R (2023)
2014	Couture relaunch under Diego Della Valle	Press releases, PR events	• Relaunched couture house with heavy emphasis on Elsa's archive and surrealist motifs	Alexander (2012)
2020	Kim Kardashian collaboration	Instagram, red carpet, fashion press	• Celebrity relaunch of couture with sculptural look	Kardashian on collaboration on Instagram (2023)
2021	Fall/Winter 2021/2022 campaign	YouTube	• High-production short film campaign, presenting Schiaparelli new collection as a must-see event, glamour, luxury	Schiaparelli Fall/Winter 2021/2022 | Film (2021)
2021	Daniel Roseberry's AW21 Couture collection promotion	YouTube	• High production, short film, behind-the-scenes, asserting legacy and heritage with new creative direction	Short film in Paris of Daniel Roseberry's Schiaparelli AW21 Couture Collection (2021)
2021–2025	Red carpet celebrity endorsements and styling collaborations	Magazine covers, music videos, press, red carpet	• Asserting legacy and positioning the brand as exclusive and luxury	Schiaparelli (n.d.) Schiaparelli (n.d._a)

(*Continued*)

Table 9.3 Continued

PERIOD	NOTABLE CAMPAIGNS	MEDIUM	STRATEGY AND MESSAGES	SOURCES
2022–2023	Exhibitions	Earned press coverage, social media	• 'Shocking! The Surreal World of Elsa Schiaparelli', Arts Museum Paris, 2022–2023	Musée des Arts Décoratifs (2022)
2024	Fall/Winter 2024 Campaign	Short film, YouTube	• Cinematic campaign shot by Johnny Dufort in Palace Vendome emphasizing surrealism • Asserting legacy and heritage blending it with modern creative direction	Schiaparelli Haute Couture Fall/Winter (2024)

Source: Author's work

DISCUSSION QUESTIONS

- How did Elsa Schiaparelli's interest in surrealism shape her approach to fashion design? In what ways did she blur the boundaries between fashion and art?
- How did Schiaparelli's personal background – aristocratic, intellectual, and rebellious – inform her brand identity and design ethos?
- What role did artistic collaboration play in establishing Schiaparelli's brand? Could you compare this to how modern designers work with artists or celebrities today?
- How did Schiaparelli use fashion shows, perfume marketing, and visual spectacle as tools of self-promotion and branding?
- In relaunching Maison Schiaparelli in the 21st century, what challenges do creative directors face in preserving Elsa's legacy while staying relevant to modern consumers?
- What role did celebrity endorsement and media coverage play in Schiaparelli's rise to fame?
- Schiaparelli's perfume campaigns, especially for Shocking (1937), used provocative packaging and surrealist visuals. What messages were conveyed through the design of her ads and product packaging? How do these tactics relate to emotional branding?
- Can Schiaparelli's perfume marketing or showmanship be considered a precursor to fashion 'happenings' or influencer culture?

Yves Saint Laurent

Yves Mathieu-Saint-Laurent, later known as Yves Saint Laurent (YSL), was born in 1936 in Algeria. He grew up as a member of the society of Oran and was initially a shy boy showing talent for the arts. His family was part of an affluent class of Oran, who attended cultural events, theater, and opera regularly (YSL Museum, n.d.), which created cultural capital for young YSL. YSL said that his mother was always dressing up, and that he was fascinated by her evening gowns (YSL Museum, n.d.), which created an interest in fashion in his early years. YSL was inspired by drawings and illustrations of Christian Bérard, who worked for Dior, Chanel, and Schiaparelli and who knew how to portray a costume and reinvent it by capturing the silhouette and the time in which the silhouette and costume existed (YSL Museum, n.d.). YSL started to sketch sets and costumes for the theater and ballet, and added drawings to books he transcribed, the latter he started at the age of 13 (YSL Museum, n.d.). According to an illustration of a book transcribed and illustrated by YSL in 1950, the drawing has a man holding a naked woman wearing just one slipper (biography available on the YSL Museum website), which signaled an early interest in unconventional sexual expressions. This will later result in a highly sexualized advertising campaign, including YSL posing naked for an advert, a first time a designer has done that in history (YSL Museum, n.d._e).

After drawings, YSL turned toward fashion, initially using paper dolls and designing an entire wardrobe for them. He created two collections, Fall/Winter 1953–1954 and 1954–1955, with over 500 garments for 11 dolls (YSL Museum, n.d.). In 1954, YSL moved to Paris, where he was introduced to Christian Dior by *Vogue Paris* editor, Michel de Brunhoff, who saw YSL's drawings and thought the style resembled Dior's style. In summer 1955, Dior hired YSL to his studio (YSL Museum, n.d.). When Dior suddenly died in 1957, YSL became his successor and the world's youngest couturier (YSL Museum, n.d._a). YSL had only a few months to prepare a new collection, Spring/Summer 1958, which was scheduled for presentation on January 30. The collection was a success. Between 1958 and 1960, YSL designed six collections for Dior, and with his designs the House of Dior changed so that 'the figure was lost in favor of style' (YSL Museum, n.d._a, n.p.). YSL distanced himself from the bourgeois elegance of the 1950s (YSL Museum, n.d._a); however, with that, he also distanced himself from Dior's New Look and an approach to femininity in fashion. This change of direction resulted in a Beatnik-inspired collection for Dior, named *Souplesse, Légèreté, Vie,* (Flexibility, Lightness, Life), and it featured purple and dark, as well as crocodile-style leather jackets and turtlenecks, which made YSL look like a provocateur. His collection for Dior, for the first time, was not well received (YSL Museum, n.d._a). In 1960, the House of Dior fired YSL and hired Marc Bohan as his replacement. YSL then founded his own haute couture house, and re-invented his style centered on colors black and purple, and shifted further toward beatnik and power girl style.

In 1965, YSL presented a collection entitled The Mondrian Revolution, featuring cocktail dresses evoking abstract canvases, simple cuts, geometrical lines, and bold colors (YSL Museum, n.d._b). YSL was open to modernity, and since the miniskirt was introduced by Mary Quant in England in 1962, skirts got shortened generally, which coincided with the women's liberation movement. Women liked wearing loose-fitted dresses that did not constrain their bodies (YSL Museum, n.d._b), which inspired YSL, who then created a collection inspired by Mondrian, an artist who was depicting nature in primary colors inside square or rectangular surfaces delineated by a thick black outline (neoplasticism).

This approach to art was meant to showcase visual stability and harmony in imbalance, and the duality of horizontal and vertical was meant to transcend feminine/masculine to material/spiritual (YSL Museum, n.d._b).

The Fall/Winter collection of 1965 featured 106 designs of classic haute couture, such as day suits, casual ensembles, formal ensembles, cocktail dresses, evening gowns, and furs, with a clean and simple silhouette (YSL Museum, n.d._b). However, what instigated attention were 26 designs that echoed Mondrian paintings, with squares delineated by thick black outline with some color inside squares, such as an all-white dress with one square having red or a similar dress with a large red square, one small blue square and four white squares, again delineated by thick black outline, and a yellow hemline (see original sketches from YSL on YSL Museum, n.d._b). This collection was a success and launched YSL's haute couture business to fame. Mondrian style remained an influence after YSL's collection. For example, in 2007, Christian Louboutin created the *Mondriana* shoe, and Francesco Maria Bandini devoted an entire show to a collection inspired by Mondrian in 1991 (YSL Museum, n.d._b). YSL also re-interpreted Mondrian in his Spring/Summer 1980 haute couture collection and a Spring/Summer 1997 rive gauche dress (YSL Museum, n.d._b). In 1966, YSL designed his *Le Smoking* jacket, the Fall/Winter 1966 haute couture collection. This jacket was a revolutionary jacket inspired by men's tuxedo, but designed specifically for women (YSL Museum, n.d._d). In the same year, YSL became the first couturier to open a ready-to-wear boutique to address the obsoleteness of haute couture during the 1960s and his desire to create clothes for everyone. This shop is known as Rive Gauche, which refers to the left bank of the Seine River in Paris, where his first ready-to-wear boutique was located (Croll, 2014). The Rive Gauche side of the Seine was also the bohemian and artistic side of Paris, whereas haute couture houses were traditionally on the right side of the Seine (Rive Droite). YSL popularized ready-to-wear and started a trend among haute couture houses. This resulted in Pierre Bergé, business and life partner of Yves Saint Laurent to form the *Chambre Syndicale du Prêt-à-Porter des Couturiers et des Créateurs de Mode* to regulate the new prêt-à-porter industry (Croll, 2014). In 1968, YSL designed another iconic item, the first Safari jacket. This was another borrowing from men's fashion and empowering women. The Safari jacket was made of cotton gabardine and was comfortable for hot summers, embodying the spirit of the 1960s while also being stylish (YSL Museum, n.d._f).

YSL was liked by Coco Chanel, who named him as her heir apparent in 1968, seven years after launching his label. Chanel saw YSL as someone like-minded because just like she revolutionized women's fashion by introducing trousers, removing corsets from dresses, which was modern at her time, YSL was modern in his approach to women because he was also seeking to free women rather than to hinder and constrain them. Like Chanel, who introduced men's trousers into women's wardrobe, YSL was also designing a wardrobe that placed women on par with men (YSL Museum, n.d._c). Pierre Berge, YSL's partner, said that 'Chanel gave women freedom. Yves Saint Laurent empowered them' (YSL Museum, n.d._c, n.p.). However, despite an affinity for Chanel and similarities between the two designers, YSL also shared something with Elsa Schiaparelli, Chanel's opposite, normally: an affection toward color pink, or shocking pink as Schiaparelli named it.

In 2002, YSL announced retirement, saying,

> I tell myself that I created the wardrobe of the contemporary woman, that I participated in the transformation of my times .... For a long time now, I have believed that fashion was not only supposed to make women beautiful, but to reassure them, to give them confidence, to allow them to come to terms with themselves. However, I have chosen today to bid adieu to this profession that I have loved so much (Kelso, 2014, n.p.).

Before his retirement, he sold his couture business to Artemis corporation, which has agreed to close the couture house to ensure no designer's name appears on YSL designs. His Rive Gauche ready-to-wear business was also sold before his retirement, and ready-to-wear continues under YSL's name and legacy up to the present day. YSL is now owned by Kering S.A., a corporation that also owns Gucci, Balenciaga, Bottega Veneta, Brioni, and Alexander McQueen. Musée Yves Saint Laurent Paris opened in 2017. The Museum is located at the historic mansion at 5 Avenue Marceau, where YSL was designing from 1974 to 2002.

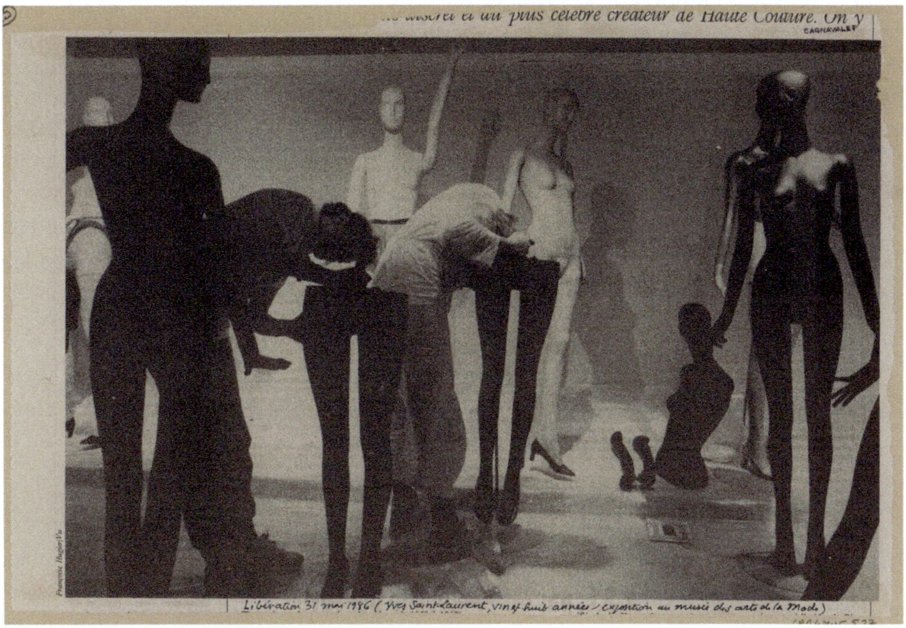

Figure 9.8 Yves Saint Laurent, Twenty-Eight Years, exhibition at the Museum of Fashion Arts

Musée Carnavalet, Histoire de Paris

REFLECT

Watch YSL runways, specifically the latest ready-to-wear fall/winter. You can find these runways on YSL's YouTube channel. When watching shows, pay attention to the colors of the collection, iconic designs previously introduced by YSL (e.g., re-interpretation of *Le Smoking* jacket, the Safari jacket, and colors, etc.). Analyze shows and new collections in line with what you know about the legacy of YSL. Consider how new collections draw from YSL's legacy designs, to what extent collections also draw from styles from various decades, and what innovative items you can recognize in a new collection.

YSL's Advertising and PR

YSL's campaigns were historically focused on collaborations and advertising in prestigious fashion magazines such as *Vogue* and *Harper's Bazaar,* using high-quality photography and communicating sensuality, sophistication, and modernity. However, YSL also has a history of provocation and scandals, such as a nude advert by YSL in the 1970s or the Opium perfume, whose name caused a scandal. The nude advert redefined the fashion relationship with the body. YSL historically blended persona with product, e.g., ready-to-wear line Rive Gauche, which launch made a political statement by being on the opposite side of the River Seine in Paris than traditional haute couture houses, with which YSL redefined and democratized fashion, creating also publicity for his brand. Celebrity friendships resulted in endorsements and earned media, thus YSL benefited from PR. The historical legacy of celebrity endorsements continues, along with a focus on rebellious substructures and identity in fashion (e.g., the Self campaign featuring artistic documentaries). The brand still focuses on luxury ready-to-wear but with a renewed focus on subcultures, mimicking YSL's beatnik inspiration and keeping the brand luxury but continually positioned differently than other luxury brands.

Table 9.4 provides a historical summary of advertising and PR efforts by YSL, starting from 1966 *Le Smoking* tuxedo invention, which challenged gender norms and put YSL on a continuous path of innovation and rebellion in fashion.

Table 9.4 YSL's Advertising and PR: A Historical Summary and Analysis of Notable Campaigns and Initiatives

PERIOD	NOTABLE CAMPAIGNS	MEDIUM	STRATEGY AND MESSAGES	SOURCES
1966	*Le Smoking* tuxedo launch	Fashion show, 'Pop Art collection'	• Introducing tuxedo suit for women • Challenging gender norms through androgynous styling	Musée Yves Saint Laurent Paris (n.d.).
1971	The Scandal collection	Runway, magazines,	• Released a retro 1940s style collection	Musée Yves Saint Laurent Paris (n.d._a).
1971	Pour Homme and Rive Gauche perfume launches with a controversial advertising campaign	Magazines	• Posed nude for a new perfume for men (photo by Jeanloup Sieff)	Musée Yves Saint Laurent Paris (n.d._b).

(*Continued*)

Table 9.4 Continued

PERIOD	NOTABLE CAMPAIGNS	MEDIUM	STRATEGY AND MESSAGES	SOURCES
1977	Opium perfume launch (perfume name caused a scandal)	Billboards, magazines, publicity stunts	• Used sensual and exotic imagery to create a sense of mystery • Controversy over name and image	Musée Yves Saint Laurent Paris (n.d._c).
1982–2023	Catherine Deneuve for YSL	Editorials, beauty campaigns, later editions YouTube and social media	• Used French film star as face of YSL fragrance and couture communicating elegance meeting celebrity	Musée Yves Saint Laurent Paris (n.d._d). Saint Laurent – Catherine Deneuve (2021) Catherine Deneuve for YSL (2023)
1999	Opium Men launch coincided with Autumn/ Winter 1977 collection	Magazines, in-store displays	• Expanding the Opium brand • Visuals emphasizing bold sensuality	Musée Yves Saint Laurent Paris (n.d._e).
2000	Sophia Dahl for Opium, controversial advertising campaign	Billboards, magazines, print adverts	• Semi-nude image of model suggestively lying, echoing 1970s shock campaign • Banned advert causing controversy	Carter (2010)
2001–2004	Tom Ford's Provocative Campaigns	Magazines, TV, stores	• Emphasizing erotica, nudity, and high luxury	Viapiana (2023)
2012–2016	Rebranding to Saint Laurent Paris	Magazines, social media	• Hedi Slimane's creative direction to modernize brand through stripped-down visuals, youth culture, and rock icons	Cartner-Morley (2012)

(*Continued*)

Table 9.4 Continued

PERIOD	NOTABLE CAMPAIGNS	MEDIUM	STRATEGY AND MESSAGES	SOURCES
2019–2022	Saint Laurent Self Campaign	Black and white short films, high-quality production Social media YouTube	• Artistic films by filmmakers (Gaspar Noe, Jim Jarmusch) exploring themes of identity and obsession	Piranha NYC (n.d.) Self Campaign (2019–2022)
2022	Podcast	YouTube	• Black and white video conversations with celebrities and personalities from cinema, photography, and arts close to St Laurent and Anthony Vaccarello • Guests are interviewed by a French journalist Augustin Trapenard	Saint Laurent Talks podcast
2024	As Time Goes By Campaign	Short films directed by Nadia Lee Cohen, inspired by Proust's In Search of Lost Time	• Exploring themes such as love and memory • Blending references to literature, cinema, salon culture, and high fashion into immersive narrative films	Saint Laurent – As Time Goes By film series (2024)

Source: author's work

DISCUSSION QUESTIONS

- How did Yves Saint Laurent challenge traditional boundaries of fashion design with pieces like *Le Smoking*, the Safari jacket, and the Mondrian dress?
- Consider the view that Chanel freed women and YSL empowered them. How did YSL's designs reflect this philosophy? How did two designers redefine femininity and power?

- How did Yves Saint Laurent use media, photography, and runway presentations to construct a strong public image for both himself and his fashion house? What made his campaigns stand out from other designers of his time?
- In what ways did Saint Laurent's use of shock, sensuality, and controversy (e.g., his nude perfume ad) function as effective PR strategies? What were the risks and rewards?
- How did the creation of the YSL Rive Gauche ready-to-wear line impact the fashion industry and the concept of democratized luxury?
- What is the role of the Musée Yves Saint Laurent in preserving and curating his legacy?
- How can fashion museums act as tools of brand building and historical canonization?

Vivienne Westwood

Vivienne Westwood, a British designer known for eccentricity, was born in 1941 in the UK. She entered the fashion world with her partner Malcolm McLaren in the early 1970s and stirred controversy with their designs of teddy boy suits, followed by biker and sado-masochist (S&M) outfits and punk fashion (Lehnert, 2000). She held her first catwalk in 1981, featuring the Pirates collection, and quickly gained recognition as a couturier. Her most notable decade was the 1970s, when she dominated punk with her punk-inspired fashion, accompanied by matching worldviews. Her fashion has been labeled as grotesque, decadent, and unwearable (Lehnert, 2000), but at the same time, she has also been called the Queen of Fashion due to eccentricity, courage, and attitudes about politics and environment often expressed in her designs, activism, and runways.

Westwood had an upbringing that can be seen as unconventional for couture. She was born to a working-class family in Northern England (Manchester area) (Lehnert, 2000), and her upbringing was not centered on gaining cultural capital that would lead one to a pathway to high fashion. She moved to London in 1958 and initially worked as a primary school teacher and married a manager of a rural dance hall (Lehnert, 2000). After divorcing Derek Westwood, she met Malcolm McLaren, who was a critic of the flower power movement, which he saw as commercial and empty; thus, the pair opened a shop in King's Road in London initially selling nostalgic fashions, and fashion that signaled rebellion against the mainstream (Lehnert, 2000; Westwood.com, n.d.). Dame Zandra Rhodes, a fashion and textile giant, said about Westwood's legacy, 'We'd had flower power … then suddenly you had this very hard-hitting punk' (Hancock, 2022, n.p.).

Westwood and McLaren initially sold Teddy Boy suits but quickly exhausted that market and moved toward the bikers' market and controversial fashions such as T-shirts with pornographic slogans that for which they were prosecuted under the 1959 Obscene Publications Act; however, they responded by making their T-shirts even more provocative (Westwood.com, n.d.). Westwood herself provoked with her outfits wearing leather miniskirts, torn T-shirts, chains, padlocks, and stilettos, pushing boundaries of good taste of the 1970s (Lehnert, 2000). However, it was the punk band Sex Pistols that launched Westwood–McLaren's career in 1975 when they started to wear their T-shirts. Sex Pistols promoted their fashion and philosophy, which increased their client base. Westwood,

> used her creations to communicate ideas – often using graphics to confront issues of political and social injustice. The swastika symbol seen on the 1977 Anarchy Shirt, designed by Westwood & McLaren, was laid over an inverted image of Christ on

> the crucifix and Queen Elizabeth II on a British stamp, with the word 'DESTROY' emblazoned above the image. The graphics were meant as a provocative act of denouncing corruption and dictatorship. More broadly, it was a meant as a means to challenge the older generation, of saying 'We don't accept your values or your taboos – you're all fascists' (Westwood.com, n.d., n.p., emphasis in the original).

Westwood was a prototype of a punk woman, 'bottle blond punk hair, pale face with dark lips, short kilt teamed with huge lace-up boots' (Lehnert, 2000, p. 109). This phase only lasted until punk subculture disintegrated, and in 1980, Westwood abandoned punk and separated from Malcolm McLaren, which resulted in new collections inspired by history and various ethnic groups, such as Native Americans, outcasts, and rebels (Lehnert, 2000). Westwood's designs are commonly referred to as the McLaren and post-McLaren eras because of a difference in creative direction. Westwood's most notable collections in the post-McLaren era include Witches (1983), Minicrini (1984), Corsets (1987), Time Machine (1988), Cut, Slash and Pull (Spring/Summer 1991), Anglomania (1993/1994), Café Society (Spring/Summer 1994), and *Les Femmes ne connaissant pas toute leur coquetterie* (Women not fully aware of their coquettishness) (Spring/Summer 1996) (V&A, n.d._b; Westwood.com, n.d.). Westwood's website divides her career and legacy into several phases, The Early Years (1981–1987), The Pagan Years (1988–1992), Anglomania (1993–1999), Exploration (2000–2016), and Andreas Kronthaler for Vivienne Westwood (2016–present) (Westwood.com, n.d.).

Westwood was voted British designer of the year several times, awarded OBE by Queen Elizabeth II, honorary membership of the Royal College of Art, and she was appointed as guest professor in many universities, including at the Academy of Applied Arts in Vienna where she met her third husband and partner Andreas Kronthaler who started to design for her in 2016, under the name Andreas Kronthaler for Vivienne Westwood. Westwood received further recognition from the Crown in 2006 when she became Dame.

REFLECT

Watch Westwood's runways, specifically the latest ready-to-wear fall/winter. You can find these runways on the brand's YouTube channel. When watching shows, pay attention to iconic designs previously introduced by Westwood. Analyze shows and new collections in line with what you know about the legacy of the brand. Consider how new collections draw from Westwood's legacy designs, to what extent collections also draw from styles from various decades, and what innovative items you can recognize in a new collection.

Westwood's Advertising and PR

Westwood's communication efforts can be mainly analyzed in the context of PR and creating publicity for the brand through provocative designs and statements, such as pornographic and political T-shirts from the 1970s punk era or posing without underwear for the Queen's honors award (Fraser, 2022). In addition to that, the brand was always activist, most notably concerning environment and political campaigning. According to the brand statement, the Vivienne Westwood brand has,

> always used our collections and catwalk shows as a platform to campaign for a better world. Vivienne herself spoke out tirelessly about the effects of climate change and over-consumption, while mobilising international attention around ecological crusading. She was very passionate about art, culture and education and advocated engaging with the world through their pursuit (Westwood.com, n.d._a, n.p.).

Westwood has supported many causes, NGOs, grassroots charities, and campaigns. Collaborations include Amnesty International, War, Child and Liberty, and Greenpeace. Westwood's own Climate Revolution campaign was launched in 2012 during the London Paralympics closing ceremony. She has written an activist Manifesto, Active Resistance to Propaganda, arguing for the protection of the planet, and including offering a strategy for a culture-led economic strategy that could save the world (Westwood.com, n.d._b; Westwood, 2007). In 2013, Westwood designed a logo for the Save the Arctic campaign, and in 2015, she launched a global campaign against industrial fishing and drilling (Westwood.com, n.d._a).

Therefore, Westwood's approach to advertising and PR can be seen through several intertwined strategies, activism as branding, earned media through controversy and PR stunts, anti-fashion messaging, collaborations with activist groups aligned with the designer's values, and narratives and cultural capital over products and consumption. This is unique in comparison to other designers, even those such as YSL who were inspired by the anti-fashion movement, the beatniks, but have still maintained the element of elegance and prestige, whereas Westwood was always a rebel and an activist brand. This makes Vivienne Westwood unique among designers of the 1970s, 1980s, and 1990s; however, her leading position did not fade with the arrival of younger designers also committed to preserving the planet and fostering diversity.

Table 9.5 provides a historical summary of advertising and PR efforts of Vivienne Westwood since the 1970s, when the brand gained traction with the SEX Boutique publicity.

Table 9.5 Westwood's Advertising and PR: A Historical Summary and Analysis of Notable Campaigns and Initiatives

PERIOD	NOTABLE CAMPAIGNS	MEDIUM	STRATEGY AND MESSAGES	SOURCES
1970s	SEX Boutique Publicity (with Malcolm McLaren)	Storefronts, punk flyers, press coverage	• Used controversial shop names and punk aesthetics to criticize establishment and instigate press attention	McLaren (2007)

(Continued)

Table 9.5 Continued

PERIOD	NOTABLE CAMPAIGNS	MEDIUM	STRATEGY AND MESSAGES	SOURCES
1981–1982	The New Romantic Look	Earned media coverage (press)	• Forging a rebel aesthetic • Positioning the brand as provocative, rebellious, and punk	V&A Museums (n.d._b)
1983-1991	Post Malcom McLaren work	Earned media coverage	• The Mini-Crini collection spring 1985 • The Time Machine Collection, Autumn/Winter 1988 • Cut, slash and pull Spring/Summer 1991	V&A Museums (n.d._a)
1989	Tatler magazine cover as Margaret Thatcher	Magazine cover, print	• Photographed style as Thatcher with the caption 'this woman was once punk'	Dobhal (2025)
1992	No Knickers Buckingham Palace PR stunt	Press photo (MBE ceremony)	• Twirled for photographers with no underwear outside Buckingham Palace	Fraser (2022)
2005	Anti-Iraq War & Climate Graphics Campaign	Runway messaging, posters, press releases	• Shirts with slogans 'I am not a Terrorist'	Istituto Marangoni (2023)
2007	Active Resistance to Propaganda Manifesto	Booklets, art film, public readings	• Merged philosophy, politics, and fashion into traveling storytelling campaign	Westwood (2007)
2013–2015	Save the Artic campaign in collaboration with Greenpeace	Fashion film, billboards, protest marches	• Collaboration with Greenpeace on climate change activism, runway shows featured Climate Revolution theme	VW – Greenpeace (n.d.)

(Continued)

Table 9.5 Continued

PERIOD	NOTABLE CAMPAIGNS	MEDIUM	STRATEGY AND MESSAGES	SOURCES
2016–2019	Vivienne Westwood x Andreas Kronthaler launch	Fashion show, mini documentaries, Instagram	• Rebranded ready-to-wear line under joint names, stylized narrative campaigns	Verner (2016)
2016	Save Venice Campaign	Spring 2016 campaign	• Campaign called Mirror the World shot by Juergen Teller in Venice, highlighting the impact of climate change and mass tourism	Marfil (2016)
2020	Julian Assange Jail Protest Appearance	Street protest, live news, social media	• Caged herself in a birdcage outside of court in protest of Assange's imprisonment	Watson (2020)
2021	Fall 2021 advert campaign (Autumn/ Winter 2021/2022)	Documentary images	• Documentary images featuring real local people in their environment highlighting punk roots of VW	Les Falcons (2021)
2022	Fall/Winter 2022 campaign with Courtney Love	Documentary images	• Documentary images featuring London area of Battersa and Courtney Love	Les Falcons (2022)

Source: Author's work

DISCUSSION QUESTIONS

- How did Vivienne Westwood's fashion philosophy challenge traditional ideas of beauty, gender, and class?
- How does the concept of 'fashion as activism' shape our understanding of Westwood's design legacy?
- What does Westwood's approach to sustainability reveal about the role of ethics in high fashion?
- Can Westwood's punk aesthetic be reconciled with her participation in the commercial fashion system?
- What elements of the Westwood brand remain consistent, even after her death?

- How does Westwood's legacy complicate the boundaries between fashion design, political protest, and performance art?
- How did Vivienne Westwood use PR stunts (e.g., the 'No Knickers' Buckingham Palace incident) to gain media attention?
- How does Westwood's use of shock, satire, and spectacle in advertising differ from more conventional luxury branding?
- How has Westwood balanced her anti-consumerist messaging with the commercial demands of running a fashion house?

Calvin Klein

Calvin Klein is known as the Master of Minimalism and the King of Clean, unfussy clothes with clean lines. His philosophy has been known as 'say more with less' and has historically focused on practical elegance and a cool, understated, chic outlook (Fraser-Cavassoni, 2017). Klein's style has been considered a uniquely American style. Klein himself praised his American background and the ability to climb the ladder on his own and succeed, thus presenting the American dream story (Fraser-Cavassoni, 2017). *Vogue* labeled Klein's fashion as modern, timeless, and easy (Fraser-Cavassoni, 2017), and Calvin Klein himself said about his fashion, 'My style, which is about purity and simplicity and less is more, has appeal all over the world' (Fraser-Cavassoni, 2017, back page).

Klein started his business in 1968 with a USD 10,000 loan from his friend Barry Schwartz (Fraser-Cavassoni, 2017). Initially, he focused on designing coats. In a January issue of *Vogue* in 1972 featuring Klein's designs, labeled the new fashion as 'the new nonchalance in fashion' (Bailey, 1972, p. 50).

> For once, it isn't a hemline or a waistline that's going to change the way you look in your clothes. It's a whole mood of dressing – a nonchalance – and it's been coming on since fall. ... Everything we're about to show you – the coats you pull on like small, cozy sweaters; the sweater offhandedness of dresses, pants suits; the hats that fit on the head the way a sweater fits on the body .... In a very quick, very vivid way fashion describes us to ourselves and how we live in our times ... which, in 1972, is faster, more freely, and more interestingly than any women in history .... This is the era of the woman who cares about how she looks but doesn't care to spend her day thinking about it. Once she's got them on, she wants to be able to relax into her clothes – forget them – know that she's correct in them, attractive, and that they will take her not only where she's going but where she just might, on the turn of a whim, decide to go instead – or as well as – or maybe not .... And this, in case it hasn't crossed your mind, is what fashion is all about today. About women .... Today (Bailey, 1972, p. 50).

This endorsement of nonchalance in fashion was written under the editorship of Grace Mirabella, who promoted American working woman style in *Vogue* (*Mirabella*, 1995), and Calvin Klein was one of the American designers who benefited from her editorship. The *Vogue* issue for January 1972 featured Klein's beige coat from his collection, which at the outset looked like a cardigan. *Vogue* said: '...no collar, no lining – something to just throw on over a shirt and pants, tie in an offhand way – and go. Great!' (Bailey, 1972, p. 56). Klein said to *Vogue* that 'American women needed to be streamlined' because 'They moved faster, they were working, they were raising kids ... they were busy – they didn't have time to change. They went to work, to the theatre, to a restaurant. That was my inspiration. What I didn't know is that there were people all over the world who were thinking the same way' (Fraser-Cavassoni, 2017, p. 13).

Klein was born in 1942 and grew up in an American, working-class Jewish family in the Bronx, New York. His father was a grocer who taught him that there are two types of customers, those willing to pay extra and those who are not (Fraser-Cavassoni, 2017). However, it was his mother who influenced his interest in fashion. His mother's colors werebeige, cream, white, and brown (Fraser-Cavassoni, 2017), which are up to this day Klein's colors, particularly for coats. Klein said, 'simplicity is how it has to be' (Fraser-Cavassoni, 2017, p. 25). He obtained the Coty award for his designs in 1973. In 1974, he got his first *Vogue* cover with a model wearing a trench coat, which *Vogue* named 'the coat of the year' (Fraser-Cavassoni, 2017, p. 27). In 1975, the most important issue of the year, September, featured a cover page focused on American women and the title 'all the clothes American women like best' (*Vogue*, 1975a). Bloomingdale's advert featured Calvin Klein collection saying, 'The suit you wished you'd always had … Fall …. it's nature at her most splendid. And splendor is second nature to Calvin Klein' (Bloomingdale's advert, *Vogue*, 1975, p. 2). Equally, Saks Fifth Avenue featured an advert promoting Calvin Klein emphasizing exclusive stock of Collection Sportswear (Saks Fifth Avenue advert, *Vogue*, 1975d, p. 35), Neiman-Marcus Calvin Klein's Fall collection, focusing on skirts and blouses for combinations (Neiman-Marcus advert, *Vogue*, 1975c, p. 71), Woodward & Lothrop promoted suits (Woodward & Lothrop advert, *Vogue*, 1975e, p. 72), Kaufmann's promoted eveningwear (Kaufmann's advert, Vogue, 1975b, p. 173), etc. In the same issue, which was already dominated by Calvin Klein's fashion due to so many adverts promoting various styles, *Vogue*'s Michals (1975) also wrote about Klein's fashion in a large article on American fashion, featuring a full page of analysis of Calvin Klein's Fall collection, and giving the brand a historical and national legacy,

> If you were around in a hundred years from now and wanted a definitive picture of the American look in the 1975, you'd study Calvin Klein: the clothes that are as easy and unstructured as sweaters, the casual turn to city dressing – the whole mood of fashion today comes through in a way that a modern woman can understand and enjoy … and even afford for a change" (p. 232).

Klein was indeed always focused on the working woman's style, something American designers are often credited for. *Vogue* said: 'He really dresses a working woman so that she can be free to work' (Fraser-Cavassoni, 2017, p. 38).

REFLECT

Watch Klein's runways, specifically the latest ready-to-wear fall/winter. You can find these runways on brand's YouTube channel. When watching shows, pay attention to the colors of the collection, iconic designs previously introduced by Klein, and note how coats feature in collections. Analyze shows and new collections in line with what you know about the legacy of Klein. Consider how new collections draw from Klein's legacy designs and a historical focus on the American working woman's style, to what extent collections also draw from styles from various decades, and what innovative items you can recognize in a new collection.

Calvin Klein's Advertising and PR

Calvin Klein is known for iconic advertising campaigns. One of Calvin Klein's advertising philosophies has historically been centered on a view that 'sex sells', a philosophy the brand particularly enforced after launching jeans in 1978 with notable campaigns with Brooke Shields famously saying, 'You want to know what comes between me and my Calvins? Nothing' (Allaire, 2021). The advert caused outrage due to a 15-year-old appearing in a highly sexualized campaign (Allaire, 2021). The advert was pulled from American networks, NBC, ABC, and CBS, leaving both Klein and Shields surprised by the backlash (Malach, 2024; Allaire, 2021). Klein told WWD in 1994 that he 'didn't set out thinking how to be controversial' but that he needed something new and thought an advert with Shields was a hoot even though he recognized it was not received that way (Allaire, 2021, n.p.). However, this campaign was not the only controversy. In 1982, Klein debuted underwear and placed an athlete, Tom Hitnaus, on a campaign poster wearing just underwear (Allaire, 2021). This campaign was followed up with Mark Wahlberg and Kate Moss underwear campaigns in 1992 (Calvin Klein advert (1992) – Marky Mark [Mark Wahlberg] & Kate Moss; Marky Mark Calvin Klein advert). In 1995, *Unbutton that top button* campaign for Klein's jeans also caused a controversy due to teenagers being asked to unbutton their jeans while seemingly looking uncomfortable and shy (Malach, 2024). Klein pushed boundaries with advertising, but his campaigns have also launched the careers of sex symbols and supermodels, such as Mark Wahlberg and Kate Moss (Malach, 2024), who starred in his underwear campaigns during the 1990s.

Calvin Klein's advertising strategy can be summarized as centered on sex appeal and provocation, minimalist visual aesthetic (the focus on products and body wearing clothes, and clean backgrounds), celebrity and supermodels featuring in campaigns (Brooke Shields and Kate Moss from 1970s–1990s, later also Justin Bieber, Kendall Jenner, the Kardashians, Jeremy Allen, etc), and cultural controversy due to scandals that adverts caused. The fashion style, however, always focused on clean lines and simplicity in clothing, which was suitable for an American working woman's style, and thus celebrated by *Vogue*, particularly under the editorship of Grace Mirabella, known for embracing practical, working woman style and endorsing American designers (Mirabella, 1995). From the 1970s, when *Vogue* frequently featured something about Calvin Klein, the brand was on the rise in establishing itself as timeless and classic, and advertising had a large role in that. Calvin Klein was dubbed a Master of Marketing (Fraser-Cavassoni, 2017, p. 63). He claimed that he never meant to create controversial advertising, and that his intention was always to create an image rather than just sell clothes with adverts (Fraser-Cavassoni, 2017).

Table 9.6 provides a historical summary of advertising and PR efforts of Calvin Klein starting with 1968 when the brand was launched.

Table 9.6 Klein's Advertising and PR: A Historical Summary and Analysis of Notable Campaigns and Initiatives

PERIOD	NOTABLE CAMPAIGNS	MEDIUM	STRATEGY AND MESSAGES	SOURCES
1968	Brand launch (coats as a focus)	Rented a showroom at Manhattan's York Hotel	• Obtaining orders from department stores to promote his fashion (the first one was Bonwit Teller)	Malach (2024), Fraser-Cavassoni (2017)
1973	Coty Award	Publicity	• Earned media	Fraser-Cavassoni (2017)
1980	Brooke Shields for Clavin Klein Jeans	Print, TV adverts, posters, billboards	• Provocation through sexualized storytelling by a young actress (15 at the time)	Allaire (2021) 1980 Calvin Klein Jeans advert featuring Brooke Shields Calvin Klein Jeans – 'Brooke Shields – Nothing' (80's advert)
1982	Men's underwear launch with Tom Hitnaus campaign	Print, posters, billboards	• The first time an athlete was turned into a sex object • Sexualized storytelling and provocation	Whitson (2024)
1985	Obsession perfume launch and an advertising campaign	Print adverts, TV adverts	• Cinematographic campaign, high-quality for the time it was released, provocative with a woman leaving family	All four Calvin Klein 'Obsession' adverts (1985)
1988–1989	Eternity perfume launch and an advertising campaign	TV adverts, print, posters, billboards	• Christy Turlington starts in adverts	Calvin Klein Eternity Cologne advert (1988) Calvin Klein Eternity Cologne advert (1989)

(*Continued*)

Table 9.6 Continued

PERIOD	NOTABLE CAMPAIGNS	MEDIUM	STRATEGY AND MESSAGES	SOURCES
1992	Mark Wahlberg and Kate Moss for Calvin Klein underwear	Billboards, TV adverts, magazines	• Athletic sex appeal, minimalism, black and white photography and TV adverts, sexual appeal	Calvin Klein advert – Marky Mark (Mark Wahlberg) & Kate Moss – 1992 Calvin Klein advert – Marky Mark
1993	Obsession advertising campaign	Billboards, TV adverts, magazines	• Kate Moss as the face of obsession • Cinematographic approach, mystery storytelling	'Obsession' from Calvin Klein
1994	CK One Fragrance Launch	TV adverts, print, MTV adverts	• Cast androgynous youth, first major gender-neutral fragrance campaign	CK One (1994) television advert
1995	Jeans advertising campaign, Unbutton that top button	TV adverts, prints, billboards	• Controversy with an advert featuring youth in a front of camera being asked by a male voice to unbutton their jeans while they appear to feel shy and comfortable • Sexualized campaign; provocative	Calvin Klein (1995) jeans advert – 'Unbutton that top button' Calvin Klein (1995) jeans advert – Doug
2006	Kate Moss advertising campaign	TV adverts, posters	• Controversy due to Moss' scandals with drug use • and a loss of other brand collaborations	Calvin Klein (2006) advert

(Continued)

Table 9.6 Continued

PERIOD	NOTABLE CAMPAIGNS	MEDIUM	STRATEGY AND MESSAGES	SOURCES
2009	Another banned ad	Only released on calvinkleinjeans.com, and never got released on TV	• A controversy with models wearing only CK jeans and nothing else	Malach (2024)
2013	The first Superbowl advert	TV adverts, print	• Matthew Terry for Calvin Klein • Black and white advert for Klein's men's underwear focusing on athleticism and male physique	Calvin Klein Concept 2013 advert debuted during the Super Bowl
2015	Justin Bieber men's underwear advertising campaign	TV adverts, print	• Black and white advert for Klein's men's underwear focusing on athleticism and Bieber's physique	Justin Bieber – Calvin Klein underwear, Spring 2015
2017	Superbowl advert		• Black and white advert for Klein's men's underwear focusing on athleticism and male physique	Calvin Klein Concept 2017 advert debuted during the Super Bowl
2019–	#myCalvins digital campaign	Instagram, Tumblr, YouTube, influencer campaigns	• User-generated content with selfie-style underwear shots • Embraced selfie culture	CalvinKlein.us (n.d.)
2020	Eternity advertising campaign	TV adverts, digital	• Christy Turlington returns for the same advert, similar story but with a modern twist	Christy Turlington and Edward Burns for Eternity | CALVIN KLEIN

(*Continued*)

Table 9.6 Continued

PERIOD	NOTABLE CAMPAIGNS	MEDIUM	STRATEGY AND MESSAGES	SOURCES
2021	#proudin-mycalvins Pride campaign	Social media, videos (short films)	• Celebration of defining moments in the queer and trans journey • Short films document cast stories	PVH (2021)
2023	Calvins or Nothing campaign	Instagram, digital	• A cast of global stars (Jennie Kim, Blackpink, Kendall Jenner, Michael B. Jordan, Aaron Taylor-Johnson).	Malach (2024)
2024	Jeremy Allen for Calvin Klein Underwear	Fashion editorials, Instagram, outdoor	• Sex appeal, minimalist styling, city landscape (modern appeal)	Jeremy Allen White in Calvin Klein underwear | Spring 2024 Campaign
2024	This is Love Pride campaign	Digital videos, social media	• Cara Delevingne for C.Klein • Pride collection for apparel and underwear with a limited edition Pride monogram	PVH (2024) Calvin Klein Pride (2024), 100% Pure Love Featuring Cara Delevingne and Jeremy Pope.

Source: Author's work

DISCUSSION QUESTIONS

- How did Calvin Klein's minimalist aesthetic shape the brand's identity, and how has it evolved over the decades?
- In what ways did Calvin Klein redefine American fashion in the 1970s and 1980s?
- How did Calvin Klein's focus on basics –such as jeans, underwear, and fragrances – contribute to redefining luxury and accessibility? What does this say about the intersection of mass-market appeal and designer credibility?
- What role did Calvin Klein himself, as a designer and public figure, play in crafting the brand's image?
- How has Calvin Klein used celebrity endorsements and models to shape its public image and connect with new audiences?

- How did Calvin Klein's advertising help normalize and commodify sexuality in fashion branding?
- In the digital era, how has Calvin Klein adapted its PR and advertising strategies for social media platforms and global audiences?
- What lessons can be drawn from Calvin Klein's use of shock value in advertising for today's brand strategists?

Ralph Lauren

Ralph Lauren was born in New York in 1939 to a family of Jewish immigrants from Belarus. Originally, his surname was Lifshitz, which Ralph and his brothers changed to Lauren, a more easily pronounceable and more American-sounding surname (Baird-Murray, 2015). Lauren's father was an artist, and he grew up in the Bronx in a middle-class family. Lauren's interest in fashion was organic, rather than influenced by his upbringing. He said, 'I didn't dream of a certain life. I wasn't obsessed. I was a happy middle-class Jewish kid in the Bronx' (Baird-Murray, 2015, p. 14). He always had a sense of style and what was suitable and fashionable to wear and started to design at the age of 15. He was known as a hipster of the Bronx and ended up fascinated by the preppy style of Brooks Brothers (Baird-Murray, 2015). Baird-Murray (2015) called Lauren 'all-American as he could be' (p. 14). He described his fashion as 'a world that we've all grown up with and love, whether … through the movies or our dreams' (Baird-Murray, 2015, p. 78). In a commentary on his 2025 ready-to-wear show, *Vogue* called Ralph Lauren's clothes 'synonymous with all-American style world over', citing also his Purple Label and Polo collections, as well as his 50th anniversary show in Central Park in 2018, as big brand achievements that make it also all-American (Phelps, 2024). *Vogue* has attached an all-American label to Lauren many times over the decades, promoting the brand to Americans as local and representative of their culture, as well as appealing to international audiences who like a leisurely style associated with the US since the rise of department stores, and Mirabella's time in *Vogue*.

Ralph Lauren launched his empire in 1967, initially focusing on men's neckties, but he soon switched to his iconic product, men's Polo shirts. He was working from the Empire State Building, taking inspiration from the glamour of Old Hollywood (Ralphlauren.com, n.d.). His first men's collection debuted in 1968, but he said that he wanted something more exciting. In 1970, Ralph Lauren opened a shop in Bloomingdale's (Ralphlauren.com, n.d.). In 1972, he launched polo shirts for men, accompanied by the first campaign that positioned Polo as a refined, Ivy League, East Coast elegance, introducing aspiration into menswear (Ralphlauren.com, n.d.). In the same year, a woman's collection was launched to great acclaim. Ralph Lauren said, 'When I started to make menswear, women were always asking, "Can you make that for me?"' (Ralphlauren.com, n.d., n.p.).

His successful campaigns resulted in awards very early in his career, such as the Coty award in 1976, when he won awards in both men's and women's fashion (Ralphlauren.com, n.d.). In 1979, Lauren launched his Americana collection by taking inspiration from the cowboy spirit and the American West. The tagline was 'made to be worn' (Crook, n.d.). Americana, up to this day, remains a notable RL collection, which has been re-interpreted in many collections. Another notable collection was the 1981 Santa Fe collection inspired by the city's artistry and free spirit, celebrating the Southwest (ralphlauren.com, n.d.). In 1984, the Safari collection was launched, evoking inspiration from African safaris, with the ad campaign featuring a reference to the film Out of Africa, which was set to come the following year (Ralphlauren.com, n.d.). In 1995, the Purple Label was introduced, inspired by European tailoring, refinement, and style (Ralphlauren.com, n.d.). Over the years, the business expanded to include not just men's and women's clothes but also home, flagship stores, and restaurants, as well as significant philanthropic activities such as The Ralph Lauren Centre for Breast Cancer Research (Ralphlauren.com, n.d.).

REFLECT

Watch Ralph Lauren's runways, specifically the latest ready-to-wear fall/winter. You can find these runways on brand's YouTube channel. When watching shows, pay attention to the iconic designs previously introduced by the brand, and note how Americana style features in collections. Analyze shows and new collections in line with what you know about the legacy of Ralph Lauren. Consider how new collections draw from Lauren's legacy designs and a historical focus on the American working woman's style, to what extent collections also draw from styles from various decades, and what innovative items you can recognize in a new collection.

Ralph Lauren's Advertising and PR

Ralph Lauren's advertising and PR are centered on lifestyle branding, rather than focusing solely on products. Lauren has historically promoted his fashion as an American lifestyle framed as one of heritage, luxury, and aspiration. In this, cinematographic advertising has been used, such as film campaigns resembling Hollywood films, particularly classic ones evoking also Ralph Lauren's collaborations with Hollywood and TV (e.g., *The Great Gatsby, Annie Hall, Friends*). However, Ralph Lauren brand is also known for excellent PR, such as publicity around flagship awards (e.g., Coty awards), creating publicity around film and TV collaborations (e.g., launching a Rachel Green collection in a *Friends* show anniversary year or the 20s style collection evoking *The Great Gatsby* collaboration). Finally, the brand has partnered with celebrities and while Ralph Lauren is not a celebrity driven brand, it has selected collaborations that match brand's focus on selling a lifestyle and values, such as Olympic athletes in Team USA uniforms Ralph Lauren designed, or Gwyneth Paltrow who famously wore Ralph Lauren's dress at the Oscars, etc. Because of a carefully crafted image and a lifestyle story, Ralph Lauren has been dubbed the synonym with American fashion by the *New York Times* (*New York Times*, 2025).

Table 9.7 provides a historical summary of notable advertising and PR campaigns by Ralph Lauren starting from 1972 Polo launch.

Table 9.7 Lauren's Advertising and PR: A Historical Summary and Analysis of Notable Campaigns and Initiatives

PERIOD	NOTABLE CAMPAIGNS	MEDIUM	STRATEGY	IMPACT
1972	Polo by Ralph Lauren launch campaigns	Print, billboards	• Positioned Polo as refined, Ivy League East Coast elegance, introduced aspirational menswear visuals	Ralphlauren.com (n.d._a)
1974	*The Great Gatsby*, costume design (fashion of the 1920s)	Film production, press coverage (earned)	• Provided menswear and tailored costumes	Corsillo (2015)
1976	Coty award for womenswear and the Coty Hall of Fame award for menswear	Earned media coverage	• Recognition • Establishing legacy	Ralphlauren.com (n.d.)
1977	*Annie Hall*, costume design	Film production, press coverage (earned), major impact on fashion (suit jackets with rolled up sleeves)	• Women started to take men's jacket and roll up sleeves like Keaton in the movie • Diane Keaton becomes a symbol for Ralph Lauren's fashion and amasses following	*Annie Hall* Official Trailer #1 – Woody Allen Movie (1977) HD Ralphlauren.com (n.d.)
1980s	Lifestyle campaigns	Print, retail displays, TV adverts	• Blended fashion with home, fragrance and accessories	Tashjian (2014)
1986	*Time* cover page	Earned media	• Recognition and establishing legacy	Ralphlauren.com (n.d.)
1992	CFDA Lifetime Achievement Award	Earned media	• Recognition • Confirmation of legacy and heritage	Ralphlauren.com (n.d.)

(Continued)

Table 9.7 Continued

PERIOD	NOTABLE CAMPAIGNS	MEDIUM	STRATEGY	IMPACT
1999-2004	*Friends* show collaboration	Rachel Green (Jennifer Aniston works as marketing director in RL Polo and wears RL designs)	• Collaboration and endorsement • Brand cemented as all-American	Season 5, episode 17, The One with Rachel's Inadvertent Kiss (Rachel's interview at RL) Employed at RL, seasons 5–10, RL featured in the show himself in S6 E8
1999	Gwyneth Paltrow endorsement	Earned media	• Red carpet (Oscar) appearance	Goldstone (2024) Ralphlauren.com (n.d.)
2007	2nd CFDA Menswear Designer of the Year Award	Earned media coverage	• Recognition and legacy	Ralphlauren.com (n.d.)
2010	Ralph Lauren receives a key to the city (NYC)	Earned media coverage	• Legacy and recognition	Ralphlauren.com (n.d.)
2011	The Great Gatsby collection, Spring/Summer 2012	Film credits, red carpet press, earned media coverage	• Remake of the Great Gatsby's collection and intertwining the brand with a popular film • Reminding audiences of Ralph Lauren's role in the first film	Freeman (2011)
2017	MoMA exhibition features Ralph Lauren's polo	Earned media coverage	• Legacy and recognition	Ralphlauren.com (n.d.)

(*Continued*)

Table 9.7 Continued

PERIOD	NOTABLE CAMPAIGNS	MEDIUM	STRATEGY	IMPACT
2018	50 years of advertising celebration in Central Park	Earned media coverage	• Legacy, heritage	Ralphlauren.com (n.d.)
2019	50th Anniversary Friends collection	Fashion show, documentary, editorials	• Staged a show in Central Park • Released branded retrospective content	Newbold (2019), Gardner (2019)
2019	Very Ralph documentary	Documentary produced by HBO	• Legacy and heritage • Recognition of contribution to American fashion	Very Ralph (2019)
2020-	Legacy campaign	Videos, documentary style, behind-the-scenes content	• Legacy campaign asserting brand's legacy, heritage, craftsmanship and tradition	The Making of a Moment: Ralph Lauren (2020–)
2022	Ralph Lauren x Morehouse & Spelman Colleges	Fashion film, Instagram, PR events	• Documentary produced by Historically Black Colleges and Universities Association (HBCU) alumni • Cast alumni and students in campaign styled on 1920s–1950s Black collegiate culture	A Portrait of the American Dream: A film by Ralph Lauren (2022)
2023	Polo Ralph Lauren 'All or Nothing at All'	Short film, social, digital	• High-style romance film set in NYC, blending fashion, jazz, and nightlife storytelling	*Runway Magazine* (2021) All or Nothing at All (2021)
2024–2025	Great Gatsby 100th anniversary collection	Lifestyle editorials, social media, capsule product drops	• Revived the 'roaring 20s' inspired styling with linen, flapper dresses, Art Deco patterns	*RL Mag* (n.d.)

Source: Author's work

DISCUSSION QUESTIONS

- How did Ralph Lauren's early life and career in tie design influence the development of his brand's aesthetic?
- What role do nostalgia and American heritage play in Ralph Lauren's collections? Can you identify recurring motifs or themes across decades?
- Ralph Lauren often blends formalwear with casual Americana (e.g., tuxedos with jeans). How does this blending reflect his broader design philosophy?
- How did Ralph Lauren's work on *The Great Gatsby* (1974) shape public perception of his brand?
- How has Ralph Lauren differentiated his brand through sub-labels (e.g., Polo, Purple Label)? What consumer identities or lifestyles do these represent?
- How does Ralph Lauren use storytelling in his ad campaigns to construct a lifestyle rather than simply market products?
- In what ways has Ralph Lauren's advertising contributed to the creation of an aspirational American identity? How does this compare to European luxury brands?
- Ralph Lauren has used relatively few celebrity endorsements compared to other luxury brands. How has this choice influenced the perception of authenticity or exclusivity in the brand?
- How has Ralph Lauren adapted its advertising and PR approach for digital platforms and global markets while maintaining brand consistency?
- Can Ralph Lauren's advertising be considered a form of cultural storytelling?
- Compare Ralph Lauren's branding strategy with another American designer (e.g., Calvin Klein). What key differences stand out in their advertising tone or PR approach?
- Is Ralph Lauren's idealized vision of American life still relevant in today's global fashion landscape?
- What challenges might Ralph Lauren face in continuing to use nostalgia and traditionalism in an increasingly sustainability- and inclusivity-driven fashion industry?

Ann Lowe

Ann Lowe (1898–1981) was an American couturier, born and raised in Clayton, Alabama. As with many Black designers, Lowe navigated a unique and often challenging path in establishing and maintaining her brand identity within the fashion landscape from the mid-20th century through to posthumous recognition in the 21st century. Lowe's brand promotion was mainly centered on discretion and exclusivity, which was suitable for the time in which she lived, when there was no recognition of Black designers. Lowe worked for elite clientele providing couture garments (Harlem World, 2017), but this work was behind the scenes, relying on word-of-mouth and private commissions rather than public campaigns (McVicker, 2020). She relied on society pages and press mentions of her work, but she was often uncredited in the mainstream press (Harlem World, 2017; Belton, 2022).

Lowe designed a wedding dress for Jacqueline (Jackie) Kennedy, a society member and later the First Lady of the US in 1953, which received press coverage, but Lowe was not credited as a designer of the iconic dress (Minutaglio, 2019; Nichols, n.d.). She designed this dress when she was operating a boutique in Harlem, New York City, where she offered couture garments (Harlem World, 2017). She also designed full bridesmaids' dresses for the Kennedy wedding and Kennedy's debutante ball before that, making Jackie Kennedy one of her most loyal and notable clients (Belton, 2022). Equally, she designed an Oscar ceremony dress for actress Olivia de Havilland in 1947, but was not credited for the design, which was wrongly attributed to another designer (Dockery Smith, 2016; Belton, 2022). From 1962 to 1966, Lowe owned a salon on Madison Avenue in New York, trying to build her business with elite consumers, but the main credit and recognition came from Black magazines, such as Ebony magazine (Way, 2024). However, some discreet credit did occasionally come from fashion magazines, such as *Vogue* in 1955 which featured a photo of Jackie Kennedy's stepsister in a dress by Lowe and mentioned her name as a designer in the photo caption (*Vogue*, August 1, 1955, cited from Belton, 2022), which eventually opened doors to more discreet recognition from other fashion magazines. In 1961, she received an award, Couturier of the Year, the first Black designer to obtain that award, which resulted in further publicity in society pages such as Park Avenue Social Review (Belton, 2022). She achieved recognition and established legacy posthumously.

Table 9.8 summarizes the advertising and PR activities of Ann Lowe, which are not as extensive as those of other designers due to a lack of exposure and opportunities; however, the publicity she obtained is remarkable due to the lack of visibility of Black designers.

REFLECT

Lowe was celebrated for her exquisite workmanship, yet often excluded from public credit.

What does Lowe's experience reveal about whose labor is seen, valued, or made invisible in fashion and creative industries? How does this shape the stories we tell about design history?

Structural Inequality in Creative Work

As a Black woman working in early–mid 20th century America, Lowe navigated a field shaped by racism, elitism, and gendered expectations. How do structural inequalities continue to shape the opportunities available to racialized and minority designers today? What forms of gatekeeping persist or have evolved?

Aesthetic Excellence vs. Economic Security

Despite her artistic success, Lowe often struggled financially because couture labor was undervalued and underpaid. How does the tension between creative excellence and economic survival appear in today's fashion labor markets—for emerging designers, freelance workers, or artisans?

Legacy and Storytelling

Lowe's legacy is now being reclaimed by museums and scholars after decades of erasure.

What responsibilities do educators, museums, and brands have in reshaping the narrative so figures like Lowe are appropriately represented? How can you contribute to more inclusive storytelling in your own work?

Figure 9.9 A dress designed by Ann Lowe, worn by Barbara Baldwin Dowd, 1066–1967

Collection of the Smithsonian National Museum of African American History and Culture, Gift of the Black Fashion Museum founded by Lois K. Alexander-Lane

Figure 9.10 A dress designed by Ann Lowe cca. 1960

Collection of the Smithsonian National Museum of African American History and Culture, Gift of the Black Fashion Museum founded by Lois K. Alexander-Lane

Table 9.8 Lowe's Advertising and PR: A Historical Summary and Analysis Of Notable Campaigns and Initiatives

PERIOD	NOTABLE CAMPAIGNS	MEDIUM	STRATEGY AND MESSAGES	SOURCES
1950	Ann Lowe's Gowns, Harlem, NYC boutique	Local press, society pages	Couture-quality garments to wealthy Black and White clients	Harlem World (2017)
1950s	Socialite commissions	Press mentions, society columns	Discreet custom design work for upper-class society, behind-the-scenes work	McVicker (2020)
1953	Wedding dress design for Jackie Kennedy	Press coverage of the wedding with no mention of the designer	Uncredited for the wedding dress	Nichols (n.d.) Minutaglio (2019)
1961–1966	Move to Madison Avenue Salon	*Ebony* magazine, fashion media	Building brand among both Black and White elite consumers Inclusive couture	Way (2024)
2016	Museum exhibitions and retrospective honors	Museum shows, *Vogue*, *New York Times*, Smithsonian	Posthumous exhibitions, restoring her legacy	Winterthur Museum The Metropolitan Museum of Art National Museum of African American History & Culture
2021	Google Arts and Culture and Black History Month recognition	Google homepage, digital education	Featured in Google Doodle and public storytelling campaigns during Black History Month	Google Arts and Culture
2021	National First Ladies Library and Museum recognition	Short documentary	Legacy established and recognized	Legacy lecture: the life and times of fashion designer Ann Lowe (2021)

(Continued)

Table 9.8 Continued

PERIOD	NOTABLE CAMPAIGNS	MEDIUM	STRATEGY AND MESSAGES	SOURCES
2022	Black Couture Fashion Designer and Fashion's Best Kept Secret	Book	Legacy honored	Belton (2022)

Source: Author's work

DISCUSSION QUESTIONS

- What barriers did Ann Lowe face as an African American woman in the fashion industry during the 20th century?
- How does Ann Lowe's story complicate mainstream narratives about American fashion history?
- Why was Ann Lowe largely unrecognized for designing Jacqueline Kennedy's wedding dress until many years later, and what does this say about media representation and race in fashion?
- How might PR and advertising strategies have changed Ann Lowe's visibility during her career, had she had access to them?
- What role does retrospective media coverage (e.g., exhibitions, documentaries, fashion journalism) play in shaping Ann Lowe's legacy today?
- If Ann Lowe were launching her brand in today's fashion industry, what public relations strategies would help elevate her work to the recognition it deserves?
- How does Ann Lowe's career contribute to our understanding of fashion as a site of both exclusion and empowerment?
- In what ways can fashion education and advertising practices become more inclusive by integrating stories like Ann Lowe's into their core narratives?

Jason Wu

Jason Wu was born in Taiwan and grew up in Vancouver, Canada. Owing to the donation of a sewing machine and encouragement from his parents, Wu began sewing and creating patterns for dolls at a very early age (Lackie, 2017). At the age of only 16, Wu became the creative director of Integrity Toys. This miniature doll craftsmanship laid the groundwork for Wu's future couture techniques, which the brand is known for.

In 2006, Wu launched his designer label. His debut was marked by acclaimed campaigns, and in 2021, he received awards such as the Fashion Group International's Rising Star Award (Ayala, 2024). He achieved global fame with an endorsement from Michelle Obama, who wore his one-shoulder white chiffon gown to the first presidential inauguration of Barack Obama as the 44th President of the United States. In 2017, Wu said to *Vogue* that despite many highs, the Obama inauguration dress is still the 'best experience of his life' (Phelps, 2017, n.p). In the second inauguration, Michelle Obama again supported Jason Wu, that time wearing a long ruby-colored chiffon gown, with a cross-halter strap neckline and deep back featuring velvet details (Smithsonian, 2014). These two gowns have been put on display in such museums as the Smithsonian National Museum of American History and Museum of the City of New York, as an important part of American history.

Wu's fashion was about fantasy-driven eveningwear, but later he switched to design fashion influenced by haute couture names such as Dior and Yves Saint Laurent, showing his creative evolution and growing up together with his brand (Phelps, 2017; The Talks, n.d.). Dave Lackie, beauty editor, called Wu on his blog as 'this generation's most talented fashion designer' (Lackie, 2017, n.p.). Wu is seen as an American designer following in the footsteps of Donna Karan, Ralph Lauren, and Michael Kors because he is based in New York City and has a feminine focus. Wu said about his designs: 'I create clothes for women who are not only fiercely fashionable but also own their power and femininity, but the heart of my collection will always be the craftsmanship: everything starts with my obsession with details' (Lackie, 2017). In the Spring 2025 collection, Wu paid homage to the heritage and artistry of fashion with a collaboration with an artist, Tong Yang-Tze, known for large-scale calligraphy. The Jason Wu studio described the collaboration as 'drawing inspiration from her monumental works, Jason Wu's designs honor identity, culture, and the enduring relationship between art and fashion' (Jasonwustudio.com, n.d.). With this, the philosophy of Jason Wu's brand matches the philosophy behind French haute couture, which has historically always been presented and celebrated as art, rather than following trends, thus seeing fashion as art and more than just a trend (in line with the view of historically most influential haute couture designers, such as Coco Chanel). In an interview with The Talks, Wu talked about his aesthetics and early influence on his philosophy:

> Well I think it's very much my personality. I don't consider myself a very trendy person. I also hate to use the word "cool." I think it has a lot to do with the way I was brought up. My mother was a huge influence on me and my aesthetics. I remember when we grew up, my mom had antique furniture in our house and I always thought it was pretty old. All my friends had glossy, newly built houses and my mom bought like a 70-year-old house. And back then I wanted what everyone else had, but as I grew up I realized that wasn't what I liked anymore. I preferred things with a history, with a point of view, things that have been touched and have been through time. And that has really helped shape my aesthetics (The Talks, n.d.).

REFLECT

Jason Wu became widely known after designing pieces for Michelle Obama, especially her 2009 and 2013 inauguration gowns. Consider the following questions:

How did this moment influence Wu's symbolic and cultural capital in the industry?

How do high-stakes political or celebrity moments shape the public's understanding of a designer's brand?

What responsibilities or constraints might arise for a designer after such rapid elevation?

Jason Wu's Advertising and PR

Jason Wu's brand is focused on using personal narratives and blending them with brand identity. He often emphasizes his personal story, common for high-end, luxury designers, starting with designing dolls and as a self-made designer in the US. His immigrant identity, as well as Taiwanese heritage, gives him a different voice in American fashion, historically dominated by European perspectives, and since the 1970s, also by American designers.

Advertising and PR strategy of Wu's brand focuses on the red carpet followed by Michelle Obama endorsement, but also editorial focus with high-quality, glossy visuals presented in advertising campaigns, lookbooks, runway photographs, cinematic aesthetic capturing clean lines of his collections, echoing high fashion and haute couture world (which inspires Wu). The communication focus, both in runways and public statements, is on craftsmanship and artistry, in line with traditional haute couture brands, also historically focused on designer persona, artisanry, and craftsmanship.

Table 9.9 presents a summary of notable advertising and PR efforts by Jason Wu's brand.

Table 9.9 Wu's Advertising and PR: A Historical Summary and Analysis of Notable Campaigns and Initiatives

PERIOD	NOTABLE CAMPAIGNS	MEDIUM	STRATEGY	SOURCE
2009	Michelle Obama's inaugural gown	Live TV, press, global press	• Celebrity endorsement	Wells (2009), Barnard (2009), Keltner de Valle (2009)
2013	Michelle Obama's second inaugural gown	News, fashion press, Smithsonian exhibit	• Celebrity endorsement signaling also loyalty to the brand	Denley (2013), CBS News (2013), Alexander (2013), Reeve (2013), Harwood (2017), Smithsonian (2014)
2013	Jason Wu for Lancôme collaboration	Print, in-store promotions	• Capsule makeup collection in signature muted tones aligned with luxury beauty	Molina (2013)

(Continued)

Table 9.9 Continued

PERIOD	NOTABLE CAMPAIGNS	MEDIUM	STRATEGY	SOURCE
2014–2015	Advertising campaigns for Spring 2015 collection	A series of adverts featuring in NY restaurants	• Capturing contrasts and attention to detail, capturing a moment in time	Les Façons (2014), Fashion Gone Rogue (2015), Okwodu (2015)
2016	Grey Jason Wu launch	Social media, editorial lookbooks, in-store PR events	• Accessible elegance with soft tailoring for everyday wear	Farra (2016)
2017–2018	Jason Wu x Eloquii collaboration	Digital adverts, social media, fashion press	• Inclusive sizing	Ogunnaike (2018)
2017	Earned media coverage	*Vogue* retrospective article	• Obama endorsement promoted	Phelps (2017)
2021	New York Fashion Week (NYFW) 'Grocery Store' Presentation (Pandemic Show)	Livestream, Instagram	• SS21 show presented inside a recreated bodega • Focus on comfort and accessibility	Rantala (2021), Thomas (2021)
2021	Haute CATure collection and advertising campaign	Digital advert	• An association with haute couture • A message of luxury • That also diversifies consumer base due to cat reference	Stanley (2021)

Source: Author's work

DISCUSSION QUESTIONS

- How does Jason Wu's personal background and early experience designing doll clothes influence the values and aesthetics of his brand? In what ways does Wu's personal story contribute to the authenticity of his brand in a competitive luxury market?
- In what ways does Jason Wu balance modern femininity with traditional luxury in his designs?
- How does Wu's identity as an Asian-American designer shape his brand narrative and position in the fashion industry?
- How do Jason Wu's advertising campaigns reflect the values of elegance, craftsmanship, and quiet luxury?
- What visual strategies does Wu use in his campaigns to differentiate his brand from trend-driven or streetwear-focused labels?
- How did Michelle Obama's 2009 inauguration gown transform Jason Wu's public image and brand trajectory?
- What role do partnerships (e.g., with Lancôme, Brizo, or Eloquii) play in shaping the public perception of the Jason Wu brand?
- How does Jason Wu's PR strategy respond to conversations around inclusivity and cultural representation in fashion?

Aurora James

Aurora James founded her brand Brother Vellies in 2013. The brand was born out of her travels to Africa, where she learned about artisans and traditional methods of design and sewing (Williams, I., 2023a). The name of the brand, Brother Vellies, is a homage to the South African term 'veldskoen' or veld shoe, which is the brand's signature item, adapted by James using locally sourced materials. The goal of Brother Vellies is to preserve traditional design practices from the African continent, support artisan communities, and champion handmade quality over fast fashion (Williams, I., 2023; Brookins, 2022).

In 2020, James also founded a 15 Percent Pledge (15PP) asking retailers to commit 15 percent of their shelves to Black-owned businesses (Williams, I., 2023). The Pledge quickly gathered responses from 29 retailers and became one of the fastest-growing NGOs (Williams, I., 2023). James said to *Fashion* that thoughtfulness about consumption has always been important to her, along with sustainability. This commitment also came from her upbringing because her father died when she was very young, and her mom raised her, instilling values of deep appreciation for sartorial craftsmanship and understanding other cultures, which she did by also purchasing and collecting items produced in various countries (Williams, I., 2023). Fifteen Percent Pledge argued that since Black people make up 15 percent of the population, retailers are asked to commit 15 percent of their shelf space to Black-owned brands (15percentpledge.org, n.d.). The initiative has 35 corporate partners who pledged support, shifting USD 14 billion of revenue to Black-owned businesses (Williams, I., 2023). The initiative's website offers a finder to find Black brands, and an opportunity to sign up to take the pledge (Williams, I., 2023). This initiative gave James recognition and media coverage that provided visibility to her brand; however, what is important to mention is that this commitment comes from James' background and values instilled in her in childhood, thus, the brand can be perceived as authentic, and it is also different and ahead of its time. James' brand is committed to social justice and supporting a minority community; thus, new designers are changing the fashion industry by showing that fashion can be luxurious and inclusive (James, n.d.).

James's debut collection (Spring 2014) featured shoes made by African artisan designers, and in 2015, she launched handbags. She also won the CFDA/*Vogue* Fashion Fund award in 2015 (Maleri, 2015), and in 2016, she was inducted into the CFDA (Council of Fashion Designers of America), where she later also became its vice-chair (2022) (Business of Fashion, n.d.).

REFLECT

Aurora James has used her platform as a designer to advocate for systemic change in fashion retail.

How does Aurora James's personal identity and lived experience inform her leadership of the 15 Percent Pledge?

In what ways do you see her activism linked to her work as a designer and founder of Brother Vellies?

What does her approach suggest about the evolving responsibilities of designers in today's fashion ecosystem?

Aurora James' Advertising and PR

James's approach to advertising and PR can be described as mission-driven branding because her brand's identity is centered on equity and heritage. As with most new designers, the communication focus seems to be on PR and generating publicity for the brand; however, this is done in a similar way to large luxury brands, by creating a designer persona. Therefore, PR messaging highlights James' personal background and how her mother influenced her values, which now feed into Brother Vellies, as well as her ethical values in artisan partnerships in Africa, commitment to cultural appreciation and not appropriation (i.e., James does not take inspiration from Africa, she hires African artisans to produce her fashion), social impact and commitment to social justice through activism (15 Percent Pledge).

Rather than using traditional advertising campaigns (which are indeed the domain of large brands with large advertising budgets), James has so far relied on celebrity placements, and organic influencer relationships, as well as through attendance at high-profile events (e.g., design she provided to Congresswoman Alexandria Ocasio-Cortez) and advocacy PR (15 Percent Pledge, public talks and engagements, etc.). She also uses media for thought leadership because in all her media interviews, she speaks about her background and values, and how they feed into her brand, providing authenticity and credibility to the brand, as well as putting the brand on par with large luxury brands who also rely on their founder stories in their PR and advertising efforts.

Table 9.10 provides a summary of notable advertising and PR efforts of Aurora James.

Table 9.10 James' Advertising and PR: A Historical Summary and Analysis of Notable Campaigns and Initiatives

PERIOD	NOTABLE CAMPAIGNS	MEDIUM	STRATEGY AND MESSAGES	SOURCE
2013	Brother Vellies launch	Website, social media	• Positioning the brand as luxury and meaningful • Artisanal empowerment • Highlighting African craftsmanship, sustainability, ethical manufacturing from Africa	Brother Vellies (n.d.)
2016	TedTalk	YouTube, live audience	• Sustainability in fashion	TedTalk (2016)
2018	Earned media coverage	Vogue Italia	• Sustainability in fashion	Di Angelo (2018)
2020–2023	The 15 Percent Pledge	Instagram campaign tagging major retailer with a viral petition	• Calling retailers to commit 15% of shelf space to Black-owned brands to match population demographics	15percentpledge.com (n.d.)
2020	Major earned media coverage	*Forbes* magazine articles	• Promotion of the 15 Percent Pledge	Robinson (2020), Simon (2020), Setiawa (2020), Eldor (2023), Okwodu (2020)
2020	Media appearance	Time100 Talks	• Promotion of the 15 Percent Pledge	Time100 Talks (2020)
2022	Earned media coverage	Forbes magazine	• Promotion of the 15 Percent Pledge	Peluso (2022)
2022	Earned media coverage	*Glamour*'s Women of the Year	• Promotion of her work and activism	Williams, I. (2023)
2023	Earned media coverage	*Vogue*, Harper's Bazaar	• Promotion of the 15 Percent Pledge	Naquian Wheeler (2023), Betancourt (2023)

(*Continued*)

Table 9.10 Continued

PERIOD	NOTABLE CAMPAIGNS	MEDIUM	STRATEGY AND MESSAGES	SOURCE
2023	Book publication and promotion, earned media coverage	Wildflower published by Crown Publishing Group, launch celebrations in NY and LA, covered by *Vogue*	• Personal PR and relationship-building	Stewart (2023) James (n.d.)
2025	Major earned media coverage	Vogue	• Diversity advocacy	Garcia-Furtado (2025)

Source: Author's work

DISCUSSION QUESTIONS

- How has Aurora James used fashion as a platform for activism?
- How does her brand Brother Vellies incorporate African craftsmanship and sustainability into luxury fashion?
- In what ways does Aurora James challenge traditional notions of luxury in the fashion industry?
- What role do heritage and culture play in Aurora James's design aesthetic?
- What motivated Aurora James to launch the 15 Percent Pledge, and how has it impacted the retail industry?
- Should designers and brands be expected to take public stands on social issues, as Aurora James has?
- How can Aurora James's approach to business serve as a model for future fashion entrepreneurs?
- How has Aurora James leveraged media and press to amplify both her fashion brand and her advocacy work?
- What communication strategies has James used to align her personal brand with her professional work?

Carla Fernández

'One day we woke up and realized we couldn't care less about what happens in Paris. We do what they told us not to do. Our way of doing things seems suicidal to business

Figure 9.11 A portrait of designer Carla Fernández
Photo courtesy of Carla Fernández Studio

schools' (Manifesto of Fashion as Resistance, n.d., n.p.). This is the opening of a Manifesto of Fashion as Resistance published by Carla Fernández, a designer based in Mexico City who promotes resistance to conventional fashion business, and advocates for ethics in trading and design, and socially responsible fashion. Fernández's fashion vision is focused on 'preserving and revitalizing the textile legacy of indigenous and mestizo communities of Mexico' (Carlafernandez.com, n.d., n.p.). Her website also states that the brand's vision

Figure 9.12 A detail shot of a piece from the Diva collection by Carla Fernández
Photo courtesy of Carla Fernández Studio

is centered on an understanding that 'manual methods prove that ethical fashion can be innovative, avant-garde and progressive' (Carlafernandez.com, n.d., n.p.). To support this brand vision, Fernández has traveled extensively in Mexico and developed collaborations with artisans who specialize in handmade textiles and centuries-old Indigenous techniques, such as embroidery or manual weaving (Carlafernandez.com, n.d.). She works with over 180 weavers, embroiderers, and sculptors from many Mexican states and uses ancestral techniques in her fashion (De Sortiraparis, 2023).

REFLECT

Carla Fernández's studio works directly with Indigenous and regional artisan cooperatives across Mexico.

How does Fernández challenge conventional Western fashion systems through her collaborative, community-based approach?

What does it mean to treat artisans as co-creators rather than suppliers?

How does her work shift the ethical conversation from 'fair trade' to deeper forms of cultural respect and reciprocity?

Carla Fernández's Advertising and PR

Fernández has used advertising and public relations campaigns to articulate her unique vision for fashion, which is deeply rooted in Mexican cultural heritage and a commitment to artisanal collaboration, making her brand ethical and authentic. Her approach transcends conventional fashion advertising and PR, positioning her brand as a force for cultural preservation and social resistance. Through a multi-faceted strategy spanning exhibitions, publications, and digital engagement, Fernández has effectively amplified her core philosophy across various global platforms.

Fernández's approach to advertising and PR can also be described as thought leadership because the designer's values are embedded into her fashion brand, and she communicates these values through everything she says and does. Fernández demonstrates how ethical practices can serve as both moral imperatives and a strategic communication asset. Her social responsibility commitments are integrated into her brand's identity, demonstrating transparency, authenticity, and social consciousness, confirmed also with B Corp Certification. Other fashion PR professionals and advertisers should follow Fernández when considering CSR engagement because Fernández demonstrates how deeply rooting CSR into brand identity can bring authenticity, result in more meaningful storytelling, and become a powerful tool for brand differentiation.

Table 9.11 summarizes advertising and PR activities and publicity of Carla Fernández, which are mainly centered on earned media and publicity, as with all younger and emerging designers.

Table 9.11 Fernández's Advertising and PR: A Historical Summary and Analysis of Notable Campaigns and Initiatives

PERIOD	NOTABLE CAMPAIGNS	MEDIUM	STRATEGY AND MESSAGES	SOURCES
2000–	Taller Flora Mobile Lab	Ethnographic workshops, documentary, press	Traveling to communities to co-create designs	Taller Flora (n.d.)
2009–2015	Fashion Manifesto and Museum Retrospectives	Press features, museum talks, exhibits	Launched Manifesto of Fashion as Resistance book and toured exhibitions	Manifesto and Retrospectives (n.d.)
2015	Design. Culture.Mexico Exhibition (Heath Ceramics)	Press, exhibition networking	Couture-meets-crafts story in San Francisco	Heath Ceramics (n.d.)
2018	Fashion as Resistance touring manifesto	Museum shows, social media press	Visited major art institutions	V&A Museums (n.d.)
2022	A Mexican Fashion Manifesto at Denver Art Museum	Exhibition, catalog, media coverage	Showcased collaborations with artisans	Denver Art Museum (2022)
2023	*El futuro es hecho a mano* (The Future is Handmade) at Galerie du 19M, Paris	Press, social media, gallery launch	Celebration of artisan textile craft with 180+ Indigenous makers	De Sortiraparis (2023)
2025	Headliner at Fashion Week Mexico	Runway, press, digital marketing	Closed FW Mexico with Teocintle Spring/Summer 2024 collection, themes around native maize protection	Garcia (2025)

Source: Author's work

DISCUSSION QUESTIONS

- How does Carla Fernández use fashion to communicate messages of cultural preservation?
- In what ways does her brand function as both a fashion label and a platform for advocacy?
- How does Fernández challenge traditional Western beauty and fashion narratives through her campaigns and imagery?
- What visual codes and casting choices does she use to communicate Indigenous pride and resistance?
- What role does storytelling play in Fernández's branding and public relations strategy?
- How are artisans, history, and place integrated into her communications materials (lookbooks, campaigns, exhibitions, etc.)?
- How does Fernández navigate the tension between visibility and appropriation in global fashion marketing?
- What can her PR strategies teach emerging designers about ethical representation?
- In what ways does Carla Fernández's brand serve as a model for CSR (corporate social responsibility) in fashion?

References

Adverts and Documentaries

CHANEL

A rendez-vous. (2024). Retrieved from https://www.youtube.com/watch?v=fo4LLux-tfM&t=3s

AdLand TV advert. (1990). Retrieved from https://adland.tv/chanel-egoiste-balcony-1990-050-uk/

Bleu De Chanel, the Martin Scorsese film starring Timothée Chalamet. (2024). Retrieved from https://www.youtube.com/watch?v=mR1fQeRqUEY

Chanel N°5, the 1998 film by Luc Besson, with Estella Warren: Le Loup – Chanel Fragrance (1998). Retrieved from https://www.youtube.com/watch?v=-0XVX-AHUbg

Chanel N°5, the 1982 film by Ridley Scott: L'invitation au Rêve, le Jardin – Chanel Fragrance (1982). Retrieved from https://www.youtube.com/watch?v=cZ3vwlhHodo

Chanel N°5, the film Train de Nuit with Audrey Tautou – Chanel Fragrance (2011). Retrieved from https://www.youtube.com/watch?v=f5r5PXBiwR0

Chanel N°5, the film with Brad Pitt: There You Are – Chanel Fragrance (2012). Retrieved from https://www.youtube.com/watch?v=mGs4CjeJiJQ

Chanel N°5, the film with Gisele Bündchen, Michiel Huisman and Lo-Fang – Chanel Fragrance (2014). Retrieved from https://www.youtube.com/watch?v=8asRWe5XNw8&list=RD8asRWe5XNw8&start_radio=1

Chanel.com. (n.d.). *Inside Chanel Campaign.* Retrieved from https://www.chanel.com/us/about-chanel/inside-chanel/

Chanel N°5, the film with Nicole Kidman – Chanel Fragrance (2004). Retrieved from https://www.youtube.com/watch?v=0hcaaKhGL00

Chanel and Literature (2024–). Retrieved from https://www.youtube.com/playlist?list=PLzZkh7mnSyo7S8gyhlJ5OE7iCylyYeyLV

Chanel Connects (2021–). Retrieved from https://www.youtube.com/watch

?v=gZgLlAaMe08&list=PLzZkh7mnSyo7uC_dbZDs_l1sVbSFIW2Fh

Inside Chanel Campaign (2012–). Retrieved from https://www.youtube.com/watch?v=5FALzu5MF-A&list=PLEE61EDB90F0AA88F

Inside Chanel – Chapter 2 – Marilyn and No.5. Retrieved from https://www.youtube.com/watch?v=Wo8UtWiYiZI

Inside Chanel – Chapter 11 – The Colors of Chanel. Retrieved from https://www.youtube.com/watch?v=TaCdAscgpU0&list=PLEE61EDB90F0AA88F&index=37

Inside Chanel – Chapter 13 – Haute Couture. Retrieved from https://www.youtube.com/watch?v=19W7fvOBG0c

Inside Chanel – Chapter 16 – The Camelia. Retrieved from https://www.youtube.com/watch?v=GiOitbvl2IU&list=PLEE61EDB90F0AA88F&index=25

Inside Chanel – Chapter 23 – Biarritz. Retrieved from https://www.youtube.com/watch?v=rUN9R-aJnXE&list=PLEE61EDB90F0AA88F&index=10

La Piscine / Share the Fantasy. (1979). Retrieved from https://www.youtube.com/watch?v=kPDlnHkEAsA

L'instant Chanel, The Chanel Moment: Film 5 – Chanel Watches (2014). Retrieved from https://www.youtube.com/watch?v=lzyKV55SrbM

New York Times. Print adverts, December 16, 1924; June 10, 1934. Retrieved from https://timesmachine.nytimes.com/browser

Shapouri, B. (2008). Do you wear perfume to bed? *Glamour*, September 29. Retrieved from https://www.glamour.com/story/do-you-wear-perfume-to-bed

The Chanel Culture Fund (2021–). Retrieved from https://www.youtube.com/watch?v=2W9xUX1WkjM&list=PLzZkh7mnSyo4uaWm_OlqBVkqMMzy5JLPA

The Land of Desire. (2020). 55. Women At War 3: The Collaborator (Coco Chanel). Retrieved from https://www.thelandofdesire.com/2020/01/16/coco-chanel/

The Last Fashion Bible. (2021, December 14). *Chanel No 5: 100 Years of Iconic Imagery.* Retrieved from https://thelastfashionbible.com/2021/12/14/chanel-no-5-100-years-of-iconic-imagery/

DIOR

'Christian Dior, Designer of Dreams' at the Musée des Arts Décoratifs (2020). Retrieved from https://www.youtube.com/watch?v=FLWDWzMrkBE

Dior ambassador Robert Pattinson stays sharp in Dior Icons #shorts. Retrieved from https://www.youtube.com/shorts/6rWf4CenEds

Dior and I documentary (2014–2015). Retrieved from https://www.youtube.com/watch?v=Sd_qAzoCpil

Dior Autumn/Winter 2020–2021 Haute Couture. (2020). Retrieved from https://www.youtube.com/watch?v=yxBFwqRbI8c&t=23s

Dior.com (n.d._a). *Beauty AR, virtual try-ons.* Retrieved from https://www.dior.com/en_us/beauty/store-page-folder/dior-virtual-try-on.html

Dior documentaries 1. Retrieved from https://www.youtube.com/@Dior/search?query=documentaries

Dior documentaries 2. Retrieved from https://www.youtube.com/@Dior/search?query=documentaries

Dior J'Adore. (1999). Retrieved from https://www.youtube.com/watch?v=tVuPEgsF-3Y

'Dior Metamorphosis': The Making of Dior Cruise. (2024). Retrieved from https://www.youtube.com/watch?v=Alv1qrV3MZg

Eau Sauvage 1980s advert ('Self Control'). Retrieved from https://www.youtube.com/watch?v=TeGd7gVhpew

Fahrenheit Dior advert. (1988). Retrieved from https://www.youtube.com/watch?v=DJKDPMV3FOA

Inside Dior. (2017). Retrieved from https://www.youtube.com/watch?v=4FIlI0VQ34I

Lady Dior campaigns video list. (2009–2016). Retrieved from https://www.youtube.com/watch?v=odPhyimb4fs&list=PLHdHHJSYoLUPrm0oc56Grewgo8Bmgt04P

Lady Dior Web Documentary Series. (2014). Retrieved from https://www.youtube.com/watch?v=dj9Hx1_54kc&list=PLJAsRfe0REKGQ5pzktXHIjZZO2Jv0gRSc

Miss Dior Chérie. (2011). Retrieved from https://www.youtube.com/watch?v=6aVP0TEe1BQ

The A.B.C. Dior Podcast Series Illustrated. (2021). Retrieved from https://www.youtube.com/playlist?list=PLzPXOOq1r2gEwCyehufdnuPrRk_uJIHM2

The Dior Book Tote Club. (2023). Retrieved from https://www.youtube.com/playlist?list=PLzPXOOq1r2gH9yO4B0a6DAVXtnpR7tuFs

The Lady Noir Affair / By Lady Dior / Chapter One / Directed by Olivier Dahan Feat. Marion Cotillard. (2009). Retrieved from https://www.youtube.com/watch?v=IL5Nnay5sKY

The Making of Dior Autumn/Winter 2023–2024. Retrieved from https://www.youtube.com/watch?v=8dyavAwmrKA

The Making of the Dior Men's Summer 2024 Show. Retrieved from https://www.youtube.com/watch?v=XbBCnlrWx6Y

The Paris Saint-Germain get dressed up in Dior. (2023). Retrieved from https://www.youtube.com/watch?v=FU6pjQtCpH4

The world of Monsieur Dior in his own words. (2020). Retrieved from https://www.youtube.com/watch?v=ZESWE3myVLk

MAISON SCHIAPARELLI

Kardashian on collaboration on Instagram. (2023). Retrieved from https://www.instagram.com/kimkardashian/p/CrzMaNIP_3G/?img_index=1

Schiaparelli – Fall/Winter 2021/2022 – Film. (2021). Retrieved from https://www.youtube.com/watch?v=cpAb-jTvu4w

Short film in Paris of Daniel Roseberry's Schiaparelli AW21 Couture Collection. (2021). Retrieved from https://www.youtube.com/watch?v=UPBwmNIEmsM

Schiaparelli Haute Couture Fall/Winter. (2024). Retrieved from https://www.youtube.com/watch?v=IyPPfF7d9SA

YVES SAINT LAURENT

Catherine Deneuve for YSL. (2023). Retrieved from https://www.tiktok.com/@toujoursdeneuve/video/7288593712131640622

Saint Laurent – Catherine Deneuve. (2021). Retrieved from https://www.youtube.com/watch?v=zQ30rbQOcuI

Saint Laurent – As Time Goes By film series. (2024). Retrieved from https://www.youtube.com/watch?v=UqjqUUHHS5U&list=PLE05euBYOyJoWmDVMKLRTLxuiDNb0jRfZ

Saint Laurent Talks podcast. Retrieved from https://www.youtube.com/playlist?list=PLE05euBYOyJqQ1WggyUPDqS1bcTHIeqym

Self Campaign. (2019–2022). Retrieved from https://www.youtube.com/watch?v=D1F-2qVh-90&list=PLE05euBYOyJrOQ0poA9mRWodq2LYxucXP

CALVIN KLEIN

All four Calvin Klein 'Obsession' adverts. (1985). Written and directed by Richard Avedon. Retrieved from https://www.youtube.com/watch?v=1m28PqHYans

Calvin Klein jeans advert featuring Brooke Shields. (1980). Retrieved from https://www.youtube.com/watch?v=AXzR5b6HolA

Calvin Klein Jeans. 'Brooke Shields – Nothing' ('80's advert). Retrieved from https://www.youtube.com/watch?v=cD3zMCWwQeo

Calvin Klein. Advert – Marky Mark. Retrieved from https://www.youtube.com/watch?v=sSWrulOaanE

Calvin Klein. Advert – Marky Mark (Mark Wahlberg) & Kate Moss – 1992. Retrieved from https://www.youtube.com/watch?v=JyGSYN5cpN0

Calvin Klein Concept 2013 advert debuted during the Super Bowl. Retrieved from https://www.youtube.com/watch?v=1yelvxwTRUY

Calvin Klein Concept 2017 advert debuted during the Super Bowl. Retrieved from https://www.youtube.com/watch?v=VMiLwRqqGtA

Calvin Klein. Eternity Cologne advert. (1989). Retrieved from https://www.youtube.com/watch?v=rnkawlsVSIA

Calvin Klein. Eternity Cologne advert. (1988). Retrieved from https://www.youtube.com/watch?v=K25e-_g16M4

Calvin Klein. Eternity Cologne advert – Christy Turlington and Edward Burns. Retrieved from https://www.youtube.com/watch?v=NN9Q2pKiDKE

Calvin Klein Pride. (2024). 100% Pure Love Featuring Cara Delevingne and Jeremy Pope Retrieved from https://www.youtube.com/watch?v=Gg5Tp6rQsBg

Calvin Klein. (2006). Advert. Retrieved from https://www.youtube.com/watch?v=-CP-8mjiGA0

Calvin Klein. (1995). Jeans advert – Unbutton that top button. Retrieved from https://www.youtube.com/watch?v=aWhOTSV5plo

Calvin Klein. (1995). Jeans advert – Doug. Retrieved from https://www.youtube.com/watch?v=Zlt-typrmBU

CK One. (1994). Television advert. Retrieved from https://www.youtube.com/watch?v=7Oskart1IGI

Jeremy Allen White in Calvin Klein Underwear | Spring 2024 Campaign. Retrieved from https://www.youtube.com/watch?v=dCbM009btVI

Justin Bieber – Calvin Klein Underwear Spring 2015. Retrieved from https://www.youtube.com/watch?v=PxMUMs8YQAk

'Obsession' from Calvin Klein. Retrieved from https://www.youtube.com/watch?v=sCqZp43vRpA

RALPH LAUREN

A Portrait of the American Dream: A film by Ralph Lauren. (2022). Retrieved from https://www.youtube.com/watch?v=6lgL NPRaio8

All or Nothing at All. (2021). Retrieved from https://www.youtube.com/watch?v=s7M_JGmDcsE&list=RDs7M_JGmDcsE&start_radio=1

Annie Hall Official Trailer #1 – Woody Allen Movie. (1977) HD. Retrieved from https://www.youtube.com/watch?v=OqVgCfZX-yE

Friends: Season 5, episode 17, The One with Rachel's Inadvertent Kiss (Rachel's interview at RL)

Employed at RL, seasons 5–10, RL featured in the show himself in S6 E8

The Making of a Moment: Ralph Lauren (2020–). Retrieved from https://www.youtube.com/playlist?list=PLhAQN8jdR-MMZAZxZ1mLelJwmN5A3GJY7

Very Ralph. (2019). Retrieved from https://www.youtube.com/watch?v=b3T8ttxTX-I

JASON WU

Les Façons. (2014, December 4). Jason Wu Spring 2015 ad campaign. Les Façons. Retrieved from https://lesfacons.com/2014/12/04/jason-wu-spring-2015-ad-campaign/

AURORA JAMES

TedTalk. (2016). Retrieved from https://www.youtube.com/watch?v=1rnnm0Ht8ZI

Time100 Talks. (2020). Retrieved from https://www.youtube.com/watch?v=8AK4b5e9VbE

CARLA FERNANDEZ

Manifesto and Retrospectives (n.d.). Retrieved from https://en.carlafernandez.com/pages/manifesto

Literature and Media Articles

Alexander, E. (2013). Jason Wu on Michelle Obama's inauguration gown. *British Vogue,* January 22. Retrieved from https://www.vogue.co.uk/article/michelle-obama-inauguration-dress-jason-wu-interview

Alexander, E. (2012). Schiaparelli Relaunch. *British Vogue,* May 8. Retrieved from https://www.vogue.co.uk/article/schiaparelli-relaunched-by-diego-della-valle

Allaire, C. (2021). Brooke Shields revisits her iconic (and controversial) Calvin Klein campaign. *Vogue,* October 28. Retrieved from https://www.vogue.com/article/behind-the-moment-brooke-shields

Anbouba, M. (2024). Chanel's New No. 5 L'Eau Drop Bottle Was Inspired by Marilyn Monroe, *Vogue,* June 3, 2024. Retrieved from https://www.vogue.com/article/chanel-leau-drop-bottle-marilyn-monroe

Ayala, G. (2024). Night of Stars 2023. Retrieved from https://www.fgi.org/tag/watch/

Bailey, D. (1972). The new nonchalance in fashion. *Vogue,* January 1. Retrieved from https://archive.vogue.com/article/1972/01/01/1972-the-new-nonchalance-in-fashion

Baird-Murray, K. (2015). *Vogue on Ralph Lauren.* Harry N. Abrams.

Baker, P. (2002). *Fashion of a Decade: The 1940s.* New York: Facts on File.

Barnard, C. (2009). Jason Wu: Straddling Park and Pennsylvania Avenues. *Vanity Fair,* January 28. Retrieved from https://www.vanityfair.com/news/2009/01/jason-wu-straddling-park-and-pennsylvania-avenues

Belton, P.A. (2022). *Colorful Designs and Illustrations of Fashion Designer Ann Lowe: America's First Black Woman Haute Couture Designer To Own a Dress Shop on Madison Ave in New York.* Belton Media.

Betancourt, B. (2023). Aurora James Has Never Claimed to Be Perfect. *Vogue*, May 9. Retrieved from https://www.harpersbazaar.com/culture/art-books-music/a43723428/aurora-james-wildflower-memoir-interview/

Borrelli-Persson, L. (2022). A Brief History of Elsa Schiaparelli's Iconic Bow Sweater. *Vogue,* March 29. Retrieved from https://www.vogue.com/article/a-brief-history-of-elsa-schiaparelli-s-iconic-bow-sweater

Bott, D. (2007). *Chanel: Collections and Creations.* London: Thames & Hudson.

Brookins, L. (2022). Aurora James Is Revolutionizing the Fashion Industry. *Business Traveler,* June 1. Retrieved from https://businesstravelerusa.com/profiles/aurora-james-is-revolutionizing-the-fashion-industry/

Brother Vellies. (n.d.). *Our Story.* Retrieved from https://brothervellies.com/pages/about-brother-vellies

Business of Fashion. (n.d.). *Aurora James – Founder, Fifteen Percent Pledge; Founder & Creative Director, Brother Vellies.* Retrieved from https://www.businessoffashion.com/people/aurora-james/

CalvinKlein.us. (n.d.). Retrieved from https://www.calvinklein.us/en/mycalvins.html

Carlafernandez.com. (n.d.). Retrieved from https://en.carlafernandez.com/

Carter, K. (2010). Fashion Statement: Banned adverts and tasteless campaigns. *The Guardian,* September 3. Retrieved from https://www.theguardian.com/lifeandstyle/2010/sep/02/banned-fashion-adverts

Cartner-Morley, J. (2012). Yves Saint Laurent to be renamed by creative director Hedi Slimane. *The Guardian,* June 21. Retrieved from https://www.theguardian.com/fashion/2012/jun/21/yves-saint-laurent-renamed

CBS News. (2013). Michelle Obama wears red Jason Wu gown to inaugural balls. *CBS News,* January 21. Retrieved from https://www.cbsnews.com/news/michelle-obama-wears-red-jason-wu-gown-to-inaugural-balls/

Clarkson, K. (2011). *Vintage Fashion Sourcebook.* London: Carlton Books Limited.

Corsillo, L. (2015). 7 Things You Didn't Know About Ralph Lauren. *GQ*, October 14. Retrieved from https://www.gq.com/story/ralph-lauren-what-you-didnt-know

Croll, J. (2014). *Fashion That Changed the World.* Munich: Prestel Verlag.

Crook, P.B. (n.d.). Made to be worn: The story of Polo Wester. *RLMAG.* Retrieved from https://www.ralphlauren.com/rlmag/the-history-of-polo-western.html?ab=en_US_rl50_Timeline_Slot_13_L1

De Sortiraparis, A. (2023). *Carla Fernández. L'avenir fait main: the free fashion and textile exhibition at Galerie du 19M.* Retrieved from https://www.sortiraparis.com/en/what-to-visit-in-paris/exhibit-museum/articles/296776-carla-fernandez-l-avenir-fait-main-the-free-fashion-and-textile-exhibition-at-galerie-du-19m

Denley, S. (2013). Inauguration 2013: Michelle Obama chooses Jason Wu gown. *Los Angeles Times*, January 22. Retrieved from https://www.latimes.com/fashion/la-xpm-2013-jan-22-la-ar-michelle-obama-chooses-jason-wu-20130121-story.html

Denver Art Museum. (2022). *Carla Fernández Casa de Moda. A Mexican Fashion Manifesto*. Retrieved from https://www.denverartmuseum.org/en/exhibitions/carla-fernandez

Di Angelo, L. (2018). Aurora James of Brother Vellies. *Vogue Italia*, April 24. Retrieved from https://www.vogue.it/en/fashion/news/2018/04/24/exclusive-interview-with-aurora-james-designer-of-brother-vellies-sustainable-brand-entirely-produced-in-africa/

DiDonato, J. (2015). The Little Black Dress: A Brief History. *Paste*, April 15. Retrieved from https://www.pastemagazine.com/style/the-little-black-dress-a-brief-history

Dior, C. (1957[1956]). *Dior by Dior*. London: Weidenfeld and Nicolson.

Dior La Galerie. (n.d.). *Discover the Richness of the House through the Work of Christian Dior and his Six Successors*. Update as available on 8 July 2025. Retrieved from https://www.galeriedior.com/en/history

Dior.com. (n.d.). *Christian Dior, Couturier-perfumer*. Retrieved from https://www.dior.com/en_us/beauty/fragrance/christian-dior-couturier-perfumer.html

Dobhal, P. (2025). How Vivienne Westwood defined fashion activism with a lifetime of rebellion and celebration of punk. *Harper's Bazaar India*, April 2. Retrieved from https://www.harpersbazaar.in/fashion/story/how-vivienne-westwood-defined-fashion-activism-with-a-lifetime-of-rebellion-and-celebration-of-punk-564974-2022-12-31

Dockery Smith, J.F. (2016). *Something to Prove: A Biography of Ann Lowe, America's Forgotten Designer*. North Charleston: CreateSpace Independent Publishing Platform.

DScene. (2021). A Closer Look at Schiaparelli SS22 Jewellery & Accessories. *DScene*, December 9. Retrieved from https://www.designscene.net/2021/12/schiaparelli-ss22.html

du Plessix Gray, F. (1996). Prophets of Seduction. *The New Yorker*, October 27. Retrieved from https://www.newyorker.com/magazine/1996/11/04/prophets-of-seduction

Eldor, K. (2023). As the 15 Percent Pledge marks its 3-year anniversary, Aurora James asserts: 'We're just getting started'. *Forbes*, June 20, 2023. Retrieved from https://www.forbes.com/sites/karineldor/2023/06/20/as-the-15-percent-pledge-marks-its-3-year-anniversary-aurora-james-asserts-were-just-getting-started/

Farra, E. (2016). See the Complete Grey Jason Wu Collection Here – Then Buy It Tomorrow. *Vogue*, June 14. Retrieved from https://www.vogue.com/article/grey-jason-wu-lookbook-exclusive-see-now-buy-now

Fashion Gone Rogue. (2015). Malgosia Bela wears the pants in Jason Wu's Fall 2015 campaign. *Fashion Gone Rogue*, July 17. Retrieved from

https://www.fashiongonerogue.com/jason-wu-fall-2015-ad-campaign/

Fifteen Percent Pledge. (2020). *Aurora James*. Retrieved from https://15percentpledge.org/team/aurora-james

Fischenich, S., Horbas, C., Kaiser, A., Kothe, R., Meisner, J., Roth, A., Willemsen, C., Wolter, G., & Zipperer, A. (2000). *A History of Fashion in the 20th Century*. Cologne: Konemann Verlagsgesellschaft.

Forsberg, J. (2024). Revisiting the storied past of Chanel's most iconic handbag through exclusive archive images. *Vogue Scandinavia*, March 28, 2024. Retrieved from https://www.voguescandinavia.com/articles/history-of-chanel-2-55-bag-through-imagery

Fraser, K. (2022). Vivienne Westwood's OBE dress goes viral 30 years later after social media praises her no-underwear style statement. *WWD*, December 30. Retrieved from https://wwd.com/eye/scoops/vivienne-westwood-obe-dress-no-underwear-queen-elizabeth-1235458358/

Fraser-Cavassoni, N. (2017). *Vogue on Calvin Klein*. London: Quadrille.

Freeman, H. (2011). Ralph Lauren offers timely take on The Great Gatsby. *The Guardian*, 15 September. Retrieved from https://www.

theguardian.com/lifeandstyle/2011/sep/15/ralph-lauren-new-york-fashion-week

Garcia, L. (2025). Carla Fernández. *Vogue*, May 12. Retrieved from https://www.vogue.com/fashion-shows/mexico-fall-2025/carla-fernandez

Garcia-Furtado, L. (2025). On the Podcast: Five Years in, Aurora James Is Still Working to Create a Diverse Meritocracy With the 15% Pledge. *Vogue*, June 10. Retrieved from https://www.vogue.com/article/on-the-podcast-aurora-james-15-percent-pledge-5-year-anniversary

Gardner, A. (2019). Ralph Lauren Launched a Collection Inspired By Rachel Green on 'Friends'. *Glamour*, September 18. Retrieved from https://www.glamour.com/story/ralph-lauren-collection-inspired-by-rachel-green-friends

Goldstone, P. (2024). The story behind Gwyneth Paltrow's iconic pink Oscars dress. *Marie Claire*, March 8. Retrieved from https://www.marieclaire.co.uk/news/fashion-news/gwyneth-paltrow-oscar-dress-732090

Google Arts and Culture. (n.d.). https://artsandculture.google.com/entity/ann-lowe/m027tz4_?categoryid=historical-figure

Hancock, S. (2022). Vivienne Westwood: Designers on her influence and legacy. *BBC News,* December 30. Retrieved from https://www.bbc.com/news/uk-64126537

Harlem World. (2017). Harlem's Ann Lowe: The Fashion Designer To First Ladies. Harlem World, March 20, 2017. Retrieved from https://www.harlemworldmagazine.com/harlems-ann-lowe-fashion-designer-first-ladies/

Harper's Bazaar historical archive. Retrieved from https://proquest.libguides.com/harpers

Harwood, E. (2017). Michelle Obama wore a red Jason Wu dress at the inauguration. *Vanity Fair,* January 20. Retrieved from https://www.vanityfair.com/style/2017/01/michelle-obama-jason-wu-inauguration-dress

Heyl, E. (2016). Christian Dior: A Look at French Fashion's Biggest Icon. *The Culture Trip*, October 18. Retrieved from https://theculturetrip.com/europe/france/paris/articles/christian-dior-a-look-at-french-fashions-biggest-icon

History.com. (2024). *Christian Dior launches his scandalizing 'New Look' postwar fashions.* Published February 13. Last update, May 27, 2025. Retrieved from https://www.history.com/this-day-in-history/february-12/christian-dior-launches-new-look-fashion-designs

History.com. (2021). *Chanel No. 5 perfume launches*. Published March 2, 2021. Last update May 28, 2025. Retrieved from https://www.history.com/this-day-in-history/may-5/chanel-no-5-perfume-launches

Istituto Marangoni. (2023). *Will fashion carry on Vivienne Westwood's activism?* February 8. Retrieved from https://www.istitutomarangoni.com/en/maze35/industry/will-fashion-carry-on-vivienne-westwoods-activism

James, A. (n.d.). Retrieved from https://aurorajames.com/

Jasonwustudio.com (n.d.). *INK*. Retrieved from https://jasonwustudio.com/

Kelso, P. (2014). Fashion archive: Yves Saint Laurent says adieu to couture. *The Guardian*, January 8. Retrieved from https://www.theguardian.com/theguardian/2014/jan/08/yves-saint-laurent-retires-2002

Keltner de Valle, J. (2009). Teen Vogue Exclusive! Jason Wu on Designing Michelle Obama's Inaugural Ball Gown. *Teen Vogue*, January 21. Retrieved from https://www.teenvogue.com/story/teen-vogue-exclusive-jason-wu-on-designing-michelle-obamas-inaugural-ball-gown

Kim, M. (2015). 5 Times Elsa Schiaparelli Revolutionized the Perfume World. *Vogue,* September 10. Retrieved from https://www.vogue.com/article/schiaparelli-perfumes-shocking-fragrance

Kotsoni, E. (2025). The V&A will host the UK's first-ever Schiaparelli exhibition next spring. *Vogue*, July 9. Retrieved from https://www.voguebusiness.com/story/fashion/the-vanda-will-host-the-uks-first-ever-schiaparelli-exhibition-next-spring#:~:text=Fashion-,The%20V%26A%20will%20host%20the%20UK's%20first%2Dever%20Schiaparelli%20exhibition,at%20the%20museum's%20Sainsbury%20Gallery.

Lackey, D. (2017). The remarkable career of Jason Wu. *Dave Lackie blog,* July 17. Retrieved from https://davelackie.com/the-remarkable-career-of-jason-wu/

Legacy Lecture: The Life and Times of Fashion Designer Ann Lowe. (2021). https://www.youtube.com/watch?v=DEjFxWqkDfk

Lehnert, G. (2000). *A History of Fashion in the 20th Century.* Cologne: Konemann.

Les Archives de la Mode. (n.d.). Retrieved from https://hprints.com/en/adverts/perfumes/Christian-Dior/

Les Archives de la Mode. (n.d._a). Retrieved from https://hprints.com/en/adverts/perfumes/Schiaparelli/

Les Falcons. (2022). Vivienne Westwood Fall 2022 Ad Campaign Featuring Courtney Love. June 28. Retrieved from https://lesfacons.com/2022/06/28/vivienne-westwood-fall-2022-ad-campaign-featuring-courtney-love/

Les Falcons. (2021). Vivienne Westwood Fall 2021 Ad Campaign. August 4. Retrieved from https://lesfacons.com/2021/08/04/vivienne-westwood-fall-2021-ad-campaign/

Malach, H. (2024). Calvin Klein Advertisements and the Stories Behind Them: More Than 50 Years of Celebrity and Controversy. *WWD,* January 19. Retrieved from https://wwd.com/pop-culture/culture-news/feature/calvin-klein-ads-1236117541/

Maleri, J. (2015). In (and Out) of Africa with Brother Vellies Designer Aurora James. *Conde Nast Traveler*, November 4. Retrieved from https://www.cntraveler.com/stories/2015-11-04/in-and-out-of-africa-with-brother-vellies-designer-aurora-james

Manifesto of Fashion as Resistance. (n.d.). Retrieved from https://en.carlafernandez.com/pages/manifesto

Marfil, L. (2016). Vivienne Westwood Focuses on Saving Venice for Spring 2016 Campaign. *WWD,* January 20. Retrieved from https://wwd.com/business-news/marketing-promotion/feature/vivienne-westwood-saving-venice-spring-2016-campaign-juergen-teller-10321423/

McLaren, M. (2007). Searching for a way to break the rules. *The Guardian,* September 15. Retrieved from https://www.theguardian.com/theguardian/2007/sep/15/greatinterviews2

McVicker, M. (2020). 1898–1981 – Ann Lowe. *Fashion History Timeline*. Last update August 4, 2020. Retrieved from https://fashionhistory.fitnyc.edu/1898-1981-ann-lowe/

Michals, D. (1975). The American look at its best ... at Calvin Klein. *Vogue,* September 1, p. 232. Retrieved from https://archive.vogue.com/issue/19750901#!&pid=232

Miller, J. (2024). The New Look Revisits Coco Chanel's Nazi Ties and Feud With Christian Dior. *Vanity Fair,* February 6. Retrieved from https://www.vanityfair.com/hollywood/the-new-look-coco-chanel-christian-dior?srsltid=AfmBOoooU8XJhJsV1BMwDBoNudVhs5HlxFTRACISsOwLRn7O8st_64OE

Minutaglio, R. (2019). Ann Lowe Is the Little-Known Black Couturier Who Designed Jackie Kennedy's Iconic Wedding Dress. *Elle*, September 12. Retrieved from https://www.elle.com/fashion/a29019843/jackie-kennedy-wedding-dress-designer-ann-lowe/

Mirabella, G. (1995). *In and Out of Vogue: A Memoir.* New York: Doubleday.

Molina, C. (2013). Why Every Woman Wants Jason Wu's Beauty Line for Lancôme. *Elle,* August 15. Retrieved from https://www.elle.com/beauty/news/a16439/jason-wu-for-lancome-collection/

Munzenrieder, K. (2016). Dior's Latest Campaign Has A Feminist Message. *W magazine,* December 20. Retrieved from https://www.wmagazine.com/story/diors-latest-campaign-has-a-feminist-message

Musée des Arts Décoratifs. (2022). 'Shocking! The Surreal World of Elsa Schiaparelli'. Retrieved from https://madparis.fr/IMG/pdf/dp-shocking-schiap-en.pdf

Musée Yves Saint Laurent Paris. (n.d.). 1966: First Tuxedo. Retrieved from https://museeyslparis.com/en/biography/premier-smoking

Musée Yves Saint Laurent Paris. (n.d._a). 1971: The Scandal Collection. Retrieved from https://museeyslparis.com/en/biography/la-collection-du-scandale

Musée Yves Saint Laurent Paris. (n.d._b). 1971: Launch of the Fragrances rive gauche and Pour Homme. Retrieved from https://museeyslparis.com/en/biography/lancement-des-parfums-rive-gauche-et-pour-homme

Musée Yves Saint Laurent Paris. (n.d._c). 1977: Opium. Retrieved from https://museeyslparis.com/en/biography/opium

Musée Yves Saint Laurent Paris. (n.d._d). The Saint Laurent women. Retrieved from https://museeyslparis.com/en/stories/new-entry-1

Musée Yves Saint Laurent Paris. (n.d._e). 1977: Opium. Retrieved from https://museeyslparis.com/en/biography/opium

Naquian Wheeler, A. (2023). Brother Vellies's Aurora James Opens Up About Her Powerful New Memoir, Wildflower. *Vogue*, April 26. Retrieved from https://www.vogue.com/article/aurora-james-wildflower-memoir

National Museum of African American History & Culture. (n.d.). https://nmaahc.si.edu/explore/stories/ann-lowe

New York Times. (2025). Ralph Lauren Makes Fashion History With Top Civilian Honor. Retrieved from https://www.nytimes.com/2025/01/04/style/ralph-lauren-presidential-medal-freedom.html

Newbold, A. (2019). Ralph Lauren is finally launching a Friends-inspired collection. *Vogue,* 19 September. Retrieved from https://www.vogue.in/fashion/content/ralph-lauren-is-finally-launching-a-friends-inspired-collection

Nichols, A. (n.d.). *Ann Lowe*. Retrieved from https://nmaahc.si.edu/explore/stories/ann-lowe

Ogunnaike, N. (2018). Jason Wu on why he never did plus size until Eloquii came calling. *ELLE,* November 1. Retrieved from

https://www.elle.com/fashion/a24508613/eloquii-jason-wu-dress-collaboration/

Okwodu, J. (2020). Aurora James on Fashion, Feminism, and the Fifteen Percent Pledge. *Vogue*, August 26. Retrieved from https://www.vogue.com/article/aurora-james-september-issue-2020-15-percent-pledge

Okwodu, J. (2015). Exclusive: Jason Wu on his latest campaign and supermodel muses. *Vogue,* July 16. Retrieved from

https://www.vogue.com/article/jason-wu-interview-campaign-supermodel-muses

Papalas, M. (2017). Fashion in interwar France: The urban vision of Elsa Schiaparelli. *French Cultural Studies, 28*(2), 159–172.

Peluso, O. (2022). Aurora James and Emma Grede know retail. Their advice on driving change in the $5.6 trillion industry? No compromises. *Forbes,* September 29. Retrieved from https://www.forbes.com/sites/oliviapeluso/2022/09/29/aurora-james-and-emma-grede-know-retail-their-advice-on-driving-change-in-the-56-trillion-industry-no-compromises/

Phelps, N. (2024). Ralph Lauren. Spring 2025 Ready-to-wear. *Vogue,* September 6. Retrieved from https://www.vogue.com/fashion-shows/spring-2025-ready-to-wear/ralph-lauren

Phelps, N. (2019). Legendary Designer Karl Lagerfeld Has Died. *Vogue,* February 19. Retrieved from https://www.vogue.com/article/karl-lagerfeld-obituary#:~:text=Karl%20Lagerfeld%2C%20one%20of%20the,%2C%20age%2Ddefying%2036%20years.

Phelps, N. (2017). 10 years in, Jason Wu has had plenty of highs, but that inauguration dress is still the "best experience of his life". *Vogue,* February 8. Retrieved from https://www.vogue.com/article/jason-wu-10-year-anniversary-interview

Philadelphia Museum of Art. (2003). Shocking! The Art & Fashion of Elsa Schiaparelli. September 28–January 4. Retrieved from https://legacyweb.philamuseum.org/doc_downloads/education/ex_resources/schiaparelli.pdf

Pike, N. (2020). 43 Classic Photographs That Prove Coco Chanel's Taste Never Wavered. *Vogue,* May 24. Retrieved from https://www.vogue.co.uk/gallery/coco-chanel-life-in-pictures

Piranha NYC. (n.d.). *Saint Laurent.* Retrieved from https://www.piranhanyc.com/saintlaurent

Pochna, M.-F. (1994). *Christian Dior: The Man Who Made the World Look New.* London: Arcade Publishing.

PVH. (2024). Calvin Klein launches 2024 This Is Love Pride campaign starring Cara Delevingne and Jeremy Pope. May 29. Retrieved from https://www.pvh.com/news/calvin-klein-this-is-love-2024-pride-campaign

PVH. (2021). *Calvin Klein Celebrates Defining Moments of the LGBTQIA+ Journey with #proudinmycalvins Campaign.* May 26. Retrieved from https://www.pvh.com/news/ck-proudinmycalvins-campaign

Ralphlauren.com. (n.d.). *The Timeline.* Retrieved from https://www.ralphlauren.com/rl-50-timeline-feat

Ralphlauren.com. (n.d._a). Retrieved from https://www.ralphlauren.com/rlmag/ralph-lauren-culture-style-polo-shirt-book.html

Rantala, H. (2021). Groceries, gowns and Coca-Cola: Jason Wu sets up shop at New York Fashion Week. *Reuters,* February 15, 2021. Retrieved from https://www.reuters.com/lifestyle/groceries-gowns-coca-cola-ja son-wu-sets-up-shop-new-york-fashion-w eek-2021-02-15/

Reeder, J. (2011). Elsa Schiaparelli (1890–1973). *The Metropolitan Museum of Art,* May 1. Retrieved from https://www.metmuseum.org/essays/elsa-schiaparelli-1890-1973

Reeve, E. (2013). Michelle Obama's dress for the second inaugural ball. *The Atlantic,* January 21. Retrieved from https://www.theatlantic.com/politics/archive/2013/01/michelle-obamas-dress-second-inauguration/319214/

RL Mag. (n.d.). The City as Inspiration. Celebrating the detail, drama, and beauty of New York's Art Deco landmarks. *RL Mag – The authentic and timeless world of Ralph Lauren.* Retrieved from https://www.ralphlauren.com/rlmag/the-city-as-inspiration.
html?ab=en_US_rlmag_culture_article48

Robinson, R. (2020). Aurora James, the designer behind the #15PercentPledge, on supporting Black-owned businesses long-term. *Forbes,* June 16. Retrieved from
https://www.forbes.com/sites/roxannerobinson/2020/06/16/aurora-james-the-designer-behind-the-15percentpledge-on-supporting-black-owned-businesses-long-term/

Runway Magazine. (2021). Ralph Lauren Spring 2021 – All or Nothing at All. *Runway Magazine*, March25. Retrieved from https://runwaymagazines.com/ralph-lauren-spring-2021-all-or-nothing-at-all/

Samaha, B., & Hyde, S.Y. (2021). The Best Coco Chanel Quotes About Fashion, Love, and Success. *Harper's Bazaar,* July 7. Retrieved from https://www.harpersbazaar.com/fashion/designers/g32971271/best-coco-chanel-quotes/

Schiaparelli, E. (2007[1954]). *Shocking Life. The Autobiography of Elsa Schiaparelli.* Victoria and Albert Museum.

Schiaparelli. (n.d.). *The story of the house.* Retrieved from https://www.schiaparelli.com/en/21-place-vendome/the-story-of-the-house/

Schiaparelli. (n.d._a). *News.* Retrieved from https://www.schiaparelli.com/en/news/2025-05-14-andie-macdowell-wears-schiaparelli-to-the-78th-cannes-film-festival

Schiaparelli.com. (n.d.). *Chapter I: Youth and initiation to the art world.* Retrieved from https://www.schiaparelli.com/en/21-place-vendome/the-life-of-elsa/#1

Schiaparelli.com. (n.d._a). *Chapter II: Discovery of fashion 1st success.* Retrieved from https://www.schiaparelli.com/en/21-place-vendome/the-life-of-elsa/#2

Schiaparelli.com. (n.d._b). *Chapter III: Inspired designer and global expansion.* Retrieved from https://www.schiaparelli.com/en/21-place-vendome/the-life-of-elsa/#3

Schiaparelli.com. (n.d._c). *Chapter IV: WWII and personal commitment.* Retrieved from https://www.schiaparelli.com/en/21-place-vendome/the-life-of-elsa/#4

Schiaparelli.com. (n.d._d). *Chapter V: Consecration and writing of her autobiography.* Retrieved from https://www.schiaparelli.com/en/21-place-vendome/the-life-of-elsa/#5

Secrest, M. (2014). *Elsa Schiaparelli: A Biography.* Penguin Random House.

Setiawan, B. (2020). Cooking and coping: Making banana bread with Aurora James in Brooklyn, New York. *Forbes,* April 6. Retrieved from https://www.forbes.com/sites/benjaminsetiawan/2020/04/06/cooking-and-coping-making-banana-bread-with-aurora-james-in-brooklyn-new-york/

Shipton, V. (2011). *The Story of Chanel.* Glasgow: Scholastic.

Simon, M. (2020). Aurora James is helping companies invest in accountability with the '15 Percent Pledge'. *Forbes,* December 21. Retrieved from

https://www.forbes.com/sites/morgansimon/2020/12/21/aurora-james-is-helping-companies-invest-in-accountability-with-the-15-percent-pledge/

Sinclair, C. (2012). *Vogue on Christian Dior.* New York: Abrams Image.

Singh, M. (2019). Dior perfume ad featuring Johnny Depp criticized over Native American tropes. *The Guardian,* August 30. Retrieved from https://www.theguardian.com/fashion/2019/aug/30/diors-fragrance-ad-draws-criticism-for-featuring-native-american-tropes

Smithsonian (2014). *Michelle Obama's Second Inaugural Ball Gown Goes on View in National Museum of American History.* January 13. Retrieved from https://www.si.edu/newsdesk/releases/michelle-obama-s-second-inaugural-ball-gown-goes-view-national-museum-american-history

Stanley, T.L. (2021). Designer Jason Wu debuts "Haute CATure" products with high-fashion ad campaign. *Adweek,* November 18. Retrieved from https://www.adweek.com/brand-marketing/designer-jason-wu-debuts-haute-cature-products-with-high-fashion-ad-campaign/

Stewart, J. (2023). On Both Coasts, Aurora James Celebrated the Release of Her Memoir Wildflower. *Vogue,* May 14. Retrieved from https://www.vogue.com/slideshow/aurora-james-wildflower-memoir-book-launch-2023

Taller Flora. (n.d.). *Mobile lab developed with Indigenous communities that researches clothing production systems. Initiator: Carla Fernández.* Retrieved from https://arte-util.org/projects/taller-flora/

Tashjian, R. (2014). 30 Iconic Ralph Lauren Ads. *Vanity Fair,* June 17. Retrieved from https://www.vanityfair.com/style/photos/2014/06/iconic-ralph-lauren-ads

The Courier Mail (1947). No knock in this knee club. *The Courier Mail,* August 19. Retrieved from https://trove.nla.gov.au/newspaper/article/49315126

Time Magazine. (1934). Schiaparelli cover. *Time Magazine,* August 13. Retrieved from https://content.time.com/time/covers/0,16641,19340813,00.html

Thomas, A. (2021). Jason Wu NYFW Fall 2021. A Grocery Store Romance. *Grazia.* Retrieved from

https://graziamagazine.com/articles/jason-wu-fall-2021-a-grocery-store-romance/

Thurman, J. (2003). Mother of Invention. *The New Yorker,* October 19. Retrieved from https://www.newyorker.com/magazine/2003/10/27/mother-of-invention

The Metropolitan Museum of Art. (n.d.). Evening Dress. https://www.metmuseum.org/art/collection/search/83961

The Talks. (n.d.). *Jason Wu: "Taste is in the eye of the beholder".* Retrieved from https://the-talks.com/interview/jason-wu/

V&A Museums. (n.d.). *Fashion in Motion: Carla Fernández.* Retrieved from https://www.vam.ac.uk/articles/fashion-in-motion-carla-fernandez?srsltid=AfmBOoq9CamhRqYMm-58N_xw8PMRXOTqjL1h0bOXvjeNp-ZXODvAAs8R

V&A Museums. (n.d._a). *Vivienne Westwood: A taste for the past.* Retrieved from https://www.vam.ac.uk/articles/vivienne-westwood-a-taste-for-the-past?srsltid=AfmBOoo4WxlJObKAyuLOxzWNSjk8LrGb5is6Khfl0z-Jpq4qXDAuQH1p

V&A Museums. (n.d._b). *Vivienne Westwood: Punk, new romantic and beyond.* Retrieved from https://www.vam.ac.uk/articles/vivienne-westwood-punk-new-romantic-and-beyond

Verner, A. (2016). Andreas Kronthaler for Vivienne Westwood. *Vogue Runway,* March

5. Retrieved from https://www.vogue.com/fashion-shows/fall-2016-ready-to-wear/andreas-kronthaler-for-vivienne-westwood

Viapiana, A. (2023). Tom Ford, the most beautiful advertising campaigns ever created between the 90s and 2000s. *L'Officiel,* 5 March 2023. Retrieved from https://www.lofficielibiza.com/fashion/tom-ford-most-popular-advertising-campaigns-photos

Vogue. (1975). Bloomingdale's advert. *Vogue*, September 1, p. 2. Retrieved from https://archive.vogue.com/issue/19750901#!&pid=2

Vogue. (1975a). Cover page. *Vogue*, September 1. Retrieved from https://archive.vogue.com/issue/19750901

Vogue. (1975b). Kaufmann's advert. *Vogue*, September 1, p. 173. Retrieved from https://archive.vogue.com/issue/19750901#!&pid=173

Vogue. (1975c). Neiman-Marcus advert. *Vogue,* September 1, p. 71. Retrieved from https://archive.vogue.com/issue/19750901#!&pid=71

Vogue. (1975d). Saks Fifth Avenue advert. *Vogue*, September 1, p. 35. Retrieved from https://archive.vogue.com/issue/19751001/print

Vogue. (1975e). Woodward & Lothrop advert. *Vogue*, September 1, p. 72. Retrieved from https://archive.vogue.com/issue/19750901#!&pid=72

Vogue. (1947). Cover page. *Vogue*, April 1. Retrieved from https://archive.vogue.com/issue/19470401

Vogue historical archive. Retrieved from https://archive.vogue.com/

VW – Greenpeace. (n.d.). Retrieved from https://www.viviennewestwood.com/en-us/contentsearch/?fdid=greenpeace

Watson, S. (2020). Designer Vivienne Westwood leads protest supporting Assange. *AP,* July 21. Retrieved from https://apnews.com/article/97f71e52065a726906778062a020c4c7

Way, E. (2024). Ann Lowe (ca. 1898–1981). The Metropolitan Museum of Art, January 24. Retrieved from https://www.metmuseum.org/essays/ann-lowe

Wells, L. (2009). At last. *Allure,* January 21. Retrieved from https://www.allure.com/story/at-last

Westwood, V. (2007). Active resistance to propaganda. *The Guardian,* May 12. Retrieved from https://www.theguardian.com/lifeandstyle/2007/may/12/fashion.features4

Westwood.com. (n.d.). *Westwood World – The Story so Far.* Retrieved from https://www.viviennewestwood.com/en-us/westwood-world/the-story-so-far/

Westwood.com. (n.d._a). *Activism.* Retrieved from https://www.viviennewestwood.com/en-us/sustainability/activism/

Westwood.com. (n.d._b). *Climate Revolution.* Retrieved from https://www.viviennewestwood.com/en-us/sustainability/activism/climate-revolution/

Whitson, L. (2024). A Quick History of Calvin Klein's Iconic Underwear Campaigns. *L'Officiel,* November, 19. Retrieved from https://www.lofficielph.com/fashion/calvin-klein-underwear-campaigns-history

Winterthur museum. (n.d.). https://www.winterthur.org/ann-lowe-american-couturier/

Williams, I. (2023). Aurora James is *FASHION*'s April 2023 Cover Star. *Fashion,* March 16. Retrieved from https://fashionmagazine.com/style/celebrity-style/aurora-james-fashion-april-2023/

Williams, R. (2023). Schiaparelli: Diego Della Valle's Vision for Scaling a 'Sleeping Beauty' Brand. *Business of Fashion,* November 14. Retrieved from https://www.businessoffashion.com/articles/luxury/schiaparelli-ready-to-wear-expansion/

YSL Museum. (n.d.). *Yves Saint Laurent, Early Years.* Retrieved from https://museeyslparis.com/en/stories/enfance-et-jeunesse-dyves-saint-laurent

YSL Museum. (n.d._a). *The Dior Years.* Retrieved from https://museeyslparis.com/en/stories/les-annees-dior-1-1

YSL Museum. (n.d._b). *The Mondrian Revolution.* Retrieved from https://museeyslparis.com/en/stories/la-revolution-mondrian

YSL Museum. (n.d._c). *The Saint Laurent Women.* Retrieved from https://museeyslparis.com/en/stories/new-entry-1

YSL Museum. (n.d._d). *1966: First Tuxedo.* Retrieved from https://museeyslparis.com/en/biography/premier-smoking

YSL Museum. (n.d._e). *1971: Launch of the Fragrances rive gauche and Pour Homme.* Retrieved from https://museeyslparis.com/en/biography/lancement-des-parfums-rive-gauche-et-pour-homme

YSL Museum. (n.d._f). *1968: First Safari Jacket.* Retrieved from https://museeyslparis.com/en/biography/premiere-saharienne-pe

15percentpledge.com. (n.d.). Retrieved from https://15percentpledge.org/

Index